Apple Devices Made Easy

A Beginners and Seniors Step by Step Guide for iWatch, iPhone, and MacBook

Jason Brown

Table of Contents

IPHONE FOR SENIORS 140

APPLE WATCH FOR SENIORS

MacBook for Seniors

A Simple Step By Step Guide For Beginners

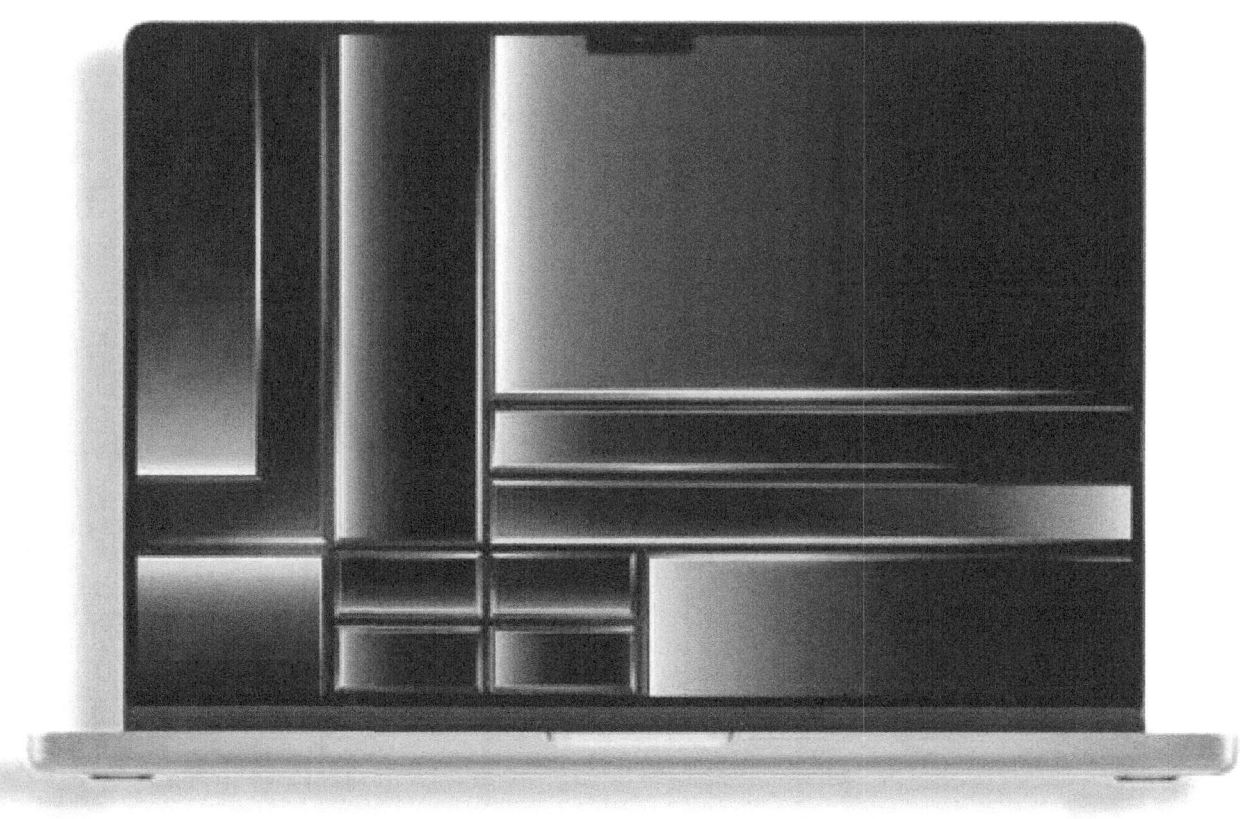

Jason Brown

SETTING UP YOUR MACBOOK

HARDWARE & SOFTWARE OVERVIEW FOR ALL MODELS

Turn on your Macbook and get started!
Set up your new Mac in a few simple steps.

MACBOOK AIR

FaceTime HD camera

Do Not Disturb

Dictation

Spotlight

MagSafe 3

Thunderbolt / USB 4

Touch ID

Force Touch trackpad

MACBOOK PRO 13"+

FaceTime HD camera

Do Not Disturb

Dictation

Spotlight

MagSafe 3

Thunderbolt 4

Headphone jack

Touch ID

HDMI port

Thunderbolt 4 (USB-C)

SDXC card slot

Force Touch trackpad

SOFTWARE OVERVIEW FOR ALL MODELS

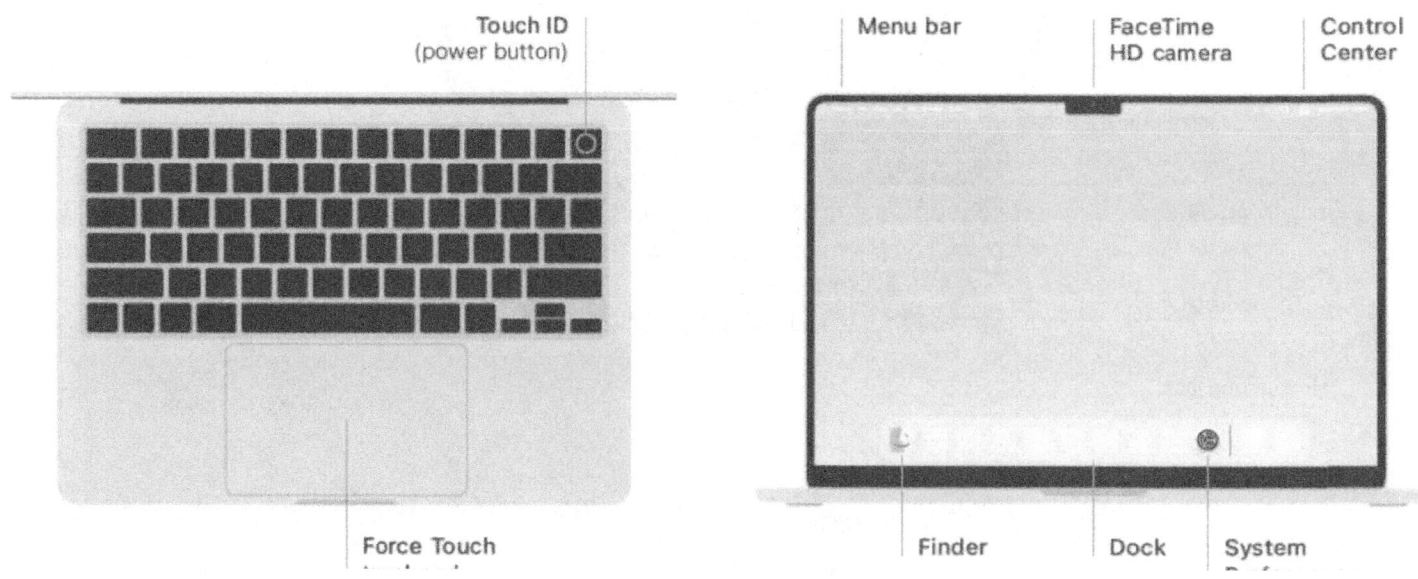

Apple menu

App menus

Finder window

Help menu

Wi-Fi

Menu bar

Spotlight

Finder

Launchpad

Desktop

System Settings

Dock

Touch ID
(power button)

Force Touch

Menu bar

FaceTime
HD camera

Control
Center

Finder

Dock

System

POWER-UP YOUR MACBOOK

To power up your MacBook, follow these straightforward steps:

1. Locate the Power Button: On most MacBook models, the power button is located at the top-right corner of the keyboard.
2. Press the Power Button: Gently press the power button. You should hear a startup chime (on older MacBooks) or see the screen illuminate.
3. Wait for Startup: Your MacBook will boot up, and you'll see the Apple logo on the screen. Depending on your MacBook's model and configuration, this process may take a few moments.
4. Log In: Once your MacBook has started up, you'll be prompted to log in with your username and password, if you have set up a password. Follow the on-screen instructions to do so.
5. You're Ready to Go: After successfully logging in, you'll be taken to your desktop, and your MacBook is now powered up and ready for use.

Remember to shut down your MacBook properly when you're done using it. To do this, click on the Apple menu in the top-left corner and choose "Shut Down." This ensures that your MacBook closes all programs and processes safely.

Charge with MagSafe 3

1. Plug the USB-C power adaptor into a plug socket.
2. Plug the USB-C end of the MagSafe 3 cable into the power adaptor.
3. Connect the other end of the cable to the MagSafe 3 port on your Mac.

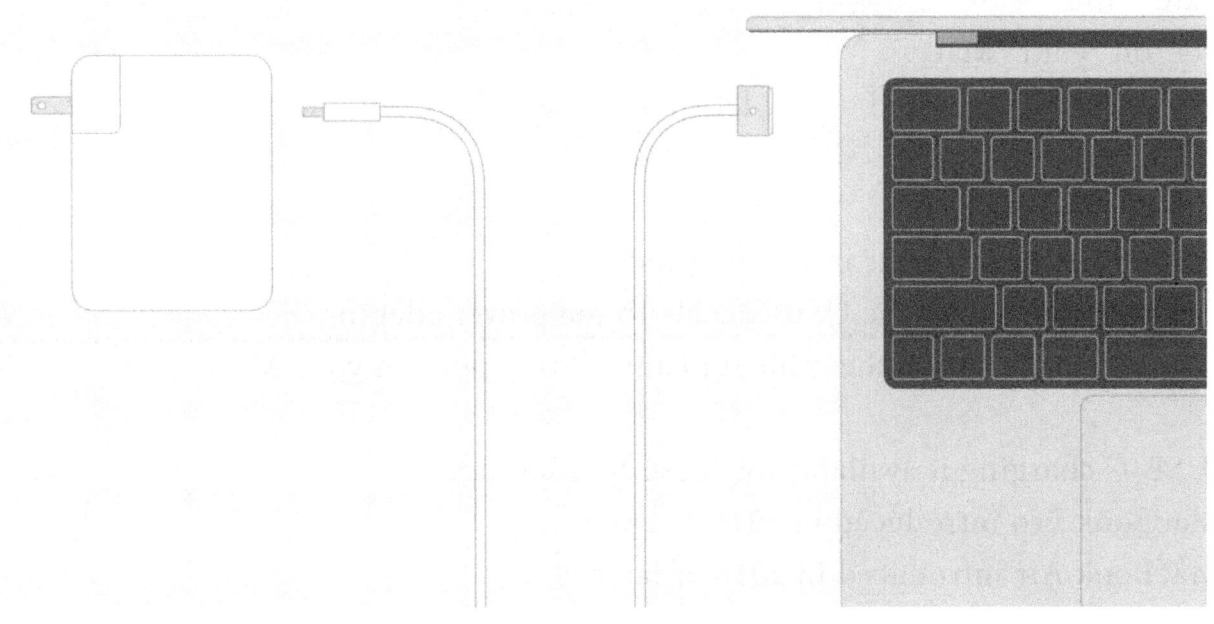

CHARGING YOUR MACBOOK

To charge your MacBook Air or MacBook Pro, follow these steps based on the type of port your Mac laptop has:

MAGSAFE 3 PORT

1. Locate the MagSafe 3 port on your Mac. It's typically found on the far left-hand side of the computer, near the escape key.

2. Charge with MagSafe 3:
   - Plug the USB-C power adaptor into a plug socket.
   - Connect the USB-C end of the MagSafe 3 cable to the power adaptor.
   - Attach the other end of the cable to the MagSafe 3 port on your Mac.

3. After connecting the charger, check the indicator light. It will glow green if your battery is fully charged or amber if your battery is charging or charging is on hold.

Note: MagSafe 3 charging is available for these Mac laptops:
   - MacBook Air introduced in 2022 or later
   - 14-inch MacBook Pro introduced in 2021 or later
   - 16-inch MacBook Pro introduced in 2021 or later

USB-C PORT

1. Locate the USB-C ports on your Mac. These ports can be found on the left-hand side or both sides of the computer.

2. Charge with USB-C
   2. Plug the power adaptor into a plug socket.
   3. Connect one end of the USB-C cable to the power adaptor.
   4. Plug the other end of the cable into any USB-C port on your Mac.

Note: USB-C charging is available for these Mac laptops:
   - MacBook Pro introduced in 2016 or later
   - MacBook Air introduced in 2018 or later

- Your Mac can only charge through one port at a time, so connecting multiple power adaptors to both USB-C ports and the MagSafe 3 port (if available) won't speed up charging.
- Different USB-C charge cables support varying maximum wattages (W). Ensure you use a cable that matches your Mac's requirements.
- If your display, such as the Apple Studio Display, provides power to your Mac, you don't need a separate USB-C power adaptor.

If the indicator light on your MagSafe 3 connector flashes amber repeatedly, try the provided troubleshooting steps. If the issue persists, contact Apple for further assistance.

GET STARTED WITH YOUR MAC

Setting up your MacBook is a straightforward process that involves several important steps. Here's a breakdown of what you'll be guided through during the initial setup:

1. Set Your Country or Region:
   - This step helps determine the language and time zone for your Mac.

2. Accessibility Options:
- You have the option to explore accessibility features for Vision, Motor, Hearing, and Cognitive abilities. If not needed immediately, you can choose "Not Now."

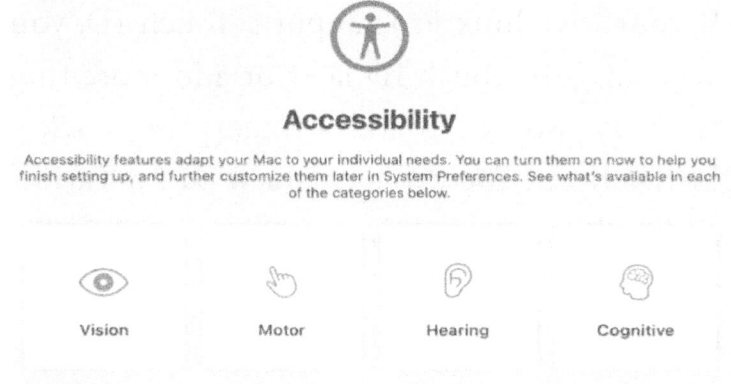

3. Connect to a Wi-Fi Network:
- Select a Wi-Fi network and enter its password, if required. If you're using an Ethernet connection, you can choose "Other Network Options." You can also change the network settings later by clicking the Wi-Fi status icon in the menu bar or going to System Preferences > Wi-Fi.
4. Transfer Information (Optional):
   - If you want to transfer data from another computer, you can do so now or at a later

time. If setting up a new computer without a previous Mac, you can choose "Not Now."

5. Sign in with Your Apple ID:
   - Your Apple ID is crucial for various Apple services. If you don't have one, you can create it during setup. Using the same Apple ID across your devices ensures seamless integration.

6. Store Files in iCloud (Optional):
   - iCloud allows you to store and access your content from anywhere. You can set this up later in System Settings.

7. Screen Time:
   - This feature allows you to monitor and receive reports on your computer usage. Details can be found in the Screen Time settings.

8. Enable Siri and "Hey Siri":
   - You can activate Siri and "Hey Siri" voice commands during setup. Instructions will be provided.

9. Set Up Touch ID:
   - If your MacBook Pro supports Touch ID, you can add your fingerprint during setup. To configure Touch ID later or add more fingerprints, go to System Settings > Touch ID & Password. To add a fingerprint, click the ╋ button and follow the onscreen instructions. You can use Touch ID for various purposes, such as unlocking your Mac and making purchases.

10. Set Up Apple Pay (Optional):
    - You have the option to set up Apple Pay for one user account. Additional users can use Apple Pay with their iPhone or Apple Watch.

11. Choose Your Desktop Appearance:
    - You can select between Light, Dark, or Auto mode for your desktop appearance. This choice can be adjusted later in System Settings.

Throughout this process, you have the flexibility to skip certain steps and complete them at a later time. Following these steps will ensure your MacBook Pro is set up according to your preferences and needs.

APPLE ID ON MAC

Your Apple ID is a crucial account that grants access to a range of Apple services. You can utilize it to download apps from the App Store, access media in Apple Music, Apple Podcasts, Apple TV, and Apple Books, synchronize content across devices using iCloud, create a Family Sharing group, and much more.

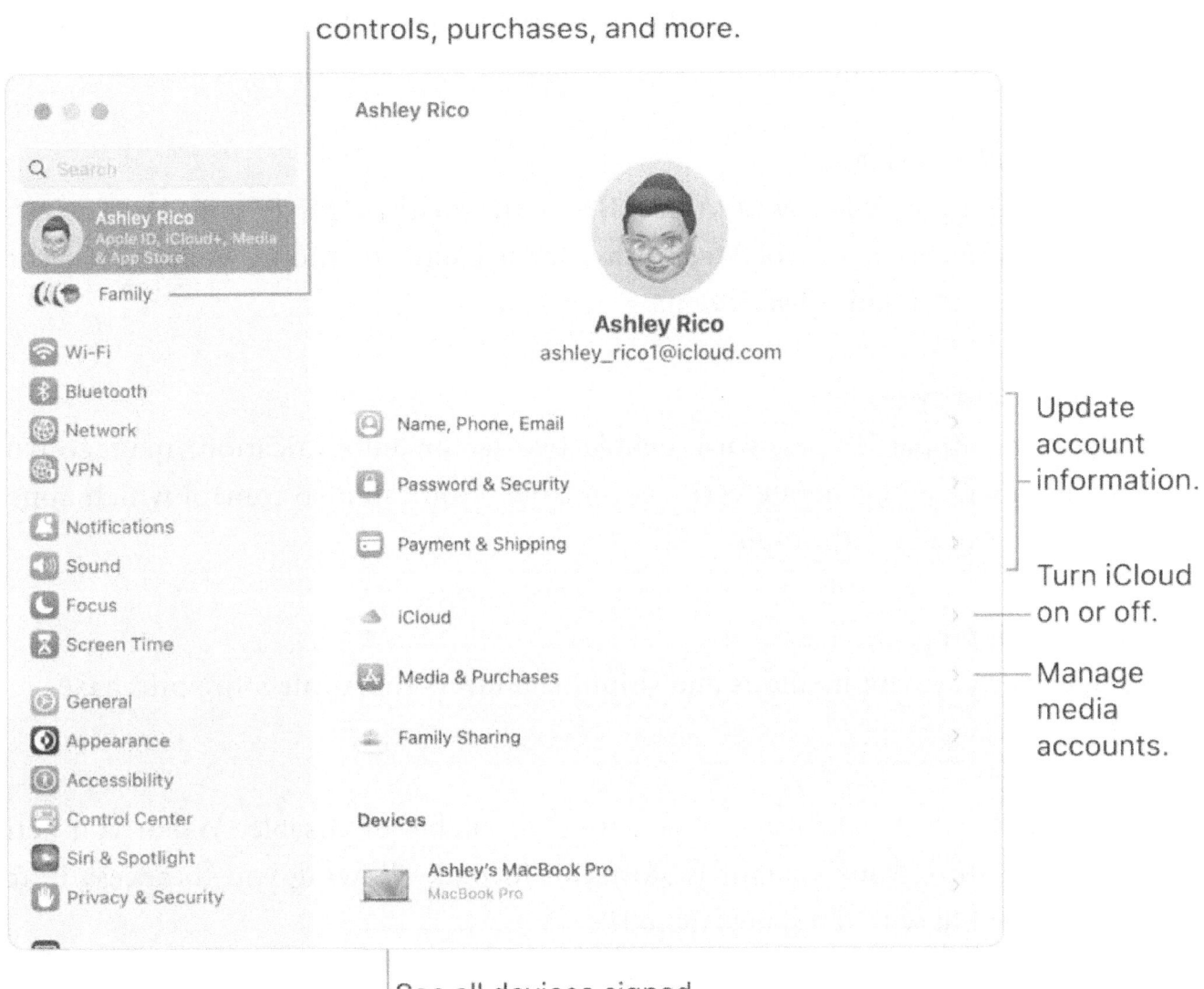

Here are some important details about managing your Apple ID:

1. Forgotten Password:
   - If you forget your Apple ID password, there's no need to create a new one. Simply click "Forgot Apple ID or password?" in the sign-in window to retrieve your password.

2. Family Members:
   - Each family member using Apple devices should have their own Apple ID. You can

create Apple ID accounts for your children and share purchases and subscriptions with Family Sharing.

3. Accessing Apple ID Settings:
   - Manage everything related to your Apple ID in System Settings on your MacBook. Your Apple ID and Family Sharing settings can be found at the top of the sidebar. To sign in with your Apple ID, if you haven't already, click "Sign in with your Apple ID" at the top of the sidebar.

4. Update Account Information:
   - In System Settings, click your Apple ID in the sidebar. Here, you can review and update the information associated with your account, including your name, contact information, and email subscriptions.

5. Password & Security:
   - Change your Apple ID password, enable two-factor authentication, manage trusted phone numbers, and generate verification codes. You can also control which apps and websites use Sign in with Apple.

6. Payment & Shipping:
   - Manage your payment methods and shipping address for Apple Store purchases.

7. iCloud:
   - Customize which iCloud features you want to enable or disable. When you activate an iCloud feature, your content is stored in iCloud, allowing you to access it across devices signed in with the same Apple ID.

8. Media & Purchases:
   - Manage accounts linked to Apple Music, Apple Podcasts, Apple TV, and Apple Books. Adjust purchasing settings and handle subscriptions.

9. Devices Associated with Your Apple ID:
   - View all the devices linked to your Apple ID. Verify that Find My [device] is activated for each one. You can also check the status of iCloud Backup for iOS or iPadOS devices and remove devices you no longer own.

10. Family Sharing:

- Set up a family group for up to six members. This allows you to share and manage purchases, share device locations, and mark devices as lost in Find My. You can also supervise how your children use their devices and set Screen Time limits.

11. Account Recovery and Legacy Contact:
- Establish recovery contacts or set up a recovery key to assist in resetting your password and regaining access to your account. Additionally, designate trusted individuals as Legacy Contacts to access your account and personal information after your passing.

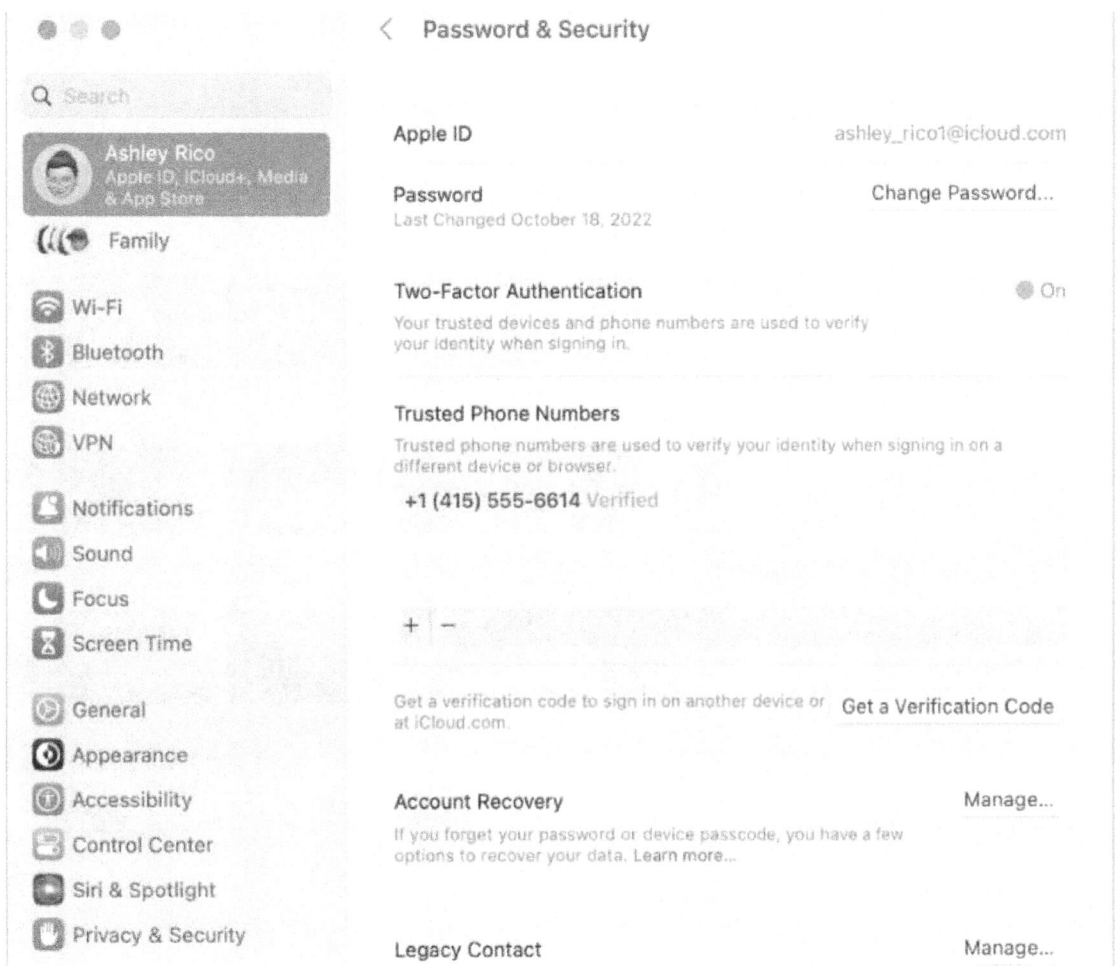

Your Apple ID is a versatile tool that enables seamless access to a variety of Apple services and allows you to manage your digital life efficiently.

CUSTOMIZE YOUR DESKTOP TO SUIT YOUR PREFERENCES

You have the option to select a basic color, use a favorite image, or even set a scenic photo that transitions with the time of day.

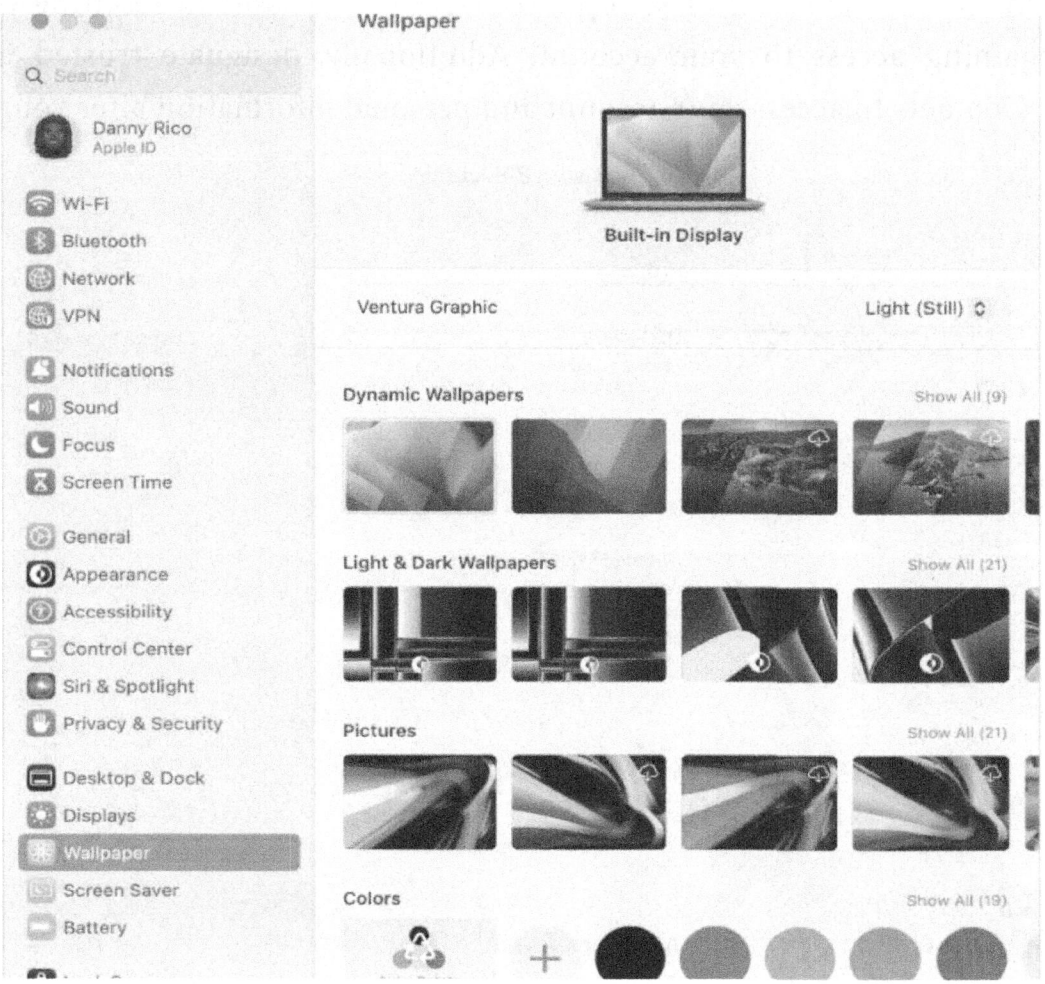

On your Mac, follow these steps to personalize your desktop:

1. Click on the Apple menu located in the top-left corner of your screen.
2. Choose "System Preferences" from the menu.
3. In the System Preferences window, find and click on Wallpaper in the sidebar. You may need to scroll down to see it.

LIGHT OR DAY

You can customize the appearance of your Mac by choosing between light, dark, or an automatic appearance that adapts based on the time of day.

Choose the color
scheme for your Mac.

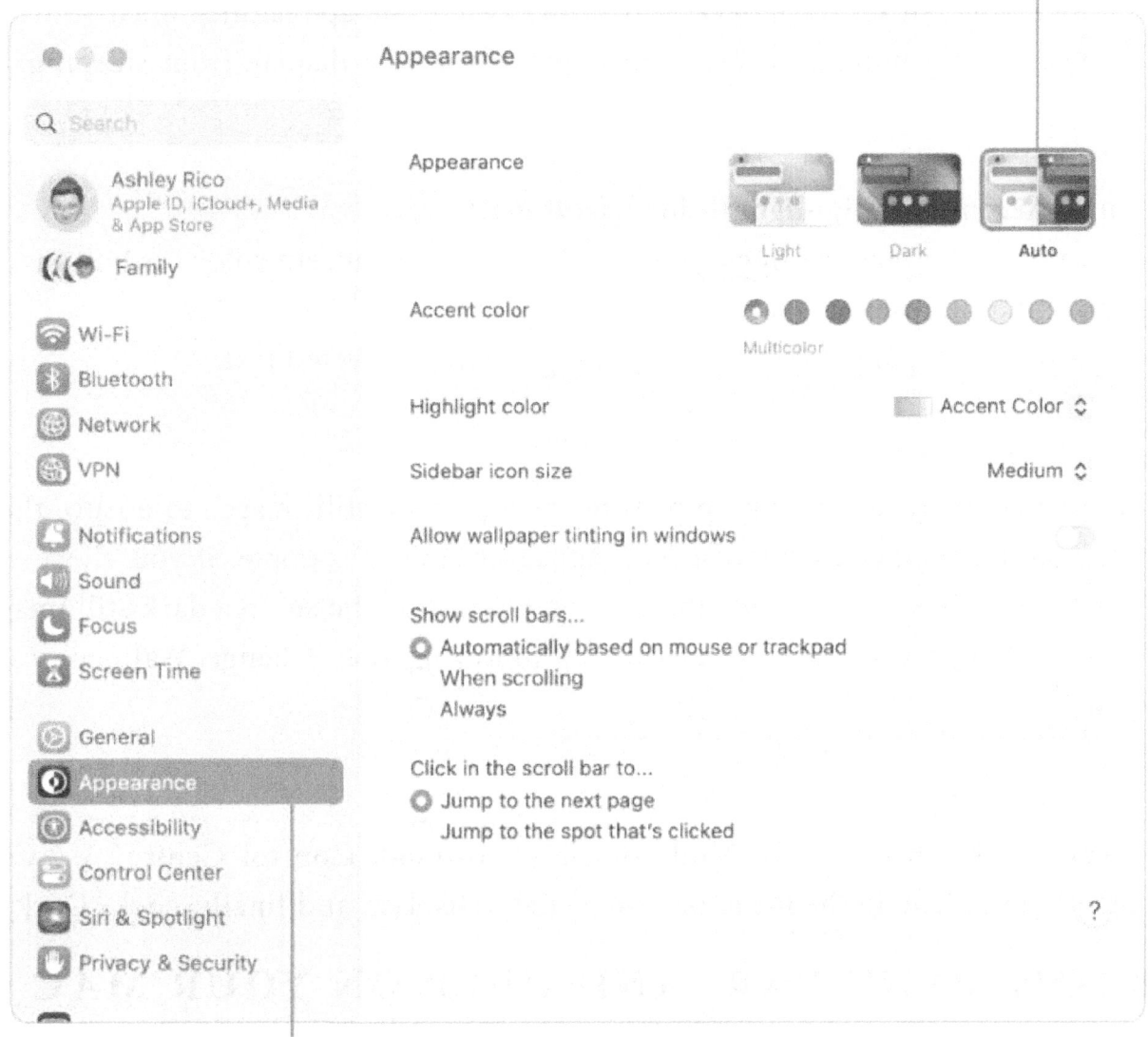

Click an item in the sidebar

1. **Open System Preferences**
   - Click the Apple menu in the top-left corner of your screen.
   - Select "System Preferences" from the dropdown menu.

2. **Access Appearance Settings**
   - In the System Preferences window, find and click on the "Appearance" icon .

3. **Choose Your Appearance**
   - In the Appearance settings, you have three options:
     - Light: This provides a light appearance that remains constant.
     - Dark: This provides a dark appearance that remains constant. Dark Mode is especially useful for tasks like viewing documents, presentations, photos, movies, and web pages.

Auto:

This automatically switches between light and dark appearances based on your Night Shift schedule, which you can set separately. Auto won't switch the appearance until your Mac has been idle for at least a minute or if an app is preventing the display from sleeping, such as during media playback.

4. **Customize Accent and Highlight Colors (Optional)**
   - In the same Appearance settings, you can also choose an accent color for buttons, pop-up menus, and other user interface (UI) controls.
   - You can select a highlight color to use for highlighting selected text.

5. **Dynamic Desktop Images**
   - Note that some dynamic desktop pictures may provide still images to ensure they don't distract from the selected light or dark appearance. For example, if you chose the dark appearance during macOS setup, the desktop picture will be set to a dark still image.
   - You can change your desktop picture by following the "Change Wallpaper settings" option.

6. **Quick Access to Dark Mode**
   - You can quickly toggle Dark Mode on or off through Control Centre ⬚ . Click the Control Centre icon in the menu bar, then click "Display," and finally, click "Dark Mode."

DESKTOP, MENU BAR, AND HELP ON YOUR MAC

The desktop is the first thing you see on your MacBook. It's where you can access apps, search for items on your Mac and the web, organize your files, and more.

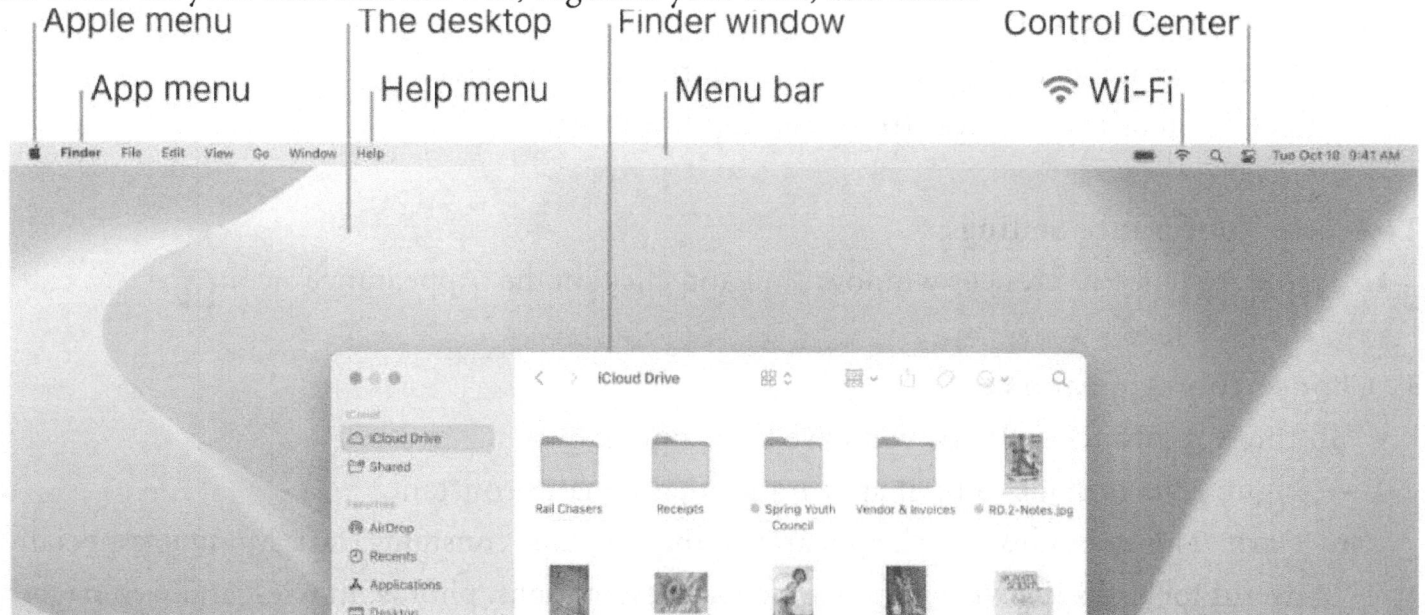

MENU BAR

- The menu bar is located at the top of the screen. It provides access to various commands and tasks within apps. The options in the menus change depending on the app you're using. On the right side of the menu bar, you'll find icons for tasks like connecting to Wi-Fi 🛜 , checking battery status 🔋 , accessing Control Center 🎛️ , and using Spotlight search 🔍 .

APPLE MENU

- The Apple menu found in the upper-left corner of the screen, contains frequently used items. Clicking the Apple icon opens this menu.

APP MENU

- You can have multiple apps and windows open simultaneously. The name of the active app appears in bold to the right of the Apple menu The app's unique menus are listed below. When you switch to a different app or window, the app menu and the menus in the menu bar adjust accordingly.

HELP MENU

- Help for your MacBook is always accessible in the menu bar. To access it, open the Finder in the Dock, click the Help menu, and select "macOS Help" to open the macOS User Guide. You can also type in the search field for suggestions. For app-specific help, open the app and click "Help" in the menu bar.

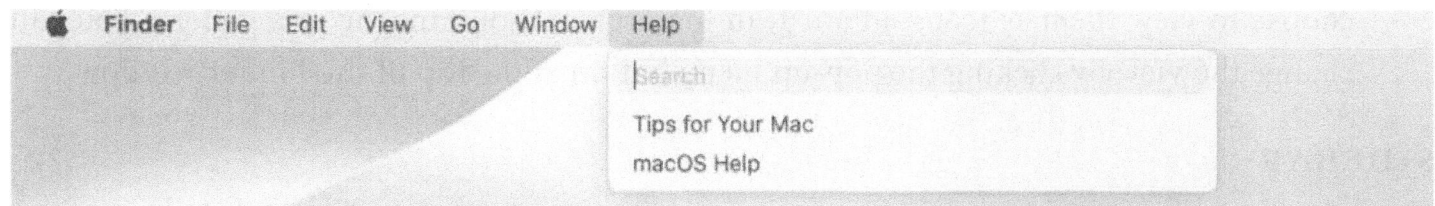

ORGANIZING WITH STACKS

- You can group files on your desktop into stacks to maintain organization. Stacks can be arranged by type, date, or tag, helping keep your desktop tidy. Clicking a stack expands its contents, and hovering over it shows thumbnail images of the files. To create stacks, click the desktop and select "View > Use Stacks." You can also set grouping options for stacks through "View > Group Stacks By." New files added to the desktop will be automatically sorted into the appropriate stack.

FINDER

The Finder, represented by the blue icon with a smiling face  is the central hub for managing and accessing everything on your Mac. Here's how you can use the Finder effectively:

OPENING FINDER

- To open a Finder window, simply click the Finder icon in the Dock at the bottom of the screen.

NAVIGATING FINDER

- The Finder window provides various ways to view documents and folders. You can choose to view them as icons, in a list, in hierarchical columns, or in a gallery. You can change the view by clicking the pop-up menu button at the top of the Finder window.

SIDEBAR

The sidebar on the left side of the Finder window displays items you frequently use or want quick access to. For instance, the iCloud Drive folder shows all your documents stored in iCloud Drive. To customize the sidebar, go to Finder > Preferences.

ORGANIZING FOLDERS

- Your Mac comes with pre-created folders for different types of content, such as Documents, Pictures, Applications, and Music. You can also create new folders to keep your files organized. To create a new folder, go to File > New Folder.

SYNCING DEVICES

- When you connect devices like an iPhone or iPad, they appear in the Finder sidebar. Click the device's name to access options for backup, updates, synchronization, and restoration.

GALLERY VIEW

- Gallery View allows you to view a large preview of selected files, making it easier to visually identify images, video clips, and other documents. The Preview pane on the right provides additional information about the selected file. You can use the scrubber bar at the bottom to quickly navigate through your files.

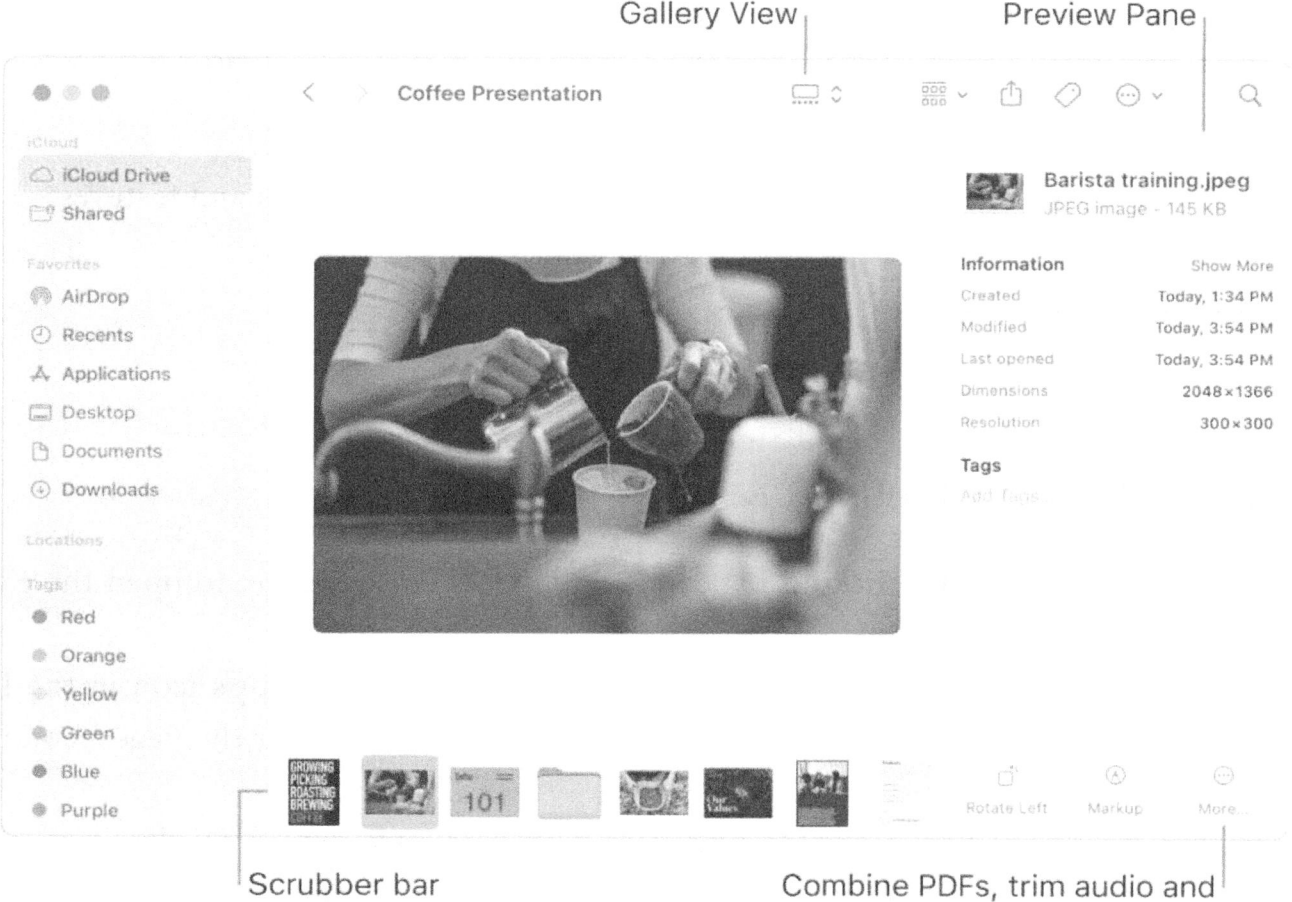

QUICK ACTIONS

- In Gallery View, you can click the "More" button ⊙ at the bottom right of the Finder window to access shortcuts for managing and editing files directly in the Finder. These actions include rotating images, annotating or cropping images using Markup, combining images and PDFs into a single file, trimming audio and video files, running shortcuts created with the Shortcuts app, and creating custom actions with Automator workflows.

QUICK LOOK

- To quickly preview a file, select it and press the Space bar. Quick Look allows you to perform actions like signing PDFs, trimming audio and video files, marking up, rotating, and cropping images without opening a separate application.

GO MENU

- The Go menu in the menu bar provides a quick way to navigate to folders and locations. For example, instead of clicking through multiple folders to find the Utilities folder, you can go directly by choosing Go > Utilities. You can also use Go > Enclosing Folder to return to the top level of nested folders or Go > Go to Folder to enter a specific folder path. *The Finder is your go-to tool for managing files, folders, and devices on your Mac.*

THE DOCK

The Dock on your Mac is a handy tool for accessing frequently used apps and features.

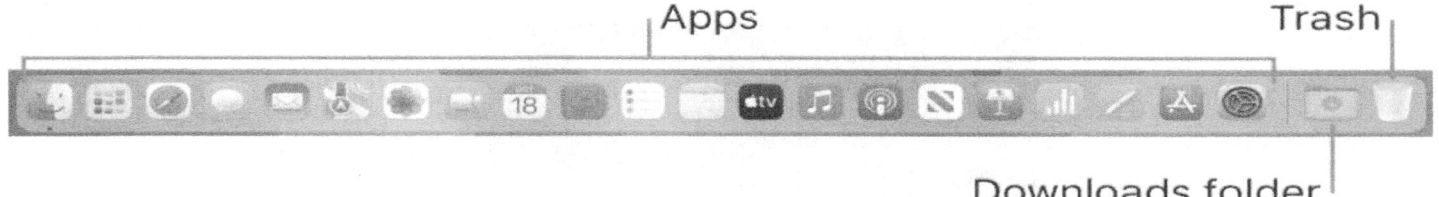

OPENING ITEMS IN THE DOCK

- To open an app, simply click on its icon in the Dock. For example, to open the Finder, click the 🙂 in the Dock.
- You can also open a file in an app by dragging the file over the app's icon in the Dock. For instance, to open a document in Pages, drag the document over the Pages icon in the Dock.
- To show an item in the Finder, Command-click the item's icon in the Dock.
- To switch to the previous app and hide the current app, Option-click the current app's icon.
- If you want to switch to another app and hide all other apps, Option-Command-click the icon of the app you want to switch to.

TAKING OTHER ACTIONS FOR ITEMS IN THE DOCK

- Control-click an item in the Dock to display a shortcut menu of actions. You can choose actions like "Show Recents" or click a filename to open the file.

- If an app becomes unresponsive, you can force it to quit by Control-clicking its icon in the Dock and selecting "Force Quit" (be aware that you may lose unsaved changes).

ADDING, REMOVING, OR REARRANGING DOCK ITEMS

- To add an item to the Dock, simply drag apps to the left side of the line that separates the recently used apps, or drag files and folders to the right side of the line.
- To remove an item from the Dock, drag it out of the Dock until you see "Remove." Note that only the alias is removed; the actual item remains on your Mac.
- If you accidentally remove an app icon from the Dock, you can easily put it back. Open the app to make its icon reappear in the Dock, then Control-click the app's icon and choose "Options" > "Keep in Dock."
- To rearrange items in the Dock, simply drag an item to a new location.

CUSTOMIZING THE DOCK

- To customize the Dock's appearance and behavior, go to Apple menu > System Preferences, then click on "Desktop & Dock" in the sidebar. You may need to scroll down to find it.
- In the "Dock" preferences, you can change how items appear in the Dock, adjust its size, choose its location (bottom, left, or right edge of the screen), or even hide it.
- Click the "Help" button at the bottom of the window to learn more about the available options.
- You can also quickly adjust the Dock's size by moving the pointer over the separator line in the Dock until a double arrow appears, then click and drag the pointer up or down.
- To navigate the Dock using keyboard shortcuts, press Control-F3 (or Control-Fn-F3 on a Mac laptop) to move to the Dock, then use the Left Arrow and Right Arrow keys to navigate between icons. Press Return to open an item.

RED BADGES IN THE DOCK

- A red badge on an icon in the Dock indicates that you have one or more pending actions in an app or System Preferences. For instance, a red badge on the Mail icon indicates that you have new emails to read.

NOTIFICATION CENTRE

Notification Centre on your Mac is a handy tool for managing notifications and accessing widgets for various purposes.

OPENING AND CLOSING NOTIFICATION CENTRE

Click the date and time to open Notification Centre.

- To open Notification Centre, click the date and time in the menu bar at the top-right corner of your screen. Alternatively, you can swipe left with two fingers from the right edge of the trackpad.
- To close Notification Centre, you can click anywhere on the desktop, click the date and time in the menu bar again, or swipe right with two fingers toward the right edge of the trackpad.

See notifications you missed and keep track of your day.

Customise widgets.

USING NOTIFICATIONS

- In Notification Centre, move your pointer over a notification to interact with it in various ways:
- To expand or collapse a stack of notifications from a single app, click anywhere in the top notification to expand it or click "Show less" to collapse the stack.
- You can take action directly from a notification by clicking on the action, such as Snooze in a Calendar notification or Reply in a Mail notification.
  - If an action has a ∨ arrow next to it, clicking the arrow provides more options. For example, in response to a call, you can click the arrow next to Decline, then choose Reply with Message.
- To see more details about a notification, click the notification itself. If there's a ⟩ arrow next to the app name, clicking it shows additional details within the notification.
- If you want to adjust the notification settings for a specific app, click the ⟩ next to the app name, click the ●●● button, and then choose options like muting or turning off notifications or accessing the app's notification settings in the Notifications preferences.
- To clear a single notification or all notifications in a stack, click the ⊗ or "Clear All"

button, respectively.

USING WIDGETS

- In Notification Centre, you can interact with widgets in the following ways:
  - To see more details or access related preferences, apps, or web pages, click anywhere within a widget. For example, clicking in a Clock widget opens Date & Time preferences, clicking the Reminders widget opens the Reminders app, or clicking the Weather widget opens a web browser to view the complete forecast.
- You can resize a widget by Control-clicking it in your set of active widgets and choosing a different size.
- If you want to remove a widget, press and hold the Option key while hovering over the widget, then click the "Remove" ⊖ button.

CONTROL CENTRE

Control Center on your Mac is a convenient way to access various settings and controls right from the menu bar.

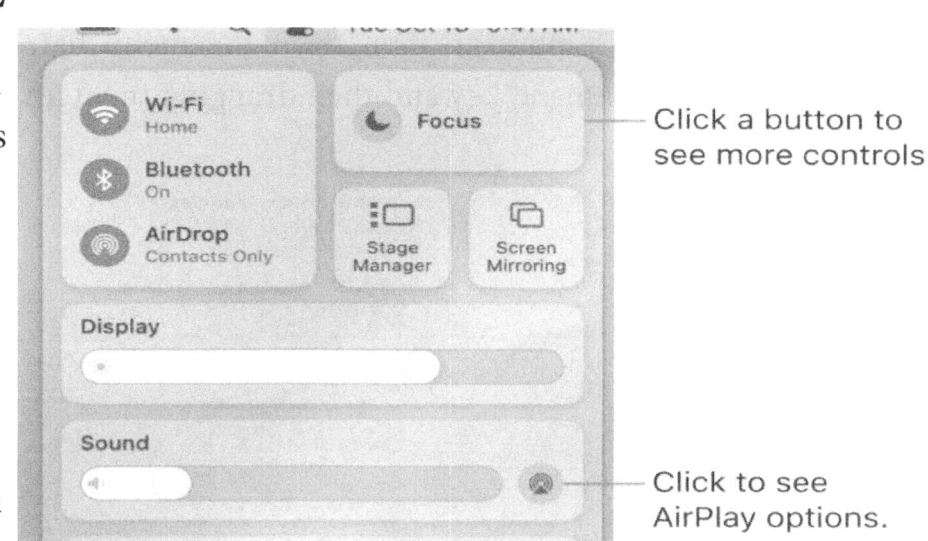

1. **Open Control Center**
   - Click the Control Center icon ⚏ located in the upper-right corner of your Mac's screen. It looks like a series of icons.

2. **Access More Options**
   - Clicking a button in Control Center allows you to access a set of related options or settings. For example, if you click the Wi-Fi button 🛜, you can view available Wi-Fi networks, your preferred networks, or open Wi-Fi Settings. To return to the main Control Center view, click the Control Center icon ⚏ again.

3. **Manage Your Desktop with Stage Manager**
   - Use Stage Manager to organize your apps and windows in a single view and switch between them quickly. You can group apps together to create workspaces that suit your workflow. This feature is especially useful for managing multiple open apps and windows efficiently.

4. Monitor Your Microphone

- The recording indicator in Control Center shows when your Mac's microphone is in use or if it was recently used. This visual indicator enhances security and privacy by informing you when an app has access to the microphone.

5. Pin Your Control Center Favorites

- You can pin your favorite Control Center items to the menu bar for quick access. To do this, simply drag a favorite item from Control Center to the menu bar. This allows you to access frequently used controls with a single click.
- To customize what appears in the menu bar, open Control Center settings, and use the dropdown menu next to each module to select "Show in Menu Bar." You'll see a preview of where the control will appear in the menu bar.

6. Removing Items from the Menu Bar

- If you want to remove an item from the menu bar, you can do so by pressing and holding the Command key and then dragging the item out of the menu bar.

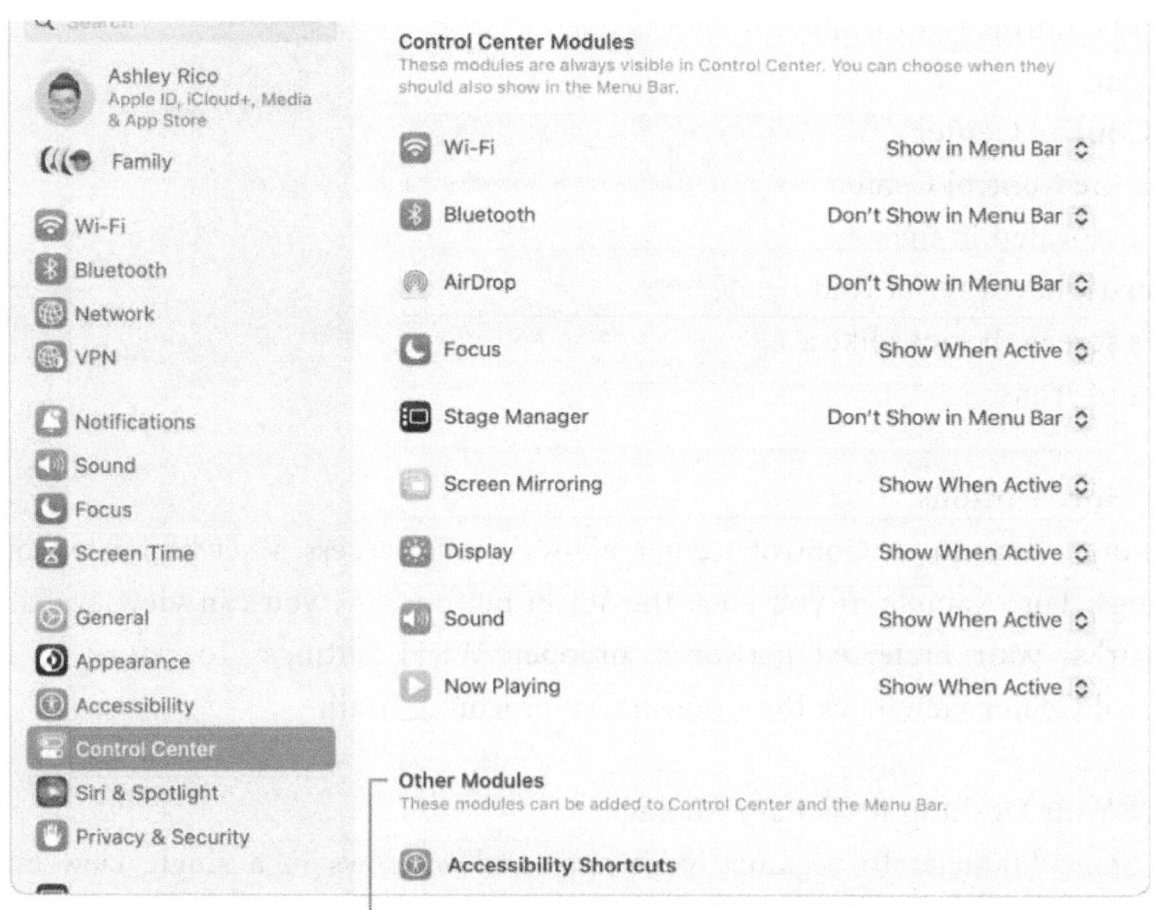

Choose additional modules

SYSTEM SETTINGS

System Settings on your Mac allow you to personalize and configure various aspects of your MacBook. Here's how you can use System Settings:

1. **Accessing System Settings**
   - To access System Settings, you can do one of the following:
     - Click the System Settings 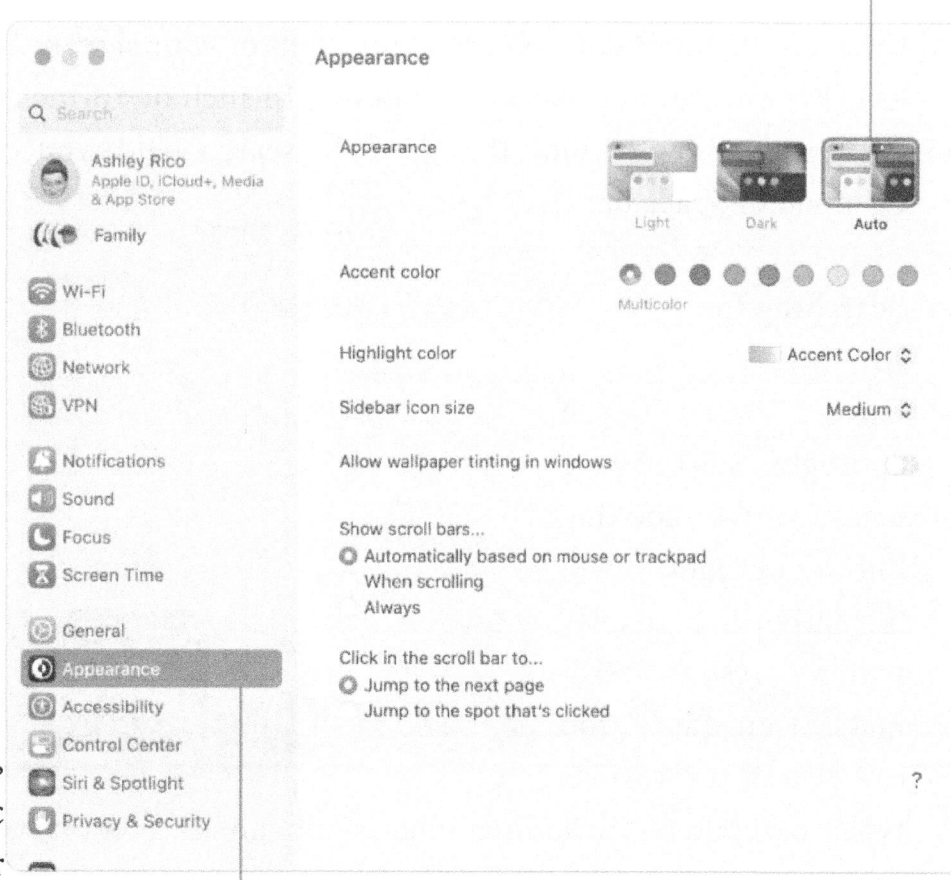 in the Dock.
     - Choose "Apple menu ⬛ > System Preferences" from the top-left corner of your screen, and then select the setting you want to adjust from the sidebar.

1. **Customizing Your MacBook**
   - Within System Settings, you can customize various settings related to your MacBook. These settings cover a wide range of options, including but not limited to:
     - Lock Screen settings: Adjust when your Mac goes to sleep.
     - Wallpaper settings: Set a custom desktop background.
     - Appearance settings: Choose between light mode, dark mode, or auto mode for your Mac's appearance.

scheme for your Mac.

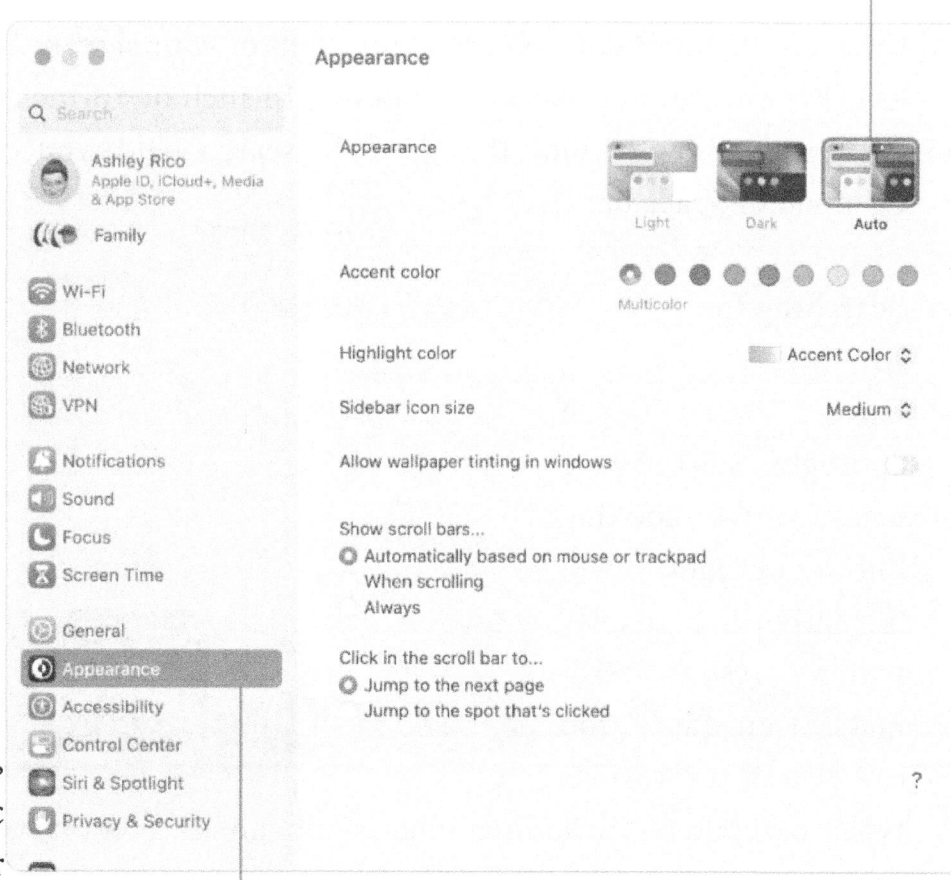

Click an item in the sidebar

   - To make adjustments, click on the specific setting in the sidebar that you want to customize. Depending on your preference, you may need to scroll down to see additional settings.

3. **Updating macOS**
   - In System Settings, you can also check for and update your macOS software. Here's how:
     - Click on "General" in the System Settings window.
     - Then, click on "Software Update" to see if your Mac is running the latest version of macOS software.
     - You can specify preferences for automatic software updates as well.

Using System Settings, you can tailor your MacBook to suit your preferences and stay up to date with the latest macOS software updates. It's a crucial tool for managing the configuration and appearance of your Mac.

SPOTLIGHT ON YOUR MAC

Spotlight 🔍 on your MacBook is a powerful tool that helps you find information, open apps, and perform quick actions quickly and easily.

1. **Accessing Spotlight**
   - Click on the Spotlight icon at the top right of your screen. You can also press the Spotlight key (F4) on your keyboard if you have a 14-inch or 16-inch MacBook.
   - To quickly show or hide the Spotlight search field, you can use the keyboard shortcut Command–Space bar.

2. **Searching for Anything**
   - Once you open Spotlight, start typing what you're looking for. Spotlight will instantly display search results that match your query. You can search for various

types of content, including images, documents, contacts, calendar events, and email messages.
   - With Live Text, Spotlight can even search for text within images. Please note that not all languages may be supported for this feature.

3. Opening Apps

- To quickly open an app, simply type its name in Spotlight, and when you see it in the search results, press the Return key.

4. Performing Quick Actions

- Spotlight allows you to perform quick actions directly. For instance, you can run a shortcut, start a Focus mode, or set an alarm without opening additional apps.
- To use these quick actions, open Spotlight, then type the action you want to perform. For example, you can type "Clock" and choose "Create Timer" to set a timer right from Spotlight.

5. Currency and Measurement Conversions

- You can use Spotlight to convert currencies and measurements. Simply enter a currency symbol (e.g., $, €, or ¥) followed by an amount, and then press Return. Spotlight will display a list of converted values.
- For measurement conversions, specify a unit of measure, and Spotlight will provide the converted result.

6. Siri Suggestions

- Spotlight also offers Siri Suggestions, which provide information from various sources such as Wikipedia articles, web search results, news, sports, weather, stocks, movies, and more when you perform a search.

7. Customizing Spotlight

- If you want Spotlight to search only for items on your MacBook and not fetch suggestions from the web, you can customize its behavior. Go to "System Preferences > Siri & Spotlight" and deselect "Siri Suggestions" in the list of Search Results. You can make other changes to the categories that Spotlight searches as well.

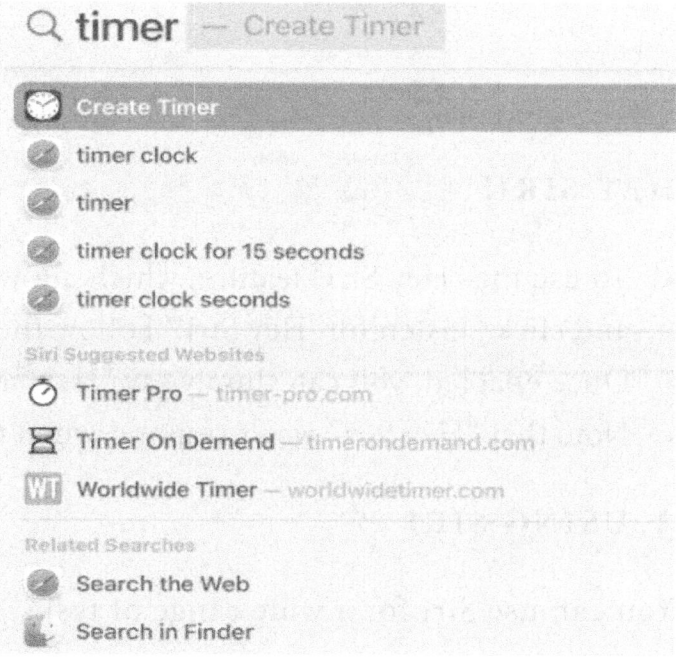

SIRI ON YOUR MAC

Siri is a powerful virtual assistant on your MacBook that you can use to perform various tasks using your voice. Here's how to enable and use Siri effectively:

ENABLE AND ACTIVATE SIRI

- Open "System Preferences" on your MacBook.
- Click on "Siri & Spotlight."
- Set your Siri preferences, including the language and voice you prefer.
- To activate Siri, you can:
  - On a 13-inch MacBook Pro: Tap the Siri button ⦿ in the Control Strip on the Touch Bar or press and hold the Command-Space bar.
  - On a 14-inch or 16-inch MacBook Pro: Press and hold the Dictation/Siri (F5) key or the microphone key 🎤 on the keyboard to open Siri.
  - You can also click "Siri & Spotlight" in System Preferences, then select "Ask Siri."

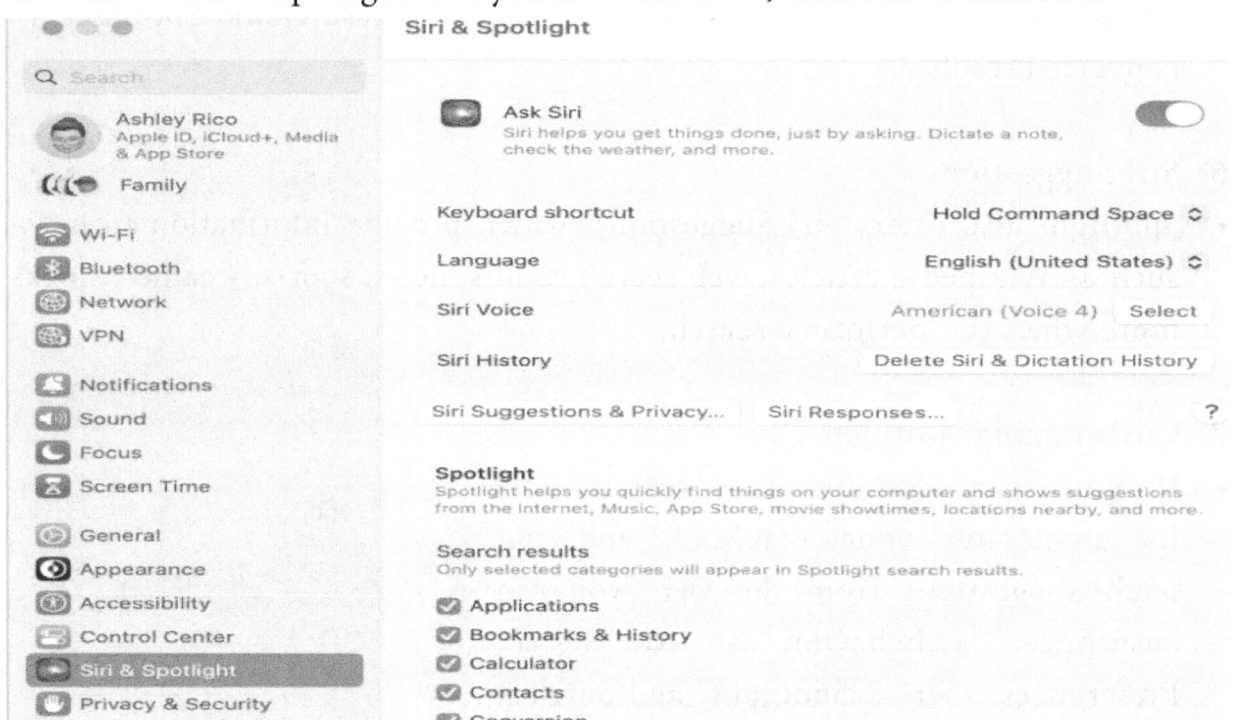

HEY SIRI!

- To use the "Hey Siri" feature, which allows you to activate Siri by voice, go to Siri settings and click "Listen for 'Hey Siri.'" Follow the prompts to set it up.
- Once enabled, you can simply say "Hey Siri" followed by your request to get a response.
- Note that "Hey Siri" won't respond when the MacBook 's lid is closed for convenience.

3. USING SIRI

You can use Siri for a wide range of tasks, including:

- Scheduling meetings and appointments.
- Changing system settings.
- Getting answers to questions.
- Making calls.
- Adding items to your calendar.
- Providing directions.

PLAY MUSIC

- To play music using Siri, simply say "Play some music," and Siri will take care of the rest. You can also request specific songs or ask for music from a particular time or genre.

DRAG AND DROP

- Siri allows you to drag and drop images and locations from the Siri window into emails, text messages, or documents. You can also copy and paste text using Siri.

CHANGE SIRI'S VOICE

- If you prefer a different voice for Siri, you can change it in the Siri settings. Go to "Siri & Spotlight" in System Preferences, then choose an option from the "Siri Voice" menu.

EXPLORING SIRI'S CAPABILITIES

- To discover more ways to use Siri, you can simply ask Siri, "What can you do?" at any time. Siri will provide you with a list of tasks and functions it can perform.

WINDOW MANAGEMENT ON YOUR MAC

Window management is crucial for efficiently organizing and navigating open apps and windows on your Mac.

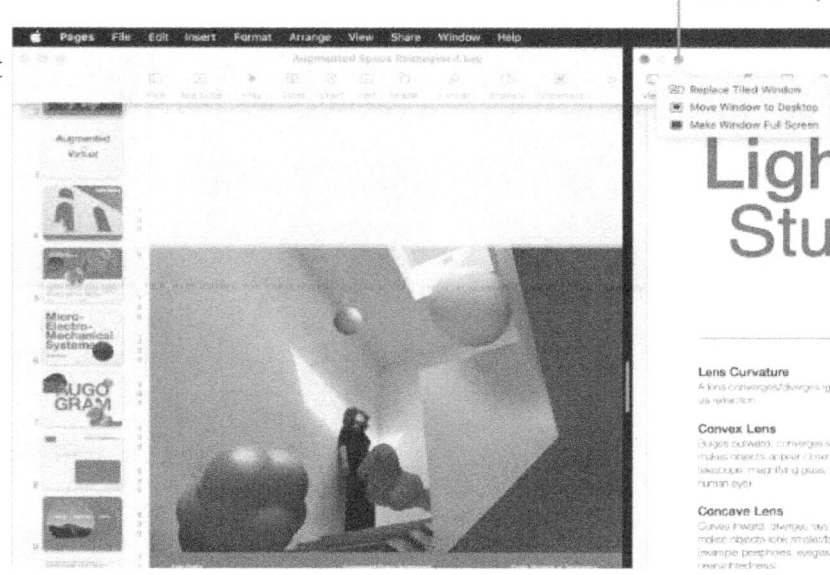

window options.

USE FULL SCREEN VIEW

- To make an app occupy the entire screen, enter full-screen view.
- Move the pointer over the green button in the top-left corner of the app window.
- Choose "Enter Full Screen" from the menu that appears.
- In full-screen view, the menu bar is hidden until you move the pointer to the top of the screen.
- This is particularly useful for apps like Keynote, Numbers, and Pages.

USE SPLIT VIEW

- Split View allows you to work with two app windows side by side, both filling the screen.
- Move the pointer over the green button in the top-left corner of a window you want to use.
- Choose "Tile Window to Left of Screen" or "Tile Window to Right of Screen" from the menu.
- Click another window to automatically fill the other half of the screen.
- The menu that appears when the pointer is over the green button offers options to switch apps and more.

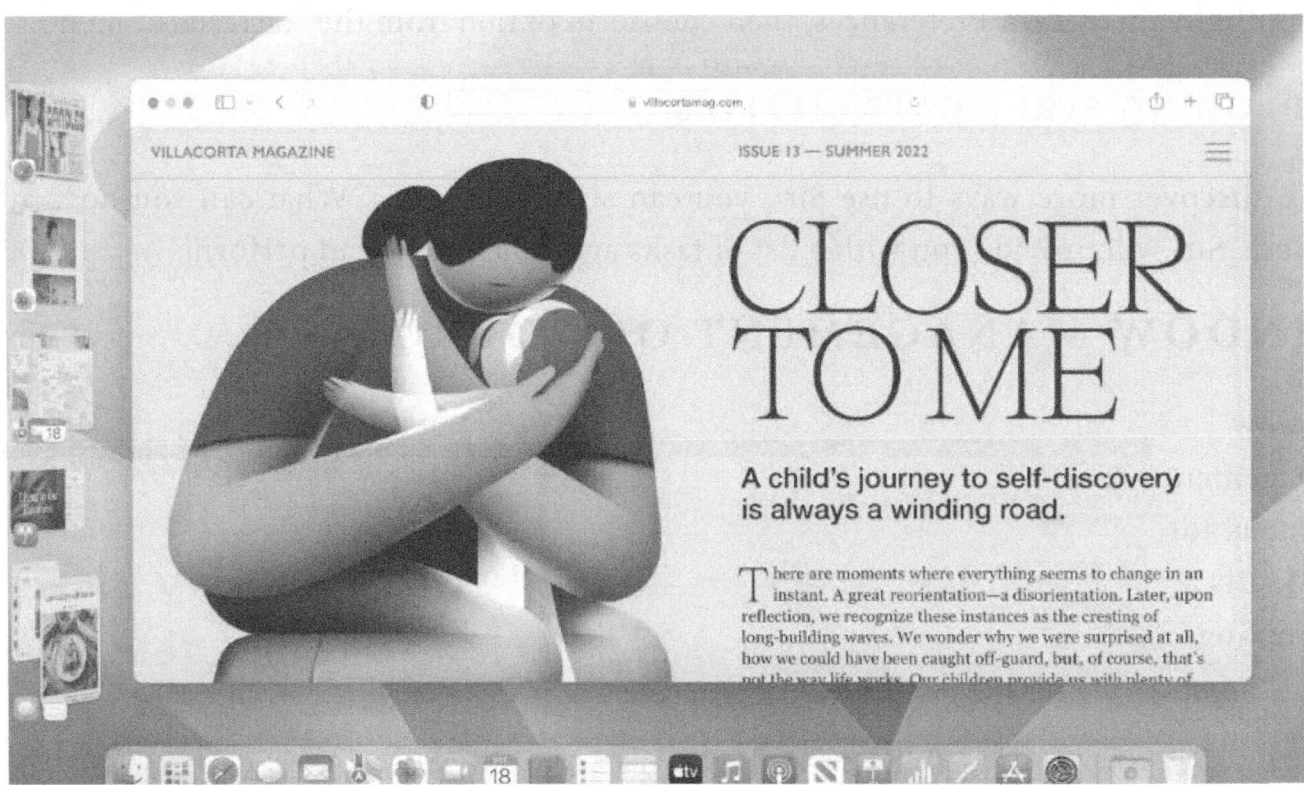

STAGE MANAGER

- Stage Manager is a feature in Control Center that automatically organizes your apps and windows to keep your desktop clutter-free.
- The focused window is front and center, while other windows are arranged on the side for easy access.
- You can access Stage Manager from Control Center.

MISSION CONTROL

- Mission Control is a powerful tool for managing open windows. It displays all open windows in a single layer.
- You can access Mission Control by pressing the Mission Control key ⌗ your keyboard or by pressing Control-Up Arrow.
- You can also add the Mission Control icon ⊞ to the Dock for quick access.
- It's useful for quickly finding and switching between open windows and desktop spaces.

MULTIPLE DESKTOP SPACES

- Organize your app windows into multiple desktop spaces to manage different tasks separately.
- To create a new space, enter Mission Control and click the "Add Desktop"   button   .
- You can switch between spaces using keyboard shortcuts and Mission Control.
- Dragging windows from one space to another is also possible.

USING THE TRAFFIC LIGHT BUTTONS

- The red, yellow, and green buttons in the top-left corner of every window have specific functions.
- Red: Closes the app window. In some apps, it quits the app entirely.
- Yellow: Minimizes the window to the right side of the Dock. Click it in the Dock to reopen it.
- Green: Maximizes the window to full screen or enters Split View, among other functions.

TRANSFER YOUR DATA TO YOUR NEW MACBOOK

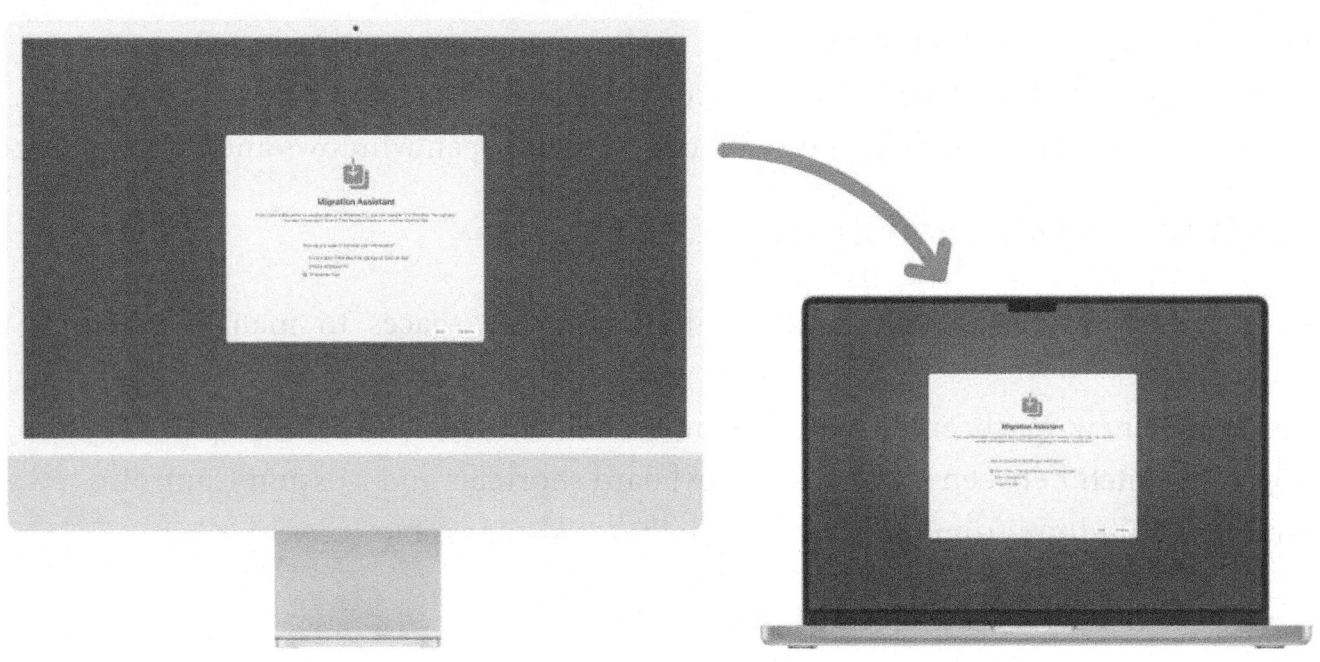

TO TRANSFER YOUR DATA TO YOUR NEW MACBOOK, FOLLOW THESE STEPS

1. Check macOS Versions

- Ensure that your older computer is running macOS 10.7 or later. It's advisable to update your older computer to the latest macOS version if possible.

2. Prepare Your New MacBook

- Make sure your new MacBook is running the latest version of macOS. To check for updates, go to System Preferences > General > Software Update.

3. Wireless Transfer

- You can use Migration Assistant to transfer data wirelessly from another Mac or PC to your MacBook.

- Open Finder, go to Applications, and open the Utilities folder.

- Double-click on Migration Assistant and follow the onscreen instructions.

- Ensure that both computers are connected to the same network and keep them near each other during the migration process.

4. Transfer from Time Machine Backup

- If you have a Time Machine backup on a USB storage device, you can transfer data from it to your MacBook.

- Connect the storage device to your MacBook using the appropriate adapter if needed.

- Drag and drop files from the storage device to your MacBook.

TRANSFER YOUR INFORMATION TO YOUR MAC FROM ANOTHER COMPUTER OR DEVICE

TRANSFER FROM A MAC

1. Upgrade both Mac computers to the latest version of macOS.
2. Connect the two computers using a cable (Ethernet, FireWire, or Thunderbolt) or ensure they're on the same network.
3. Open System Preferences on your new Mac, click on General, then select "Transfer or Reset" on the right and click "Open Migration Assistant."
4. Click Continue and follow the onscreen instructions.
5. On the other Mac, open Migration Assistant and follow the onscreen instructions.
6. Select the information you want to transfer:

- Apps, user accounts (and specific content like apps, documents, etc.)

- Documents and files from apps

- Computer settings

7. Follow any additional instructions and click Continue to start the transfer.

8. Once completed, review the migration summary for any issues and click Done to exit Migration Assistant.

TRANSFER FROM A PC

1. Ensure both computers are on the same network (wired or wireless).
2. Download and install the Windows Migration Assistant for your macOS version on your PC.
3. Close any open Windows apps on your PC.
4. Open Windows Migration Assistant and follow the onscreen instructions.
5. Select the information to transfer:
   - User accounts (and specific content)
   - Computer settings
   - Additional shared files, apps, and documents
6. Click Continue to start the transfer.
7. Once completed, click Done to exit Migration Assistant.

TRANSFER FROM A TIME MACHINE BACKUP OR STORAGE DEVICE

1. Connect the storage device to your Mac (using an appropriate adapter if needed).
2. Open System Preferences on your new Mac, click on General, then select "Transfer or Reset" on the right and click "Open Migration Assistant."
3. Click Continue and follow the onscreen instructions.
4. Select the information you want to transfer.
5. Follow any additional instructions and click Continue to start the transfer.
6. Once completed, review the migration summary for any issues and click Done to exit Migration Assistant.

TRANSFER YOUR DATA TO A NEW MAC USING MIGRATION ASSISTANT

To transfer your data to a new Mac using Migration Assistant, follow these steps:

ON YOUR NEW MAC:

1. Open Migration Assistant on your new Mac. You can find it in the Utilities folder within the Applications folder.
2. When prompted for permission to make changes, enter your administrator password and click "OK."
3. Choose the option to transfer from a Mac, Time Machine backup, or startup disk and click "Continue."

ON YOUR OLD MAC

4. Open Migration Assistant on your old Mac, located in the Utilities folder within the Applications folder, and click "Continue."
5. Select the option to transfer to another Mac and click "Continue."

BACK ON YOUR NEW MAC:

6. When asked to select a source, choose the old Mac and click "Continue."

ON YOUR OLD MAC:

7. If you see a security code, ensure it matches the one displayed on your new Mac and click "Continue."

BACK ON YOUR NEW MAC

8. Migration Assistant will catalog the content on your old Mac and calculate the storage space used by apps, user accounts, files, folders, and settings. This process may take a few minutes.
9. Select the specific information you want to transfer, such as user accounts and folders.
10. Before clicking "Continue," consider what to do if there are accounts with the same name on both Macs:

   • Rename: The account on your old Mac will appear as an additional user on your new Mac with a separate login and home folder.

   • Replace: The account on your old Mac will replace the identically named account on your new Mac.

11. Initiate the transfer by clicking "Continue." Large transfers may take hours to complete, so you might want to start in the evening and allow it to finish overnight.

AFTER THE TRANSFE

12. Once Migration Assistant finishes, close it on both computers.
13. Log in to the migrated account on your new Mac to access its files and settings.

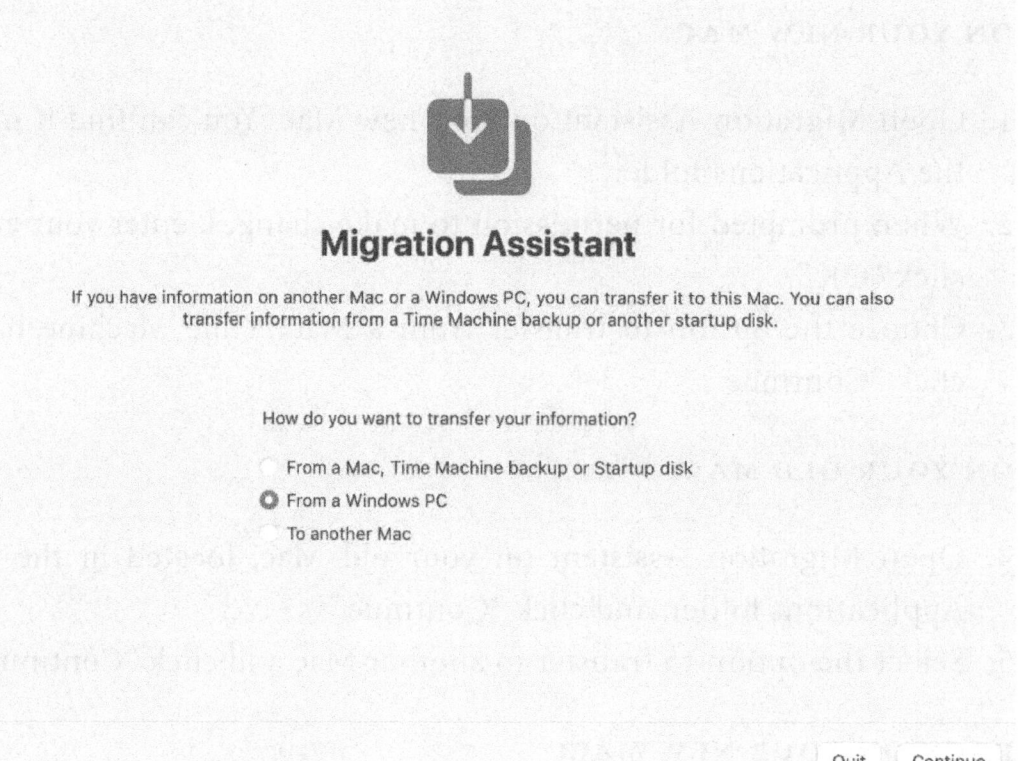

BACKING

UP YOUR MACBOOK WITH TIME MACHINE

To keep your files safe, it's essential to back up your MacBook regularly. The easiest way to do this is by using Time Machine, which is built into your Mac. Time Machine can back up your apps, accounts, settings, music, photos, movies, and documents (excluding the macOS operating system). You can back up to an external storage device connected to your MacBook or a supported network volume. Check Apple Support for a list of devices compatible with Time Machine.

SETTING UP TIME MACHINE

Ensure your MacBook is on the same Wi-Fi network as your external storage device, or connect the external storage device to your MacBook.

1. Open System Settings, click General > Time Machine.
2. Click "Add Backup Disk."
3. Select the drive you want to use for backup, and you're all set.

Files in iCloud Drive and photos in iCloud Photos are automatically stored in iCloud and don't need to be part of your Time Machine backup. However, if you want to back them up:

FOR ICLOUD DRIVE

1. Open System Settings, click Apple ID.
2. Click iCloud and deselect "Optimize Mac Storage."

FOR ICLOUD PHOTOS

1. Open Photos, choose Photos > Settings.
2. Click iCloud and select "Download Originals to this Mac."

You can use Time Machine to restore your files easily:

1. Click the Time Machine icon in the menu bar.
2. Choose "Browse Time Machine backups."
3. Select the items you want to restore (individual folders or your entire disk).
4. Click "Restore."

Note: If your operating system or startup disk is damaged, you must first reinstall macOS before restoring your files using Time Machine.

To restore your Mac to its original state. *(WARNING: Erasing your Mac removes all the information from it. Before you start, back up your Mac with Time Machine.)*

On a Mac with Apple silicon or an Intel-based Mac with the Apple T2 Security Chip, use Erase Assistant to reset your Mac to factory settings before you trade it in or sell it. You can also use Erase Assistant to erase your Mac before reinstalling macOS. Erase Assistant removes your content and settings, and any apps that you installed.

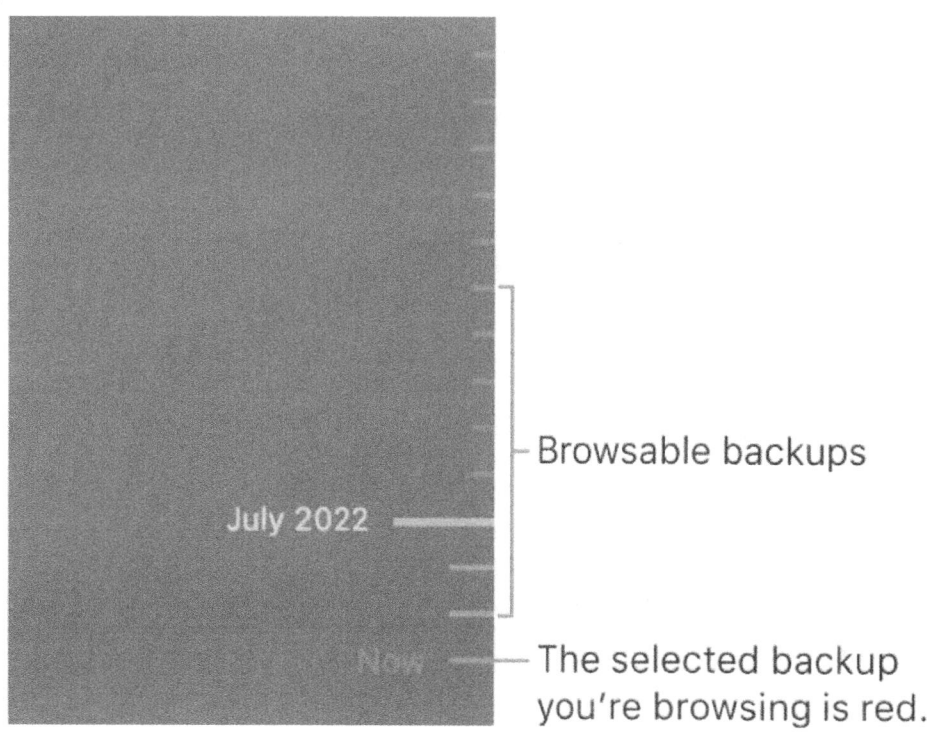

July 2022

Now

— Browsable backups

— The selected backup you're browsing is red.

What does Erase Assistant do?

Erase Assistant does the following things on your Mac:

- Signs you out of Apple services, such as iCloud.

- Turns off Find My and Activation Lock, so the Mac you're erasing is no longer associated with you.

- Erases your content and settings, and any apps that you installed.

- Erases all volumes (not just the volume you're on). If you installed Windows on your Mac using Boot Camp Assistant, the BOOTCAMP volume is also erased.

- Erases all user accounts and their data (not just your own user account).

ERASE YOUR MAC

1. Choose Apple menu > System Preferences.
2. In the menu bar, choose System Preferences > Erase All Content and Settings.
3. In Erase Assistant, enter your administrator information.
4. Review items that will be removed in addition to your content and settings.
5. If your Mac has multiple user accounts, click the arrow next to your account name to review the items.
6. Click Continue, then follow the on-screen instructions.

Note: If your version of macOS has been modified, Erase Assistant can't erase your Mac and displays an alert indicating you need to first reinstall macOS. Reinstall macOS, then use Erase Assistant.

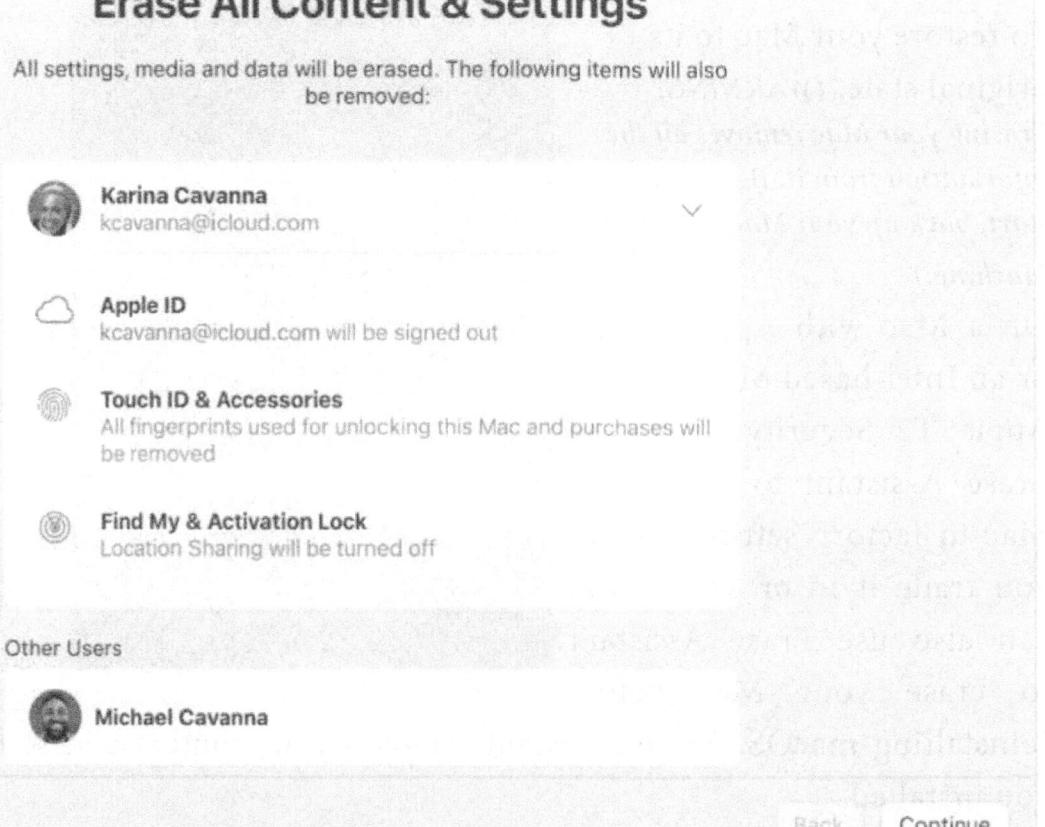

CONNECTING YOUR MAC WITH OTHER DEVICES

AIRDROP ON YOUR MAC

USING AIRDROP TO SHARE CONTENT

1. Open the file you want to send, then click the Share button. For files in the Finder, you can also Control-click the file, then choose "Share" from the shortcut menu.
2. Choose "AirDrop" from the sharing options listed.
3. A recipient list will appear in the AirDrop sheet. You can select a recipient from this list.

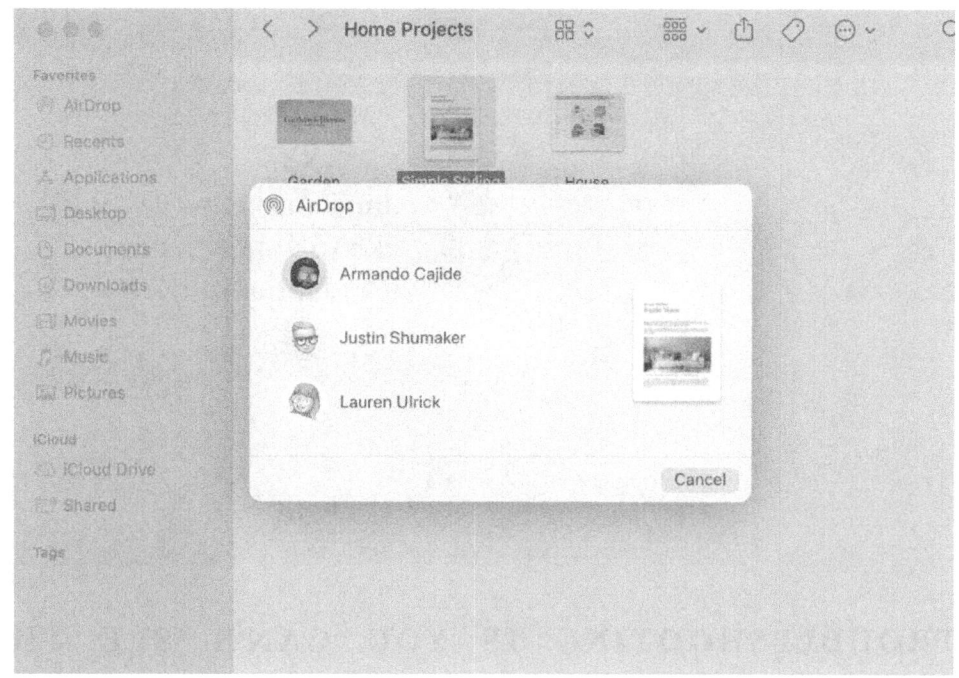

Alternatively, you can open an AirDrop window by selecting "AirDrop" in the sidebar of a Finder window or choosing "Go > AirDrop" from the menu bar.

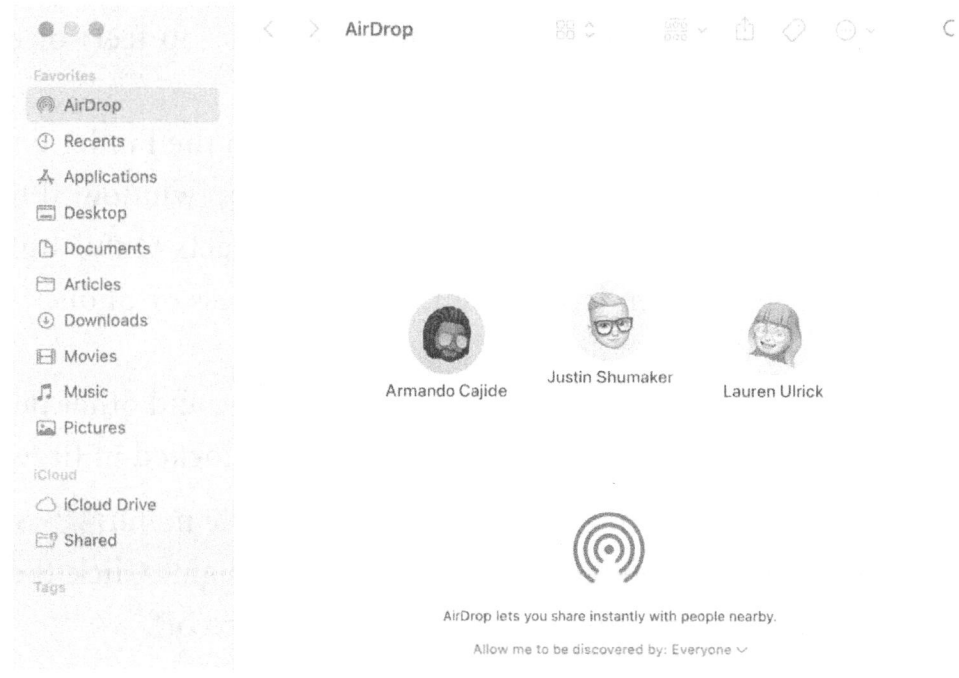

The AirDrop window will display nearby AirDrop users. To send files, drag one or more documents, photos, or other files to the recipient's name shown in the window.

RECEIVING CONTENT WITH AIRDROP

1. When someone nearby attempts to send you a file using AirDrop, you'll see their request as a notification or as a message in the AirDrop window.
2. Click "Accept" to save the file to your Downloads folder.

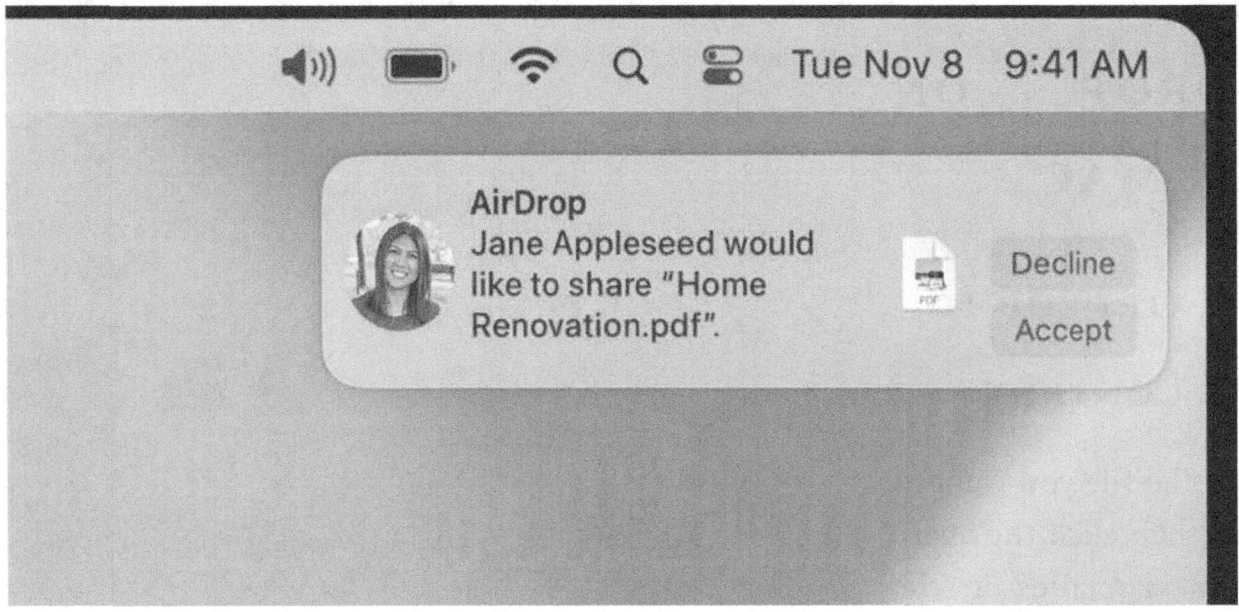

TROUBLESHOOTING IF YOU CAN'T SEE THE OTHER DEVICE IN AIRDROP

1. Ensure that both devices are within 9 meters (30 feet) of each other and have Wi-Fi and Bluetooth turned on.
2. Choose "Go > AirDrop" from the menu bar in the Finder on your Mac, then tick the "Allow me to be discovered by" setting in the AirDrop window. iPhone, iPad, and iPod touch have a similar setting. If set to receive from "Contacts Only," both devices must be signed in to iCloud, and the sender's Apple ID email address or phone number must be in the Contacts app of the receiving device.
3. Install the latest software updates for your Mac and other devices.
4. Make sure that incoming connections aren't blocked in firewall settings:

    •   For macOS Ventura or later: Choose Apple menu > System Settings, click "Network" in the sidebar, then click "Firewall" on the right. Click the "Options" button, and ensure that "Block all incoming connections" is turned off.

    •   For earlier versions of macOS: Choose Apple menu > System Preferences, then click "Security & Privacy." Click the "Firewall" tab, click the lock icon and enter your administrator password when prompted. Click "Firewall Options," then make sure that

"Block all incoming connections" is deselected.

AIRPLAY TO MAC

You can also airplay videos or movies from your iPad or iPhone to your Mac. See below:

STREAM VIDEO FROM IPHONE OR IPAD

1. Ensure your device is connected to the same Wi-Fi network as your Apple TV, AirPlay-compatible smart TV, or Mac.
2. Find the video you want to stream on your iPhone or iPad.
3. Tap the AirPlay button
   In some apps, you may need to tap a different button first. For example, in the Photos app, tap the Share button, then tap the AirPlay button.
4. Choose your TV or Mac from the list of available devices.

5. To stop streaming, tap the AirPlay button in the app you're using, then select your iPhone or iPad from the list.

STREAM VIDEO AUTOMATICALLY

Depending on your settings, your iPhone or iPad can suggest or automatically connect to

45

devices you use with AirPlay regularly. Here's how to adjust these settings:

1. Go to Settings 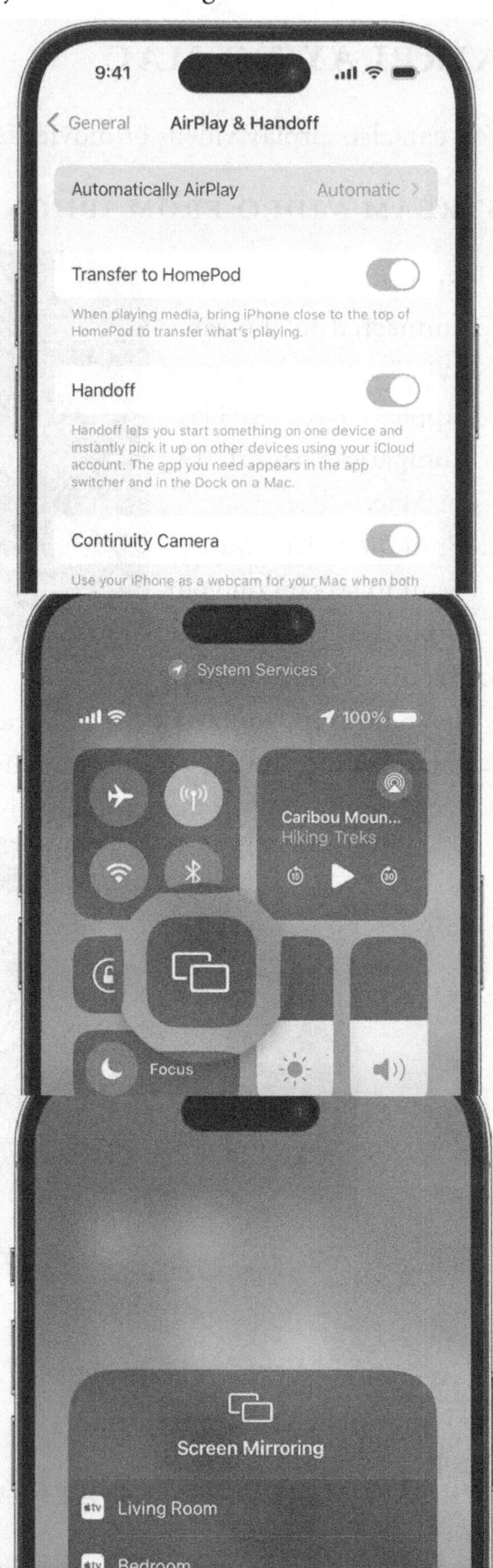 on your iPhone or iPad.
2. Tap General.
3. Tap AirPlay & Handoff, then tap "Automatically AirPlay."
4. Choose a setting:

   • Never: Manually choose a device for AirPlay.

   • Ask: Get suggested AirPlay connection notifications.

   • Automatic: Get suggested and automatic AirPlay connection notifications.

Ensure both your iPhone or iPad and your AirPlay-enabled device are on the same Wi-Fi network for automatic and suggested AirPlay connections.

MIRROR IPHONE OR IPAD TO A TV OR MAC

1. Connect your iPhone or iPad to the same Wi-Fi network as your Apple TV, AirPlay-compatible smart TV, or Mac.
2. Open Control Centre:

   • On iPhone X or later, or iPad with iPadOS 13 or later: Swipe down from the upper right-hand corner of the screen.

   • On iPhone 8 or earlier or iOS 11 or earlier: Swipe up from the bottom edge of the screen.
3. Tap the Screen Mirroring button.
4. Select your TV or Mac from the list of available devices.
5. If an AirPlay passcode appears on your TV screen or Mac, enter the passcode on your iPhone or iPad.
6. To stop mirroring, open Control Centre, tap

Screen Mirroring, then tap Stop Mirroring. Alternatively, press the Menu button on your Apple TV Remote.

Please note that not all video apps support AirPlay, so be sure to check the App Store on your Apple TV for app availability. You can also find out which macOS versions and Mac models are compatible with AirPlay to Mac and how to set up your Mac as an AirPlay receiver if needed.

APPLEPAY ON YOUR MAC AND OTHER DEVICES

Shopping online using Apple Pay on your Mac and completing the purchase with your iPhone or Apple Watch is a convenient and secure way to make online transactions. Here's how you can do it:

STEP 1: SET UP APPLE PAY ON YOUR MAC

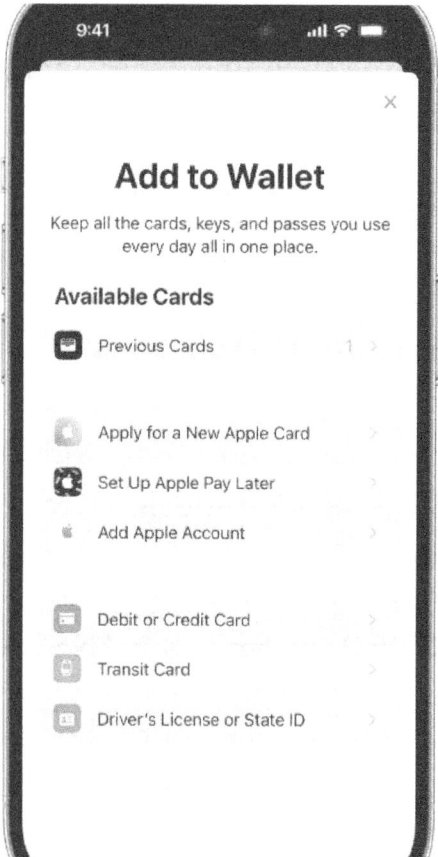

- Ensure you have Apple Pay set up on your Mac. You can do this by going to System ⚙ > "Wallet & Apple Pay."

- Add your debit or credit cards to Apple Pay by pressing on the add button ➕ on the top right of Wallet & Apple Pay on your Mac or other Apple device.

STEP 2: START SHOPPING ON YOUR MAC

1. Open your web browser on your Mac and go to the online store where you want to make a purchase.
2. Browse the website, select the items you wish to buy, and add them to your cart.
3. Proceed to the checkout page.

STEP 3: CHOOSE APPLE PAY

1. On the checkout page, look for the Apple Pay option.
2. Click on the Apple Pay button. This will initiate the payment process.

STEP 4: CONFIRM YOUR PURCHASE ON YOUR IPHONE OR APPLE WATCH

1. Shortly after clicking the Apple Pay button on your Mac, a payment prompt will appear

on your iPhone or Apple Watch if they are nearby and signed in to the same account.On your iPhone, use Face ID, Touch ID, or your passcode to authorize the payment.

2. On your Apple Watch, double-click the side button to confirm the payment.

STEP 5: COMPLETE THE TRANSACTION

1. Once you've confirmed the payment on your iPhone or Apple Watch, your Mac will receive the confirmation, and your purchase will be finalized.
2. You'll typically receive an email or on-screen confirmation of your successful transaction.

That's it! You've successfully shopped online on your Mac and used Apple Pay on your iPhone or Apple Watch to complete the purchase. This method ensures a quick and secure online shopping experience without the need to manually enter your payment details on the Mac.

HOTSPOT CONTINUITY

Using Instant Hotspot to connect to your Personal Hotspot without entering a password is a convenient way to share your iPhone or iPad's internet connection with your Mac, iPhone, iPad, or iPod touch. Here's how to set it up and use it:

STEP 1: SET UP INSTANT HOTSPOT

1. Ensure that your iPhone or iPad (Wi-Fi + Cellular) has an activated service provider plan that includes Personal Hotspot service.
2. Make sure all devices you want to connect are signed in to iCloud with the same Apple ID.
3. Enable Bluetooth and Wi-Fi on all devices involved.

STEP 2: USE INSTANT HOTSPOT

To connect from your Mac

1. Click on the Wi-Fi icon 📶 in the Control Center or the menu bar 🔲 your Mac.
2. You'll see the name of the iPhone or iPad providing your Personal Hotspot ⌘ listed there with a personal hotspot icon next to it.
3. Click on the name of your iPhone or iPad.

TO CONNECT FROM ANOTHER IPHONE OR IPAD

1. Open the "Settings" ⚙ app on your iPhone or iPad, tap "Wi-Fi."
2. You'll see the name of the iPhone or iPad providing your Personal Hotspot listed there with a personal hotspot icon next to it. Tap on the name of your iPhone or iPad.

CAMERA CONTINUITY

You can easily use your iPhone or iPad to scan documents or take pictures on your Mac using Continuity Camera. Here's how to do it:

STEP 1: USE AN APP THAT SUPPORTS CONTINUITY CAMERA

You can use Continuity Camera to scan or take a picture in these built-in apps on your Mac:

Finder	Notes
Keynote 8.2 or later	Numbers 5.2 or later
Mail	Pages 7.2 or later
Messages	TextEdit

STEP 2: TAKE A PHOTO

To take a photo and have it instantly appear on your Mac:

1. Open a supported app on your Mac.
2. You can either:

Control-click where you want the photo to be inserted in the app window. From the shortcut menu, choose "Insert from iPhone or iPad" > "Take Photo." You can do this in a Finder window or on the desktop.

From the File menu (or Insert menu, if applicable), choose "Insert from iPhone or iPad" > "Take Photo."

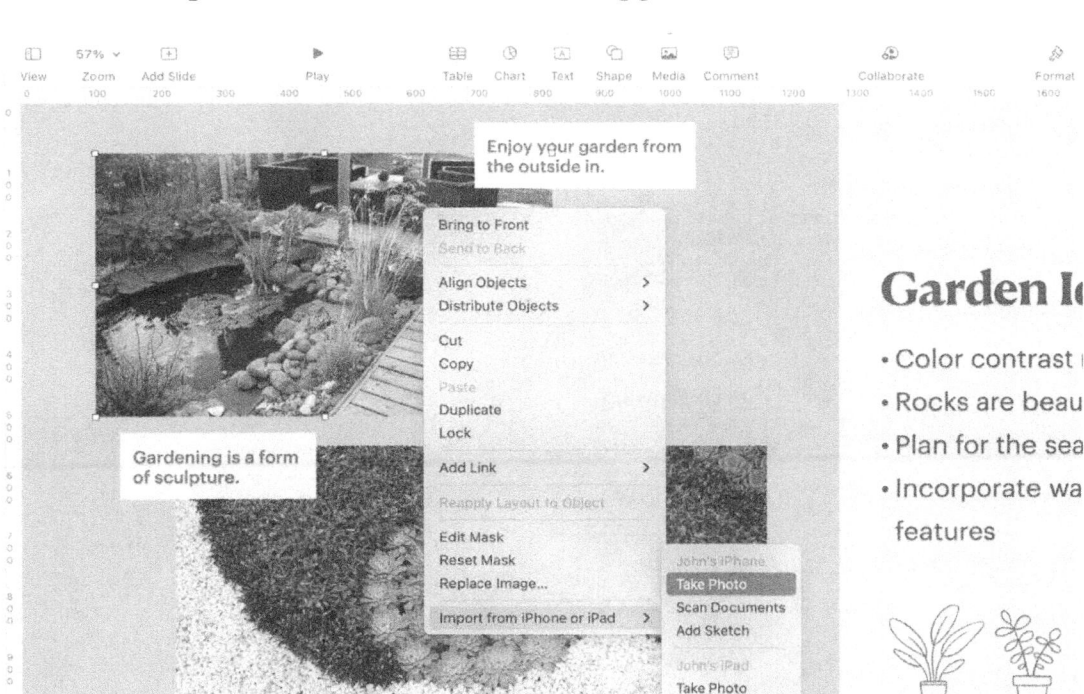

3. The Camera app will open on your iPhone or iPad.
4. Tap the Shutter button ⬤ to take a photo.
5. After taking the photo, tap "Use Photo" on your iPhone or iPad.
6. Your photo will instantly appear in the window on your Mac.

STEP 3: SCAN DOCUMENTS

To scan documents and have them appear on your Mac:

1. Open a supported app on your Mac.
2. You can either:

   • Control-click where you want the scan to be inserted in the app window. From the shortcut menu, choose "Insert from iPhone or iPad" > "Scan Documents." You can do this in a Finder window or on the desktop.

   • From the File menu (or Insert menu, if applicable), choose "Insert from iPhone or iPad" > "Scan Documents."

3. The Camera app will open on your iPhone or iPad.
4. Place your document in view of the camera and wait for the scan to complete.
5. If needed, tap the Shutter button ⬤ to manually capture a scan.
6. Adjust the scan to fit the page by dragging the corners, then tap "Keep Scan" to save it.
7. You can add additional scans to the document or tap "Save" when you're finished.
8. Your scans will appear as a PDF in the window on your Mac.

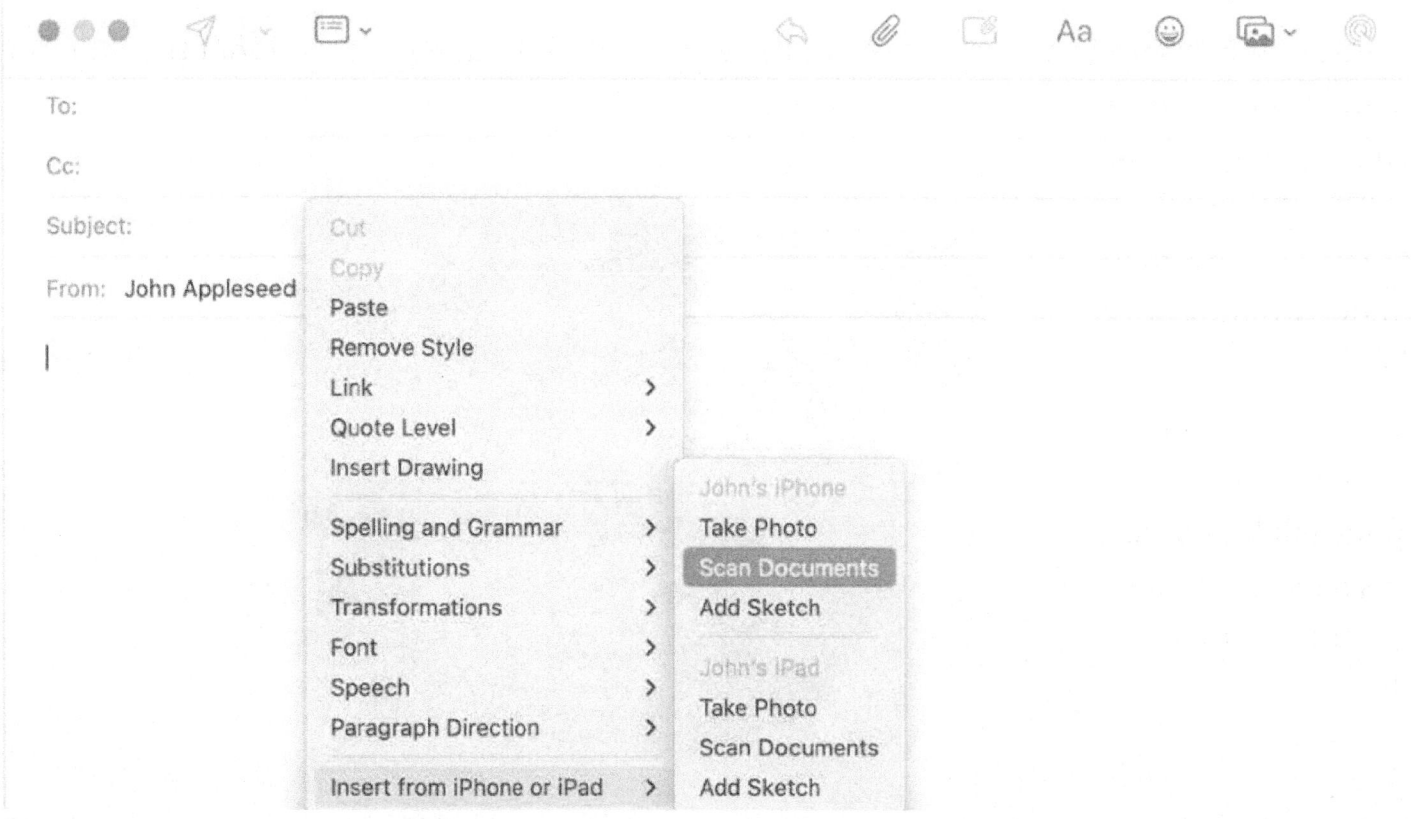

STEP 4: USE YOUR IPHONE AS A WEBCAM

You can also use your iPhone as a webcam for your Mac, but please note that this feature has different system requirements.

STEP 1: MOUNT YOUR IPHONE

Continuity Camera mounts and other iPhone-compatible mounts and stands are available from various manufacturers. When mounting your iPhone, make sure it meets the following criteria:

- It should be placed near your Mac.

- Ensure it's locked for security.

- Keep it stable to avoid movement.

- Position your iPhone with its rear cameras facing you and unobstructed.

- It can be mounted in landscape orientation to allow apps to choose your iPhone automatically, or in portrait orientation.

You can use Continuity Camera wired or wirelessly. To keep your iPhone charged while using it, you can plug it into your Mac or a USB charger. Your Mac will notify you if the iPhone battery level gets low.

STEP 2: CHOOSE YOUR IPHONE AS YOUR CAMERA OR MICROPHONE

When your iPhone is properly mounted, its camera and microphone are available to apps that can use them.

- To choose your iPhone camera, open an app like FaceTime or any other app that uses the camera. If the app doesn't automatically start using your iPhone camera, you can select it from the app's video menu or camera menu.
- To choose your iPhone microphone, go to Apple menu > System Settings, click on Sound in the sidebar, then select your iPhone microphone in the Input tab.

You don't need to manually select your iPhone microphone unless your Mac has no built-in or external microphone. In that case, your app might choose your iPhone microphone automatically.

Privacy Note: When the camera or microphone is in use, a privacy indicator appears in the iPhone status bar and next to Control Centre n the Mac menu bar. When used wirelessly, the iPhone emits a brief sound when an app begins using its camera or microphone.

STEP 3: USE EFFECTS AND FEATURES

macOS offers various video and audio features that you can use in FaceTime and many other video-conferencing apps. These features include Reactions, Presenter Overlay, camera modes, and microphone modes.

STEP 4: PAUSE, DISCONNECT, OR TURN OFF

If you receive a call while using your iPhone camera or microphone:

- If you answer the call on your iPhone, video and audio will pause until you end the call and lock and mount your iPhone.
- If you answer the call on your Mac, the current video and audio session pauses. When you end the call, you might need to choose your iPhone again in your app.

OTHER WAYS TO PAUSE, DISCONNECT, OR TURN OFF:

- Use your app's controls to stop video, mute audio, or end the call, or simply quit the app.

- Unlock your iPhone. To resume, lock and mount your iPhone. You may need to stop and restart video or audio in your app as well.

- Tap the Pause button on your iPhone screen. To resume, tap Resume and mount your iPhone.

- Tap the Disconnect button on your iPhone screen, or move it out of Bluetooth range of your Mac. The current video and audio session pauses or switches to another camera or microphone, if available. Your iPhone is removed from camera and microphone lists on your Mac. To add it back, plug your iPhone into your Mac and mount your iPhone.

If you want to prevent your Mac from recognizing your iPhone as a camera or microphone, even when it's plugged in and mounted, you can turn off Continuity Camera:

1. On your iPhone, go to Settings ⚙ > General > AirPlay & Handoff.
2. Turn off Continuity Camera.

CONTINUITY CAMERA SYSTEM REQUIREMENTS

When used for scanning and taking photos on your Mac, Continuity Camera works with the following devices and operating systems:

macOS Mojave or later	MacBook Pro introduced in 2012 or later
Mac mini introduced in 2012 or later	iMac Pro
Mac Studio introduced in 2022 or later	iPhone
iPod touch	MacBook introduced in 2015 or later
MacBook Air introduced in 2012 or later	iMac introduced in 2012 or later
Mac Pro introduced in 2013 or later	iOS 12 or later
iPad	

Additional Requirements

- Both devices must have both Wi-Fi and Bluetooth turned on.
- Both devices must be signed in with the same Apple ID using two-factor authentication.
- Ensure your Mac is using the latest version of macOS.

APPLE ID & ICLOUD SETTINGS

iCloud is a powerful service that keeps your important data safe, up-to-date, and accessible across all your Apple devices. It provides 5 GB of free storage for your files, documents and photos, and your purchases from Apple's digital stores don't count towards your available space. You can upgrade to iCloud+ for more storage and premium features.

SIGNING IN TO ICLOUD.COM

1. Open a web browser on your computer.
2. Go to [iCloud.com](https://www.icloud.com).
3. Sign in with your Apple ID using one of the following methods:

   • Enter your Apple ID (or a Reachable At email address or phone number associated with your Apple ID) and password.

   • If you're using Safari and are already signed in to a device that supports Face ID or Touch ID, you can use Face ID or Touch ID to sign in.

   • In supported versions of Google Chrome or Microsoft Edge, you can enter your Apple ID and click "Sign in with Passkey" to scan a QR code (if you have iCloud Keychain enabled and an iPhone or iPad with iOS 17, iPadOS 17, or later).

4. If prompted, follow the on-screen instructions to verify your identity. This may involve entering a code sent to a trusted device or phone number, or using a security key. If you've lost your trusted device, you can use the "Find Devices" button for assistance.

APPS AND FEATURES AVAILABLE ON ICLOUD.COM

Once you sign in, you can access various apps and features on iCloud.com, depending on your account and device, such as:

SWITCHING BETWEEN APPS AND FEATURES ON ICLOUD.COM:

Once logged in to iCloud.com, using different apps and features is easy:

- Click on the app or feature tile on the iCloud.com homepage.

- You can also click within a tile, for instance, to open a specific note directly.

- Use the App Launcher button in the toolbar to select another app or feature.

SIGNING OUT OF ICLOUD.COM

To sign out of iCloud.com, follow these steps:

1. Click your Apple ID photo or the Account button in the top-right corner of the iCloud.com window.

2. Choose one of the following options:

- Sign out from the browser you're currently using: Select "Sign Out."

- Sign out from all browsers where you're signed in: Click "iCloud Settings," then "Sign Out Of All Browsers," and finally, "Sign Out."

Calendar	Contacts	Custom Email Domain (iCloud+)	Find Devices
Keynote	iCloud Mail	Hide My Email (iCloud+)	iCloud Drive
Notes	Numbers	Pages	Photos

SETTING UP ICLOUD DRIVE ON YOUR MAC OR WINDOWS COMPUTER

ON A MAC

macOS 13.3 or later:

1. Click the Apple menu located at the top-left corner of your screen.

2. Choose "System Preferences."

3. Click on your name located at the top of the sidebar.

4. Click on "iCloud" on the right.

5. Select "iCloud Drive."

6. Turn on the "Sync this Mac" option.

macOS 13 to 13.2:

1. Click the Apple menu located at the top-left corner of your screen.
2. Choose "System Preferences."
3. Click on your name located at the top of the sidebar.
4. Click on "iCloud" on the right.
5. Select "iCloud Drive."
6. Click "Turn On."
7. Click "Options" to configure your preferences.

macOS 12 or earlier

1. Click the Apple menu located at the top-left corner of your screen.
2. Choose "System Preferences."
3. Click "Apple ID."
4. Click "iCloud."
5. Select "iCloud Drive."
6. Click "Options" to configure your preferences.

In the options, you have the ability to select or turn on various features, including "Desktop & Documents Folders," which allows you to access files on your desktop and in the Documents folder on any device with iCloud Drive enabled.

To access your iCloud Drive files and folders, open the Finder, and you'll find "iCloud Drive" in the sidebar.

ON A WINDOWS COMPUTER

If you're using a Windows computer, you can set up iCloud Drive by following these steps:

1. Download iCloud for Windows from the [official Apple website](https://support.apple.com/en-us/HT204283) if you haven't already.
2. Install and open iCloud for Windows.
3. Select "iCloud Drive," and then click "Apply."

To access your iCloud Drive files and folders on your Windows computer, open File Explorer, and you'll find "iCloud Drive" in the Navigation pane.

ACCESS DESKTOP AND DOCUMENTS FILES THROUGH ICLOUD DRIVE

ON YOUR MAC

1. Click on the Apple menu 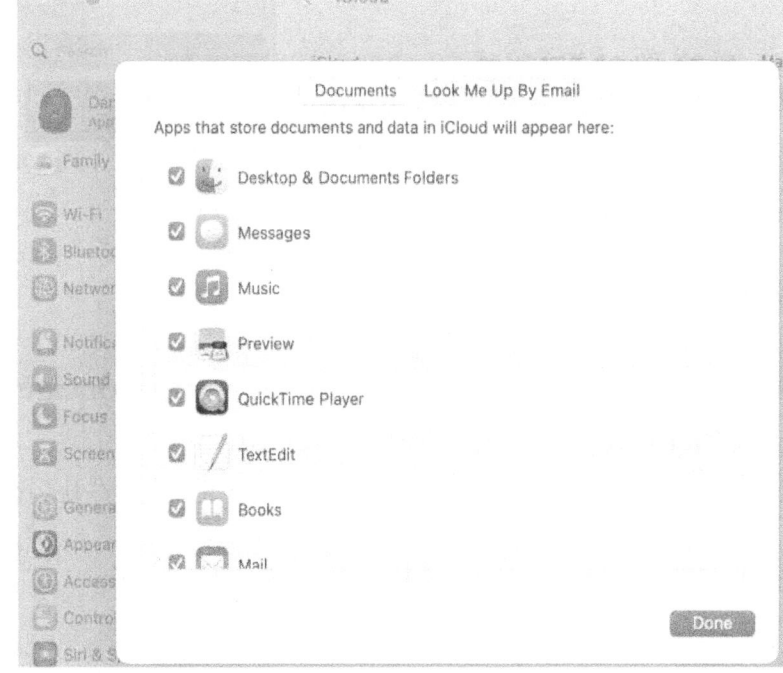 in the top-left corner of your screen.
2. Click on "System Preferences" Click on "Apple ID," then select "iCloud."
3. Ensure that iCloud Drive is turned on.
4. Click on "Options" next to iCloud Drive.
5. Choose "Desktop & Documents Folders."
6. Click "Done."

By doing this, your Desktop and Documents files will be synchronized with iCloud Drive, making them accessible from all your devices.

ON YOUR IPHONE, IPAD, AND IPOD TOUCH

To set up iCloud Drive on your iPhone, iPad, or iPod touch, follow these steps:

1. Open the Settings app on your device.
2. Scroll down and tap on "[your name]" at the top of the settings.
3. Tap "iCloud."
4. Under "iCloud Drive," tap "Sync this [device]" to turn it on.

After you've turned on iCloud Drive, you can access your iCloud Drive files and folders by opening the "Files" app on your device. You'll find the iCloud Drive section within the app, where you can view and manage your files.

ON ICLOUD.COM

1. Sign in to iCloud.com using your Apple ID & go to iCloud Drive.
2. Double-click on the Desktop or Documents folder.
3. To use a file or make edits, click to download it. Once you've finished making edits, upload the file to iCloud Drive to ensure the latest version is available on all your devices.

By storing your files in iCloud Drive, you can save space on your devices. The files you keep in iCloud Drive use your iCloud storage, so ensure you have enough space available.

You can delete files in iCloud Drive to free up space, but keep in mind that when you delete a file on one device, it will be deleted on all devices signed in with the same Apple ID. Deleted files are stored in the "Recently Deleted" folder for 30 days before permanent removal.

TURNING OFF DESKTOP AND DOCUMENTS FEATURES:

1. Click on the Apple menu and select "System Preferences"
2. Click on "Apple ID," then select "iCloud."
3. Click on "Options" next to iCloud Drive.
4. Deselect "Desktop & Documents Folders."
5. Click "Done."

This will turn off the feature. Your files will remain in iCloud Drive, and a new Desktop and Documents folder will be created on your Mac in the home folder.

If you decide to turn off iCloud Drive or sign out of iCloud, a new Desktop and Documents folder will be created in your home folder, and you'll have the option to keep a local copy of your iCloud Drive files. These files will be copied to a folder called "iCloud Drive (Archive)" in your home folder. You can move any files that were in your iCloud Desktop and Documents to your new local Desktop and Documents.

HANDOFF ON MAC

If you have multiple Apple devices and want to seamlessly switch between them while using an app, you can use Handoff.

TO USE HANDOFF

1. Make sure that your devices meet the Continuity system requirements and have Wi-Fi, Bluetooth, and Handoff turned on.
2. Sign in with the same Apple ID on all your devices.

TO TURN HANDOFF ON OR OFF

On your Mac

1. Click on the Apple menu  in the top-left corner of your screen.
2. Select System Preferences
3. Click on "General" in the sidebar.
4. In the "Allow Handoff between this Mac and your iCloud devices" section, turn the toggle on or off.

On your iOS or iPadOS device

1. Open the Settings
   .
2. Scroll down and select "General."
3. Tap "AirPlay & Handoff."
4. Turn Handoff on or off.

On your Apple Watch (configured through your iPhone):

1. Open the Apple Watch app on your iPhone.
2. Go to "My Watch."
3. Choose "General."
4. Turn "Enable Handoff" on or off.

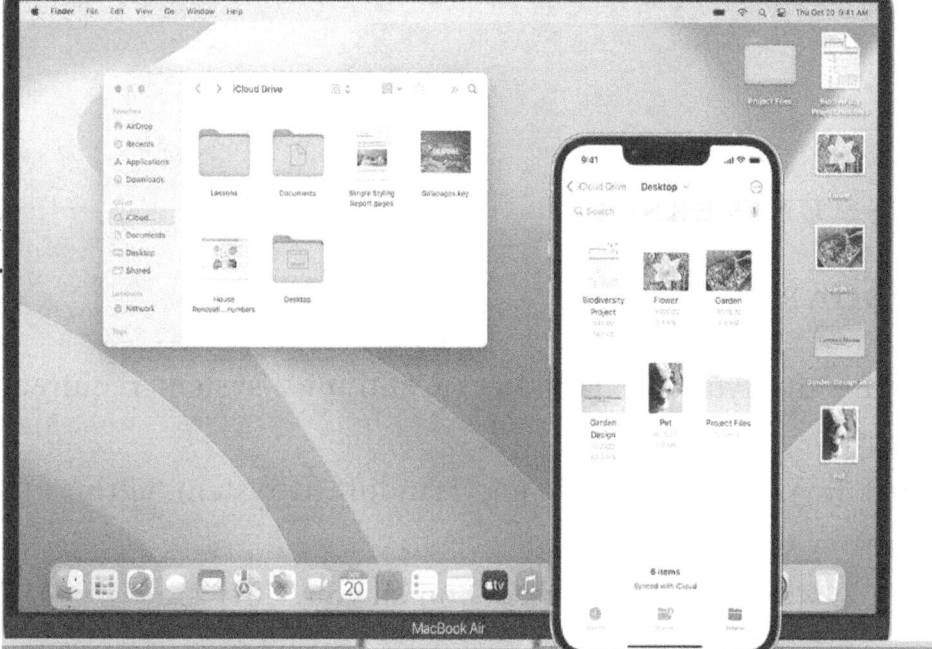

Click to continue what you were doing on your iPhone.

TO HAND OFF AN APP FROM ONE DEVICE TO ANOTHER

From your Mac to an iOS or iPadOS device

The Handoff icon of the app you're using on your Mac will appear on your iPhone or iPad. You can continue working in the app by tapping on the Handoff icon.

From an iOS or iPadOS device or Apple Watch to your Mac

The Handoff icon of the app you're using on your iPhone, iPad, iPod touch, or Apple Watch will appear on your Mac's Dock. You can continue working in the app by clicking the Handoff icon.

You can also use the Command-Tab shortcut on your Mac's keyboard to quickly switch to the app that has the Handoff icon.

UNIVERSAL CLIPOARD

Universal Clipboard is a feature that allows you to seamlessly copy and paste content between your Apple devices, provided they are signed in with the same Apple ID and have the necessary settings turned on.

TO USE UNIVERSAL CLIPBOARD

1. Ensure that your devices meet Continuity system requirements(Explored in Coninuity chapter).
2. Turn on Wi-Fi, Bluetooth, and Handoff in System Settings (on your Mac) and in Settings (on your iOS and iPadOS devices).
3. Sign in with the same Apple ID on all your devices.

COPYING ON A DEVICE

To copy content on a device, follow these steps:

1. Select the content you want to copy, just as you would with any copy action (e.g., on your Mac, press Command-C or choose Edit > Copy).
2. The copied content will be available for pasting on your other devices for a short time.

PASTING ON A DEVICE

1. Position the pointer or cursor where you want to paste the content.
2. Initiate the paste action. For example, on your iPad, you can double-tap and then choose "Paste" from the available options.

TYPES OF CONTENT

With Universal Clipboard, you can copy and paste various types of content, including:

- Text
- Images
- Photos
- Videos
- Files

You can copy and paste these types of content between apps that support copy and paste on your Mac, iPhone, iPad, and iPod touch.

UNIVERSAL CONTROL

Universal Control is a fantastic feature that lets you use a single keyboard, mouse, or trackpad to control multiple devices.

TO USE UNIVERSAL CONTROL

1. Check that your Mac has macOS version 12.3 or later, and your iPad has iPadOS 15.4 or later.
2. Ensure that both your devices have Bluetooth turned on and are connected to Wi-Fi.
3. Verify that Handoff is turned on in your General settings on your MacBook and in Settings > General > AirPlay & Handoff on your iPad.
4. Sign in with the same Apple ID on both devices and enable two-factor authentication.

CONNECTING DEVICES

1. Click on Control Center in the menu bar of your Mac.
2. Select "Screen Mirroring."

3. Under "Link Keyboard and Mouse," choose a device to link your keyboard and mouse to.

MOVING BETWEEN SCREENS

1. On your Mac, use your mouse or trackpad to move the pointer to the right or left edge of the screen closest to your iPad.
2. Pause briefly and then continue moving the pointer slightly past the edge of the screen.
3. When you see a border appear at the edge of the iPad screen, keep moving the pointer to the iPad screen.

DRAG AND DROP

1. Select the text, image, or object you want to move.
2. Drag it to the location on your other device where you want it to appear. For example, you can drag a sketch drawn with Apple Pencil from your iPad to the Keynote app on your MacBook. You can also copy content on one device and paste it on the other.

SHARING A KEYBOARD

1. With the pointer in a document or any area where you can enter text, start typing.
2. The keyboard input will be registered on the device where the pointer is active.

Universal Control is a simple yet powerful tool that lets you work seamlessly between your Mac and iPad. By following this guide, you can easily set it up and enjoy enhanced productivity and workflow.

HOW TO SET UP YOUR IPHONE TO MAKE PHONE CALLS AND SEND TEXT MESSAGES ON YOUR MAC

Using FaceTime on your Mac is a convenient way to have video or audio calls with friends and family.

MAKING A FACETIME CALL

1. Open the FaceTime app on your Mac.
2. Click the "New FaceTime" button to initiate a call.
3. Enter the name, email address, or phone number of the person you want to call.
4. Click the FaceTime button to make a video call. Alternatively, click the arrow ⌄ next to it and choose FaceTime Audio for an audio call. If you can't see these options, click either the Video or Audio button.

If you're making a group call, you'll see a tile for each person in the group, which will say "Waiting" until they answer.

LEAVING A CALL

To leave a call, simply click the "End" button. If you leave a group call, others will remain on the call until they choose to leave.

MANAGING GROUP FACETIME CALLS

During a Group FaceTime call, the video tiles work as follows:

- The most active speakers appear in live video tiles, while other participants are in a row of tiles below.

- You can click a tile to show that person's name, or double-click it to make the tile larger.

- A ⚠ symbol indicates a slow internet connection.

ADDING A PERSON TO A FACETIME CALL

1. While on a call, click the sidebar button ⊟ n the FaceTime app and then click the add button . ⊕
2. Enter the new person's name, email, or phone number, and then click "Add."
3. Click the "Ring" button next to their name to call them. If a FaceTime link was created for the call, participants can share it to invite others to join.

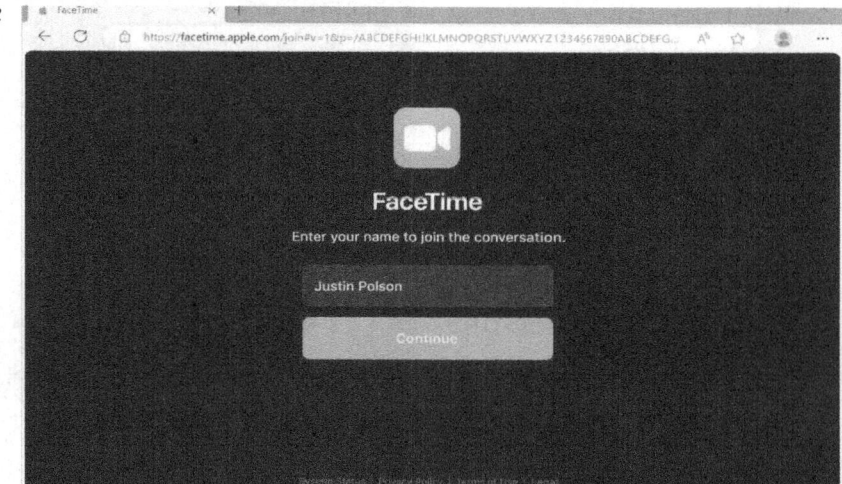

USING FACETIME LINKS

FaceTime links simplify planning for calls and allow participants with Android and Windows devices to join via their web browser. Here's how to create and use FaceTime links:

1. Open the FaceTime app and click 🔗 to generate a sharing menu or choose other sharing options.
2. The link will appear in the FaceTime window's sidebar.
3. Double-click the FaceTime Link to start the call.
4. Participants who click the link need to be allowed into the call.

- To let a participant join the call, click the tick ✓ next to their name.

- If you want to decline a participant's request to join the call, click the decline button ✕ next to their name.

- If you need to remove a participant from the call within 30 seconds of them joining, click the remove button ✕.

ANSWERING A FACETIME CALL

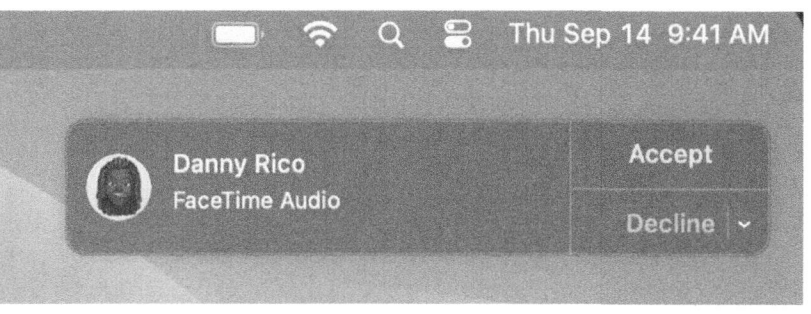

When you receive a FaceTime call, a notification will appear on your Mac. Click "Accept" to answer the call in the FaceTime app. You can also choose to accept it as an audio call or send a message or reminder to call back later. Group FaceTime calls display a "Join" button to open the FaceTime app and join the call.

HANDING OFF THE CALL

With macOS Ventura or later, iOS 16 or later, and iPadOS 16 or later, you can hand off active calls to your other devices. This works similarly to handing off other tasks. Click the notification on the device you want to transfer the call to, and then click "Join" or "Switch" to complete the handoff. If you're using a Bluetooth headset, the call audio will also switch to the other device, provided that your phone number or Apple ID is selected for FaceTime in the settings on both devices.

SMS & MMS FROM YOUR MAC

To set up SMS and MMS messaging on your Mac using your iPhone, follow these steps:

1. On your iPhone, open Settings and select Messages.
2. Tap on Text Message Forwarding.
3. If you don't see the Text Message Forwarding option, ensure that you have signed into iMessage using the same Apple ID on both your iPhone and your Mac.
4. Turn on your Mac in the list of devices.
5. If you're not using two-factor authentication, you will see a six-digit activation code on your Mac. Enter this code into your iPhone when prompted and tap Allow.

When the message bubbles are green, it means they were sent as SMS text messages.

UNLOCKING YOUR MAC WITH YOUR APPLE WATCH

Unlocking your MacBook and approving tasks with your Apple Watch is a convenient and secure way to enhance the usability of your devices. Here are the steps to set up and use these features:

1. Ensure that you are signed in to both your Mac and Apple Watch using the same Apple ID.
2. Turn on two-factor authentication for your Apple ID. You can do this by opening System Preferences, clicking your Apple ID in the sidebar, and selecting "Password & Security." Then, choose "Set Up Two-Factor Authentication."
3. Make sure the "Disable automatic login" option is selected. If you're using FileVault, you won't see this option, but you can still use the Auto Unlock feature. Set up Auto Unlock. Sign in on all your devices with the same Apple ID, then open System Preferences on your MacBook. Click "Touch ID & Password" in the sidebar, and turn on the unlock settings for Apple Watch.

Now, when you approach your sleeping MacBook wearing your authenticated Apple Watch, simply lift the cover or press a key to wake it up, and your Apple Watch will unlock it, allowing you to start working immediately.

APPROVING TASKS WITH APPLE WATCH

If you're prompted for a password, you can use your Apple Watch to authenticate on your Mac:

1. 1. Double-click the side button on your Apple Watch to authenticate your password on your Mac.
2. 2. You can use this feature to view passwords in Safari, approve app installations, unlock locked notes, and more (requires watchOS 6).

These features work seamlessly when your Apple Watch is authenticated with a passcode, and there are no extra steps required after you enter your passcode.

Double-click the side button to approve requests from your Mac.

AIRPRINT

Printing documents and photos wirelessly without the need for printer drivers is easy with AirPrint on your Mac. Here's a simple guide on how to use AirPrint:

PRINTING WITH AIRPRINT

1. Make sure your printer is AirPrint-enabled.
2. You can print wirelessly using AirPrint to:

   • An AirPrint-enabled printer on your Wi-Fi network.

   • A network printer or a printer shared by another Mac on your Wi-Fi network.

   • A printer connected to the USB port of an AirPort base station.
3. Open the app where your document or photo is located.
4. Click on "File" and select "Print" or press Command-P to open the Print dialog.
5. In the Print dialog, click on the "Printer" pop-up menu.
6. Choose your printer from the "Nearby Printers" list.

TROUBLESHOOTING

If you can't find your printer in the Nearby Printers list, follow these steps:

1. Make sure that your printer is connected to the same Wi-Fi network as your MacBook.
2. If the printer is connected to the same network and still isn't visible, you can add it manually:

   • Open System Settings.

   • Click on "Printers & Scanners" in the sidebar.

3. On the right, click on "Add Printer, Scanner, or Fax."
3. 4. If necessary, you may have to temporarily connect the printer to your MacBook using a USB cable and an adapter.

By following these steps, you can easily use AirPrint to print wirelessly from your Mac to your compatible printer.

APPS

Enjoy Apple's pre-installed apps and in-app functionalities for entertainment, seamless connections, and enhanced productivity.

App Store

Included Apps

Icon/App name	Icon/App name	Icon/App name
App Store	Books	Calendar
FaceTime	Find My	Freeform
GarageBand	Home	iMovie
Keynote	Mail	Maps
Messages	Music	News
Notes	Numbers	Pages
Photos	Podcasts	Preview
Reminders	Safari	Shortcuts
Stocks	TV	Voice Memos

Apart from the apps mentioned in the table on the left, your Mac also has other apps and utilities that could be useful. These include Calculator 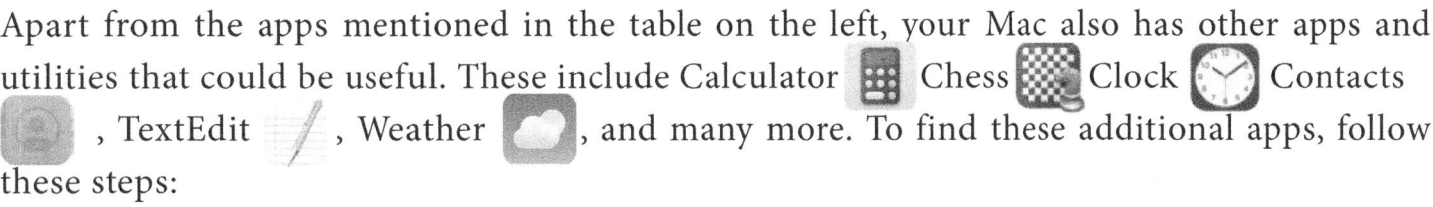 Chess Clock Contacts , TextEdit , Weather , and many more. To find these additional apps, follow these steps:

1. Open your Applications folder. You can do this by clicking on the desktop or using Finder from your Dock, then selecting "Go" from the menu bar and choosing "Applications."

2. Inside the Applications folder, you'll find a wide range of apps and utilities, some of which may not be featured in the table mentioned earlier.

3. If you want to explore a complete list of all the apps and utilities installed on your Mac, refer to the macOS User Guide for a detailed inventory.

4. Additionally, if you're looking for more apps to enhance your Mac's capabilities, you can visit the App Store. To access the App Store, click on its icon in your Dock. The App Store offers a vast selection of apps to fulfill almost any task you have in mind. For a comprehensive guide on how to browse and download apps from the App Store, please explore the dedicated section in the guide.

APP STORE

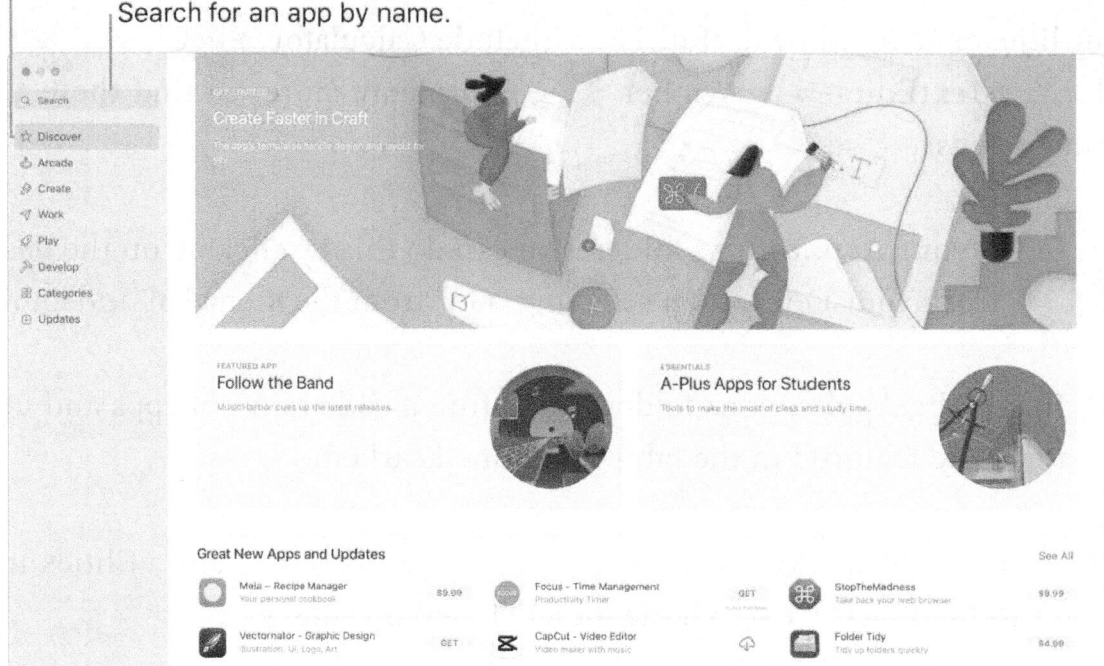

The App Store on your MacBook is where you can discover, download, and keep your apps up-to-date. Here's how to make the most of it:

FINDING APPS

To search for a specific app, type its name in the search field and press Return. When you download an app from the App Store, it will automatically appear in Launchpad for easy access.

You can also explore new apps by selecting a tab in the sidebar, such as Create, Work, or Play, and browse through the results.

USING SIRI

If you prefer using voice commands, you can ask Siri to help you find apps. For example, you can say, "Find apps for kids."

APPLE ID

To download free apps, sign in with your Apple ID. Click "Sign In" at the bottom of the sidebar in the App Store. If you don't have an Apple ID yet, click "Create Apple ID." If you have an existing Apple ID but can't remember your password, you can recover it by clicking "Forgot Apple ID or password." You'll also need to set up an account with purchasing information to buy fee-based apps.

72

IPHONE AND IPAD APPS ON MAC

Many iPhone and iPad apps are compatible with your MacBook. Any apps you've previously purchased for your iPhone or iPad will appear on your Mac. Search the App Store to see if they're available for Mac.

APPLE ARCADE

Click the Arcade tab to explore Apple Arcade, a subscription service that offers a collection of games to play. You can also find games popular among your Game Center friends, track your achievements, and more. Games you download from the App Store will automatically appear in the Games folder in Launchpad for easy access.

GAME CAPTURE

For gaming enthusiasts, you can capture up to a 15-second video clip of your gameplay by pressing the share button on supported third-party game controllers. This allows you to review your strategy or keep memorable gaming moments.

You have available updates.

APP UPDATES

Keep your apps up-to-date by checking the App Store icon in the Dock. If it has a badge, it means there are updates available. Click the icon to open the App Store, then click "Updates" in the sidebar.

TOUCH BAR (ON 13-INCH MACBOOK)

If you have a 13-inch MacBook with a Touch Bar, you can use it to quickly navigate to different tabs within the App Store, such as Discover, Arcade, Create, Work, Play, Develop, Categories, and Updates.

The App Store is your one-stop-shop for all app-related needs on your MacBook, from finding new apps to keeping your current ones up-to-date.

BOOKS

If you want to buy books and audiobooks using the Books app on your Mac, it's a piece of cake.

SEARCHING FOR BOOKS OR AUDIOBOOKS

1. Open the Books app 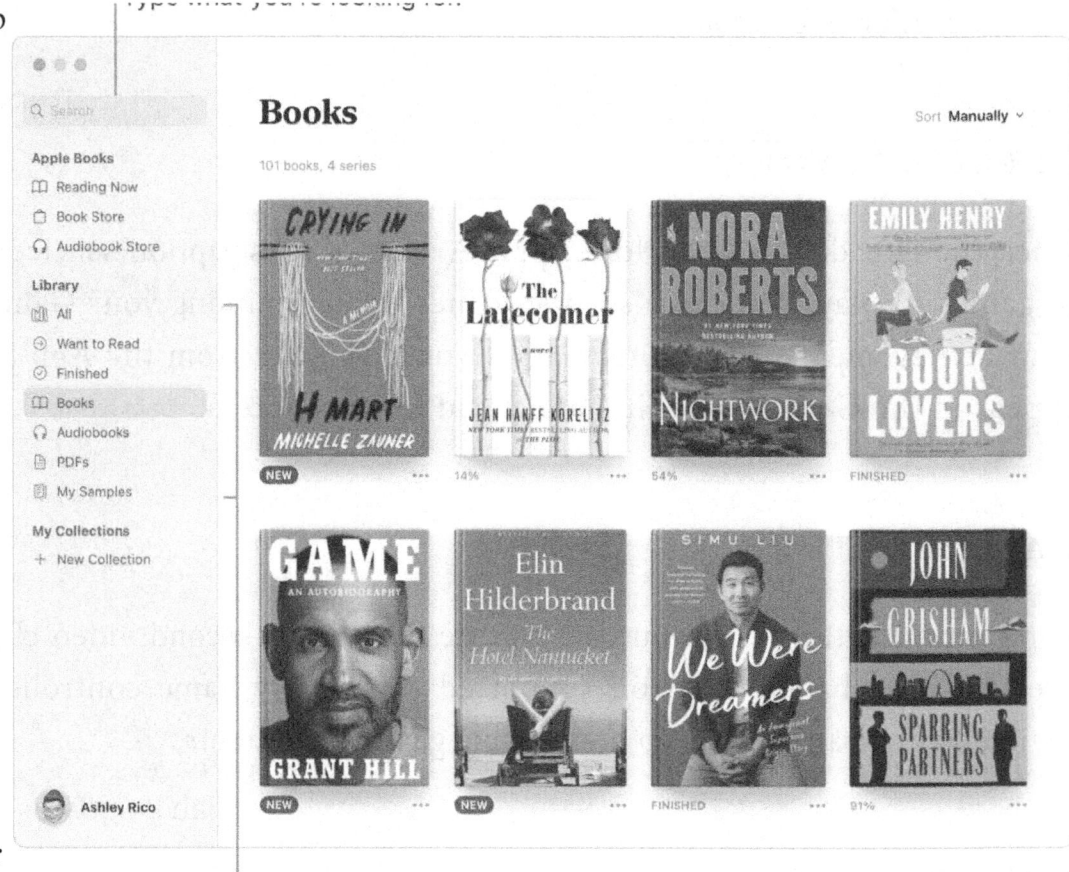 on your Mac.
2. Click on the search field.
3. Start typing, and you'll see suggestions. You can search by title, author, genre, or publisher.
4. Select a suggestion or press Return to perform the search.
5. To filter your results, use the options in the "Filter by" menu, or click "All" to see all results.

BROWSING THE STORES

1. In the Books app , you can access the Book Store or Audiobook Store from the sidebar.
2. Scroll down or click "Browse Sections" in the upper-right corner.
3. Choose a store section, such as "For You" or "Top Charts," or select a genre like "History" or "Romance."

SETTING READING GOALS

If you want to motivate yourself, set daily reading goals. By default, it's set to 5 minutes a day, but you can adjust it by clicking the "Adjust Goal" button in the Reading Goals section of "Reading Now." If you wish to turn off reading goals or clear reading goal data, you can do so in Books settings.

ADDING BOOKMARKS, NOTES, AND HIGHLIGHTS

To add bookmarks, notes, and highlights, move your pointer to the top of the book you're reading to show controls. Click the Add Bookmark button to bookmark a page, and tap the bookmark again to remove it. To go to a bookmarked page, show the controls, tap the Show Bookmarks button, and then click the bookmark

You can also add notes and highlights by selecting the text and choosing a highlight color or "Add Note" from the pop-up menu. To access your notes later, show the controls and click the Notes and Highlights button.

SYNC ACROSS DEVICES

Your purchased books, collections, bookmarks, highlights, notes, and the current page you're reading are available automatically on your Mac, iOS devices, and iPadOS devices as long as you're signed in with the same Apple ID.

BUYING, DOWNLOADING, OR PRE-ORDERING BOOKS

1. In the Books app, go to the Book Store from the sidebar.
2. Search for or select a book you're interested in.
3. Click the book's price or the "Get" button.
4. To save a book for later, click "Want to Read." It will be added to the "Want to Read" collection in your library.
5. If available, you can also try out a book by clicking "Sample." The sample will be added to the "My Samples" collection in your library.

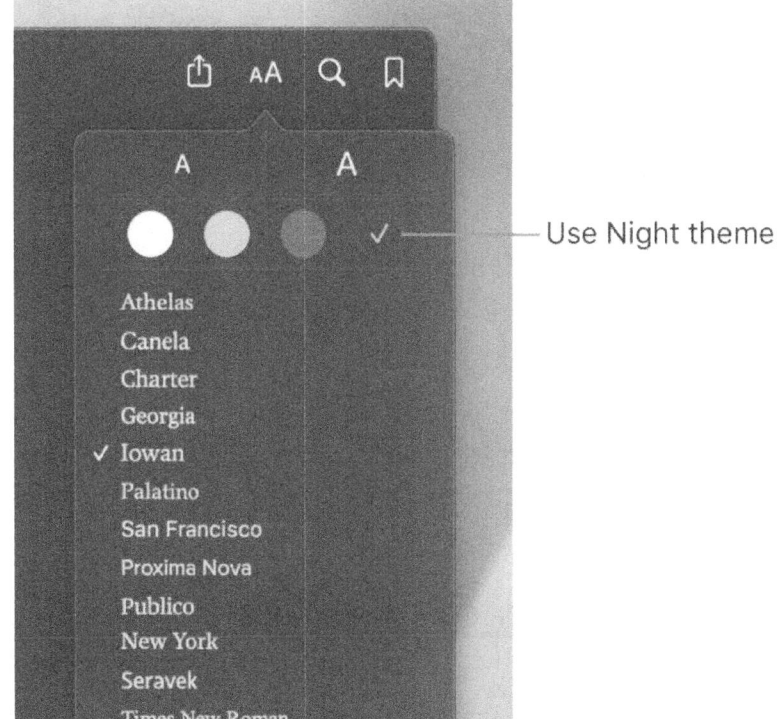

Use Night theme.

NIGHT THEME

For easier reading in low-light conditions, you can change to Night theme. Simply choose View > Theme, then select "Night." However, please note that not all books support this theme.

CALENDAR

Using the Calendar app on your Mac can help you stay organized to create events, customize calendars, add holiday calendars, and filter your calendars with Focus

CREATING EVENTS

- Click the Add button ✛ or double-click anywhere in a day to create an event.

- To invite someone, double-click the event, click the "Add Invitees" section, then type their email address.

- The Calendar app will keep you informed about their responses.

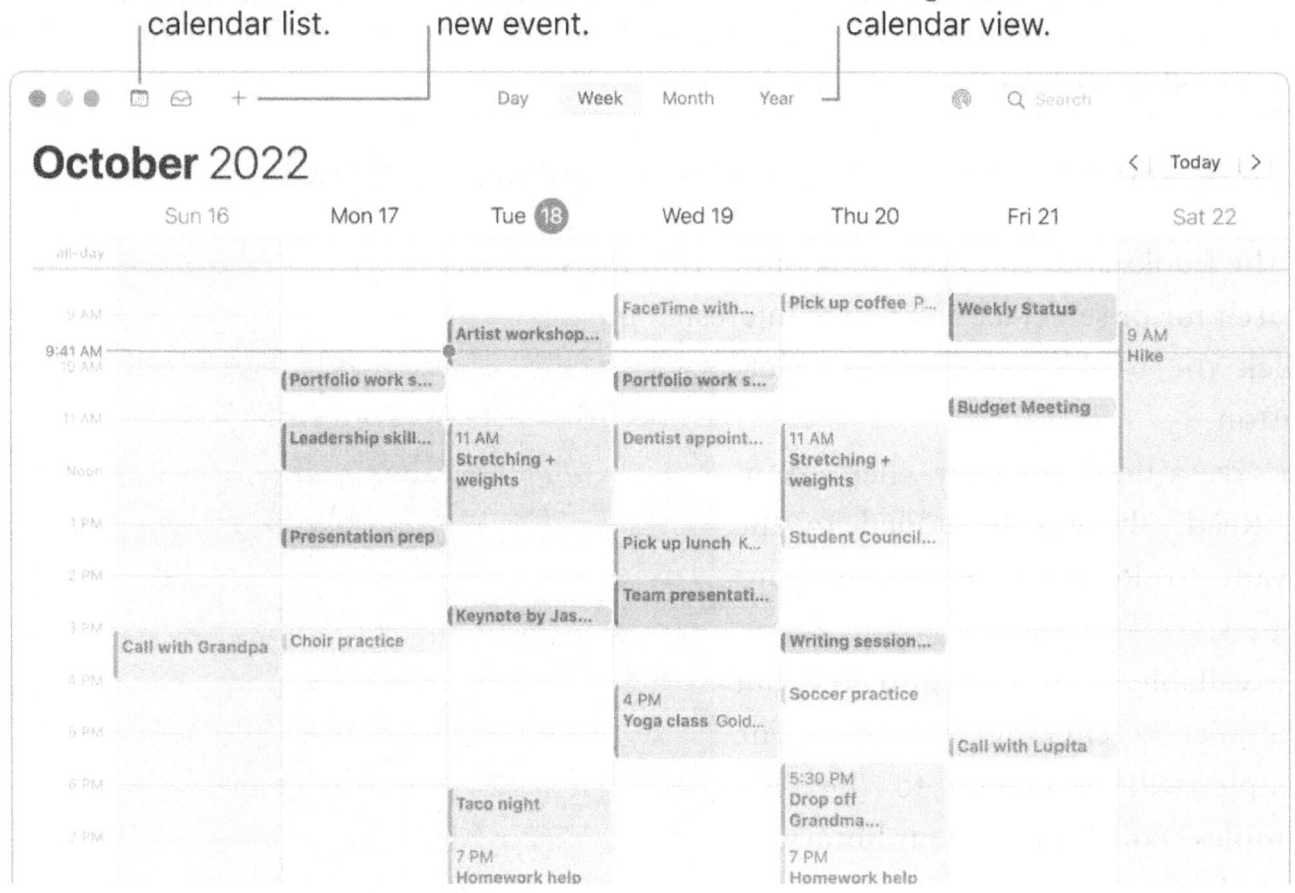

CUSTOMIZING CALENDARS

- Create separate calendars for different parts of your life by choosing File > New Calendar.

- Assign each calendar a different color by Control-clicking the calendar and choosing a new color.

ADDING HOLIDAY CALENDARS

- View holiday calendars from different regions worldwide by choosing File > New Holiday Calendar.
- Select the holiday calendar you want to add.

FILTERING CALENDARS WITH FOCUS

- Choose which calendars to display during a specific Focus.
- To access this feature, choose Apple Menu > System Preferences, then click Focus in the sidebar.
- Select a Focus, click the Right arrow, and choose Add Filter under Focus Filters.

SHARING CALENDARS

- Sign in to iCloud to synchronize your calendars across all your devices with the same Apple ID.
- Share calendars with other iCloud users.

Using the Touch Bar (on the 13-inch MacBook):

- Tap the Today button on the Touch Bar to view or edit today's events.
- Use the slider to select the month, either past or future.
- Select an event in your calendar and tap buttons on the Touch Bar to specify the calendar, view event details, edit time or location, and manage invitees.

By following these steps, you can efficiently manage your schedule, color-code your events, and stay on top of important dates.

FACETIME

Making video, audio, and group calls directly from your Mac is simple, all with just a few simple steps.

1. SIGN IN TO FACETIME

- Open the FaceTime app on your Mac, enter your Apple ID and password in the FaceTime window and then click "Next."

2. MAKE A CALL

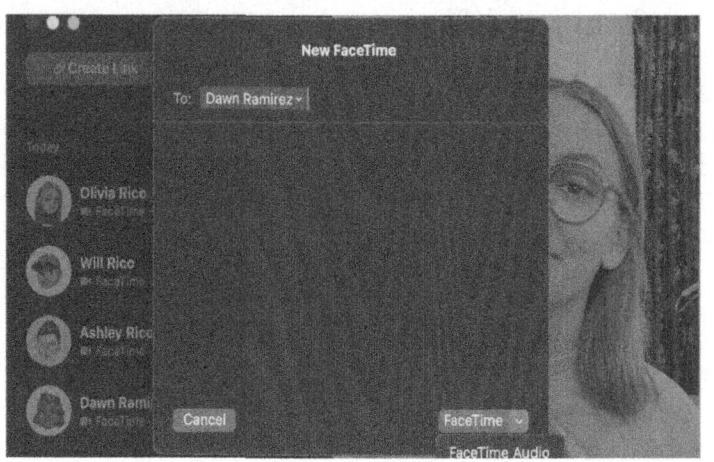

- Click the "New FaceTime" button.
- Enter the phone number, email address, or name from your Contacts list for the person you want to call.
- Click the "FaceTime" button to make a video call or click ⌄ "FaceTime Audio" for an audio-only call.

3. ACCEPT OR DECLINE CALLS

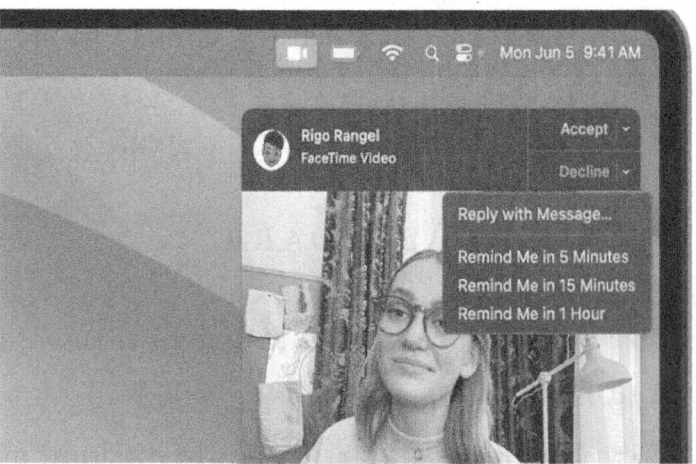

When you receive a FaceTime call, you have options.

- Click "Answer" to accept the call immediately.
- Click ⌄ to accept an audio-only call.
- Click "Decline" to decline the call.
- Alternatively, message the caller or set a reminder to call them later.

4. ADD PEOPLE TO A CALL

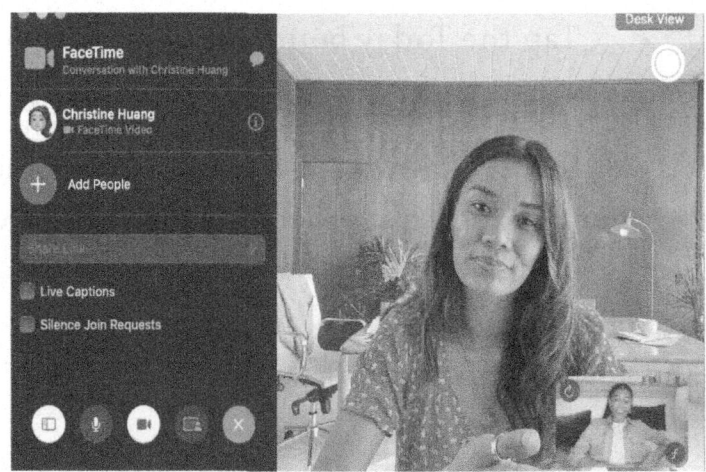

- Click the "Sidebar" button.
- Click the plus button ⊕ next to "Add People" for a video call.
- For an audio-only call, click the "Audio" button in the menu bar, then the arrow in the window that appears, and then "Add."

5. USE VIDEO EFFECTS

During a FaceTime video call, you can use video effects on compatible Macs to enhance your experience. Click the "Video" button in the menu and choose from available video effects, such as reactions, blur your background with Portrait mode, turn on Centre Stage, and more.

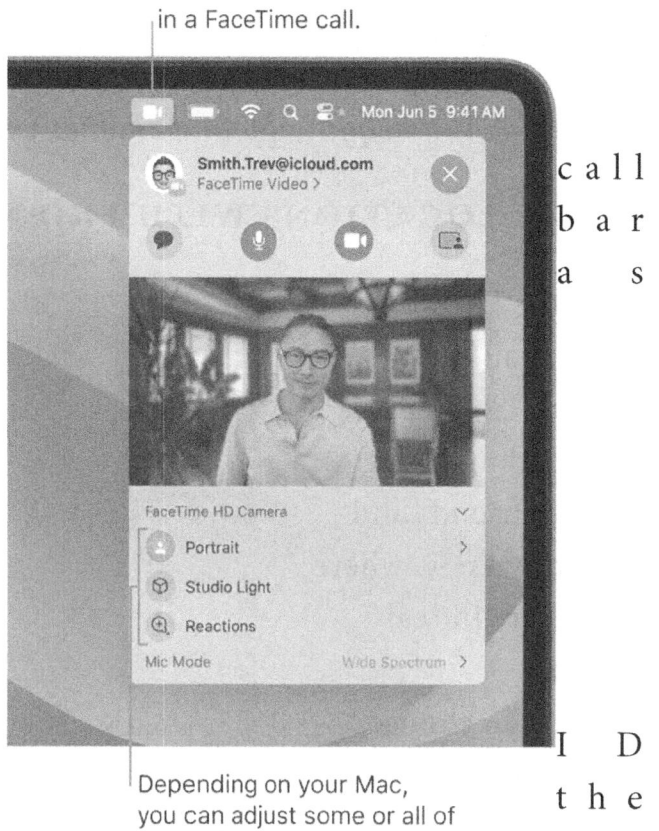

in a FaceTime call.

Depending on your Mac, you can adjust some or all of

6. CREATE A FACETIME LINK (MACOS 12 OR LATER)

In the FaceTime app 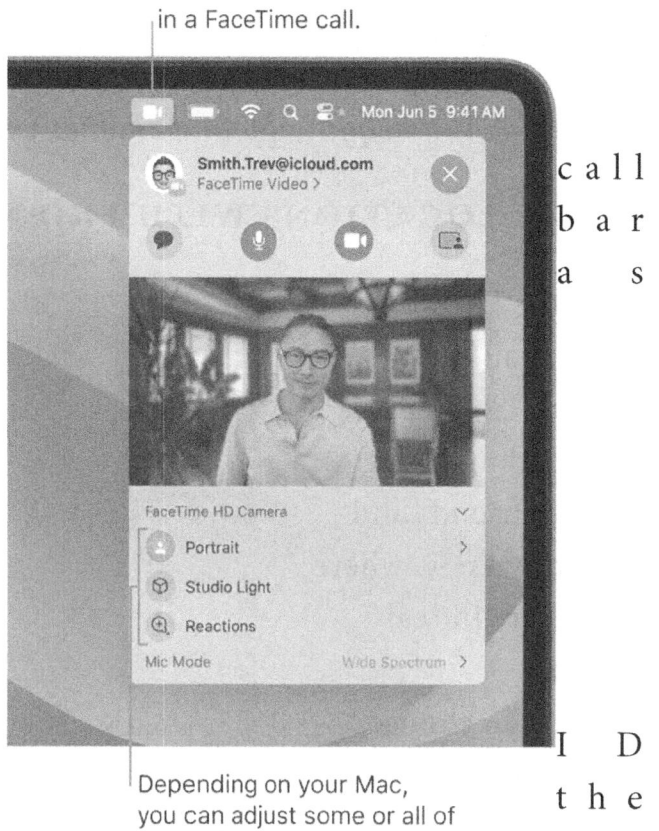, sign in to your Apple ID and click "Create Link" to generate a link for the FaceTime call.

7. START A CALL FROM A FACETIME LINK

If you created a FaceTime link, you can start the call from an app 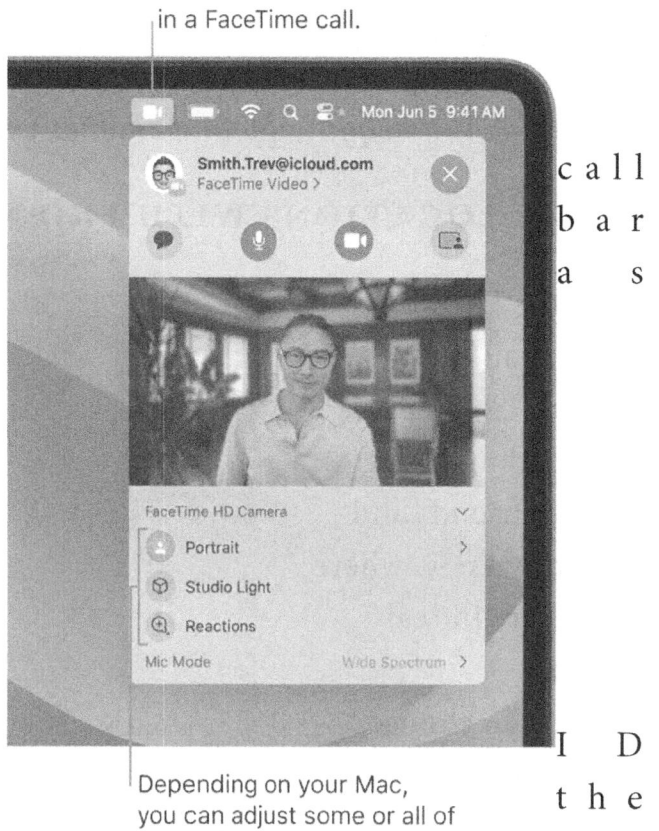 or from FaceTime itself. Double-click the FaceTime call link or find it in the list of recent calls in the "Upcoming" section. Click the "Video" button and then "Join" to start the call.

8. LET CALLERS JOIN THE FACETIME CALL

As the originator of the FaceTime link, you can allow others to join the call immediately. When a new caller is waiting, you'll see a badge on the "Sidebar" button . Click the "Sidebar" button and choose to "Allow the caller to join the call" or "Don't allow the caller to join the call."

9. DELETE A FACETIME LINK

To delete a FaceTime link you created, you can delete it. Check the list of callers for the call made with a FaceTime link, click the "Info" button, and select "Delete Link."

FIND MY APP

Find My is a helpful app that enables you to locate your friends, family, and Apple devices.

SHARE LOCATIONS WITH FRIENDS

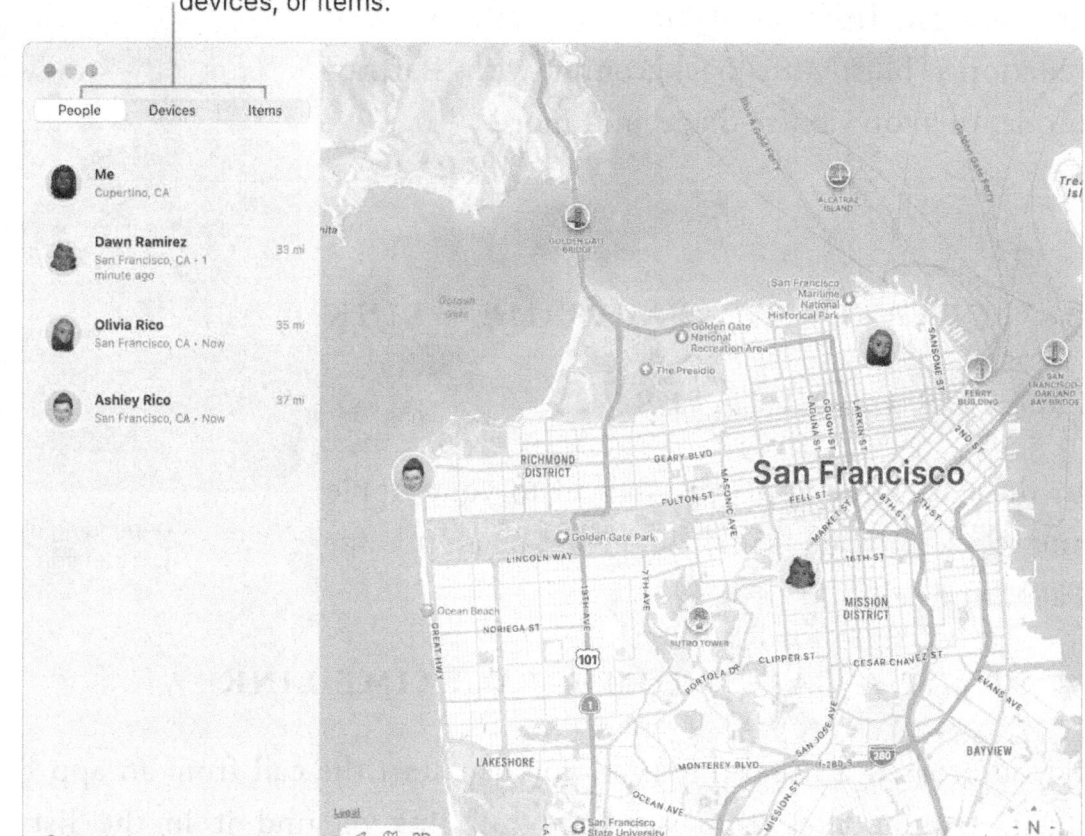

devices, or items.

- In the People list, you can click "Share My Location" to let your friends and family know where you are in real-time.
- You can choose to share your live location for an hour, a day, or indefinitely and stop sharing whenever you want.
- You can also ask to follow a friend, allowing you to see their location on a map and receive step-by-step directions to their whereabouts.

SET LOCATION ALERTS

- You can configure location alerts to notify your friends when you arrive at or leave a specific location.
- You can also receive notifications when your friends arrive or leave particular places.
- If your friends create notifications about your location, you can find them all in one place by clicking "Me" in the People list and scrolling to "Notifications About You."

GET NOTIFIED WHEN YOU LEAVE SOMETHING BEHIND

- To avoid leaving your devices, such as your MacBook, behind, you can set up separation alerts on your iPhone, iPad, or iPod touch.
- These alerts will notify you when you move away from your device.

- To set up separation alerts for a device, click the Info icon for that device and select "Notify When Left Behind." Follow the onscreen instructions.

SECURE A LOST DEVICE

- Find My allows you to locate and protect lost devices, such as your Mac, iPhone, or AirPods.
- Click on a device in the Devices list to locate it on the map. You can play a sound on the device to help you find it.
- You can also mark the device as lost, preventing others from accessing your personal information, and even erase the device remotely for added security.

LOCATE DEVICES, EVEN WHEN THEY'RE OFFLINE

- Find My uses Bluetooth signals from nearby Apple devices to locate your device, even when it's not connected to a Wi-Fi or cellular network.
- These signals are anonymous and encrypted to protect your privacy.
- You can even locate a device that has been erased, provided it meets the compatibility requirements.

FIND EVERYDAY ITEMS

- You can attach an AirTag to items like your keychain to find them quickly when they go missing.
- Use your iOS or iPadOS device to register an AirTag and compatible third-party items to your Apple ID. In Find My on your Mac, you can click the "Items" tab to view the location of your items on a map.

If an item can't be located, you can check its last known location and receive a notification when it's found. You can also activate Lost Mode for an item, including a custom message and contact number for recovery.

FREE FORM

Freeform is a powerful and versatile tool that allows you to organize your ideas and collaborate with others on macOS Ventura 13.1 or later.

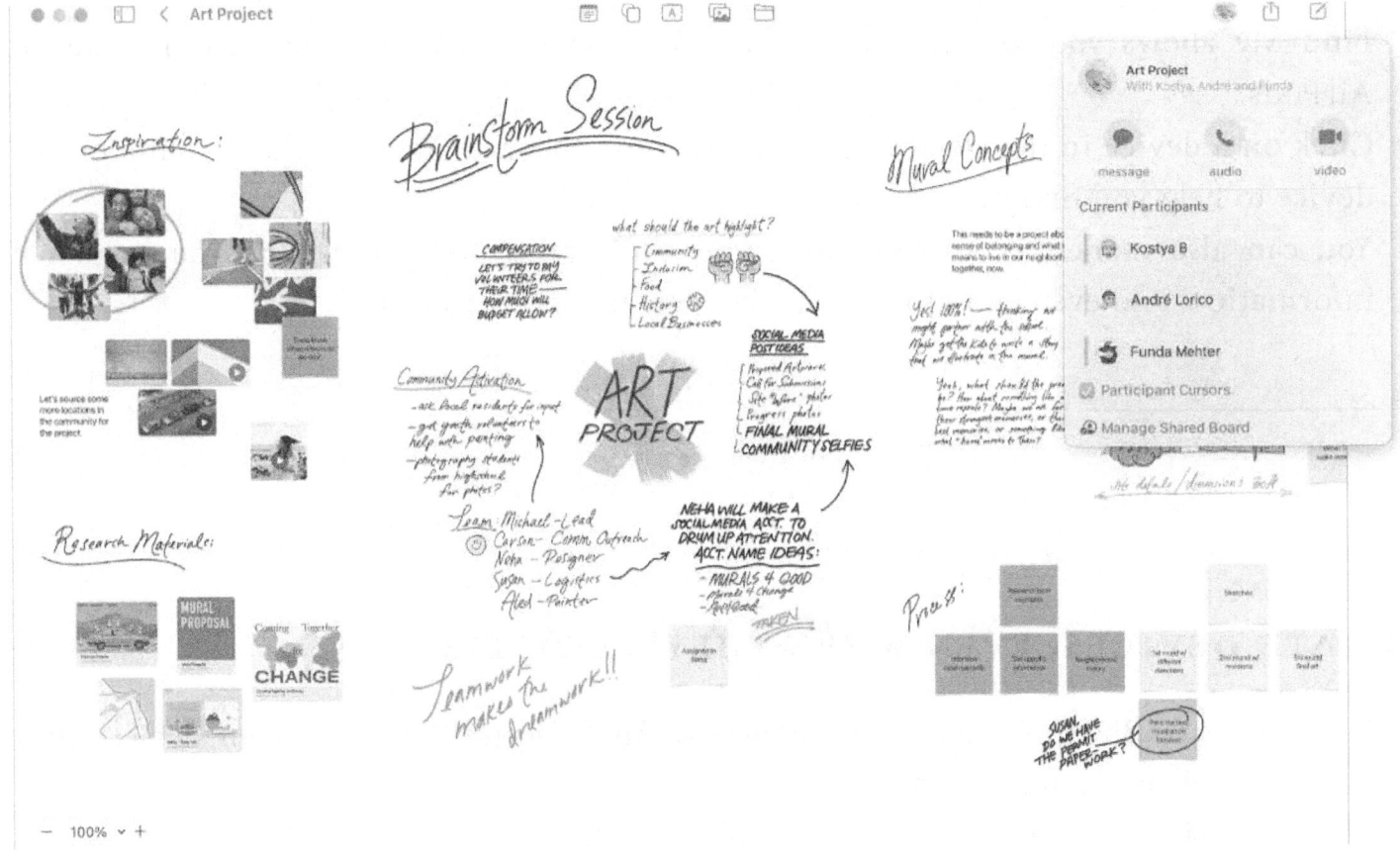

CREATE A BOARD

To create a new board, simply click the "New Board" button located in the toolbar. You don't need to worry about saving your board as it is done automatically. To give your board a name, click on "Untitled" in the top left of the title bar and enter the desired name.

ADD CONTENT

Use the toolbar to insert different types of elements into your board such as text, sticky notes, photos, links, and files. You can also drag items from other apps onto your board.

ORGANIZE YOUR BOARD

Freeform provides tools for arranging and managing items on your board. You can move, resize, group, and align items as needed. You can also choose to view your board with a grid or use alignment guides to help you position items accurately.

COLLABORATION

Freeform allows you to collaborate with others in real-time. You can invite people to collaborate on a board through Messages or Mail, or by sharing a link. To invite collaborators, click the share button in the toolbar, select "Collaborate," and then choose to share via Messages, Mail, or by copying the link. When you share in Messages, everyone on the thread is invited to the board.

EXPORT AS A PDF

If you want to create a PDF of your Freeform board, you can do so by choosing "File" and then selecting "Export PDF."

Your Freeform boards sync across all your devices, ensuring easy access and consistent collaboration. If you experience syncing issues, you can enable Freeform in iCloud Settings. Also, Freeform is available on iOS 16.2 and iPadOS 16.2 or later, allowing you to work seamlessly across different Apple devices.

GARAGEBAND

GarageBand is an amazing application that allows you to create, record, and share your music. Whether you are an aspiring musician or a seasoned artist, unleash your creativity and build your own home recording studio.

CREATE A NEW PROJECT

- Start by creating a new project. You can either begin from scratch or use a pre-made song template.

- Customize your project by selecting the tempo, key, and other options that suit your music style. Tap the ? button if you need any help with how items work.

- Click "Record" to start playing and building your song. GarageBand offers various tracks and loops to help you craft your musical masterpiece.

View Editors.   Tracks area   Open the Note Pad.

ADD INSTRUMENTS AND LOOPS

- Quickly enhance your project with drums and other instruments using Loops.
- Click the "Loop Browser" ◯ to explore a vast collection of loops categorized by instrument, genre, or descriptor.
- Drag and drop the desired loop into an empty section of the Tracks area.
- You can customize loops to seamlessly blend with your composition using straightforward controls.

RECORD YOUR VOICE

- To record your voice, go to "Track" and choose "New Track."
- Select the microphone under "Audio."
- Click the triangle next to "Details" to set various options for input, output, and monitoring.
- Click "Create" to confirm the settings.
- Hit the "Record" button ● to begin recording your voice, and press the "Play" button ▶ to stop the recording.

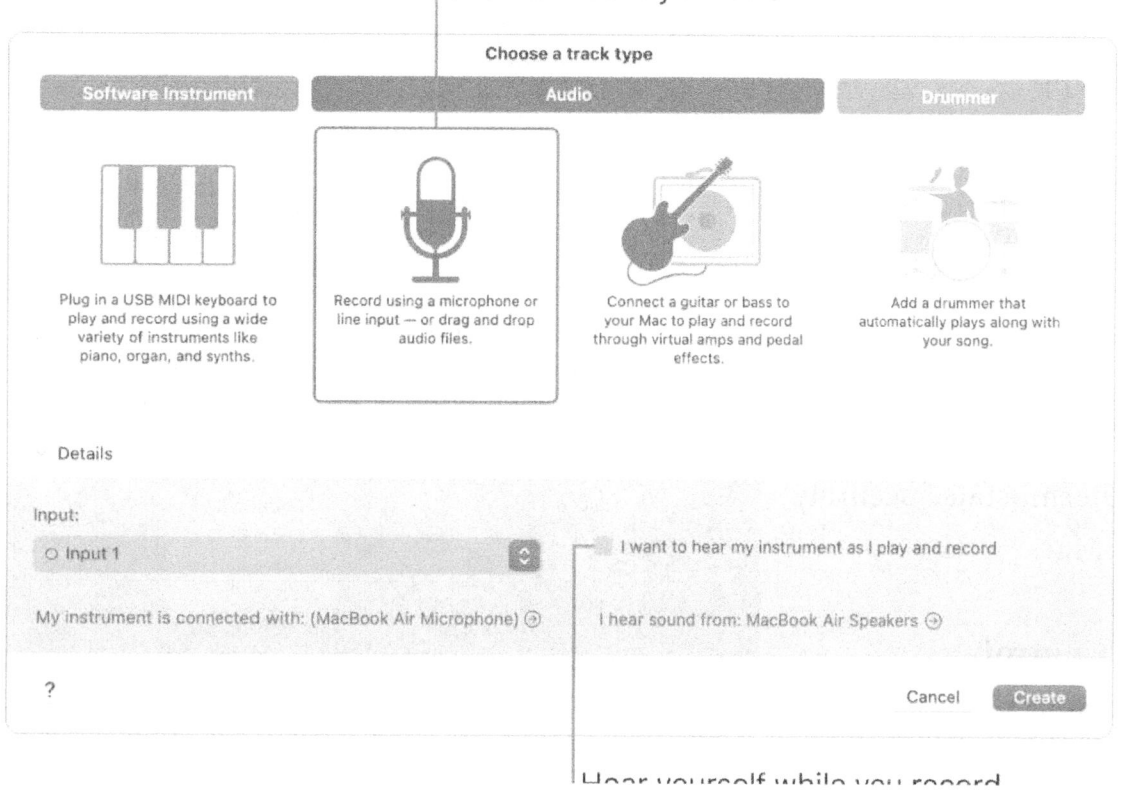

SMART CONTROLS AND EFFECTS

- Take advantage of the Touch Bar on your 13-inch MacBook to fine-tune the sound of your selected track.
- Easily adjust Smart Controls to modify the instrument's sound, enable or disable effects, or adjust track volume.

GarageBand is an excellent platform for musicians of all levels to express their creativity and bring their musical ideas to life. Whether you're a singer, instrumentalist, or music producer, GarageBand offers a user-friendly and feature-rich environment for music creation.

HOME

Control your home accessories, safely, with your MAC!

Siri can help you control your smart home accessories using your Mac. Besides setting reminders and answering questions, Siri is here to make your life more convenient by allowing you to control your home devices. This chapter explores how you can use the home app 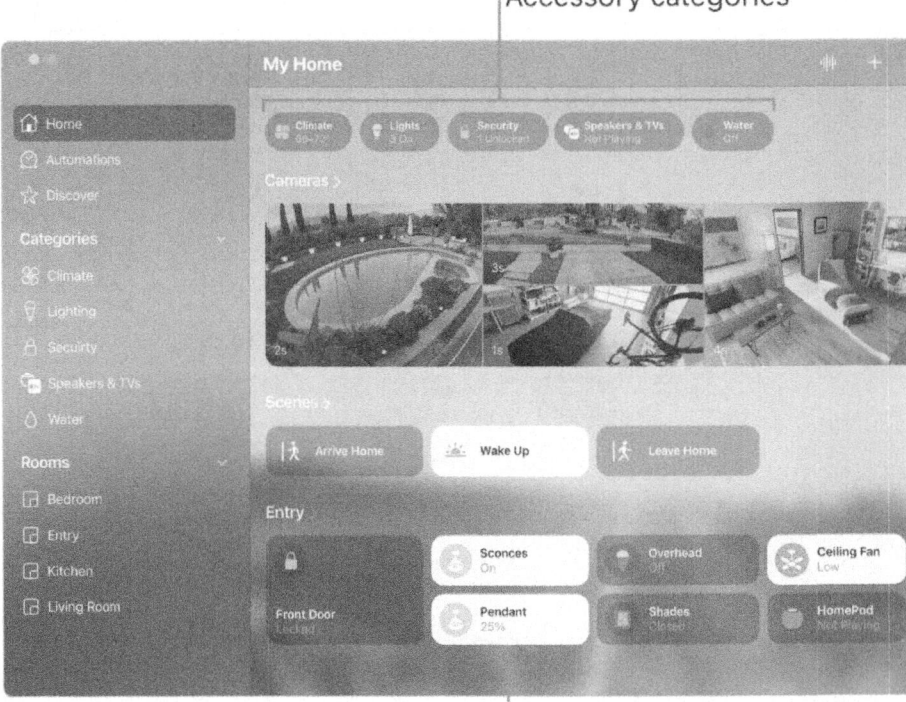 to control your accessories and scenes with Siri on your Mac.

The Home app on your Mac provides a whole-house view, allowing you to see your entire home at a glance, including cameras, scenes, and accessories organized by room. You can easily control your HomeKit accessories, from lights to thermostats, securely using your Mac.

Accessory Control

The Home app offers accessory control through tiles with icons, making it intuitive to interact with your devices. You can turn lights on or off, lock or unlock doors, open or close blinds, and more. Adjusting brightness and temperature is also a breeze.

Categories

Categories such as Lights, Climate, Security, Speakers & TVs, and Water help you quickly access relevant accessories organized by room, along with detailed status information.

Scenes

Create scenes in the Home app to make multiple accessories work together with a single command. For example, you can create a "Good Night" scene that turns off all lights, closes shades, and locks the door when it's time for bed.

Home Security Cameras

With the ability to view your cameras and HomeKit Secure Video, you can connect your home security cameras to record footage and view it securely from anywhere. Up to nine camera views are displayed in the Home tab, end-to-end encrypted.

Adaptive Lighting

Adaptive lighting is another feature, allowing you to set smart light bulbs to adjust the color temperature throughout the day to enhance comfort and productivity.

USING SIRI:

Light Control:
- "Turn off the lights."
- "Turn on the lights."
- "Dim the lights." Then specify the brightness, for example, "Set brightness to 55 percent."

Checking Light Status:
- "Is the hallway light on?"

Thermostat Control:
- "Set the temperature to 20 degrees."

Garage Door Control:
- "Close the garage door."

Room and Scene Control:
If you've set up rooms or scenes, you can use commands like "I'm home" or "I'm leaving."
- "Turn down the kitchen lights."
- "Turn on the fan in the office."
- "Set my reading scene."

It's important to note that Siri can work with some third-party accessories as well. If prompted, you can set up these accessories and control their settings using Siri.

EMAILS

Apple's Mail app 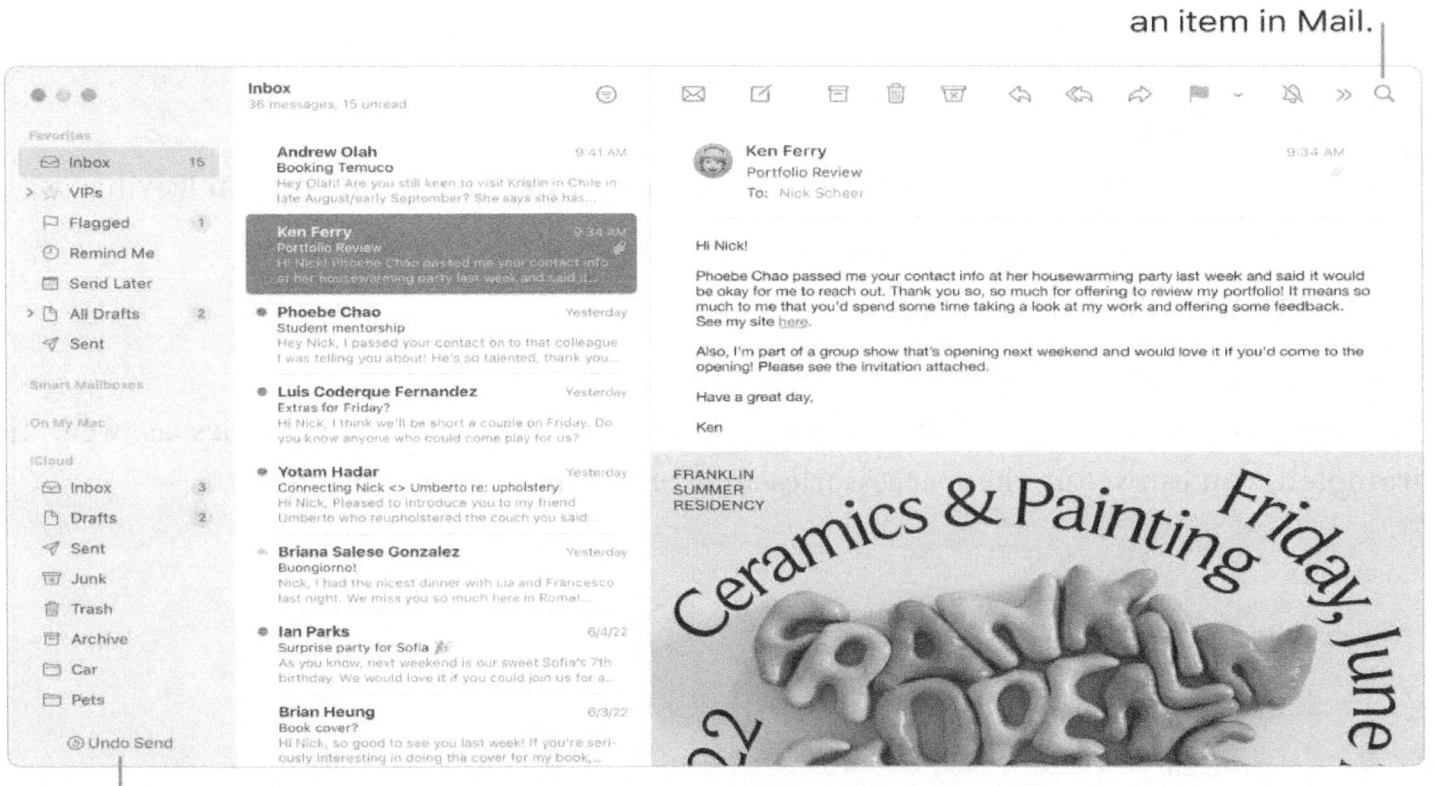 is a powerful tool for managing your email accounts efficiently. It supports popular email services like iCloud, Gmail, Yahoo Mail, and AOL Mail, allowing you to consolidate all your emails in one place on your Mac.

ONE-STOP EMAIL

Instead of logging into multiple websites to check your email accounts, you can set up all your email accounts in the Mail app. This way, you can access all your messages in one convenient location. To add an account, go to Mail > Add Account.

SIRI INTEGRATION

You can use Siri to compose and send emails effortlessly. For example, you can say, "Email Laura about the trip," and Siri will help you draft the message.

SMART SEARCH

The Mail app features a smart search that provides accurate results, corrects typos, and even suggests synonyms for your search terms. This makes it easier to find the messages you're looking for. Smart search also offers a richer view of shared content as you search for email messages.

an item in Mail.

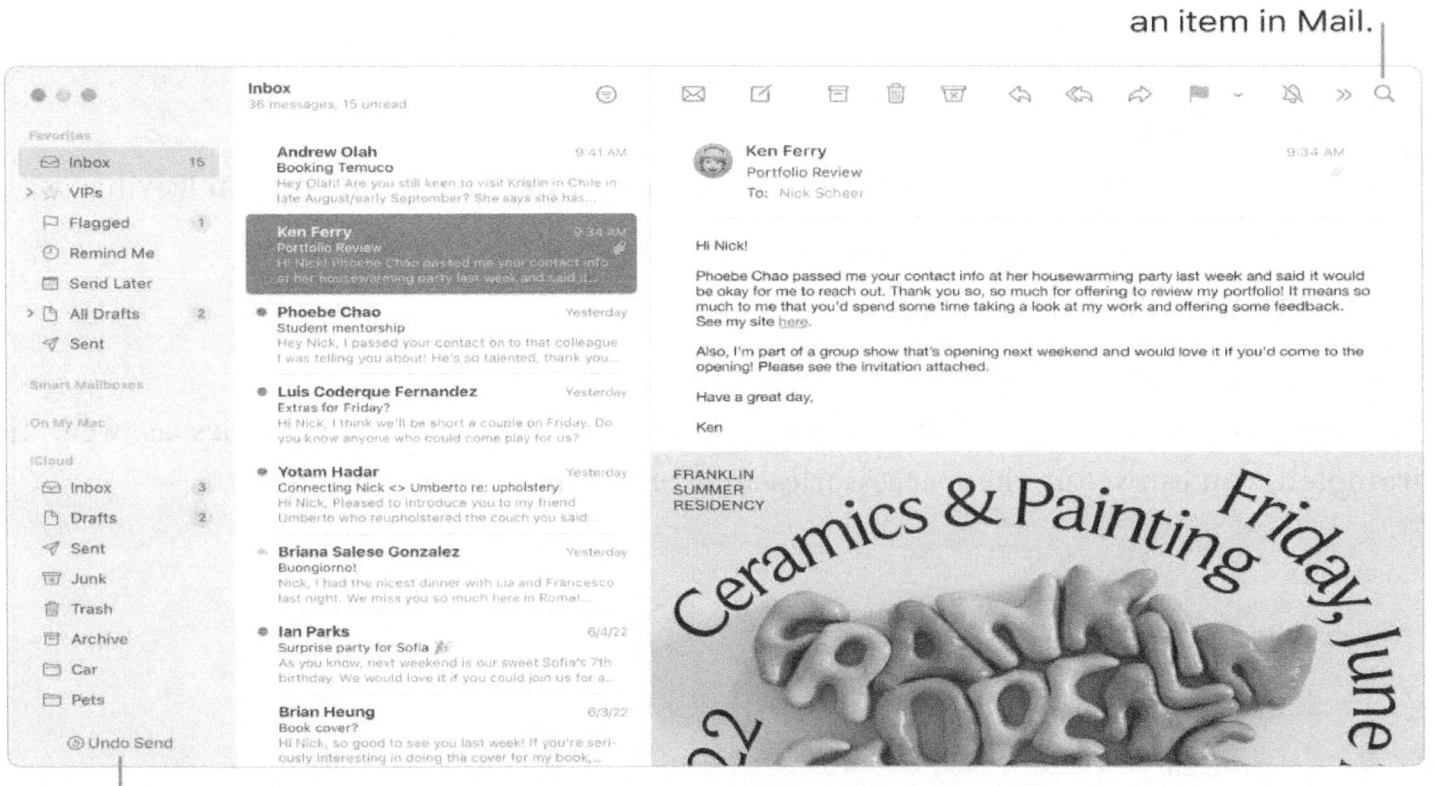

Click to Undo Send

MESSAGE MANAGEMENT

Keep your inbox organized by blocking messages from specific senders, moving their emails to the Trash. You can also mute overly active email threads and unsubscribe from mailing lists directly within the Mail app.

SCHEDULED SENDING

You can schedule your emails to be sent at the perfect time. When composing a message, click the dropdown menu next to the Send button and select a suggested time or choose "Send Later" to set a specific date and time.

UNDO SEND

If you accidentally send an email before it's ready, you can easily unsend it within 10 seconds after sending. Customize the time frame for undoing sends by going to Mail Settings > Composing.

EFFICIENCY AND ORGANIZATION

Mail helps you stay efficient and organized. It notifies you when you forget to include important parts of your message, like a recipient. Sent email messages that don't receive a response are intelligently moved to the top of your inbox for easy follow-up.

REMINDERS

If you opened an email and didn't respond, you can set a date and time to be reminded to follow up. Just right-click the email in your inbox, select "Remind Me," and choose when you'd like to be reminded.

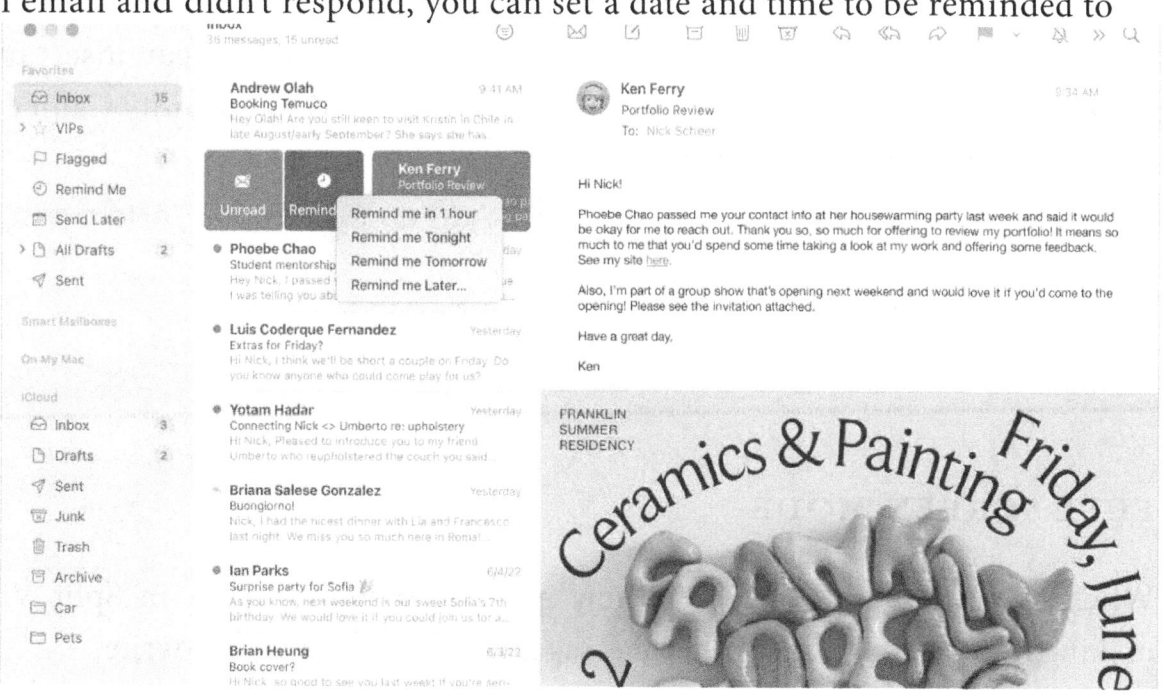

EVENTS AND CONTACTS INTEGRATION

Add events and contacts directly from emails. If you receive a message containing a new email address or event, you can click "Add" within the message to add it to Contacts or Calendar.

PRIVACY PROTECTION

Protect your privacy with the Privacy Protection feature, which hides your IP address from email senders. It also prevents senders from knowing if you've opened their emails. Turn this feature on in Mail Settings > Privacy.

HIDE MY EMAIL

With an iCloud+ subscription, you can create unique, random email addresses for added privacy when interacting with websites. This feature allows you to send and receive messages without sharing your real email address. You can create, manage, or disable Hide My Email addresses in iCloud settings.

TRANSLATION

Translate text quickly by selecting the text, right-clicking it, and choosing "Translate." You can also download languages to work offline. on your Mac, choose Apple Menu > System Settings, then click General in the sideba

PERSONALIZATION

Add emoji, photos, or sketches to your messages with ease. You can insert photos from your library or take new ones using your iPhone or iPad. Continuity Camera lets you insert photos and sketches from other devices.

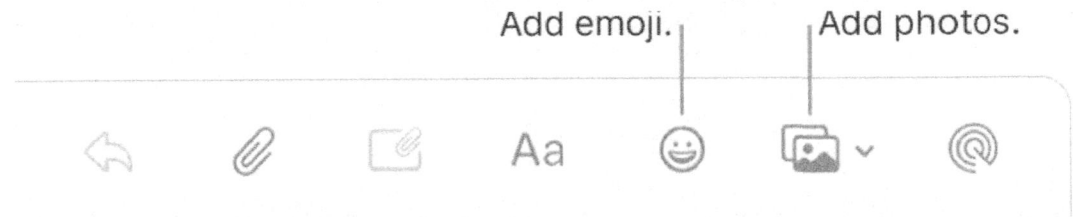

FULL SCREEN MODE

When using Mail in full screen, new message windows open in Split View on the right, making it easy to reference other messages in your inbox as you write.

MAPS

Maps on your Mac provides a great way to explore and organize places using curated Guides and your own custom Guides. If you're planning a trip or just want to discover new places, you can use Food and Travel Guides in Maps.

EXPLORE PLACES WITH GUIDES

1. Launch 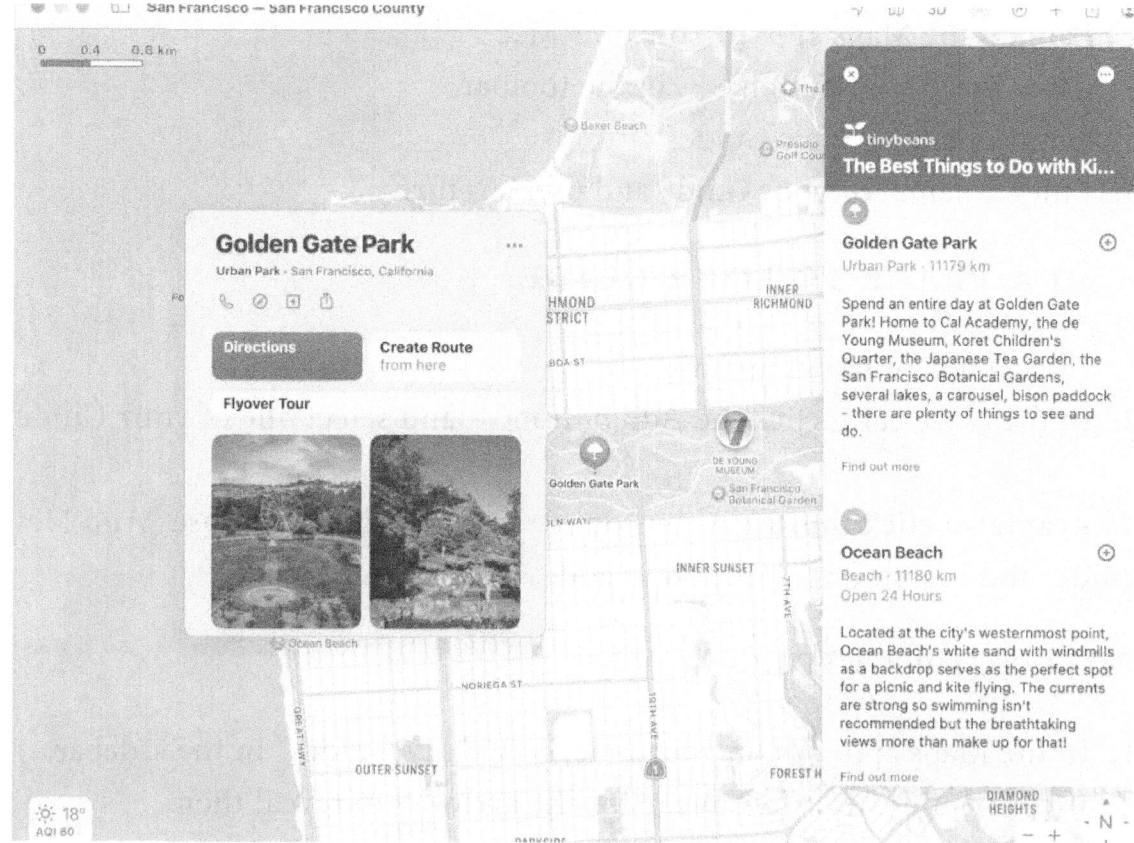 Maps app on your Mac.
2. In the search field, you can:

   • Click a Guide that appears under "Guides We Love."

   • Click "See All" and choose a Guide.

   • Scroll down and click a publisher, then select a Guide.

   • Enter a word or phrase in the search field and click a Guide from the search results.

3. When you have a Guide open, you can:

   • Scroll up or down to view locations.

   • Save the Guide by clicking the "More" button ⋯ in the upper-right corner and then selecting "Add to My Guides."

   • Add a location to one of your Guides by clicking the "Add" button ⊕ next to the location and selecting a Guide. If you don't have any Guides, you can create one first.

   • See other Guides from the same publisher by clicking the "More" button and then selecting "See Publisher's Guides." If the publisher has no other guides, you can click "Publisher's Website" to visit their website.

   • See Guides for a specific location by clicking the "More" button ⋯ , selecting "See All Guides," clicking "Editors' Picks," and then choosing a location from the menu.

- Share the Guide by clicking the "Share" button ⬆ under the guide's title and selecting an option.

- Explore related media by clicking links to find relevant music, books, and more.

- Close the Guide by clicking the "Close" button ⊗.

CREATE YOUR OWN GUIDE

1. Launch the Maps app 🗺 on your Mac.
2. Click the "New" button ✛ in the toolbar.
3. Choose "Create New Guide."
4. Enter a name for your Guide and press Return.

ADD A PLACE TO YOUR GUIDE

1. Click a location on the map.
2. In the place card, click the Add button ⊞ and select one of your Guides.

You can also click the "New" button ✛ in the toolbar, choose "Add New Place To," select a guide, and search for a location to add.

EDIT YOUR GUIDE

1. In the Maps app 🗺 on your Mac, go to "My Guides" in the sidebar.
2. If your Guides aren't visible, click the arrow ❯ to reveal them.
3. To perform various actions on your Guide, you can:

- Rename the Guide by control-clicking it, choosing "Edit Guide," and entering a new name.

- Change the Guide cover photo by control-clicking it, selecting "Edit Guide," and choosing "Change Key Photo."

- Delete the Guide by tapping ❯ and control-clicking it and choosing "Delete Guide."

- Remove a place from the Guide by moving the pointer over the Guide, clicking the arrow ❯ control-clicking the place, and selecting "Remove from Guide."

- Change the sort order by moving the pointer over the Guide, clicking the arrow, clicking the "Sort Order" button, and choosing "Name," "Distance," or "Date Added."

- Move a place to another Guide by moving the pointer over the Guide, clicking the arrow ❯, control-clicking the place, and choosing "Move to," then selecting another Guide.

SHARE YOUR GUIDE

1. In the Maps app 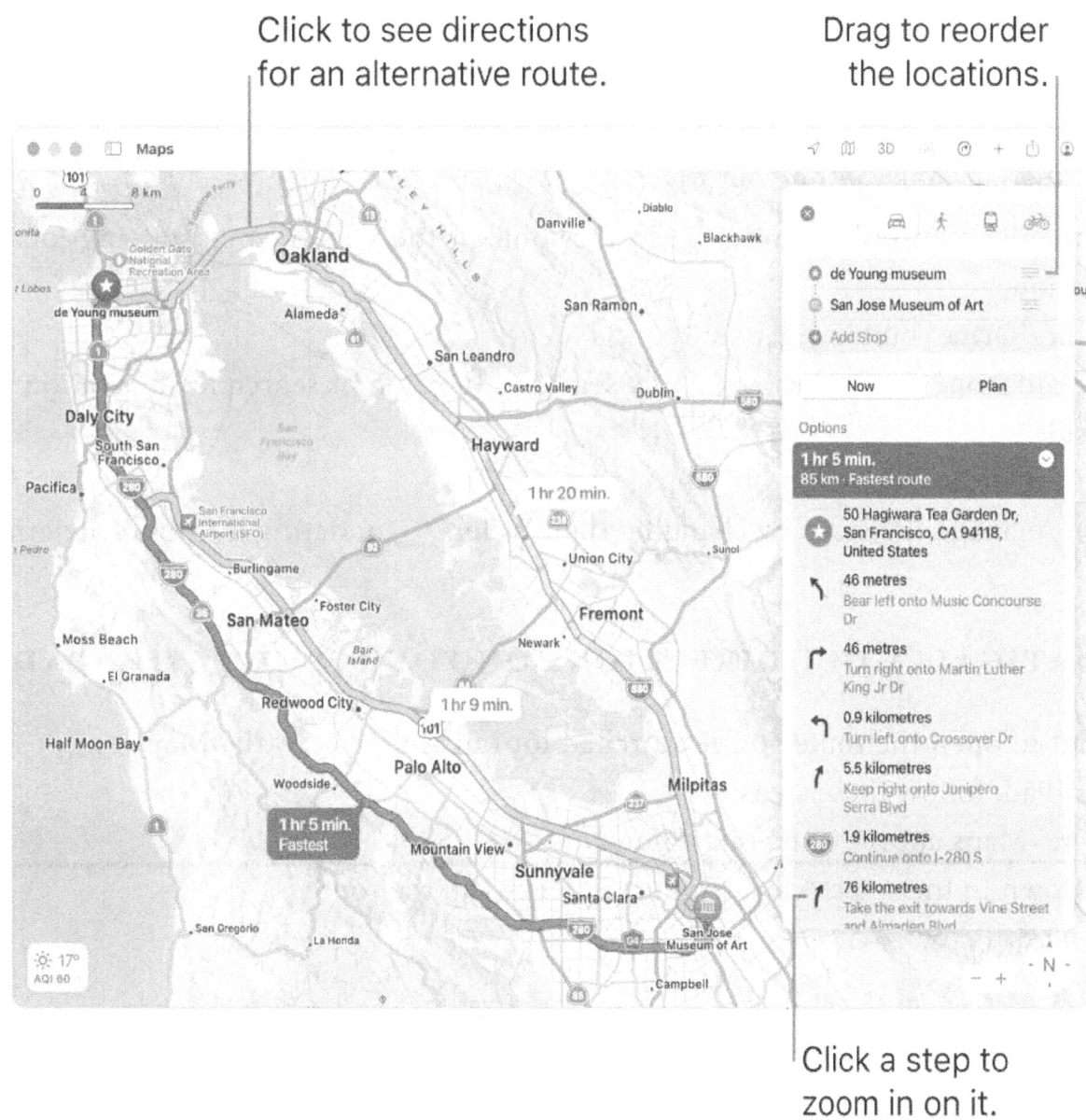 on your Mac, go to "My Guides" in the sidebar.
2. If your Guides aren't visible, click the arrow ❯ to reveal them.
3. Control-click the Guide you want to share, choose "Share," and then select an option.

Your Guides are automatically updated when new places are added, ensuring that you always have access to the latest recommendations for your food and travel adventures.

GET DIRECTIONS IN MAPS ON MAC

If you need to navigate your way around a new place, you can easily get directions in Maps on your Mac for driving, walking, public transport, or cycling. Moreover, you can even send the directions to your iPhone, iPad, or Apple Watch for convenient access while on the go.

Click to see directions for an alternative route.

Drag to reorder the locations.

Click a step to zoom in on it.

Here's how to use the Maps app for directions:

1. Open the Maps app ⬛ n your Mac.

2. There are several ways to get directions:

   • Click the "Directions" button ⬛ n the toolbar, then enter your starting location and destination.

   • Click on your destination on the map, such as a landmark or pin, and in the place card, click "Directions."

   • If Maps displays your current location, it will use it as your starting point. You can drag the "Reorder" button ▬ next to a location to swap your starting and ending points.

3. Click the appropriate button to choose the mode of transportation: "Drive," "Walk," "Public Transport," or "Cycle".

4. To view the directions list, click the "Trip Details" button next to a route.

If you're driving, directions may include additional features like electric vehicle routing, congestion zones, and number plate restrictions in specific regions.

GET DIRECTIONS TO MULTIPLE STOPS WHEN DRIVING

1. Open the Maps app ⬛ on your Mac.

2. Click the "Directions" button ⬛ in the toolbar, then enter your starting location and destination.

3. Click the "Drive" button 🚗.

4. Click "Add stop," then select a recently searched location or search for a location and click the result.

5. Repeat the process to add more stops as needed.

6. You ⬇ manage the stops by changing their order ▬ updating a stop, or deleting a stop .

AUTOMATICALLY GET DIRECTIONS ON YOUR IPHONE OR IPAD

If you want to open the route you've searched for on your Mac in the Maps app ⬛ on your iPhone or iPad, follow these steps:

1. Open the Maps app ⬛ on your iPhone or iPad.

2. Scroll down in the search card to "Recent," then tap the route.

SEND DIRECTIONS TO YOUR IPHONE, IPAD, OR APPLE WATCH

1. In the Maps app on your Mac, select a location on the map, and click "Directions."

2. Make any necessary adjustments.
3. Click the "Share" button ⬆️ in the toolbar.
4. Choose the device to which you want to send the directions.

To easily share and access directions across your Apple devices, ensure you sign in using the same Apple ID on both your Mac and your device.

LOOK AROUND IN MAPS ON MAC

1. Open the Maps app 🅐 on your Mac.
2. In the search field, enter an address, intersection, landmark, or business.
3. If available, you can click on "Look Around" below the location in the search results, select a location and then click on the "Look Around" button in the toolbar or click on the image with the "Look Around" button in the lower-left corner of the place card.

While Using Look Around, you can:

• Drag the image left or right to look around (Pan).

• Click in front of you in the Look Around view to move forward (Move Forward).

• Pinch two fingers open to zoom in or close them to zoom out (Zoom In or Out).

• Click on another location on the map to explore a different area (View Another Point of Interest).

• Click the "Enter Full Screen" button to view ↗️↘️ the location in full screen. To exit full screen, click the "Exit Full Screen" button ↘️↖️

• Click the "Close" button ⓧ to exit the Look Around view when you're done.

MESSAGES

Sending messages on your Mac is a convenient way to communicate with others. Below is a detailed guide on how to send messages on your Mac using the Messages app

1. Open the Messages App

    • First, locate and open the Messages app on your Mac.

2. Compose a New Message:

    • Click the "Compose" button (icon with a pencil) located in the top-right corner or use the Touch Bar if your Mac supports it.

3. Choose Recipient

    • Type the name, email address, or phone number of the person you want to send a message to in the "To" field. As you type, Messages will suggest matching addresses from your Contacts or previous conversations.

    • Alternatively, click the "Add" button located to the right of the "To" field, select a contact from the list, and click on their email address or phone number.

4. Compose Message

    • Type your message in the field located at the bottom of the window. You can use typing suggestions if available.

5. Send Message

    • Press the "Return" key on your keyboard or click the "Send" button to send the

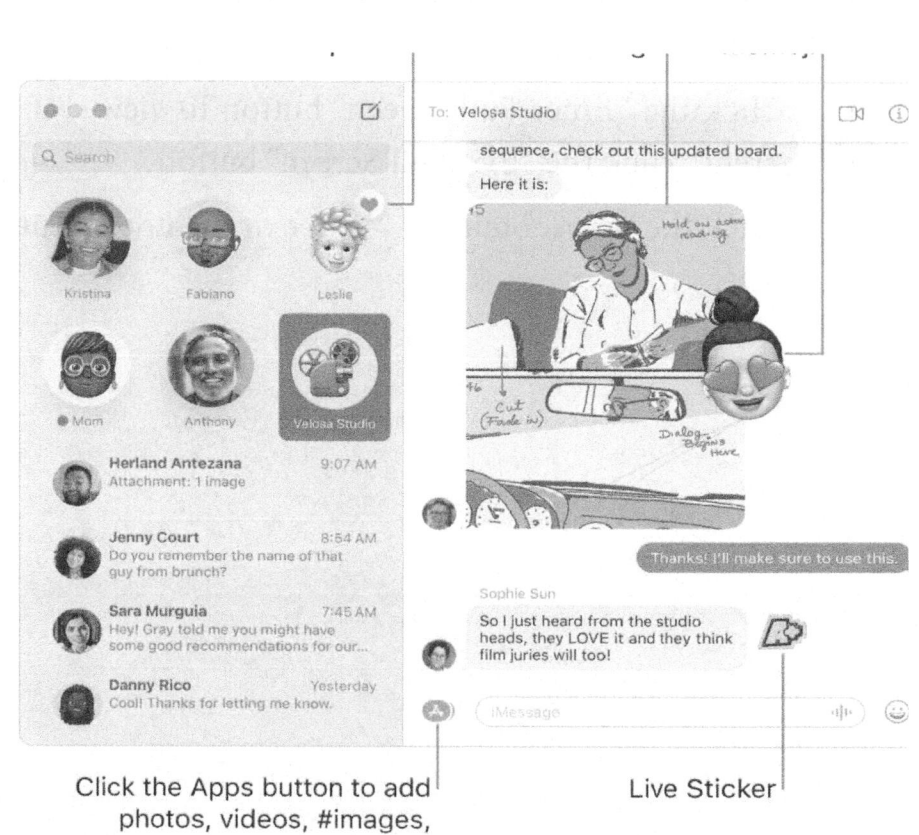

Start a conversation.

Manage a conversation, share your location, and more.

Start a FaceTime call.

Click the Apps button to add photos, videos, #images,

Live Sticker

message.

6. Additional Features

- Messages on Mac offers various features to enhance your messages, such as Tapbacks, sending photos, videos, stickers, audio messages, and using message effects. You can use these options to make your messages more engaging.

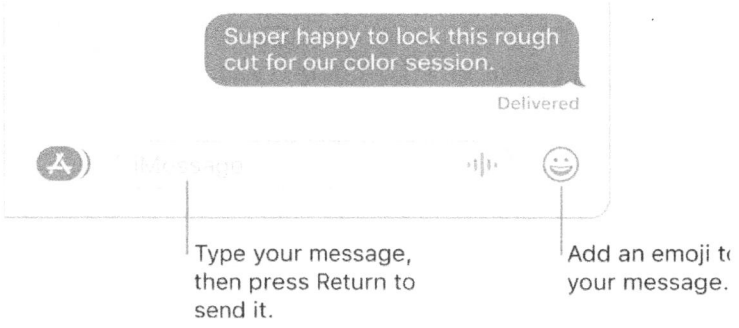

Super happy to lock this rough cut for our color session.

Delivered

Type your message, then press Return to send it.

Add an emoji to your message.

7. Managing Conversations

- Messages on Mac keeps track of your conversations in the sidebar. You can easily switch between different conversations and manage your messages.

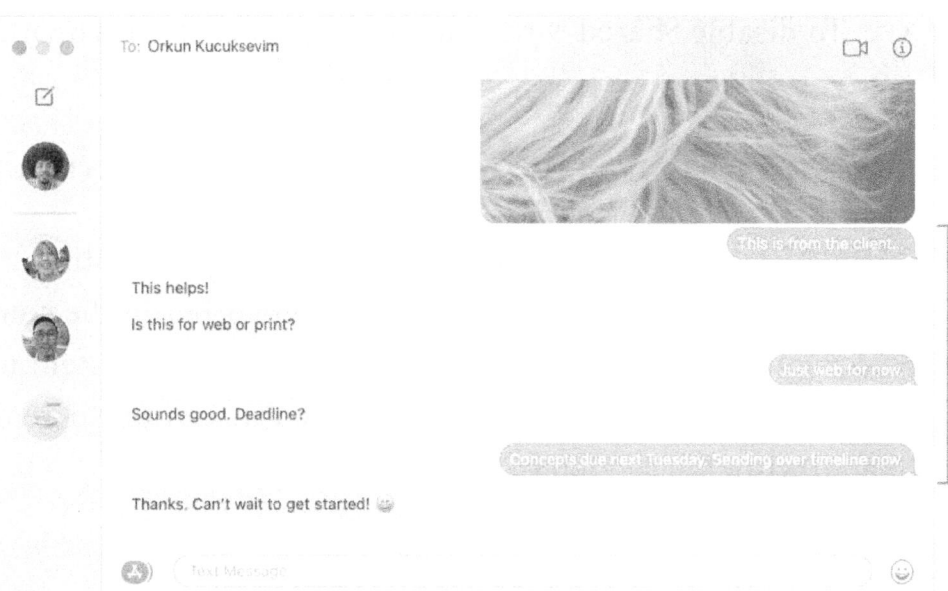

When the message bubbles are green, it means they were sent as SMS text messages.

To: Orkun Kucuksevim

This helps!
Is this for web or print?

Sounds good. Deadline?

Thanks. Can't wait to get started!

This is from the client.

Just web for now.

Concepts due next Tuesday. Sending over timeline now.

8. Using Siri

- If you prefer voice commands, you can use Siri to send messages. Just say something like, "Message Mum that I'll be late."

Please note that to send SMS and MMS messages on your Mac, your iPhone must have iOS 8.1 or later, and both your iPhone and Mac must be signed into iMessage using the same Apple ID. This allows you to receive and send text and multimedia messages on your Mac.

If you want to make FaceTime video calls using Messages on your Mac, you can do so by selecting a conversation, sending a message to a person or group, and a message to a person or group, and clicking the "Video" button to initiate a FaceTime Video call with the selected contacts.

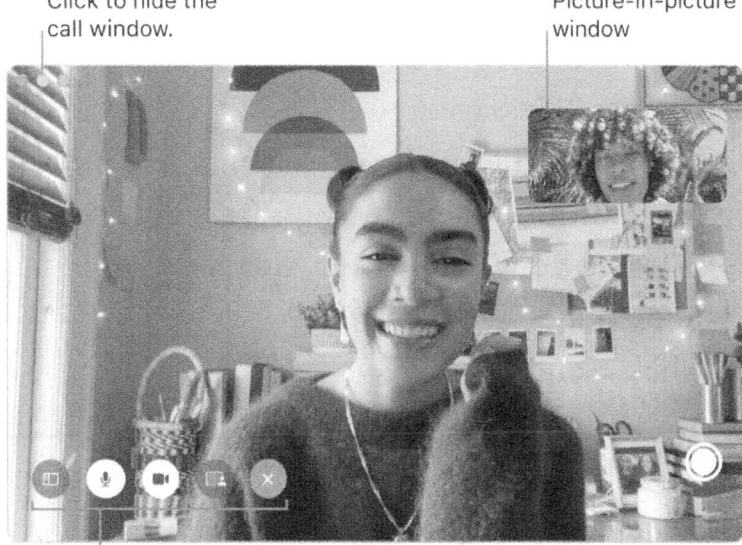

Click to hide the call window.

Picture-in-picture window

Move the pointer over FaceTime to see call options.

The Messages app ⬜ on your Mac is equipped with a helpful feature called "Shared with You" that allows you to keep track of all the content that others have shared with you in your messages. You can access this content in various apps, and this is how you can make the most of it:

TURN SHARED WITH YOU SETTINGS ON OR OFF FOR ALL APPS

1. Open the Messages app ⬜ on your Mac.
2. Go to Messages > Settings, then click "Shared with You."
3. Choose one of the following options:

   • To enable Shared with You for all apps, click "Turn On."

   • To disable Shared with You for all apps, click "Turn Off."

TURN SHARED WITH YOU ON OR OFF BY CONVERSATION

1. In the Messages app ⬜ on your Mac, select a conversation.
2. Click the "Info" button ⓘ in the top-right corner of the conversation.
3. Select "Show in Shared with You" to enable shared content to appear in the corresponding app's Shared with You section. Deselect this option to remove shared content from the Shared with You section.

SHARE CONTENT WITH OTHERS

1. Select the content you want to share, such as a link, and click the "Share" button ⬆ or choose "Share."
2. Choose "Messages."
3. In the "To" field, type the name, email address, or phone number of the person you want to send the content to. Messages will suggest matching addresses from your Contacts or previous conversations as you type.
4. Enter a message if desired.
5. Click "Send."

VIEW SHARED CONTENT

You can view the content that others have shared with you either in your Messages conversation or later in the corresponding apps. The Shared with You section is available in various apps, including Apple TV, Books, Finder, Freeform (macOS 13.1 or later), News,

Notes, Photos, Podcasts, Reminders, Safari, iWork apps, and some third-party apps.

For example, to view shared content in the Apple TV app tv click "Watch Now," then scroll down to the "Shared with You" row.

CONTINUE THE CONVERSATION

In the corresponding apps, shared content includes a button with the name of the person who sent it. You can click this button to continue the conversation about the shared content. For example, in the News app , click the "From" label to send a reply in Messages.

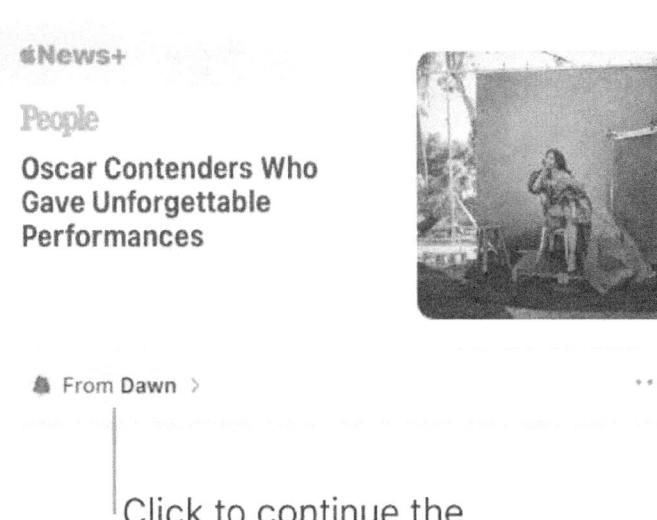

Oscar Contenders Who
Gave Unforgettable
Performances

From Dawn >

Click to continue the
conversation in Messages.

PIN SHARED CONTENT

If you find shared content particularly interesting, you can pin it in Messages, and it will be highlighted in Shared with You, Messages search, and the Info view of the conversation.

1. In the Messages app on your Mac, select a conversation.
2. Control-click the shared content, then choose "Pin."

This way, you can easily keep track of the content shared with you and access it when it's convenient for you in various apps.

MUSIC

If you want to access a vast library of songs, listen to music offline, create playlists, and enjoy various features, subscribing to Apple Music on your Mac is an excellent option.

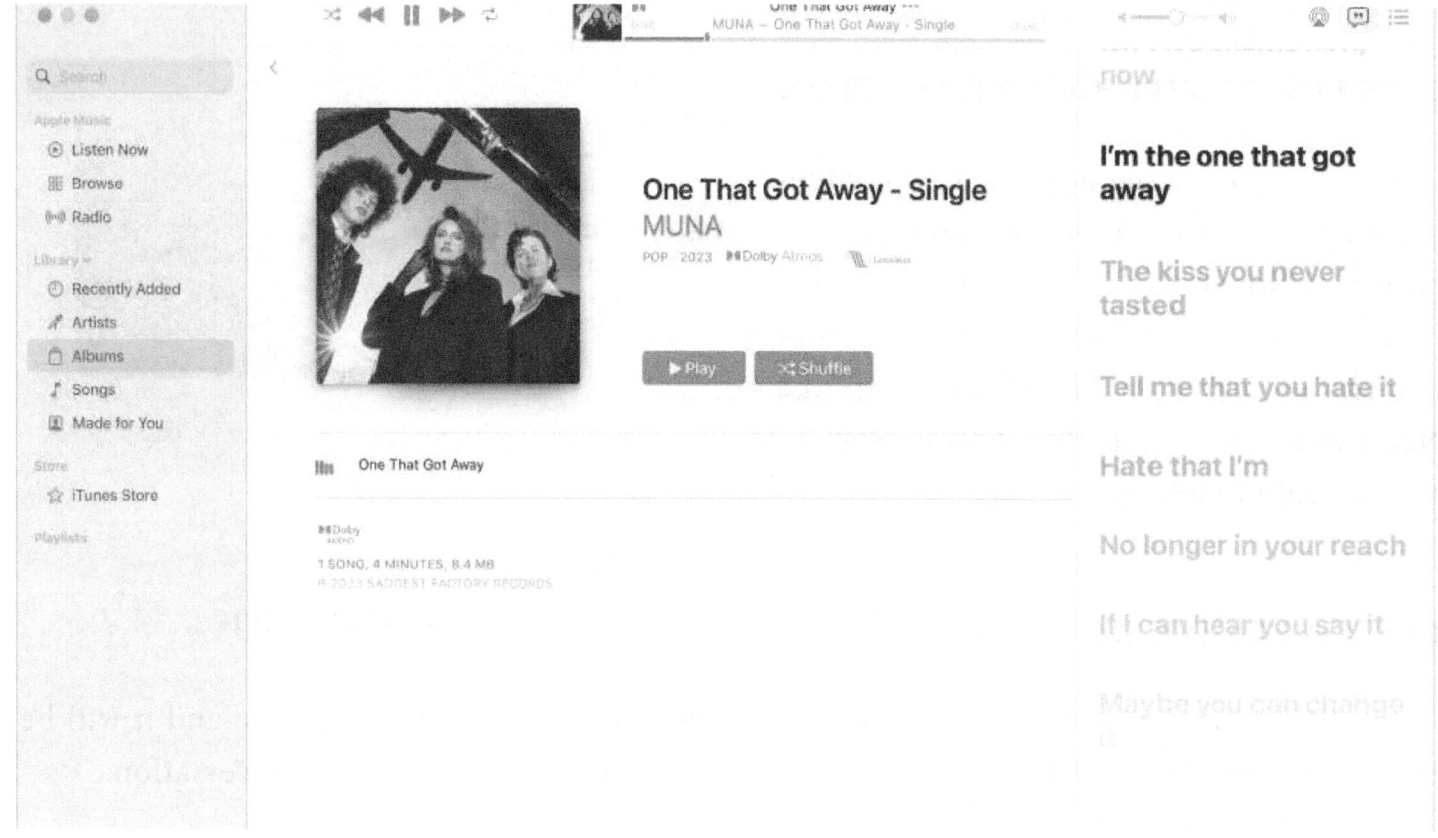

SUBSCRIBE TO APPLE MUSIC ON YOUR MAC

1. Open the Music app 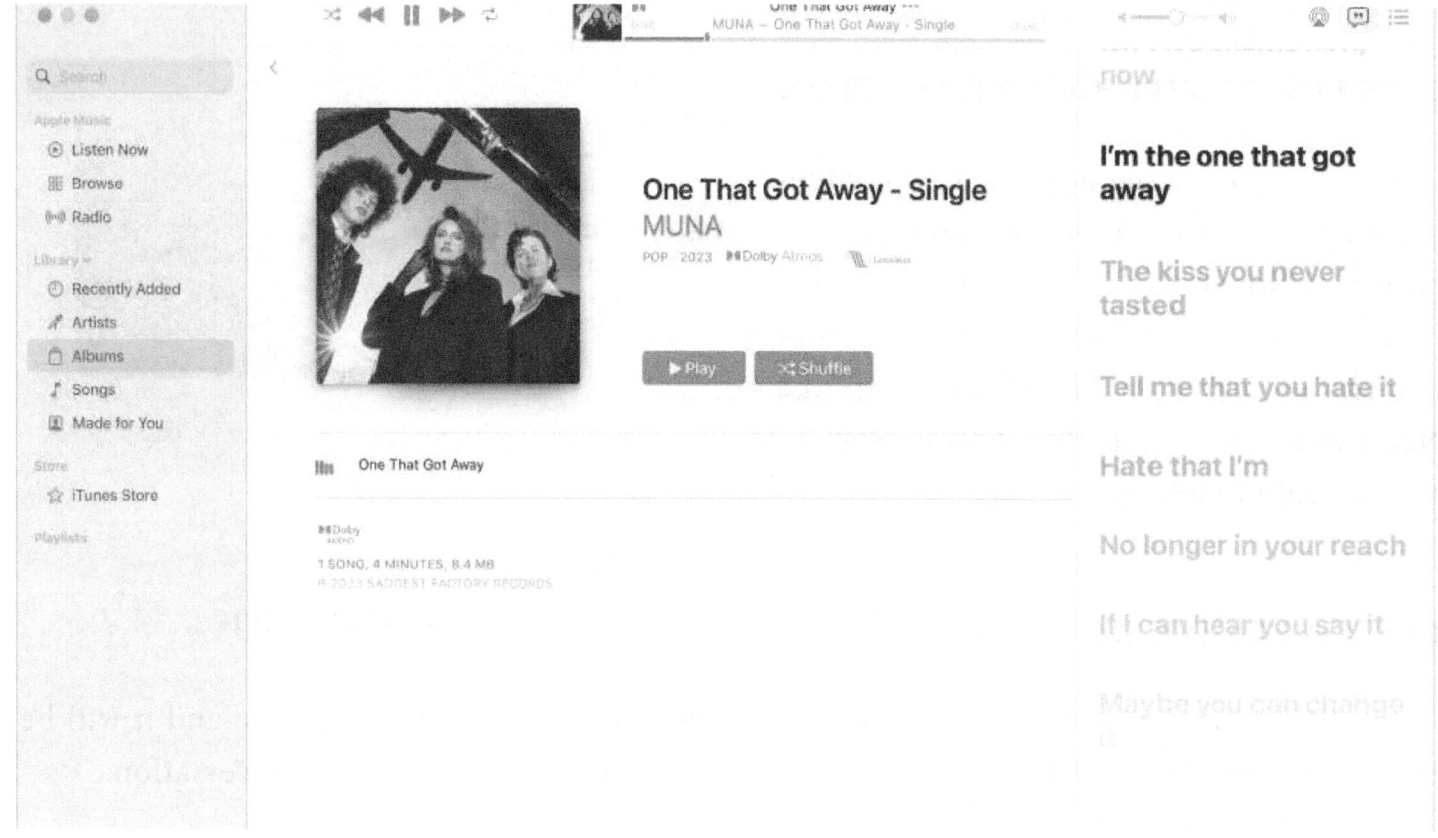 on your Mac.
2. In the menu bar, go to "Account" and select "Join Apple Music."
3. Follow the on-screen instructions.
4. If prompted, sign in with your Apple ID. If you don't have an Apple ID, you can create one during the setup.

Once you become an Apple Music subscriber, you can enjoy the following benefits:

• Stream recommended songs on up to 10 computers and devices.

• Select artists as favorites to receive notifications about them and easily find their music.

• Download songs for offline listening.

• Access your music library on all your devices.

- Play Apple Music radio stations.

- Listen to music together using SharePlay on a FaceTime call.

- Listen to and download songs in lossless audio and Dolby Atmos (spatial) audio.

- Create an Apple Music profile and share music with friends.

- Allow third-party apps to access Apple Music.

- View song lyrics.

- Use Autoplay to automatically add similar songs to the end of the queue.

If you ever need to cancel or change your Apple Music subscription, follow these steps:

1. In the Music app 🎵 on your Mac, go to "Account" > "Account Settings" and sign in with your Apple ID.
2. In the "Settings" section, click "Manage" next to Subscriptions.
3. Click "Edit" next to Apple Music, Apple Music Voice, or Apple One.
4. Choose to cancel your subscription or change your plan as needed.

Please note that the availability of Apple Music, Apple Music Voice, and Apple One may vary by country or region. To get more details, you can refer to the Apple Support article on the Availability of Apple Media Services.Subscribing to Apple Music on your Mac allows you to access a vast library of songs, listen to music offline, create playlists, and enjoy various features. Here's how to subscribe to Apple Music on your Mac:

SUBSCRIBE TO APPLE MUSIC

1. Open the Music app 🎵 on your Mac.
2. In the menu bar, go to "Account" and select "Join Apple Music."
3. Follow the onscreen instructions.
4. If prompted, sign in with your Apple ID. If you don't have an Apple ID, you can create one during the setup.

ABOUT YOUR APPLE MUSIC SUBSCRIPTION

Once you become an Apple Music subscriber, you can enjoy the following benefits:
Stream recommended songs on up to 10 computers and devices.
Select artists as favorites to receive notifications about them and easily find their music.
Download songs for offline listening.

ACCESS YOUR MUSIC LIBRARY ON ALL YOUR DEVICES

- Play Apple Music radio stations.
- Listen to music together using SharePlay on a FaceTime call.
- Listen to and download songs in lossless audio and Dolby Atmos (spatial) audio.
- Create an Apple Music profile and share music with friends.
- Allow third-party apps to access Apple Music.
- View song lyrics.
- Use Autoplay to automatically add similar songs to the end of the queue.

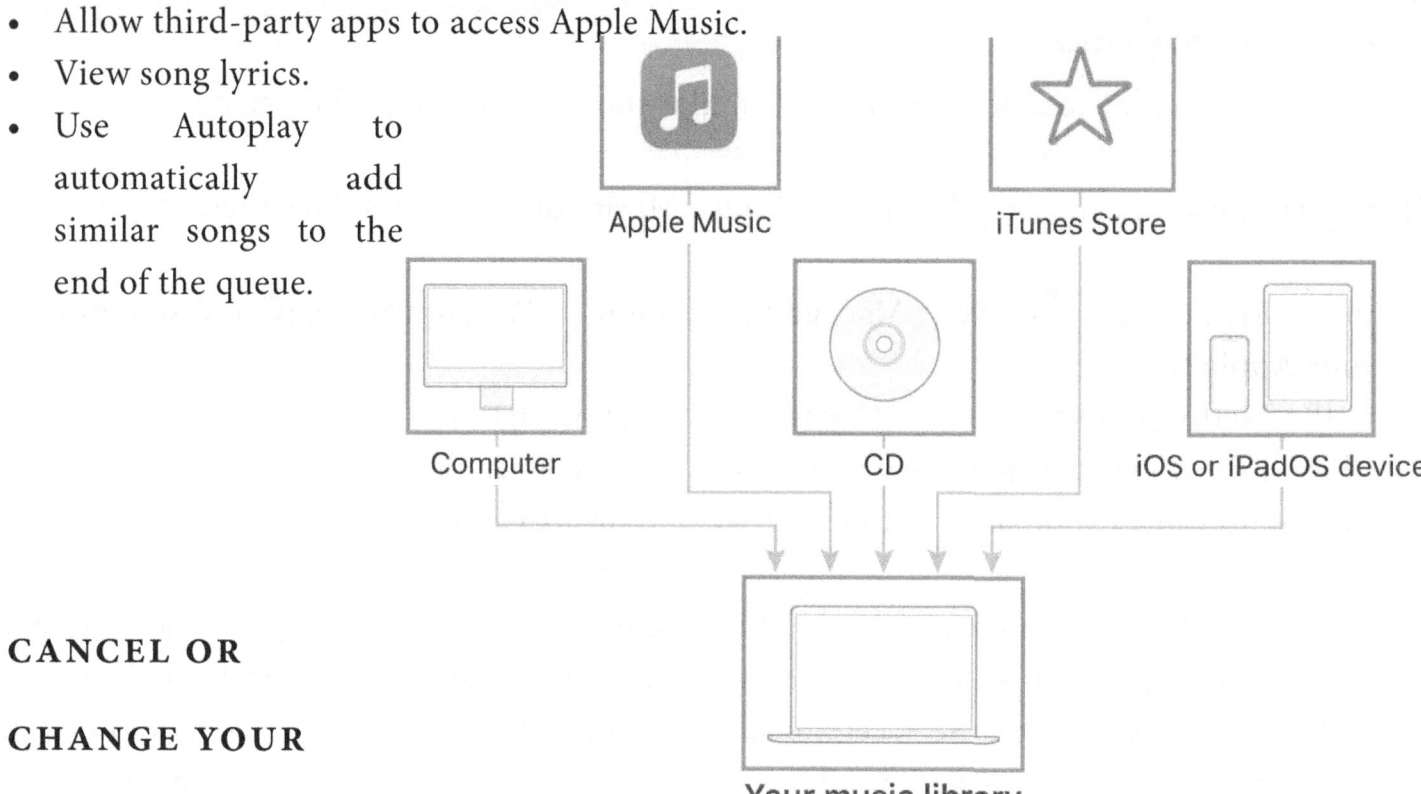

Apple Music   iTunes Store

Computer   CD   iOS or iPadOS device

Your music library

CANCEL OR CHANGE YOUR APPLE MUSIC SUBSCRIPTION

If you ever need to cancel or change your Apple Music subscription, follow these steps:

1. In the Music app on your Mac, go to "Account" > "Account Settings" and sign in with your Apple ID.
2. In the "Settings" section, click "Manage" next to Subscriptions.
3. Click "Edit" next to Apple Music, Apple Music Voice, or Apple One.
4. Choose to cancel your subscription or change your plan as needed.
5. Please note that Apple Music, Apple Music Voice, and Apple One availability may vary by country or region. To get more details, you can refer to the Apple Support article on the Availability of Apple Media Services.

NEWS

SIDEBAR

NAVIGATION

1. Open the News app  on your Mac.

2. Click an item in the sidebar to access different sections.

- If the sidebar isn't shown, click the Sidebar button ⊟ in the toolbar.

Today

- Features top stories selected by Apple News editors.

- Displays stories from the channels and topics you follow.

- In some regions, it includes personalized local news and weather reports based on your location.

- If you're an Apple News+ subscriber, My Magazines shows issues from magazines you follow.

News+

- Provides access to hundreds of magazines, popular newspapers, and other publications available through Apple News+.

- Subscribers can browse recent issues, download them, and read publications.

Puzzles

- Exclusive to Apple News+ subscribers, where you can solve daily crossword and crossword mini puzzles.

Shared with You

- Shows stories shared with you by others via the Messages app ⬜.

- Conveniently aggregates shared stories in one location.

Sport

- Allows you to follow your favorite sports, leagues, teams, and athletes.

- Receive stories from top sporting publications, local newspapers, and more.

- Access scores, fixtures, standings for professional and college leagues.

- Watch highlights.

Favourites

- Lists the channels and topics you've marked as your favorites.

- You can customize this list at any time.

- You may already have some channels and topics that were automatically added to Favourites.

Suggested

- Lists channels and topics suggested by Siri or based on your interactions within Apple News.

- May include local news suggestions in some regions based on your location.

Search and Discover Channels

- If a specific channel or topic isn't shown, use the search field at the top of the sidebar to search within Apple News.

- You can also choose "File" > "Discover Channels" to explore more content.

WHILE READING A STORY

- Watch videos, ask for more or fewer stories like it, share it, or save it for later.

- Navigate to the next or previous story using the arrow keys.

- Access the story's channel by clicking the Share button in the toolbar and choosing "Go to Channel."

FOLLOW CHANNELS OR TOPICS

1. Open the News app ◣ on your Mac.
2. To follow channels or topics, you can:

- Choose "File" > "Discover Channels," select the channels you want to follow by the ＋ icon should change to ✅, and click "Done."

- In the Today feed, click the "Add" button ⊕ next to a channel or topic, or click the More button ⋯ and choose "Follow Channel" or "Follow Topic."

- While viewing stories for a specific topic or channel, choose "File" > "Follow Topic" or "Follow Channel."

- If you're reading a story, choose "File" > "Follow Channel" or click the Share button ⬆ in the toolbar and select "Follow Channel."

- If the channel, topic, or story you want to follow isn't shown, you can search for it in Apple News and follow it from the search results.

UNFOLLOW CHANNELS OR TOPICS

To unfollow a channel or topic, do the following:

- In the sidebar (if not shown, click the Sidebar button ⊟ in the toolbar), select the channel or topic, swipe with two fingers (on a trackpad) or one finger (on a mouse), then click "Unfollow."

- Choose "File" > "Unfollow Channel" or "File" > "Unfollow Topic."
- If you're reading a story from a channel you want to unfollow, choose "File" > "Unfollow Channel" or click the Share button in the toolbar and select "Unfollow Channel."

MANAGE YOUR FAVOURITES

- The "Favourites" section displays the channels and topics from your Following list that you like the most. You can customize this list at any time.
- To add a channel or topic to your Favourites, go to "Following," Control-click the channel or topic, and click "Add to Favourites."
- To remove a channel or topic from your Favourites, go to "Favourites," Control-click the channel or topic, and click "Remove from Favourites."
- You can also rearrange the items you follow in the sidebar by dragging an item below "Favourites" or "Following" to a different position.

SAVE STORIES

1. In the News app on your Mac, to save a story, you can:
   - In the Today feed, click the ellipsis ••• for a story, then choose "Save Story."
   - While reading a story, click the "Save" button in the toolbar, or press Command-S.

VIEW SAVED STORIES

1. Open the News app on your Mac.
2. In the sidebar (if not shown, click the Sidebar button in the toolbar), click "Saved Stories."
3. You will see a list of saved stories.
4. Click on a saved story to view it.
5. To return to the list of saved stories, click the "Back" button in the toolbar.

UNSAVE STORIES

1. To unsave a story, view the saved story in the News app on your Mac.
2. Click the "Save" button in the toolbar, or press Command-S.

By saving stories, you can easily access and read them later, even without an internet connection. This feature allows you to catch up on articles of interest at your convenience.

NOTES

Notes app 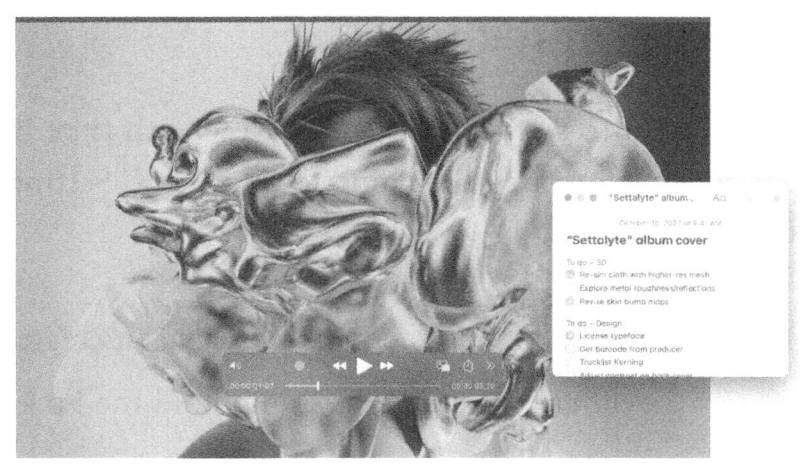 is an efficient and versatile application that provides a great platform for jotting down quick thoughts or saving longer notes with checklists, images, web links, and more. It offers a wide range of features to enhance your note-taking experience, such as:

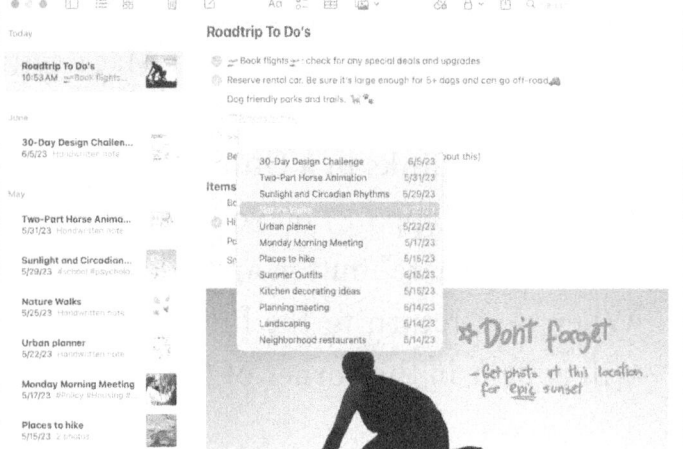

Collaboration Features

You can collaborate with others by sharing notes and folders. This allows multiple people to work on and update a note, making it a valuable tool for team projects.

Mentions

You can mention specific individuals in a note, making it easy to direct their attention to specific content within the note. This is particularly useful for communication and task assignment.

Tags

Tags help you categorize and organize your notes. You can assign tags to notes based on topics, projects, or any other criteria that make sense to you. This enhances your ability to find and manage your notes effectively.

Smart Folders

Smart Folders are a convenient way to automatically arrange your notes based on specific criteria, such as whether a note contains checklists or attachments, or when the note was created or last edited. This helps you keep your notes organized and easy to access.

iCloud Sync

With iCloud integration, your notes are seamlessly synchronized across all your Apple devices. This means you can access your notes from any device where you're signed in with your Apple ID, ensuring that your important information is always at your fingertips.

Siri Integration

You can use Siri voice commands to create a new note quickly. Just say something like, "Create a new note," and Siri will assist you in setting up a new note.

START A QUICK NOTE

If you want to start a fresh Quick Note each time instead of reopening the previous one, you can make this change by going to "Notes" > "Settings" and unselecting "Always resume to last Quick Note."

If you're working in another app and want to create a Quick Note, you have a few options:

- Keyboard Shortcut: Press and hold the Fn key or Globe key and then press Q.
- Hot Corners: Move your mouse pointer to the bottom-right corner of the screen (the default hot corner for Quick Note) and click the note that appears. You can customize or turn off this hot corner in your Mac's settings.

Adding Safari Links to a Quick Note

1. In the Safari app on your Mac, open the webpage you want to link to.
2. Click the "Share" button and choose either "New Quick Note" or "Add to Quick Note."
3. When you return to the linked content on the webpage, a thumbnail of the Quick Note will appear in the corner of the screen as a reminder of what you noted earlier.

Adding Content from Safari to a Quick Note

1. In the Safari app on your Mac, open a web page and select the text you want to add to a Quick Note.
2. Control-click the selected text, then choose "New Quick Note" or "Add to Quick Note."
3. A link will appear in the Quick Note, and the text in Safari will be highlighted. The highlighted text remains when you revisit the webpage later.

CLOSING AND REOPENING QUICK NOTES

- To close a Quick Note, click the red "Close" button ocated in the top left corner of the note.
- To reopen a Quick Note, use any of the methods mentioned above.

MANAGING NOTES

Managing your accounts and enhancing your note-taking experience in the Notes app on your Mac can be made easier by adding, temporarily stopping, or removing accounts. Here are the steps to perform these actions:

ADDING AN ACCOUNT

1. Open the Notes app   on your Mac.
2. In the app's menu, go to "Notes" and select "Accounts."
3. Click on "Add Account." You have the option to add various account types, including iCloud, Google, Yahoo, and others.
4. Follow the onscreen instructions to enter your account information and sign in. If you use Safari to sign in, you may need to return to the settings window to complete the process.
5. Ensure that the "Notes" option is selected for the account.
6. Click "Done" to finish the account setup.

Each account you add will be listed separately. To keep your notes synchronized across all your Apple devices, remember to set up your iPhone, iPad, and iPod touch with the same notes accounts.

TEMPORARILY STOPPING AN ACCOUNT

1. In the Notes app   on your Mac, click on "Notes" in the menu.
2. Select "Accounts."
3. Choose the account you want to temporarily stop using.
4. Turn off "Notes" for that account.

This action will make the account's notes unavailable while "Notes" is turned off. To access the notes from that account again, simply turn "Notes" back on.

REMOVING AN ACCOUNT

1. Open the Notes app   on your Mac.
2. In the app's menu, go to "Notes" and select "Accounts."
3. Click on the account you want to remove.
4. Click "Delete Account."

Please note that when you remove an account, the notes associated with that account will be deleted and will no longer be available on your Mac. Copies of the notes will remain on your internet account (e.g., iCloud.com or Yahoo) and any other devices where you had previously set up the account.

ADDING FILES AND IMAGES TO NOTES

1. Open the Notes app ▢ on your Mac.
2. Select the note where you want to add attachments or create a new note.

Note: If the note is locked, you must unlock it before adding attachments, tables, or links.

3. To add an attachment, do any of the following:

   a.   Add a File from the Desktop or Finder: Drag the file you want to attach into the note.

   b.   Add a File from Your Mac: Choose "Edit" from the menu. > Select "Attach File." > Choose the file you want to attach and click "Attach."

   c.   Add a Photo from Your Photos Library: Drag a photo directly from your Photos library into the note.

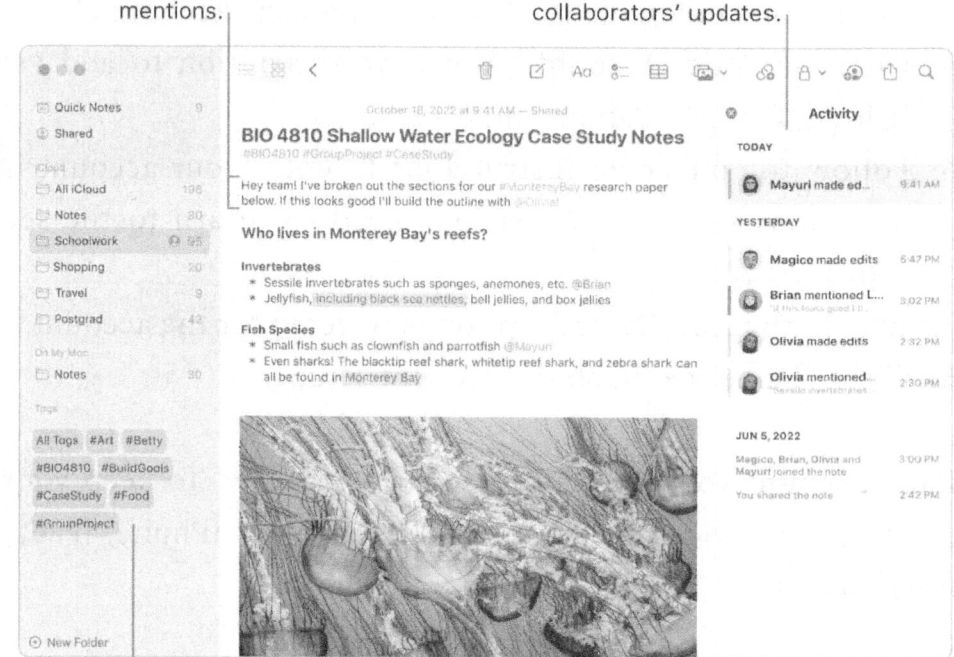

Alternatively, in the Notes app, click the 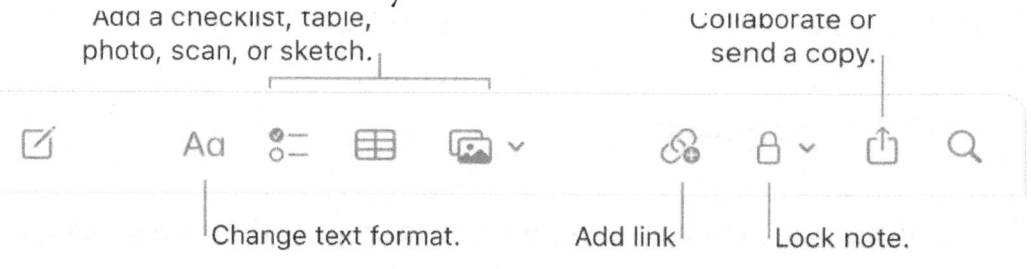 button in the toolbar, then click "Photos," and drag a photo from the window that appears.

   d. Insert a Photo or Scan from Your iPhone or iPad Camera: Click at the beginning of a line in your note > Choose "File" from the menu > Select "Insert from iPhone or iPad" > Choose to "Take Photo" or "Scan Documents" to capture a picture or scan a document with your iPhone or iPad. This will insert it into your note.

   e. Insert a Sketch from Your iPhone or iPad: Click at the beginning of a line in your note > Choose "File" from the menu > Select "Insert from iPhone or iPad" > Choose "Add Sketch" to draw a sketch using your finger or Apple Pencil on your iPad. The sketch will be inserted into your note.

You can change the size of all images, scanned documents, or PDFs in a note with attachments by going to "View," selecting "Attachment View," and then choosing "Set All to Small" or "Set All to Large." You can also adjust the size of individual attachments by Control-clicking them, choosing "View As," and selecting an option. Note that you can't change the size of drawings in notes.

ADDING ITEMS FROM OTHER APPS TO A NOTE

You can also attach items like map locations or webpage previews to a note directly from other apps. Here's how:

From another app (e.g., Maps, Safari, Preview, or Photos), you can do the following:

a. Share from the Toolbar: Click the "Share" button (please note that not all apps have this option) > Choose "Notes."

b. Share from a Selection: Select the text or images you want to share > Control-click your selection > Choose "Share" and then "Notes" > Click "Save" to add the item to a new note.

If you want to add an attachment to an existing note, click the "Choose Note" pop-up menu, select the name of the note, and then click "Save."

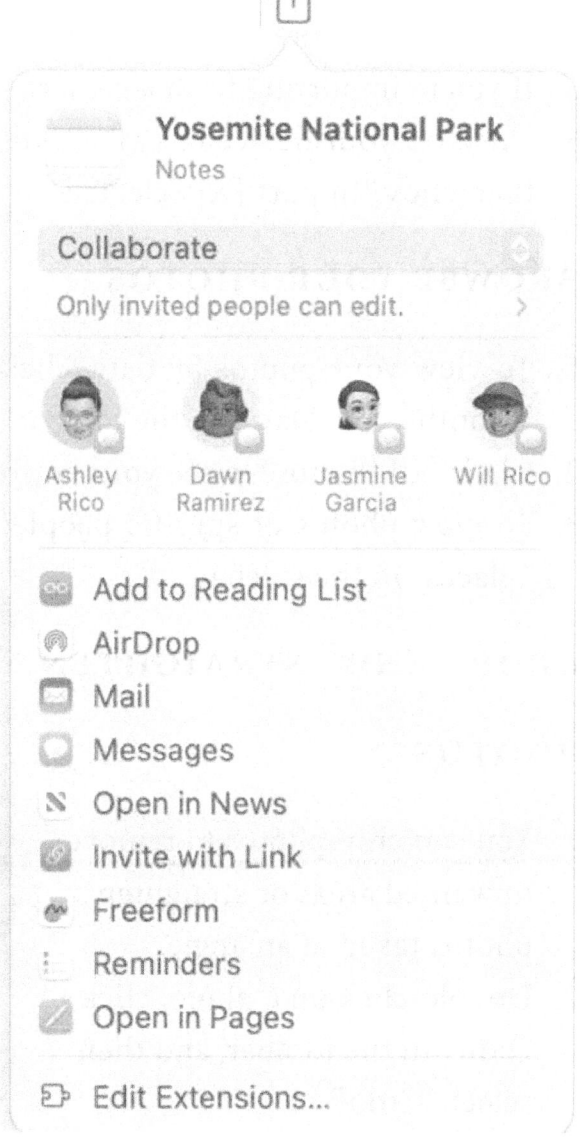

A Shared icon shows the note is shared with one or more people.

Summer Outfits
Yesterday 2 photos

PHOTOS

PHOTOS TO YOUR

MAC FROM ICLOUD

If you use iCloud, you
can access your photos
across all your devices by
enabling iCloud Photos on

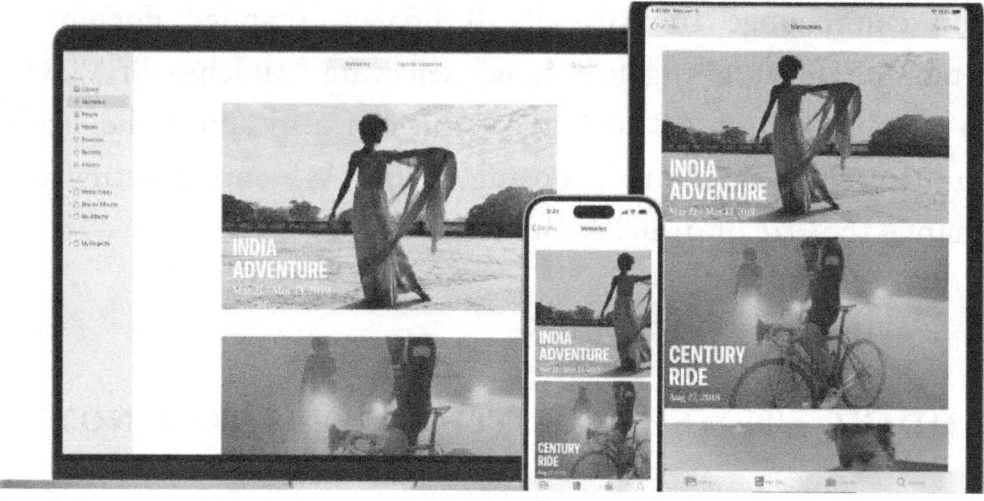

your Mac, iPhone, and iPad. Go to Photos > Settings in the Photos app on your Mac, click on
iCloud, and select iCloud Photos.

IMPORT PHOTOS

1. To import photos from your iPhone, iPad, or camera, connect your device or camera to
   your Mac, ensure it's turned on, and open Photos.
2. If you're importing from a camera, set it to download photos.
3. Click on your device or camera in the sidebar, select the photos you want to import, and
   then click "Import [X] Selected."

BROWSE YOUR PHOTOS

1. To view your photos by date, click "Library" in the sidebar. You can then select "Years,"
   "Months," or "Days" in the toolbar.
2. Click "All Photos" to see your entire collection.
3. To view photos of specific people or those taken in specific locations, click "People" or
   "Places" in the sidebar.

CROP AND STRAIGHTEN

PHOTOS

1. You can crop photos to remove
   unwanted areas or straighten
   photos taken at an angle.
2. Double-click on a photo, click
   "Edit" in the toolbar, and then
   select "Crop."

3. Drag the selection rectangle to enclose the area you want to keep and use the "Straighten" slider to adjust the photo's angle.

IMPROVE THE LOOK OF PHOTOS

1. Enhance your photos by adjusting brightness, color, and more.
2. Double-click on a photo, click "Edit" in the toolbar, and choose the "Light" or "Colour" options.
3. Drag the slider to achieve the desired look, or use the "Auto" option to let Photos make automatic adjustments.

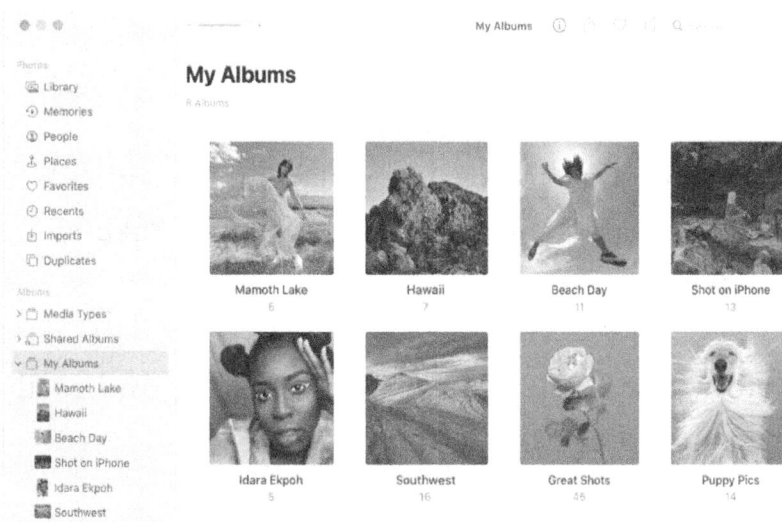

ORGANIZE PHOTOS IN ALBUMS

1. To organize your photos, create albums as you like.
2. Go to "File" > "New Album," provide a name for the album, and press Return.
3. To add photos to the album, click "Library" in the sidebar, and then drag photos to the new album in the sidebar.

PHOTO STORAGE

To optimize storage in the Photos app 🌸 on your Mac when using iCloud Photos, follow these steps:

1. Open the Photos app 🌸 on your Mac.
2. In the menu bar at the top of your screen, click "Photos."

3. Select "Preferences."then in the Preferences window, click on the "iCloud" tab.

4. Ensure that the "iCloud Photos" checkbox is selected. This enables iCloud Photos, which is required for optimizing Mac storage.

5. Below the checkbox, you'll find an option called "Optimise Mac Storage." Select this option.

6. Once you've selected "Optimise Mac Storage," your Mac will store smaller versions of your photos locally when storage space is limited, while keeping the original, full-size photos in iCloud. This helps free up space on your Mac.

TO RESTORE THE ORIGINAL, FULL-SIZE PHOTOS TO YOUR MAC, FOLLOW THESE STEPS

1. In the Photos app 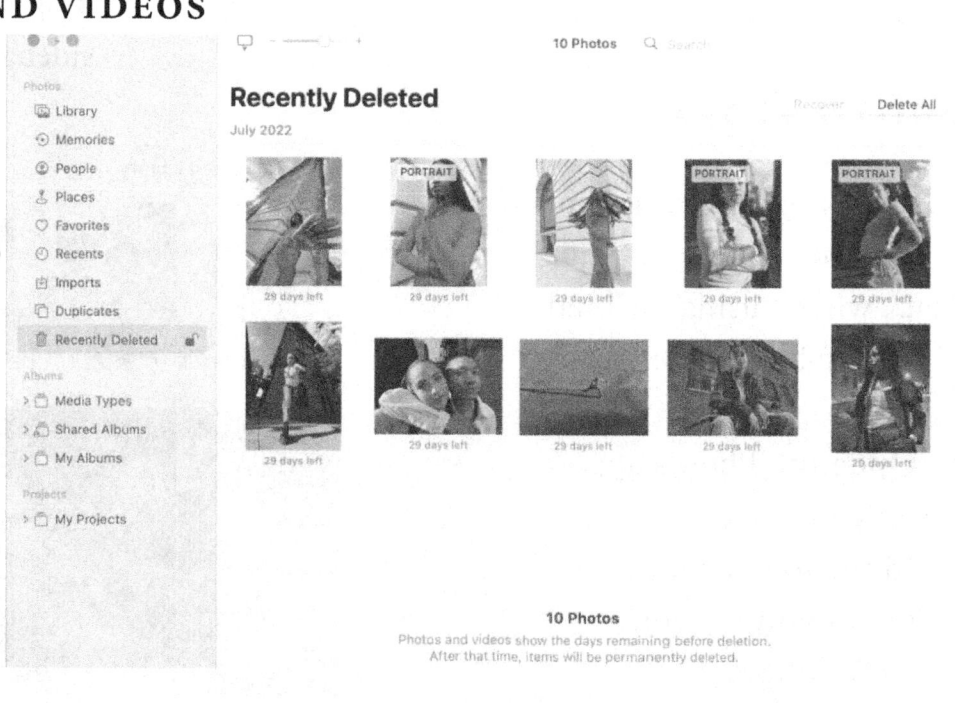 on your Mac, go to the menu bar and click "Photos."

2. Select "Preferences" to open the Preferences window.

3. Click on the "iCloud" tab.

4. Locate the "Optimise Mac Storage" option, and this time, unselect it.

5. After you've turned off the optimization feature, the Photos app will begin downloading the original, full-size photos to your Mac. Be patient, as this process might take some time depending on the number and size of your photos.

By following these steps, you can optimize storage in the Photos app on your Mac and easily manage your photo library while conserving local storage space.

DELETING PHOTOS AND VIDEOS

1. Open the Photos app on your Mac.

2. Choose the items (photos or videos) that you want to delete by clicking on them in your library.

3. To delete the selected items and move them to the "Recently Deleted" album, you can either:

• Press the Delete key if you're in "Days" view, and

then click the Delete button that appears.

- Press Delete to remove items from an album, but they'll remain in your library.

- To permanently delete items from the "Recently Deleted" album, press Command-Delete, then open the "Recently Deleted" album.

RESTORING RECENTLY DELETED ITEMS

1. In the Photos app 🌸 , you can find the "Recently Deleted" album in the sidebar. Click on it to access recently deleted items.
2. If the "Recently Deleted" album is locked, you can unlock it either by using Touch ID or by entering your password.
3. Select the items that you want to restore to your Photos library.
4. Click the "Recover" button to restore the selected items.

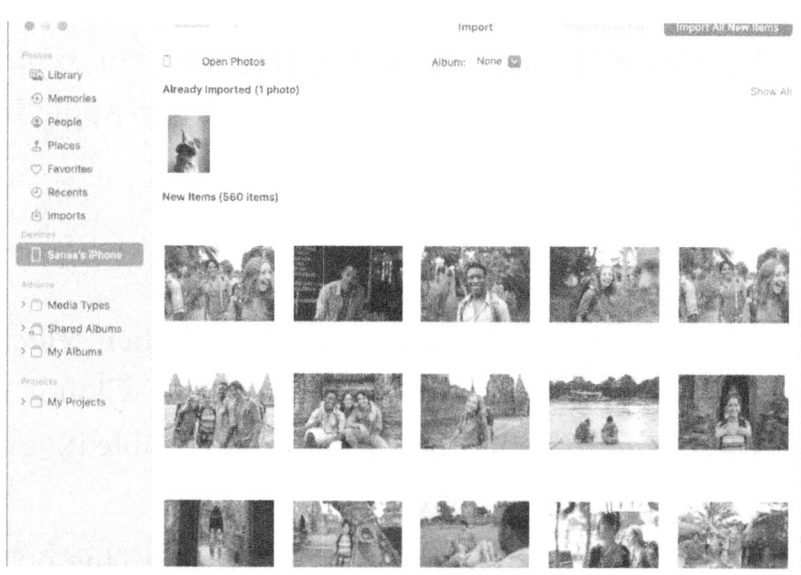

If you use iCloud Photos, you can recover photos and videos from iCloud within 30 days of deletion. If you don't use iCloud Photos, deleted items will be removed from your Mac only.

In addition, if you've set up Time Machine to back up your Mac, you may be able to recover items that have been permanently deleted from your Mac or iCloud using your backups. You can refer to the "Restore a Photos library from Time Machine" feature for this purpose.

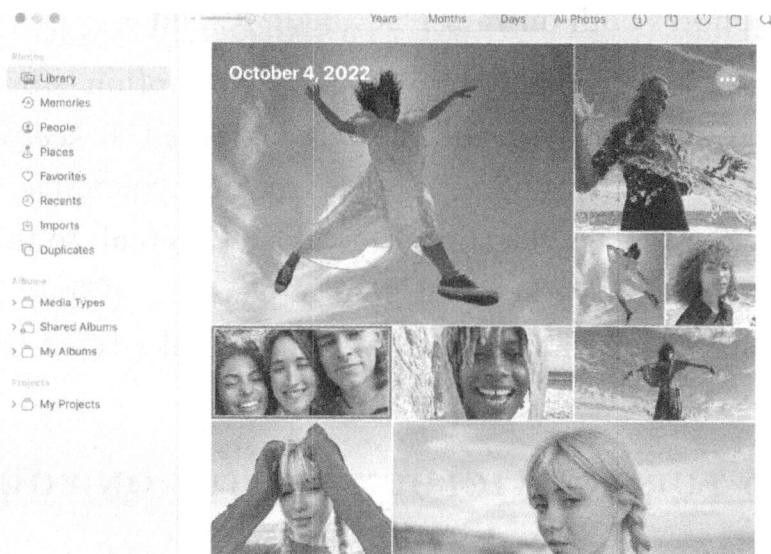

ICLOUD

Using iCloud Photos on your Mac is a convenient way to store and access your photos and videos across multiple devices.

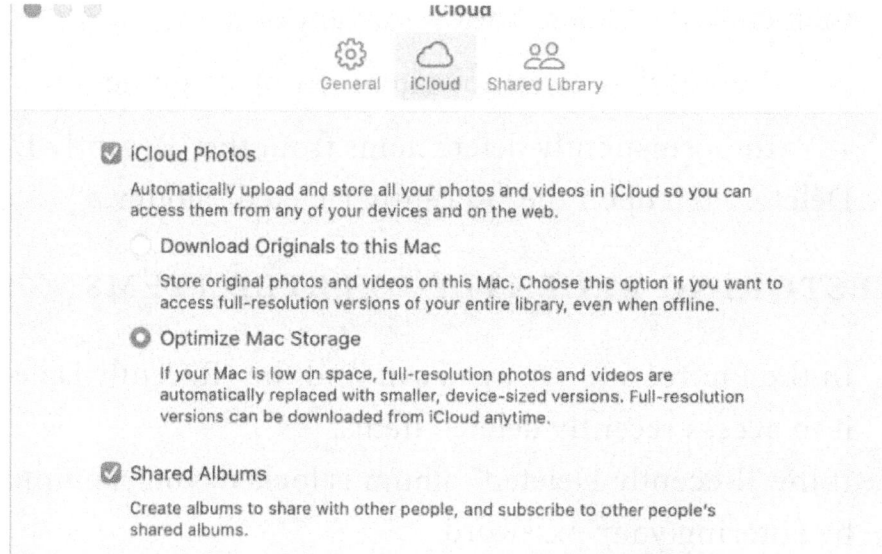

BEFORE YOU BEGIN

1. Ensure that your Mac and other devices have the latest software updates.

2. Sign in with your Apple ID. If you're not signed in, go to Apple menu > System Preferences, then click "Sign in with your Apple ID" and follow the prompts.

TO TURN ON ICLOUD PHOTOS

1. Open the Photos app on your Mac.
2. Click on "Photos" in the top menu bar, then select "Preferences."
3. In the Preferences window, click on the "iCloud" tab.
4. Check the "iCloud Photos" option to enable it.
5. You'll have two options:

   • "Download Originals to this Mac": This option stores the full-size versions of your photos both on your Mac and in iCloud.

   • "Optimise Mac Storage": This option stores smaller versions of your photos on your Mac when storage space is limited. It keeps the original, full-size photos in iCloud. Choose this option to save space on your Mac. You can always restore the originals to your Mac by selecting "Download Originals to this Mac."

6. Once you've selected your preference, iCloud Photos will start syncing your photos to iCloud. This initial upload may take some time, but you can continue using Photos during this process.

TO TURN OFF ICLOUD PHOTOS ON YOUR MAC

1. Open the Photos app on your Mac.
2. Click on "Photos" in the top menu bar, then select "Preferences."
3. In the Preferences window, click on the "iCloud" tab.
4. Uncheck the "iCloud Photos" option to disable it.

5. You can choose to download photos and videos from iCloud to your Mac by clicking "Download" or remove photos and videos that haven't been fully downloaded by clicking "Remove."

Please note that turning off iCloud Photos on your Mac doesn't delete your photos from iCloud. They'll still be available to your other devices that use iCloud Photos.

TO STOP USING ICLOUD PHOTOS ON ALL YOUR APPLE DEVICES

1. Click the Apple menu ![Apple logo] on your Mac and choose "System Preferences."
2. Click on your name at the top of the sidebar. If your name isn't visible, you may need to sign in with your Apple ID.
3. Click on "iCloud" on the right.
4. Click "Manage," then select "Photos." and then tap "Turn Off and Delete."

Warning: If you turn off iCloud Photos on all your devices, your photos and videos will be deleted from iCloud after 30 days. Be sure to click "Undo Delete" within that time frame if you want to recover them.

VIEWING MEMORIES & HOW TO PLAY A MEMORY

1. Open the Photos app ![Photos icon] on your Mac and tap "Memories" in the sidebar.
2. Scroll through the various memories.
3. Double-click the memory you want to play.
4. While the memory is playing, you can start or stop it by clicking the Play button or pressing the Spacebar. You can also navigate through individual photos in the memory by using the arrow keys or trackpad swipes. To display memory photos in a grid, click the "Grid View" button. You can exit a memory by clicking the left arrow in the toolbar.

HOW TO CREATE YOUR OWN MEMORY FROM AN ALBUM

1. Select an album in the sidebar.
2. Click "Play Memory Video" from the toolbar.
3. If you want to add the new memory to your Memories collection, click the "Favourite" button. If you change your mind, you can click the "Favourite" button again to remove it as a favorite.

HOW TO SHARE A MEMORY

1. Click "Memories" in the sidebar.
2. Find and double-click the memory you want to share.
3. Press the Spacebar to stop playing the memory, then the "Share" button in the toolbar.
4. Choose how you want to share the memory, whether it's through Messages, Mail, or AirDrop.

HOW TO SHARE PHOTOS FROM A MEMORY

1. Click "Memories" in the sidebar.
2. Find and double-click the memory containing the photos you want to share.
3. Press the Spacebar to stop playing the memory then click the "Grid View" button.
4. Select the photos you want to share and click the "Share" button in the toolbar.
5. Choose your preferred sharing method, like Messages, Mail, or AirDrop.

HOW TO ADD A MEMORY AS A FAVORITE

1. Click "Memories" in the sidebar.
2. Scroll to the memory you want to make a favorite.
3. Click the "Favourite" button on the memory. You can also do this while viewing the memory.
4. To access your favorite memories, click "Favourite Memories" in the toolbar.

PODCASTS

Do you want to explore, subscribe to, and enjoy your favorite podcasts on your Mac? Then Apple Podcasts is the perfect platform for you!

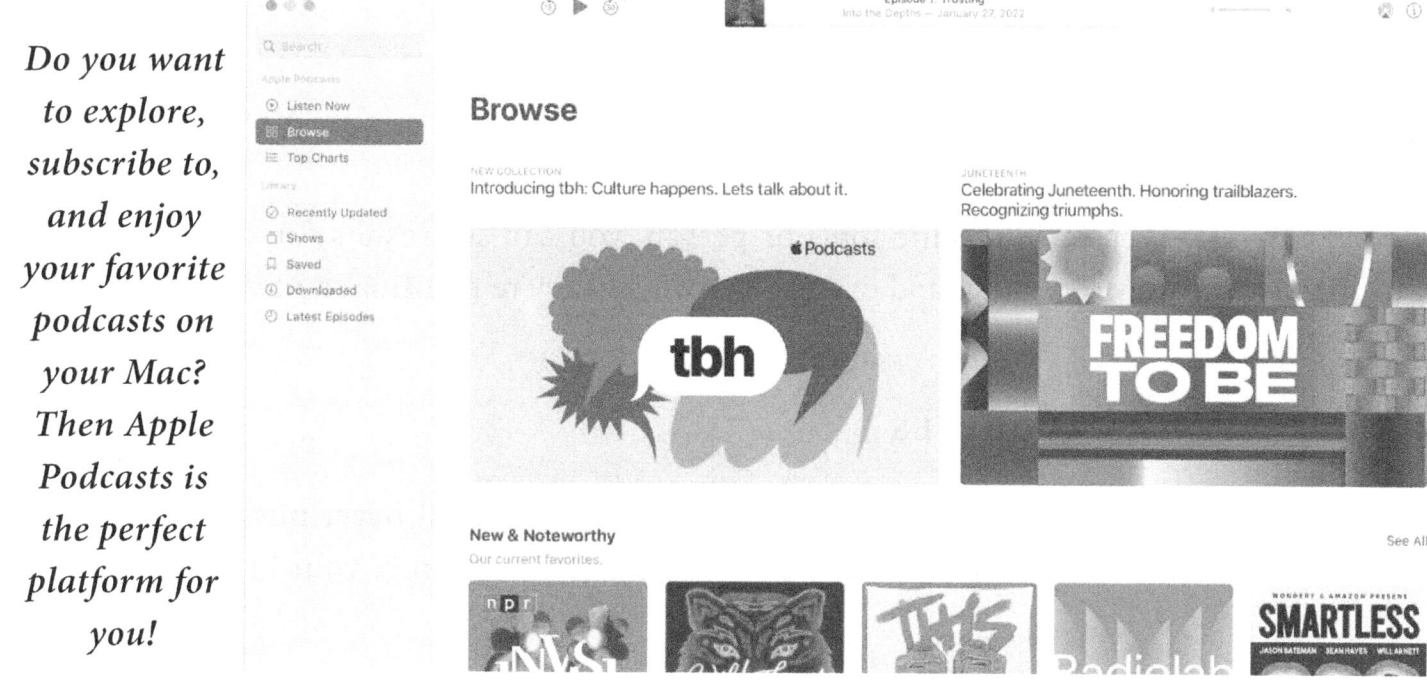

Here's a guide to help you get started with Apple Podcasts and make the most of its features:

- Listen Now: This is where you can start exploring your subscribed podcasts, and also find personalized recommendations for new podcasts based on your interests. It's your one-stop-shop for all your listening needs. You can even use Siri to interact with your podcasts and pick up where you last left off.

DISCOVER NEW PODCASTS

- Use the "Listen Now" section to discover new and interesting podcasts based on topics or shows you enjoy. If you find a show you like, you can subscribe to it or add an episode to your library for later. You'll also get suggestions for similar topics and shows based on what you enjoy. Check out the "Top Charts" to see which podcasts are currently trending.

SHARED WITH YOU

- If your friends share podcasts with you in Messages, those episodes will appear in the "Shared with You" section of Listen Now.

SAVE EPISODES TO YOUR LIBRARY

- You can save individual episodes to your library by clicking the "Add" button $+$. To keep up with all new episodes for a podcast, click "Subscribe." If you want to listen offline, click the "Download" button

SEARCH BY HOST OR GUEST

- When you search for a specific topic or person, you can see results for shows they host, shows where they're a guest, and even shows where they're mentioned or discussed.

FOLLOW YOUR FAVORITES

- Click "Follow" to add a show to your favorites. This way, you'll never miss a new episode. You can easily see what's new in the "Recently Updated" section of your library.

SAVE IDEAS WITH QUICK NOTE

- If you come across a podcast you want to remember for later, you can create a Quick Note. This helps you save the information, and you can find it later in the sidebar of the Notes app. To create a Quick Note, press Fn-Q or use a specified Hot Corner.

USE AIRPLAY

- You can use AirPlay to play a podcast through an external speaker. Click the Control Center icon in the menu bar, then click Screen Mirroring to select an available speaker.

With Apple Podcasts, you can enjoy a wide range of podcasts, discover new content, and keep up with your favorite shows. It's a great way to stay informed and entertained while using your Mac.

PREVIEW

As a Mac user, you can take advantage of the Preview app to view and edit PDFs and images, fill out and sign forms online, annotate PDFs, convert graphic file types, password protect PDFs, highlight and translate text, and more.

View and Edit PDFs and Images: You can easily open and view PDF and image files using Preview, and make simple edits to these documents.

Fill in PDF Forms: Interactive PDF forms can be filled in by clicking on form fields and typing your text directly into them.

Password Protect PDFs: To secure a PDF, you can assign a password that users must enter before they can view the contents, which is ideal for protecting sensitive information.

Add and Remove PDF Pages: You can manipulate the pages in a PDF by adding, deleting, or rearranging them, making it easy to customize a PDF document.

Copy Pages from One PDF to Another: Preview allows you to copy pages from one PDF and paste them into another, which is handy when you need to combine content from multiple PDFs.

Translate Text: You can highlight text in a PDF, right-click, and select the "Translate" option to get a translation. Plus, you can download languages for offline use.

View and Convert Image Files: Preview can open and convert images to various file types, including JPEG, PDF, PNG, TIFF, and more. This feature is helpful for converting and saving images in different formats.

REMINDERS

The Reminders app ⬚ on your Mac is a useful tool for keeping track of tasks and to-dos. To make the most of the app, here are some key features and tips you can use:

Tags: You can add tags to your reminders to help organize them. By clicking on one or more tags in the sidebar, you can quickly filter reminders based on those tags.

Custom Smart Lists: Smart Lists automatically sort your upcoming reminders based on criteria like dates, times, tags, locations, flags, or priority. To create your own Custom Smart Lists, simply add filters to suit your specific needs.

Save Lists as Templates: If you have a list that you want to reuse in the future, you can save it as a template. Simply select the list in the sidebar, then choose "File > Save as Template."

Today and Scheduled Lists: The Today and Scheduled lists in the sidebar group reminders based on their due dates and times. This helps you keep track of what's coming up and ensures you don't miss any important tasks.

Smart Suggestions: Reminders can automatically suggest dates, times, and locations for a reminder based on your past reminders. This feature can save you time when creating new reminders.

Collaboration: You can collaborate with others on a list by sending invitations through Messages or Mail, or by sharing a link. Click the Share button ⬆ then choose how to share the list. Once others are invited, you can track activity and manage collaboration using the Collaborate button 👥

Assign Responsibility: When sharing a list, you can assign reminders to specific people, ensuring that they receive notifications. This is useful for dividing tasks and clarifying responsibilities.

Subtasks and Groups: You can create subtasks by pressing Command-] or dragging one reminder on top of another. Subtasks are indented under their parent reminders. You can also organize your lists by creating groups. To create a group, choose "File > New Group."

Completed Smart List: The Completed Smart List in the sidebar allows you to review all your finished reminders, including their completion dates.

Reminder Suggestions in Mail: When using Mail, Siri can recognize potential reminders and make suggestions for creating them. This feature can be especially helpful during email correspondence.

Adding Reminders Quickly: You can add reminders quickly using natural language. For instance, you can type "Take Amy to soccer every Wednesday at 5 PM" to create a repeating reminder for that specific day and time.

By using these features and tips, you can stay organized with your tasks and to-dos and make the most of the Reminders app on your Mac.

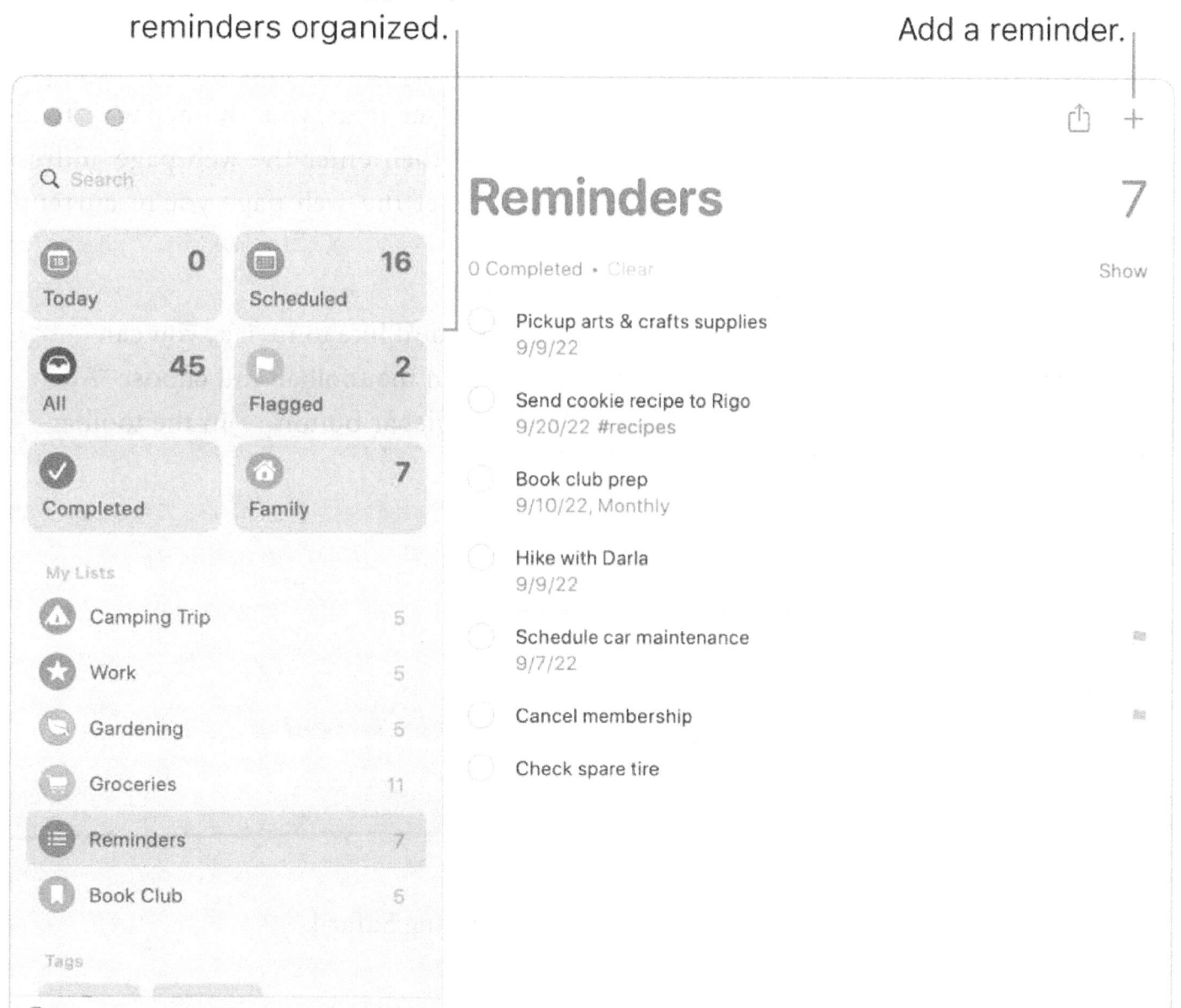

SAFARI

If you're using a Mac, Safari is a great browser to use for browsing the internet and finding information.

1. **Search for Information:** You can use the Smart Search field at the top of the Safari window to search the web for almost anything. Simply type in what you're looking for, such as "ice-cream near me," and then click on one of the suggested search results that appear.

Type what you're looking for.

2. **Go to a Website:** The Smart Search field also allows you to visit a specific website. Simply enter the website's name or web address, and Safari will take you there.

3. **Choose a Homepage:** If you frequently visit a particular website and want it to appear every time you open a new Safari window, you can set it as your homepage. To do this, go to Safari > Preferences, click on General, and then enter the web page address. Alternatively, you can click "Set to Current Page" to set the web page you're currently viewing as your homepage.

4. **Bookmark Websites:** When you come across websites you'd like to revisit, you can bookmark them for easy access. Click the Share button in the toolbar and choose "Add Bookmark." To access bookmarked websites, click the Sidebar button ▤ in the toolbar, then click the Bookmarks button ⬕.

5.

WEBSITE INTO AN APP

You can convert a website to be like an app on your Mac using Safari!

1. Open Safari 🧭 on your Mac.

2. Visit the website that you want to convert into an app.
3. Click the Share button 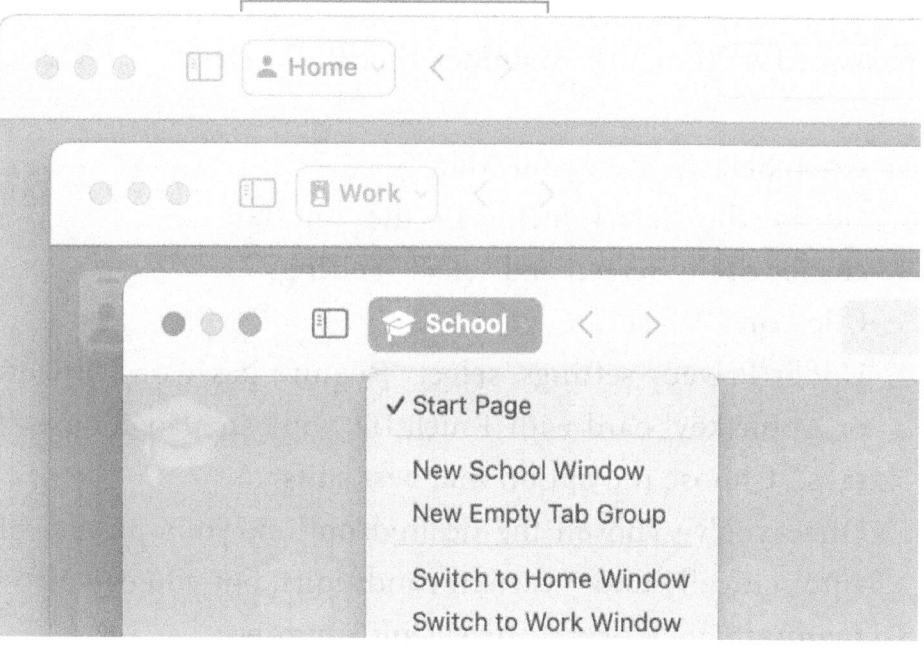 located in the toolbar, which looks like a square with an arrow pointing upwards.
4. From the Share menu, select "Add to Dock."
5. Click "Add" to confirm.

After completing the above steps, the web app will be added to your Dock and Launchpad. If you were previously signed in to the website, you'll likely be automatically signed in to the web app. Your username and password will remain the same.

The web app will have a simplified toolbar and you'll receive notifications from it, just like in any other app. This allows you to easily access your favorite websites as standalone applications.

BROWSING PROFILES

If you want to keep your personal browsing separate from other aspects of your life, you can create a profile in Safari on your Mac. Here are the steps to follow:

1. Open Safari 🧭 on your Mac.
2. In the Safari app, go to the menu and choose "Safari" located at the top left corner of the screen.
3. From the Safari menu, select "Settings," then click on "Profiles."
4. If you haven't used profiles before, you'll be prompted to "Start Using Profiles." Click on it to begin setting up your profiles.
5. Next, click the "Add" button below the profiles list to create a new profile.
6. Enter a name for this profile. You can also choose an icon and color to make it easily identifiable.
7. Select a bookmarks folder for your favorite websites to be associated with this profile.
8. Click "Create Profile" to finish the setup.

9. If you have browser extensions, you can click on "Extensions" to select the ones you want to use with this profile.
10. Keep in mind that if you store passwords in iCloud Keychain, they will be available in any profile you create.

It's important to note that, in addition to any profiles you create, you always have a "Personal (Default)" profile. You can change the name, icon, and color of your personal profile as well. This way, you can keep your browsing organized and separate for different aspects of your life.

LOCK PRIVATE BROWSING

WINDOWS

Here's how to lock private browsing windows in Safari on your Mac and require your password or Touch ID to unlock them:

Private Browsing Is Locked

Touch ID or enter the password for the user "Danny Rico" to view locked tabs.

Enter password

1. Open Safari on your Mac.
2. Go to the Safari menu in the top left corner of the screen and select "Settings."
3. Click on "Privacy."
4. Under Privacy settings, select "Require password to view locked tabs." If you have a Mac or Apple keyboard with Touch ID, you can also choose "Require Touch ID to view locked tabs." Choose the option that best suits you.
5. Once you've chosen the desired option, your private browsing windows will be locked automatically under certain conditions, but you can also manually lock them.

To manually lock private browsing windows:
Go to the Safari menu and select "Window." > Choose "Lock All Private Windows."

This will immediately lock all your private browsing windows, and they will require your password or Touch ID to unlock.

Keep in mind that private browsing windows will also lock automatically under the following conditions:

- When you lock your screen.

- When a password is required after the screen saver starts.

- When a password is required after the display is turned off.

- When you minimize the windows and leave them inactive for a period of time.

- When you leave the windows open in the background but don't interact with them for a period of time.

If you ever want to allow private browsing windows to remain unlocked, you can go back to the Privacy settings in Safari and unselect the "Require password to view locked tabs" or "Require Touch ID to view locked tabs" option, depending on your preference.

ALLOW OR BLOCK POP-UPS ON ALL WEBSITES

1. Open Safari  on your Mac.
2. Click on Safari in the menu bar, then select "Settings."
3. Choose "Websites."
4. Click "Pop-up Windows" on the left. If you don't see "Pop-up Windows," make sure you scroll to the bottom of the list.
5. If there are websites listed below "Configured Websites," and you want to change the settings for these sites (for example, changing from Allow to Block), select each website, then click "Remove."
6. If you don't see "Configured Websites," it means you haven't set pop-up blocking for any sites yet or you've cleared the list.
7. Click the "When visiting other websites" pop-up menu, then choose one of the following:

- Allow: Pop-ups for all websites will appear.

Click to show the blocked
pop-up windows.

- Block and Notify: Pop-ups for all websites won't appear, but you'll be notified when a pop-up is blocked, and you can choose to show it by clicking the "Show" button [icon] in the Smart Search field.

Show blocked pop-up window ↻ 🗗 ⚫

- Block: Pop-ups for all websites won't appear.

Remember that blocking pop-ups may also prevent some content you want to see. If you continue to see pop-ups on a website that you've set to block, it could be due to unwanted software on your Mac, and you might need to address that separately.

GOT COOKIES??

If you want to clear cookies in Safari on your Mac, follow these easy steps:

1. Open Safari 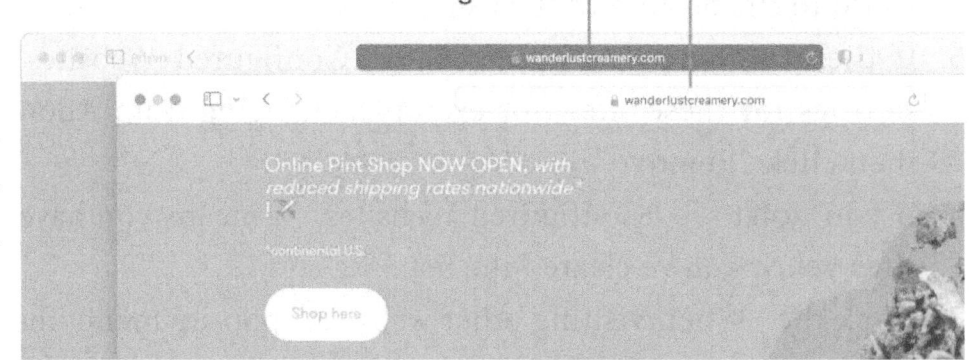 on your Mac.
2. Click on "Safari" in the menu bar located at the top left corner of your screen.
3. From the drop-down menu, select "Preferences."
4. In the Preferences window, choose "Privacy" from the toolbar.
5. Under the "Privacy" tab, you will see an option labeled "Manage Website Data." Click on it.
6. A new window will appear, displaying a list of all websites that have stored cookies and website data on your Mac.
7. To remove data from a specific website, select the website from the list.
8. Click on the "Remove" button to remove data for the selected website.
9. If you want to remove data for all websites, click on the "Remove All" button.

Please keep in mind that deleting cookies and website data may affect your experience on certain websites, such as logging you out or altering website behavior. Furthermore, removing cookies in Safari may also affect cookies in other apps.

Private browsing window   Normal window

BROWSE PRIVATELY

If you want to browse the internet privately on your Mac, you can follow these steps:

1. First, open Safari  on your Mac.
2. Next, click on "File" in the Safari menu at the top left of your screen.
3. Then, select "New Private Window".
4. A new window will open with a dark Smart Search field, indicating that you are browsing privately.
5. When you use Private Browsing, the following happens:

   • Browsing in one tab is isolated from browsing in other tabs, preventing websites from tracking your activity across multiple sessions.

   • Webpages you visit and your AutoFill information aren't saved.

- Your open web pages aren't stored in iCloud, so they won't appear on other Apple devices.

- Your recent searches aren't included in the Smart Search field's results list.

- Items you download aren't included in the downloads list (but remain on your computer).

- Changes to cookies and website data aren't saved.

6. To always browse privately, you can go to Safari 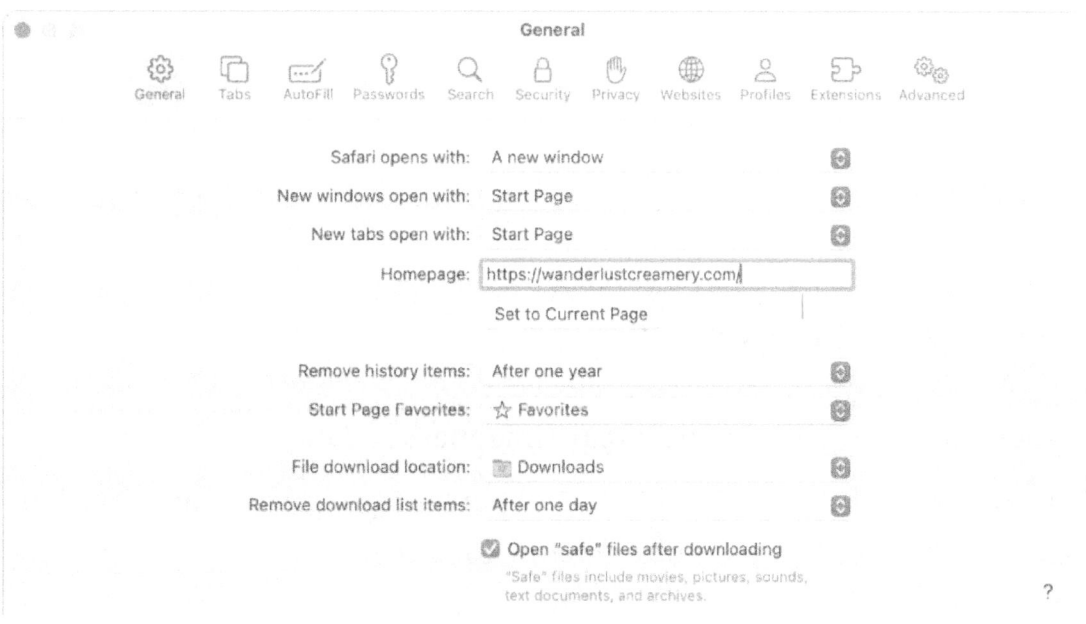 > Settings > General and choose "A new private window" under "Safari opens with."

7. To stop browsing privately, close the private window, switch to a non-private Safari window, or open a new non-private window using File > New Window.

Remember that when you browse privately, your browsing history and website data won't be saved, providing you with enhanced privacy during your online activities.

STOCKS

The Stocks app your Mac is a useful tool for keeping track of financial markets and your investments.

Below are the key features and how to use them:

CREATE AND

CUSTOMIZE

WATCHLISTS

- To create a new watchlist, click on "My Symbols" and then select "New Watchlist."

- Add stocks to your watchlist by entering a company name or stock symbol in the search field.

- Double-click the stock symbol in the search results to view detailed stock information.

- To add a stock to a watchlist, click the "Add" button ╋ in the top-right corner and choose the watchlist you want to add it to.

- To remove a stock from a watchlist, Control-click the stock symbol and select "Manage Symbol." Then, deselect the checkbox next to the watchlist you want to remove it from.

- Control-clicking a stock in your watchlist will allow you to open it in a new tab or window.

MONITOR MARKET CHANGES

- In your watchlist, you can view real-time market data.

- You can switch between price change, percentage change, and market capitalization by clicking on the green or red button below each price.

- Color-coded sparklines provide a visual representation of the stock's performance throughout the day.

change, percentage change, and market capitalization.

READ ARTICLES

- Click on a stock in your watchlist to access an interactive chart and additional details about that stock.

- You can also read the latest news related to the company.

- To access curated business articles from Apple News, click "Business News" at the top of your watchlist.

GET A DEEPER VIEW

- The Stocks app allows you to explore historical data. You can switch between different timeframes (e.g., last week, last month, or last year) by clicking the buttons above the chart.

SYNC WATCHLISTS ACROSS DEVICES

- Signing in with the same Apple ID on multiple devices ensures your watchlist remains consistent across all of them, providing you access to the same information on all your Apple devices.

Please note that Apple News stories and Top Stories are available in the U.S., Canada, the UK, and Australia, while news stories in other countries and regions are provided by Yahoo.

APPLE TV

The Apple TV app on your Mac is the hub for all your TV and streaming content. It offers a range of features that make it easy for you to access your favorite content.

Here's what you can do with the Apple TV app:

1. **Apple TV+:** Subscribe to and watch Apple TV+, Apple's streaming service featuring original TV shows and movies created by some of the most creative people in the entertainment industry. Note that the availability of Apple TV+ varies by country and region.

2. **MLS Season Pass:** If you're a fan of Major League Soccer (MLS), you can subscribe to MLS Season Pass in the Apple TV app. This provides access to all MLS regular season and playoff matches and hundreds of MLS NEXT Pro and MLS NEXT games. Note that the availability of MLS Season Pass may differ depending on your location.

3. **Apple TV Channels:** You can subscribe to various Apple TV channels, such as Paramount+ and STARZ, to access additional content. The availability of Apple TV channels may differ by country and region.

4. **Personalized Recommendations:** The app offers content recommendations based on your viewing history and preferences, making it easier to discover new shows and movies you might enjoy.

5. **Content Sharing:** You can watch movies and shows shared with you from the Messages app.

6. **Watch Together with SharePlay:** The Apple TV app integrates with SharePlay and the FaceTime app, allowing you to watch content with friends and family, even if you're not in the same location.

7. **Access the Store:** You can access the Apple TV Store to purchase, rent, or subscribe to

the world's best movies and TV shows, including Apple TV channels that you haven't subscribed to yet.

8. **Manage Your Collection:** The app provides access to your entire movie and TV show collection, making it easy to organize and access your media.

Keep in mind that the availability of some features, such as Apple TV+ and MLS Season Pass, may vary by country or region. This means that the content and subscriptions available to you in the Apple TV app could differ based on your location.

SIGN IN TO START WATCHING NOW

To buy, rent, or subscribe to content on Apple TV app using your Mac, you need to sign in with your Apple ID. Here's how you can sign in or create a new Apple ID if you don't have one yet:

CREATING A NEW APPLE ID

1. Open the Apple TV app  on your Mac.
2. Click on "Account" in the menu bar at the top of the screen.
3. Choose "Sign In."
4. Click on "Create New Apple ID."
5. Follow the on-screen instructions to set up a new Apple ID.

Please note that PayPal is available as a payment method in some regions. However, it may not be accepted in all countries.

SIGNING IN OR OUT OF THE APPLE TV APP

Once you have an Apple ID, you can use it to sign in or out of the Apple TV app. Here's how:

1. In the Apple TV app on your Mac, click on "Account" in the menu bar.
2. Select either "Sign In" or "Sign Out," depending on your current status.
3. If you can't remember your Apple ID or password, click on "Forgot Apple ID or

Password?" and follow the instructions to recover your credentials.

We recommend signing out of the app if you share your computer with others to prevent unauthorized purchases using your account.

By signing in, you can easily access your account information, purchase history, and enjoy a seamless experience when renting or buying movies and TV shows through the Apple TV app

WATCH TOGETHER

Watching movies or TV shows with your friends or family can be a fun activity, especially when you are not together physically. With SharePlay in the Apple TV app, you can enjoy synchronized viewing while on a FaceTime call.

WATCH TOGETHER WITH SHAREPLAY

1. Open the FaceTime app on your Mac and start or answer a call.
2. Open the Apple TV app on your Mac or another caller's device and start watching a movie or show.
3. If prompted, click "View" to open the TV app on your Mac and then click "Join."

The video will start playing in sync on all devices participating in the FaceTime call. Each person can control the playback using their respective devices while the FaceTime app window remains open.

To modify the SharePlay settings, you can click the SharePlay button 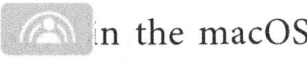 in the macOS menu bar.

LEAVING THE CALL OR SHARED VIEWING SESSION

Anyone can leave the FaceTime call while continuing the shared viewing session or leave both. Here is how you can do it:

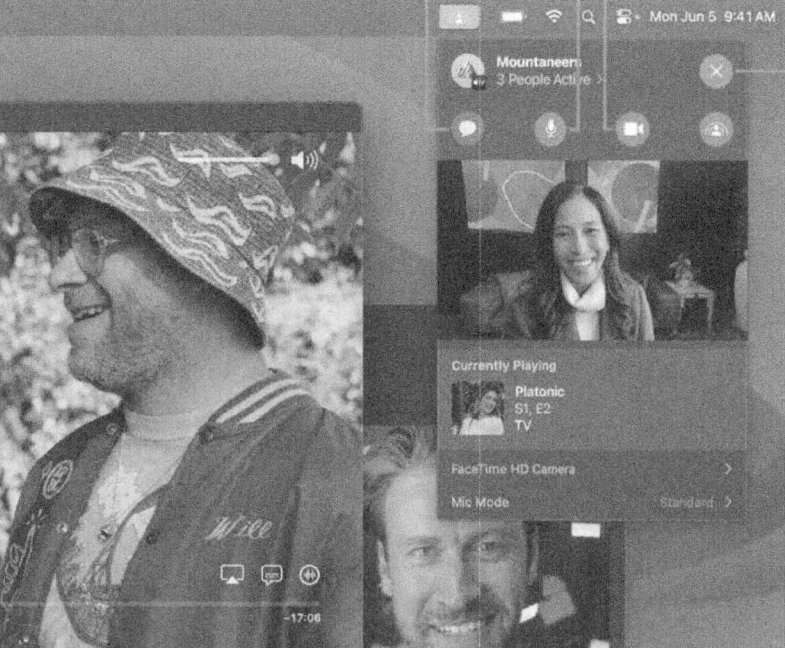

Click to mute your microphone.

Click to open Messages.

Click to leave the call.

1. While using SharePlay in the Apple TV app on your Mac, click the SharePlay button in the macOS menu bar.
2. Click the "Leave Call" button .
3. Choose to either "Continue" or "Leave SharePlay."

If you initiated the shared session and choose "Leave SharePlay," the shared session will end for everyone.

START A TEXT CONVERSATION

During a SharePlay watch session in the Apple TV app n your Mac, you can initiate a text conversation in Messages with all the participants:

1. Click the SharePlay button in the macOS menu bar.
2. Click the "Messages" button .
3. The Messages app will open, allowing you to enter your messages in the text field.

ADD VIDEO EFFECTS

While watching with SharePlay, you can add video effects and animated reactions to your live video in the FaceTime app window (requires macOS 12 or later and Apple silicon):
1. Click the SharePlay button in the macOS menu bar.

2. Click the disclosure arrow to the right of "FaceTime HD Camera."

3. Choose video effects such as Portrait, Studio Light, or Reactions (animated effects created using hand gestures).

ADJUST MICROPHONE SENSITIVITY

You can adjust the sensitivity of your microphone to isolate your voice or capture surrounding sounds (requires macOS 12 or later and Apple silicon):

1. Click the SharePlay button in the macOS menu bar.
2. Click the disclosure triangle to the right of "Mic Mode."
3. Select a microphone option: Standard, Voice Isolation, or Wide Spectrum.

USE AIRPLAY

If you want to share what you're watching during SharePlay with an Apple TV on the same network:

1. While using SharePlay in the Apple TV app on your Mac, move your pointer over the viewer window to show playback controls.
2. Click the AirPlay button d choose the Apple TV you want to use for watching.

Please note that SharePlay may not be available in all countries or regions, and the availability of specific content and features may vary.

VOICE MEMOS

Recording audio on your MacBook becomes easy with the help of Voice Memos. Let's take a look at some of the major features and actions that you can perform with Voice Memos:

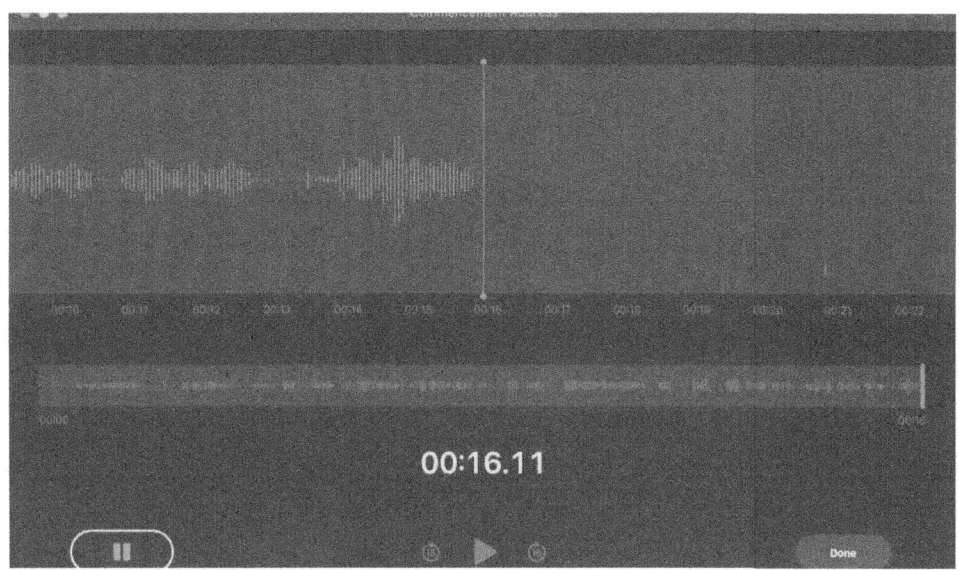

RECORDING

1. To start recording, click on the Record button ⬤ .
2. Click Done when you are finished with recording.
3. You can rename your recording by clicking on the default name and entering a new one for better identification.
4. To play back a recording, click on the Play button ▶ .

ACCESS ON ALL DEVICES

When you sign in using the same Apple ID, your voice memos become available on all your devices. This means that you can access recordings made with your iPhone or iPad right from your Mac.

ORGANIZE WITH FOLDERS

1. Create folders to keep your Voice Memos organized. Click on the Sidebar button, then the New Folder button at the bottom of the sidebar.
2. Enter a name for the folder and click Save.
3. To add a recording to the folder, press and hold the Option key while dragging the recording to the folder.

MARK AS FAVORITE

1. You can mark a recording as a favorite for quick access later.
2. Select a recording, then click the Favorite button ♡ in the toolbar.
3. Click the Sidebar button 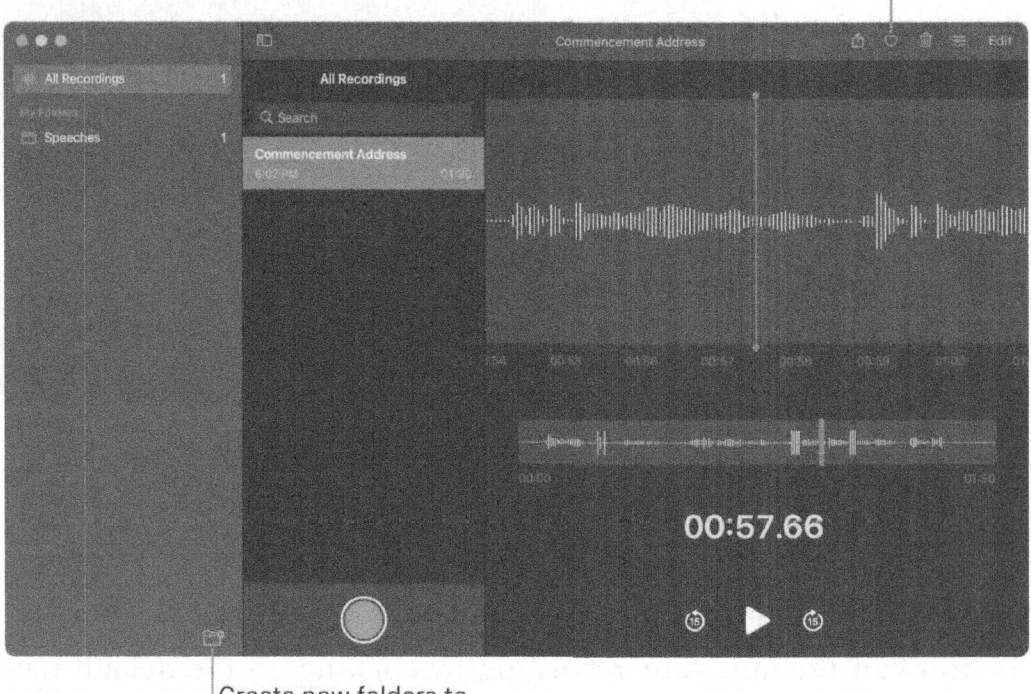 to see all your favorites.

Create new folders to organize your recordings

SKIP SILENCE

1. Skip over gaps or silent portions in your audio.
2. Click the Playback Settings button at the top of the Voice Memos window and turn on "Skip Silence."

CHANGE PLAYBACK SPEED

1. Speed up or slow down the playback speed of your audio.
2. Click the Playback Settings button at the top of the Voice Memos window.
3. Drag the slider left or right to adjust the speed.

ENHANCE A RECORDING

1. Improve the sound quality of your Voice Memos by reducing background noise and room reverberation.
2. Click the Playback Settings button at the top of the Voice Memos window and turn on "Enhance Recording."

These features allow you to record, manage, and enhance your audio recordings with Voice Memos on your MacBook.

Dear Apple Pro!
I hope you are
enjoying exploring
the world of Apple
devices thus far! Your
feedback means a
lot to me and it can
be a valuable gift to
fellow readers who are
considering this guide. Writing a review on Amazon is a simple yet incredibly helpful way to
pay it forward. Scan this QR code to take you straight there!

Your words have the power to inspire confidence in others, just as I've aimed to do with this
book. Whether you found the content insightful, the instructions clear, or if you have any
suggestions for improvement (I WILL incorporate it into following books), your review will
be appreciated.

By sharing your thoughts, you not only assist other seniors in making an informed choice
but also support the author (that's me!). Your review provides insights that can guide
prospective readers, making their journey with the Apple products more enjoyable and
stress-free.

Thank you for considering this request. Your words
can make a big difference, and together, we can make
the Apple world even more accessible and enjoyable for
everyone, everywhere!

Thank you,
Jason Brown

iPhone for Seniors

A Simple Step By Step Guide For Beginners

Jason Brown

 Apple Store App

 Clock App

 Apple TV App

 Maps App

 Books App

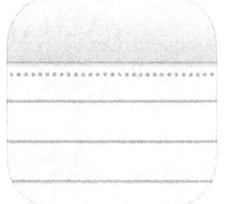 Notes App

 Calendar App

 Files App

 Camera App

iTunes App

 Calculator App

 News App

 Weather App

 Messages App

 Wallet App

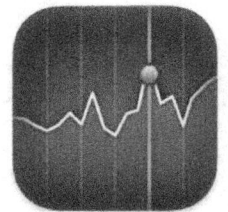 Stocks App

 Audio Recorder App

 Music App

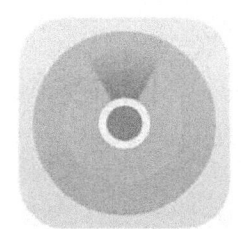 My iPhone App

 Photos App

 Mail App

 Video Call App

 Translate App

 Health App

 Contacts App

 Podcasts App

 Reminder App

 Settings App

 Compass App

 Phone App

 Tips App

 Safari App

SETTING UP YOUR iPHONE

Turn on your iPhone and get started! Set up your new phone in a few simple steps.

POWER-UP YOUR IPHONE

Turn on your iPhone by long-pressing the side button on your iPhone. The side button also functions as a sleep/wake button. Press it once to wake your iPhone or lock the screen after use.

If your phone does not turn on, it may be because of the low battery. Connect it to the power supply and wait for the phone to charge. If it still does not turn on, contact Apple Support using another phone or visit the nearest Apple Store.

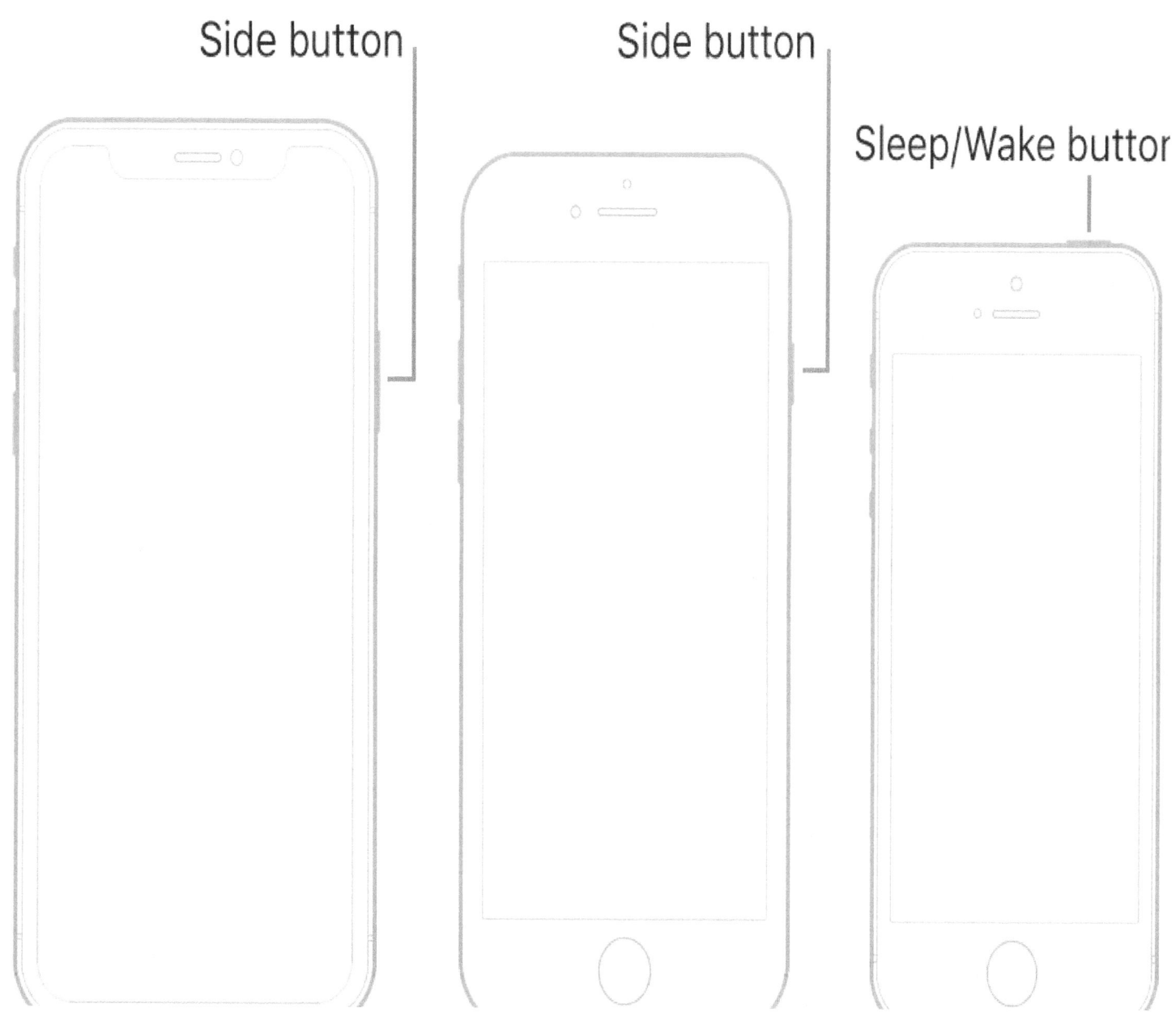

BASICS FOR SETUP

For a seamless setup of your iPhone, make sure you have a few things ready and working properly:

- Make sure you have an internet connection. In the case of a Wi-Fi network, you need to have the name of the network (Network ID) to identify it on the setup screen and the passwc 📶 Network Key) to let the iPhone connect to it. Look for the Wi-Fi symbol on the top right corner of your screen. It indicates that the iPhone is connected to the network.

- You can also set up your iPhone on a cellular connection provided by your service carrier. To set up an iPhone over a cellular connection, insert your SIM card in the iPhone before setup.

- Log in with your Apple ID. If you do not have an Apple ID, you can create one during the setup process. We'll discuss Apple ID in the setup section.

- Keep your debit or credit card ready in order to set up a payment method for App Store & Service or Apple Pay (optional).

- If you are an android user moving to iPhone, keep your Android device with you during the iPhone setup.

- For android devices, download the "Move to IOS" app from the Google Play Store. If you are not moving from an Android Device, you can skip the last two steps.

GUIDE FOR A MANUAL SETUP

Once you make sure that you have all the items ready, we can move on to setting up your iPhone. Here's a step-by-step guide to your iPhone for a manual setup.

SETTING LANGUAGE & REGION

Once your iPhone is turned on, it will ask you to choose a language and region. Choose your preferred language & region from the provided list on your screen.

"QUICK START" OR "SET UP MANUALLY"

If you are already an iPhone user, unlock your old device and bring it near to your new iPhone. A new screen on your old device will appear. Follow the instructions on the screen to complete the "Quick Start" setup.

For 1st time users of IOS devices or iPhones, tap "Set Up Manually" on your screen. Follow the instructions on the screen to set up your iPhone manually.

CONNECTING TO THE INTERNET

Choose a Wi-Fi network from available networks. You need to provide a Wi-Fi key to your network in order for the iPhone to connect to your network. After putting the password (Network Key), look for the Wi-Fi symbol 📶 on the top right corner of your iPhone. The symbol indicates a successful connection of your iPhone to the internet.

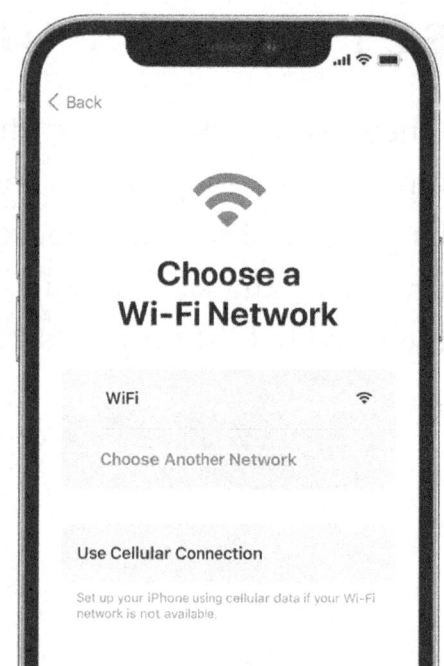

SETTING UP SECURITY ON YOUR IPHONE

In the next step, you will be asked to set up a Face ID & a Passcode to secure your iPhone.

In 1st step, you can use your face to set up a Face ID for unlocking your iPhone. Tap "Continue" and follow the instruction to scan your face for a successful Face ID setup.

In the 2nd step, you need to create a passcode for your iPhone. You can opt for a 6 digit or a 4 digit unique

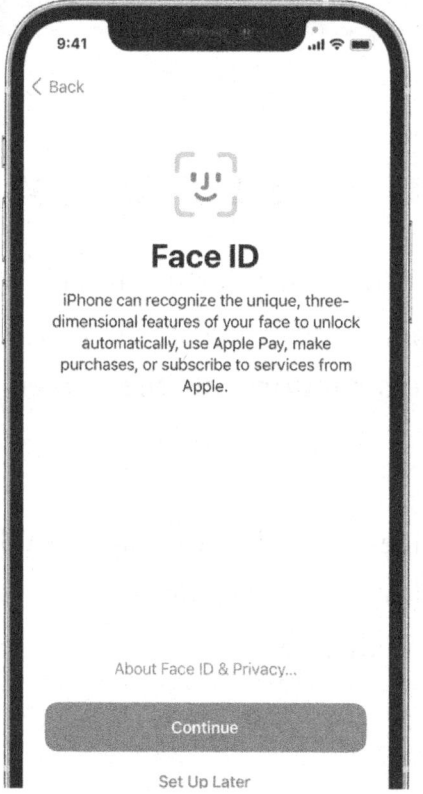

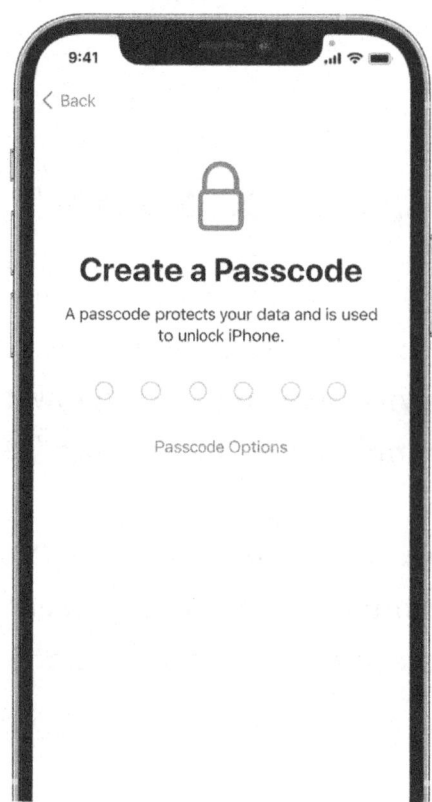

number to set up a passcode. Do not forget the passcode! It will be used to unlock your iPhone.

Note: Face ID will be used to process the transactions on the App Store & Apple Pay.
If you do not want to set up any security on your iPhone. You can tap "Set up later" on both screens.

148

"RESTORE" OR "TRANSFER DATA"

For previous IOS & iPhone users, you can transfer data from your older device to your new one using different options provided on your screen. The methods include restoring from iCloud, transferring from a PC, Mac or Android.

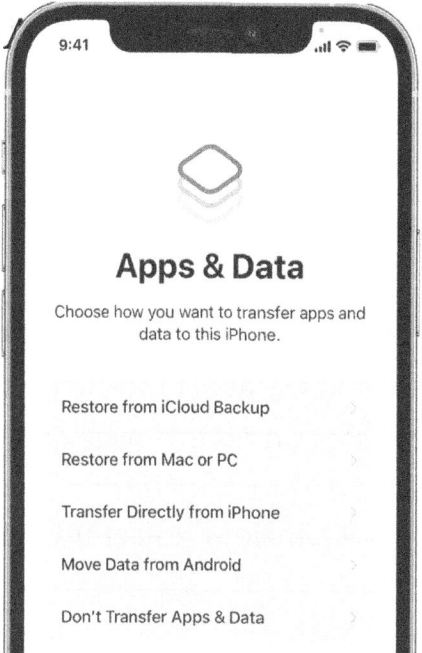

If you are new to IOS & iPhone, tap "Don't Transfer Apps & Data". It will take you to the next step.

CREATING OR SIGNING IN WITH APPLE ID

You'll be asked to sign in to your existing Apple ID. Provide the Apple ID & Password in order to sign in to your existing Apple ID.

If you don't have an Apple ID, tap "forgot the password or don't have an Apple ID." On the next screen, tap "Create a Free Apple ID."

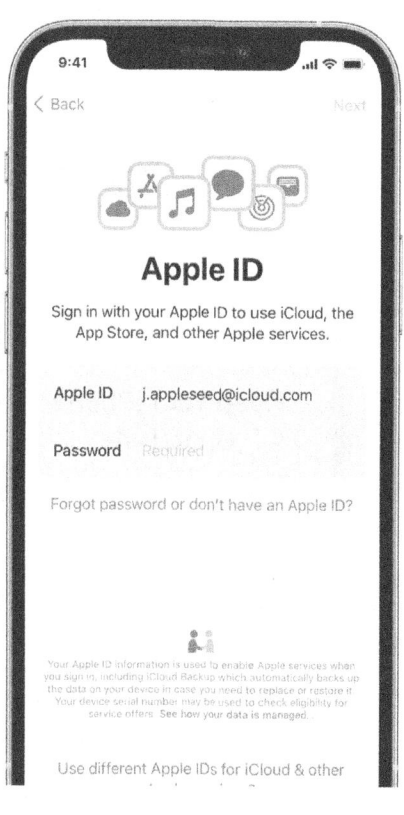

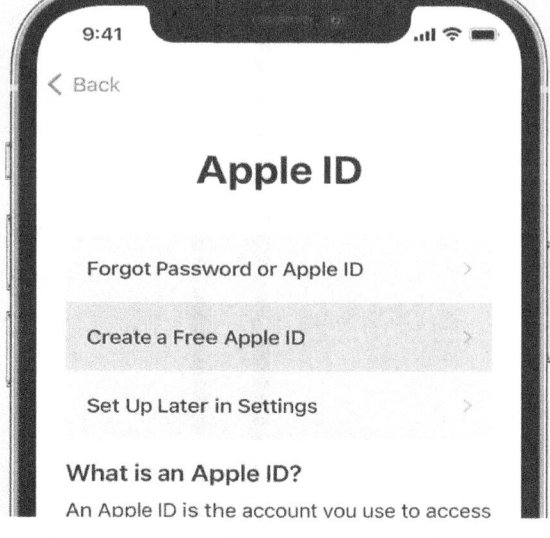

Provide basic information about yourself such as your name, birthday, and email address. If you have used an already existing email for signup, a prompt screen will ask you to verify your email. Follow the on-screen instruction to verify your email.

However, if you do not have an email address, tap "Get a free iCloud email address" to generate a new ID.

UPDATES & OTHER FEATURES

Here, you can set up auto-updates, Siri (a virtual voice assistant), and screentime.

For automatic updates tap "Continue" and your iPhone will automatically set it up for you.

For Siri, tap "Continue" and follow the on-screen instructions to set up and enable Siri as your voice assistant. Siri can help you call or send a text to your contacts or even give you updates on your device and weather (and much more).

Tap "Continue" to set up the "Screen Time" feature for insights on how you use your phone.

YOUR SETUP IS COMPLETE

Welcome to your new iPhone! Your setup is complete now. You can begin using your phone to connect to your loved ones, take pictures of your precious life moments and anything in between.

BASIC BUTTONS & GESTURES ON YOUR iPhone

Learn to engage with your iPhone. Basic gestures and buttons to help you with simple tasks.

BUTTONS & CAMERAS ON YOUR IPHONE

iPhone has different buttons that perform various functions. These buttons can easily be located and identified on the sides. Each button can perform one or more functions.

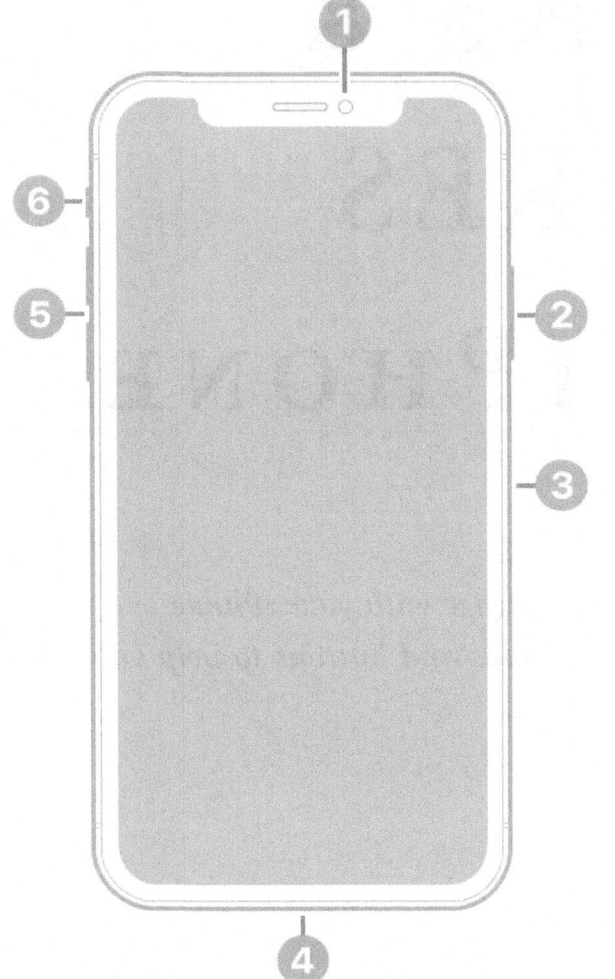

1. Front Facing Camera for selfies and videos.

2. A side button for Sleep/Wake function. You can also use it to turn your phone on and off.

3. SIM tray - Use it insert a physical SIM card to set up cellular connection.
A lighting cable connector which is used to charge your phone or connect it to your computer or other devices via lightning cable.

4. Volume buttons to adjust the ringtone volume or media volume on your iPhone.

5. Ring/Silent mode with lets you put your phone insolent mode or ing mode without having to unlock it first.

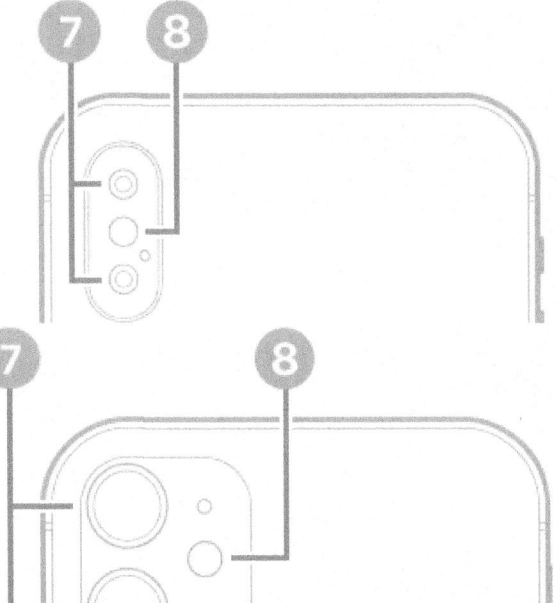

Front Facing Camera for selfies and videos.

A side button for Sleep/Wake function. You can also use it to turn your phone on and off.

Back Facing Camera for selfies and videos.

The back camera formation on your iPhone can be different depending on the model that you have.

BASIC GESTURES

iPhone uses specialized gestures to perform simple tasks. These gestures help users open or close apps, switch between apps, access Siri and Apple pay options, and much more. These gestures are as simple as pressing buttons and swiping your fingers. Here is a list of simple and basic gestures to help you interact with your iPhone.

Touch any icon on the screen with one finger. You can tap an App's icon to open it or enable or disable any feature.

The touch and hold gesture is used to reveal more options for apps or actions in the control center. Tap and hold the item until more options appear on your screen.

A swipe is a quick finger move across the screen. You can swipe from top to bottom or from left to right to scroll, move, or open another screen. For more functions, see the advanced gestures list below.

To scroll through the list of items like settings, webpages, or photos, swipe your finger from the top to bottom or from the bottom to the top without lifting it off the screen.

Bring your two fingers together and place them on the screen. Move them apart from each other while keeping them on screen. It will zoom in the picture or a webpage in the browser. Move the fingers towards each other to zoom out of the photo or webpage.

Here are some additional gestures that come in handy for an iPhone user.

SWIPE – Swipe up from the bottom edge of the screen. It will take you from a lock screen to your home screen where you can access apps and other features.

Use the same swipe gesture to close the already opened apps.

APP SWITCHER – Swipe up your finger from bottom to the center of the screen and then lift your finger. This will open the app switcher. Use it to access all the recently opened apps. Swipe through these apps from left to right and then tap the one you want to open.

If you wish to close an app, access the app switcher, tap and hold the app you wish to close, then swipe toward the top of the screen.

CONTROL CENTER – To access the "Control Center," swipe down with one finger from the top-right corner of the phone. Here you can access quick action controls of your iPhone. Touch and hold any icon to bring out more options.

To customize your control center go to Settings > Control Center > Customize Control center

SWITCH BETWEEN APPS – You can switch between your opened apps by swiping from left to right or right to left on the bottom of your screen. You can only switch between the apps that are already opened in the background.

ACCESS "SIRI" – For "Siri," press and hold the power button & wait for Siri to appear and listen to your request. Siri listens as long as you are holding the button. It will complete your request once you release the button.

You can also set up "Hey Siri" to access Siri using your voice.

Go to Settings ⚙ > Siri & Search

APPLE PAY – If you have set up Apple Pay using your credit card, you can quickly access it by double-clicking the side button. Your phone will ask you to provide a Face ID to process the payments.

SCREENSHOT – Take a screenshot of your current screen by pressing the power button & volume up button and then quickly releasing them simultaneously.

EMERGENCY SOS – In case of an SOS call, press and hold the power button along with any one of the volume buttons until the iPhone screen shows sliders. Swipe the SOS slider from left to right to make the call.

TURN OFF – Repeat the steps described for the SOS call in the previous step. Press & hold the side button and any of the volume buttons until sliders on the screen appear. This time, drag the power slider from left to right to turn off the iPhone.
You can also shut down your iPhone by:
Going to Settings ⚙ > General > Shut Down

RESTART YOUR iPhone – If you need to force restart your phone for any reason, press & let go of the volume up button followed by doing the same for the volume down button (press & let go instantly), and lastly press & hold on the side button and wait for the Apple logo to appear on your screen before releasing the side button.

APPLE ID & ICLOUD SETTINGS

Your Apple ID is your key to using different Apple services. Apple ID is used to access apps and services. The Apple ID also keeps your private data and information safe and stored on a cloud storage named "iCloud." Here you can learn everything about your Apple ID and iCloud services to help you secure data and use your iPhone to its full potential.

APPLE ID SIGN IN & SETTINGS

You can create and sign in to your Apple ID while setting up the iPhone or later in Settings. If you have completed the setup without Apple ID, here's how to create or sign in to your Apple ID from Settings.

CREATE, SIGN IN, OR RECOVER YOUR APPLE ID

To create an Apple ID after the setup:

- Go to Settings ⚙ > Tap "Sign in" at the top of the screen.
- On the next screen tap "Don't have an Apple ID".
- Tap "Create Free Apple ID".
- Follow the steps provided on your screen to create a new Apple ID for your iPhone.

If you have already created an Apple ID but did not sign in during setup, you can sign in to your ID by following the simple steps given below:

- Go to Settings ⚙ > Tap "Sign in" at the top of the screen.
- Enter your Apple ID and Password.
- Tap "Sign in."

In case you have forgotten your Apple ID or password, you can recover your ID in Settings. To recover an Apple ID follow the instructions below:
Go to Settings ⚙ > Tap "Sign in" at the top of the screen.

- If you have forgotten Apple ID, tap "Don't have an Apple ID" or "Forgot it."
- On the next screen, tap "Forgot Apple ID."
- Provide your personal information, such as your name, used while creating your

157

Apple ID to help Apple support find your ID.

- Follow the step-by-step procedure to recover your Apple ID.

To reset a forgotten password, the steps are almost similar and as easy as recovering an Apple ID:

- Go to Settings ⚙ > Tap "Sign in" at the top of the screen.

- Enter your Apple ID and tap "Next."

- Tap "Forgot Apple ID or Password."

- Follow the steps shown on the screen to recover the password.

Note: Keep your Phone number and email that you used in Apple ID ready, as you'll use it to reset your password. You will receive some confirmation codes in order for Apple to confirm that it's you resetting your password.

CHANGE APPLE ID INFORMATION

Once logged in, you can change or update your Apple ID information in Apple ID settings.

If you wish to see or update your Apple ID information or settings on your iPhone:

- Go to Settings ⚙ > Tap "Your Name" appearing at the top of the settings screen.

- The option of your personal information will appear on the next screen.

- These options include;
    ▷ Name, Phone Numbers, Email
    ▷ Password & Security
    ▷ Payment & Shipping
    ▷ Subscription

- Tap any of the above options to see your currently used information or update it to your needs.

You can also manage and see your iCloud storage, App store purchases, Find My, or manage family sharing under this section. These features are all related to the Apple ID and iCloud.

ICLOUD STORAGE & SERVICES

iCloud is your personal cloud storage provided to you by Apple. iCloud can be used in many ways for different purposes. iCloud stores your photos, documents, music, messages, notes, backups, and even personalization on your home screen, all secure and accessible to you at any instant. It also keeps your data updated across all your IOS devices including iPhone, iPad, Macbook, and iMac.

ICLOUD+

Apple provides 5 GB of free iCloud space. To get more storage, you need to purchase an iCloud+ service. Currently, this is the iCloud+ pricing from Apple:

- 50 GB for $0.99
- 200 GB for $2.99
- 1 TB for $9.99

ICLOUD+ SETTINGS

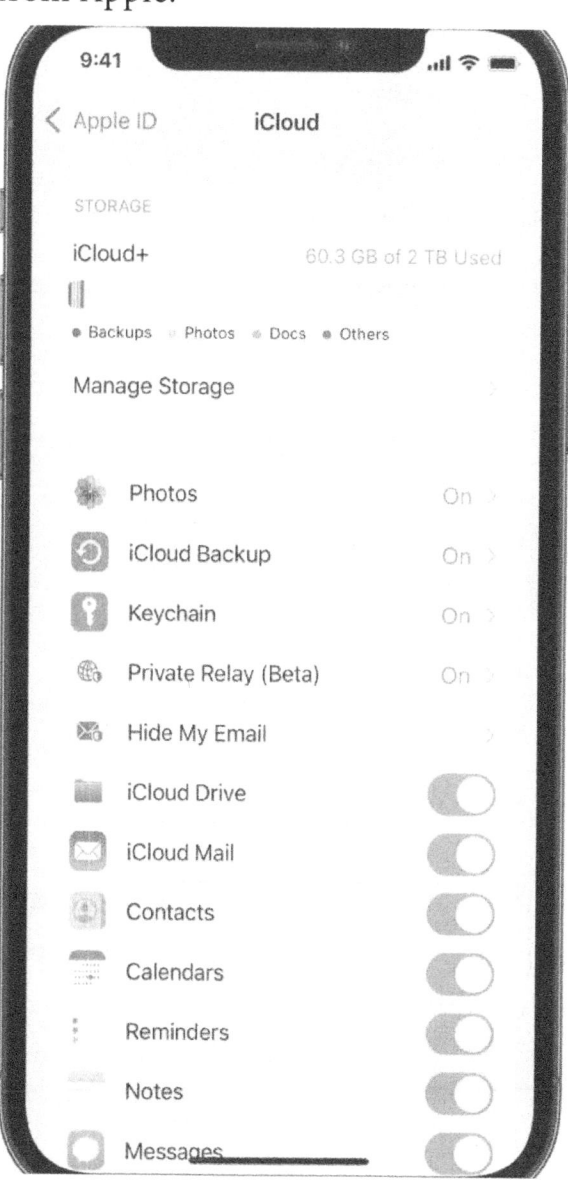

To access your iCloud settings

Go to Settings ⚙ > Tap "Your Name" appearing at the top of settings screen > Tap "iCloud."
You can access the following settings & information under your iCloud section.

Photos - Turning the feature on will let you store your personal photos on iCloud saving you space on your iPhone. You can also turn it off if you don't want to store your date on iCloud.

iCloud backup - The feature turns your personal apps and date automatically on iCloud so you don't los data even if you lose your phone.

Keychain - Save and sync your passwords and login information across IOS devices.

Private Beta Replay - (Only on iCloud+) - hide your IP address while using the internet.

Hide my Email - Hides your email address from potential scammer sand marketing campaigns.

To save and sync your other data across all your IOS devices, enable all the following features in your iCloud or iCloud+ settings list:

- iCloud Drive
- Contacts
- Calenders
- Reminders
- Notes
- Messages
- Safari
- Stocks
- Home
- Health
- Wallet
- Game center
- Siri
- Books
- Shortcuts
- Weather

iCloud also stores app data from apps other than default apps on Apple. All the apps that support the iCloud feature will appear in the list under the iCloud settings. You can enable or disable backup or data sharing according to your preferences and use.

PERSONALIZATION

Personalize your iPhone the way you like.

Learn how to change the wallpaper, ringtones, date, time, and more.

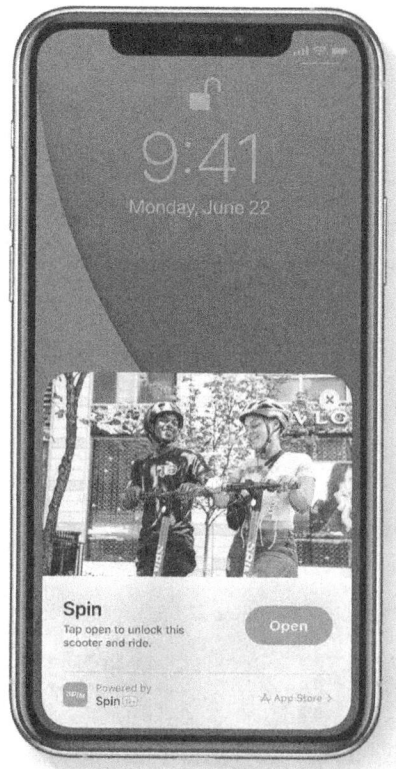

HOW TO CHANGE THE WALLPAPER ON IPHONE?

You can change your display background from the default picture to any picture you like. The iPhone gives plenty of pictures in the wallpaper gallery to choose from. You can choose your next wallpaper from three categories: dynamic, still, or live. Don't like pictures from the default gallery? You can also set your favorite picture from your photo gallery as your next wallpaper too.

WALLPAPER SETTINGS

To open wallpaper settings, go to Settings ⚙ > Wallpaper

Your screen will look like this:

Tap "Choose a New Wallpaper" to access more options related to Wallpaper.

Choose your new wallpaper by clicking any of the above-given groups i.e. Dynamic, Stills, or Live. Each category contains different wallpapers to let you pick the one you like. Simply tap the wallpaper to set it as your new wallpaper.

Below these three groups, you can see your photo gallery albums. If you wish to put one of your pictures from the gallery as your wallpaper, tap "All Photos" or tap the "Album" the image is in, then tap the desired picture to set it as your wallpaper.

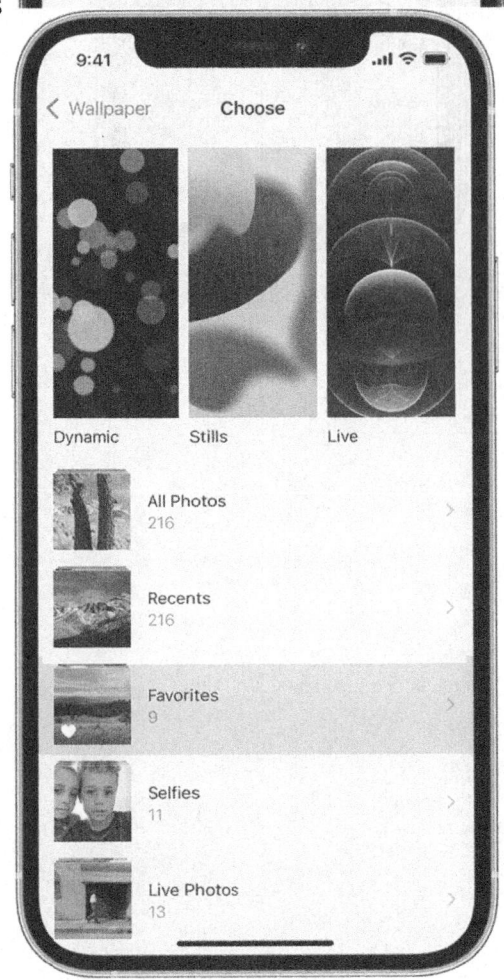

Once you tap the new wallpaper or picture, you'll be asked to choose the following options on the next screen.

You'll see a symbol of "Perspective Zoom" at the bottom of your wallpaper screen while setting it up. The option is available for some wallpapers and may not be able to see it with others as they don't support the feature.

Perspective Zoom changes the angle of the wallpaper as you change the angle of your iPhone while holding it in your palm. This gives your wallpaper a more realistic view
You'll also see some of the wallpaper with "Dark Mode" ◑. Wallpapers with the Dark Mode symbol change their appearance from bright colors to darker ones.

After adjusting zoom and light or dark mode, tap "Set" at the bottom right corner. The iPhone will ask whether you want the desired wallpaper to be set as your home screen background, lock screen background or both. Tap any of the desired options, and it will change your wallpaper to a new one.

ADJUST COLOR & BRIGHTNESS TO YOUR PREFERENCES

The iPhone uses three modes to adjust the color and brightness according to your needs. These modes are Dark Mode, Night Shift, and True Tone. All three modes work differently. Your iPhone also adjusts brightness according to your surroundings once you enable the option from settings.

The following are your brightness and color options on your iPhone:

ADJUST BRIGHTNESS MANUALLY OR AUTOMATICALLY

For a manual adjustment of your screen brightness:

- Swipe your finger from the top-right corner towards the bottom to open the control center.
- Look for the brightness bar with the ☀ symbol.
- Drag it up or down to manually adjust the brightness of your screen.

To let your phone adjust the brightness automatically according to your surroundings:

- Go to Settings ⚙ > Tap "Accessibility"
- From the list showing on your screen, tap "Display & Text Size."
- Enable the "Auto-Brightness" feature.

DARK MODE

In Dark Mode, your phone changes the light colors to darker ones (everything that has a white background will now have a black background). It helps you use your phone in low light. With Dark Mode turned on, you can use your phone in the dark without the lighter colors being hard on your eyes.

You can turn Dark Mode on & off from the control center or by going into the Settings. You can even set it to change automatically depending on what time of the day it is.

DARK MODE IN CONTROL CENTER

- Open the control center and long press ☀ to show more options.
- Tap 🌓 to turn the Dark Mode on or off.

TURN ON DARK MODE IN SETTINGS OR SCHEDULE IT

- Go to Settings ⚙ > Tap "Display & Brightness."
- At the top of the next screen, you can see the option of "Light Mode" or "Dark Mode."
- Tap any of the two to switch between the two modes.

To automatically turn Dark Mode on or off, enable the "Automatic" feature just below the light & dark mode option, then follow the instructions below to schedule it.

- After you enable "Automatic," tap the "Options" that will appear below the toggle button.
- Choose "Sunset to Sunrise" to let the iPhone switch the modes depending on the sunset and sunrise time.
- To schedule the modes at your preferred times, tap "Custom Schedule."
- You'll see two options, light mode and dark mode, with a clock option in front of both the options.
- Enter the time for both modes to let your phone switch between modes at your given time.

NIGHT SHIFT

Night shift makes the screen light dimmer and less hard on your eyes, especially when you are using your phone in darker places. Here's how to turn it on, off, or schedule it to your needs.

- Open control center, long press to show more options on the screen.
- Tap "Night Shift" to turn it on or off.

To turn Night Shift on manually or to schedule it, you need to turn it on from settings. In settings, it also gives you the option to adjust the tone of the night shift by sliding the adjustment slider between less warm or more warm options.

- Go to Settings ⚙ > tap "Display & Brightness"
- Tap "Night Shift" to reveal more options.
- Tap "Scheduled" to set the time to turn Night Shift on & off.
- Slide the adjustment slider to set the color that best suits your eyes.

TRUE TONE

True Tone gives your document, photo, or any content on your screen a more natural display using the true tone feature. Enabling True Tone will allow your iPhone to adjust the color and brightness of the content on the screen according to the external environment.

To turn True Tone on & off, follow the steps below:

- Go to Settings ⚙ > tap "Display & Brightness."
- Tap the "True Tone" toggle button to turn it on or off.

ORGANIZE THE HOME SCREEN ON YOUR IPHONE

You can organize your apps on the home screen where they are more accessible and adjusted to your use. You can move, remove, create folders, or add widgets on your home screen.

To move apps from one place on the screen to another, or even on the next page:

- Tap and hold any app icon on the home screen until it reveals more options
- Tap "Edit Home Screen," and the icon will start to wobble.
- Tap and hold the app you want to move, and drag it across the screen to change its place on the same page, or drag it to the edge of the screen and hold your finger for a moment until your phone automatically moves to the next page on the home screen.
- Release the icon to place the app in its new place.

- Tap "Done" at the top-right corner when you have finished organizing the apps.

- You can also add widgets to your home screen. A widget is a small window-like display on your home screen that can show your app's data without having to open the app.

To add an app's widget:

- Tap and hold any app icon on the home screen until it reveals more options.

- Tap "Edit Home Screen," the icon will start to wobble.

- Tap the " + " at the top-right corner of the screen.

- It will show you the list of widgets that you can use on your screen.

- Here, you can choose any widget of your desired app and you can also choose the widget style.

- Simply tap the desired widget to show on your home screen. Drag the widget to adjust its place on the home screen and then tap "Done" when finished.

ADJUST SOUND & VIBRATION ON YOUR IPHONE

The iPhone gives you plenty of options in sound and vibrations too. You can adjust the volume and vibration (called haptic feedback by Apple), according to your needs.

ADJUST OR CHANGE THE SOUND & VIBRATION

You can change the ringtone or adjust the volume of the ringtone and other notifications under iPhone sound settings. To see & change all the options related to sound and vibration:

- Go to Settings ⚙ > tap "Sound & Haptics."

- Drag the slider to adjust the volume for all notifications on your iPhone.

- To change the ringtone for different notifications, tap the notification type such as ringtone, text tone, voicemail, mail, calendars, reminder, and airdrop.

- Scroll through all the given ringtones from the list, tap one of them to have a listen, and set the tone you like as your new ringtone or notification tone.

- To change the vibration pattern, tap the notification type as mentioned above i.e. ringtone, text tone, voicemail, mail, calendar, reminder, or airdrop.

- Tap "Vibration" at the top of the ringtone list to change the vibration pattern or create your own vibration pattern for a specific notification type.

HAPTIC FEEDBACK

Haptic feedback is the vibrational feedback that your iPhone generates while performing certain tasks such as using long-press or refreshing your Facebook or Twitter timeline.
You can turn this feature on and off as follows:

- Go to Settings ⚙ > tap "Sound & Haptics."
- Tap "System Haptics" toggle button to turn the feature on & off.

Note: "Sound & Haptic" feature controls all the vibrations on your phone. If you turn the feature off, it will also turn the vibration for all notifications including incoming calls & messages off.

CHANGE DATE, TIME, REGION, LANGUAGE & DEVICE NAME

You can change your device information including date & time, language & region, and even your device name that appeared while setting up Bluetooth or hotspot connections. This information changes depending on your location, but sometimes the iPhone may not be able to automatically update this information. You can update the information as follows:

DATE & TIME

The iPhone sets the time automatically depending on your location. If you want to change the time manually, you can do it by following these instructions:

- Go to Settings ⚙ > General > tap "Date & Time."
- Enable "Set Automatically" to let your iPhone set the time automatically according to your location.
- If you wish to manually set your time, disable the automatic option and it will allow you to set the time manually.
- You can also decide whether you want your iPhone's clock to show time in 12 hours

time format or 24 hour format. To show time in 12 hour format, disable the 24 hour time button. If you wish to see your time in 24 hour time format, simply enable the option.

REGION & LANGUAGE

To manually set your region and language differently, do the following:

- Go to Settings ⚙ > General > tap "Region & Language."
- You can change Region, Languages, Calendar, and even Temperature Units.
- Below the list, you can see how your iPhone will present the region, language, and calendar information after finishing the new changes.

DEVICE NAME

iPhone will automatically set your device name picking it up from your Apple ID information. This information will show while using Airdrop, Bluetooth connections, and personal hotspot. You can change the name of the device to whatever name you want.
To change your device name, simply:

- Go to Settings ⚙ > General > tap "About" > tap "Name."
- Clear the older name and type a new one of your choice.
- Tap "Done" in the lower-right corner of the keyboard and it will change your device name.

APP STORE

Get your favorite apps with just one tap.

*Discover new apps, services, and subscriptions
in one place.*

App Store is your one-stop for every app you love. You can download apps, games, fonts, and much more with a single tap. The App Store offers more than two million apps for you to enjoy. To enjoy your favorite apps & games or discover new ones, all you need is your Apple ID and a working internet connection

HOW TO DISCOVER NEW APPS?

Apple divides its App Store into four main categories to help you discover new apps & experiences. It also offers a search option to find apps by name so you can find & download

170

apps that you want on your phone with ease. Here's how the categories on the App Store works:

Today – Here you can find apps and in-app events featured by Apple itself. The featured apps and events update by time so you can come across new and better apps every day.

Games – App Store offers exciting games for you to enjoy. You can download your favorite games from different categories including online, multiplayer, action-adventure, racing, and more.

Apps – Never miss any new release or top-rated apps that can be helpful for you. You can see top-chart apps, look for a new release or browse by the category to find the best apps.

Arcade – Apple Arcade offers a collection of premium games without ads or in-app purchases. A subscription is required to access the Apple Arcade.

Search – Go to search bar up the top to find apps using names or keywords.

PURCHASE OR DOWNLOADING APPS

Getting apps on your phone is simply a one-tap process. Purchase or download the desired app by following these easy steps:

- Open the App Store by clicking the app store icon , find the app that you want to download.
- Tap "[App's Name]" to discover more information about the app such as app size, rating, reviews, developer information, compatibility, and language.
- If the app is free, tap "Get" to download the app. If the app is paid you'll see the "Price" of the app instead of "Get." Simply tap the price and confirm the payment by face ID or your Apple ID password to start downloading it.

Note: If you have already downloaded the free app or purchased it from the App Store you'll see icon in place of price or get.

HOW TO SEND OR REDEEM AN APPLE GIFT CARD IN THEAPP STORE?

Apple Gift cards are used to put money directly into your Apple ID. The balance can later be used to make purchases or buy other subscriptions on the App Store. You can get gift cards from the Apple website or the nearest Apple Store. You can even send a gift card to any family member, friend, or other Apple users.

To Redeem or Send an Apple Gift card:

- Go to App Store 🅰 Tap your "Profile Icon" on the top-right corner of your screen.
- On the next screen, tap "Redeem Gift Card or Code" or "Send Gift Card By Email."
- Follow the on-screen instructions or redeem or send a gift card.

ADD FUNDS TO APPLE ID

You can add funds to your Apple ID. These funds can also be used to purchase apps or games and pay for your subscriptions or complete in-App purchases. Just like your debit/credit card payment or an Apple Gift card, Apple ID Funds add to your balance that you can use to make purchases on the App Store.

To Add Funds to your Apple ID, make sure you have added a payment method such as your debit or credit card to your Apple ID. Follow these steps to add funds:

- Go to App Store 🅰 > Tap your "Profile Icon" 🔘 at the top-right corner of your screen
- Tap "Add Funds To Apple ID"
- Choose from the amount shown on your screen or choose "Other" to enter your desired amount to add.
- Tap "Next" and confirm your purchase through face ID or password. This will add the funds to your Apple ID.

MANAGE YOUR SUBSCRIPTIONS, DOWNLOADS & PURCHASES IN THE APP STORE

App Store settings let you see or change your subscriptions, downloads, and purchases all in one place. You can even customize your App Store to only see the apps and features that you like.

To see all your purchased apps:

- Go to the App Store ![icon] > Tap your "Profile Icon" ![icon] on the top-right corner of your screen

- Tap "Purchased."

- You'll see two categories on the next screen. "All" where you can see all your downloaded & purchases you've made using your Apple ID. "Not on this iPhone" where you can see the purchases that you've made using your Apple ID on other devices but haven't downloaded onto your iPhone.

To manage your subscription with Apple ID:

- Go to the App Store ![icon] > Tap your "Profile Icon" ![icon] on the top-right corner of your screen.

- Tap "Subscription." The iPhone may ask you to sign in again.

- Here you can see all your subscriptions and you can renew or cancel your subscriptions made in the App Store.

CUSTOMIZE OR RESTRICT YOUR APP STORE

You can customize and restrict how your App Store works. To see & change the App Store settings, go to Settings ![icon] > Tap "App Store ![icon] > choose from the following to customize the App Store to your needs:

AUTOMATIC DOWNLOADS

Under Automatic Downloads, turn on "Apps" to let your iPhone download apps and purchases made on your other IOS devices.
Turn "App Updates" on so your phone downloads and installs new updates automatically.

MOBILE DATA

Turn on "Automatic Downloads" to allow your phone to download and update apps while you are on a cellular connection (not recommended unless you have sufficient monthly data. If you're unsure it's best to keep it off and download/update apps when you're at home with your wifi).

Tap "Apps Downloads" to choose if you want your phone to download bigger apps on your iPhone using cellular data.

VIDEO AUTOPLAY

Choose the "On," "Off," or "Wi-Fi Only" option. App Store will play apps' preview video while downloading, depending on what option you choose.

IN-APP RATINGS & REVIEWS

Turn the option "On" if you want to review your favorite apps.

OFFLOAD UNUSED APPS

Turning the option on will remove the unused apps after some time but will keep the data. You will still be able to see the App's icon on your home screen. If you wish to download it again, simply tap its icon and the iPhone will download the app again if it's still available on the App Store. Turn the feature "On" to save storage on your iPhone.

APPS ON YOUR iPHONE

Use Apple's default apps & In-app features for entertainment, connectivity & productivity.

App Store

BOOKS

You can purchase your favorite book and read or listen to them on the go. You can even read, print, or mark up any PDF using "Books."

To purchase your books or Audiobooks

- Go to Books 📖 Tap "Book Store" or "Audiobooks" to discover books in both stores.
- Tap on any title to preview it or listen to a sample preview on the Audiobook store.
- Tap "Buy" and proceed to payment or tap "Get" if the book is free to download.
- Tap "Library," to read, listen, or organize your purchased books & audiobooks.

READ, PRINT, OR SHARE A PDF

To open and read your PDF file in Books:

- Open PDF file > Tap 📤 > Tap "Books to open your pdf in Books app.
- To Share or Print your PDF file through different apps:
- Open PDF file > Tap 📤 from the share sheet, and choose the apps you want to share your PDF with.
- To print your PDF, tap the "Print" option from the share sheet and then choose the available printers to print the document.

CALCULATOR

The calculator app performs every basic function that a standard calculator can. It can perform a range of calculations, from simple arithmetic calculations to trigonometric, exponential, or even logarithmic calculations.

Tap the "Calculator"  app icon or open the control center and tap the "calculator icon" to open the app.

To use the simple calculator for standard arithmetic functions, use the calculator while holding the phone upright (portrait orientation)

To change the standard calculator into scientific mode, simply rotate your iPhone sideways (landscape orientation).

ADDITIONAL FUNCTIONS ON THE CALCULATOR

• Tap and hold the current calculation result on the screen, tap "Copy" to get the results on the clipboard. Go to another app such as messages or notes, tap & hold the cursor and then tap "Paste," to copy the results to your desired location.

• To delete any wrongly typed numbers during your calculation, simply swipe right or left while keeping your finger over the numbers. This will delete one number at a time.

• Tap "C" to clear the last calculation and tap "AC" to clear all the previous calculations on the calculator.

CALENDAR

Your iPhone calendar keeps track of all your events such as appointments, meetings, invitations, and more.

Here are some of the basics on your calendar's app ^{WED}28 :

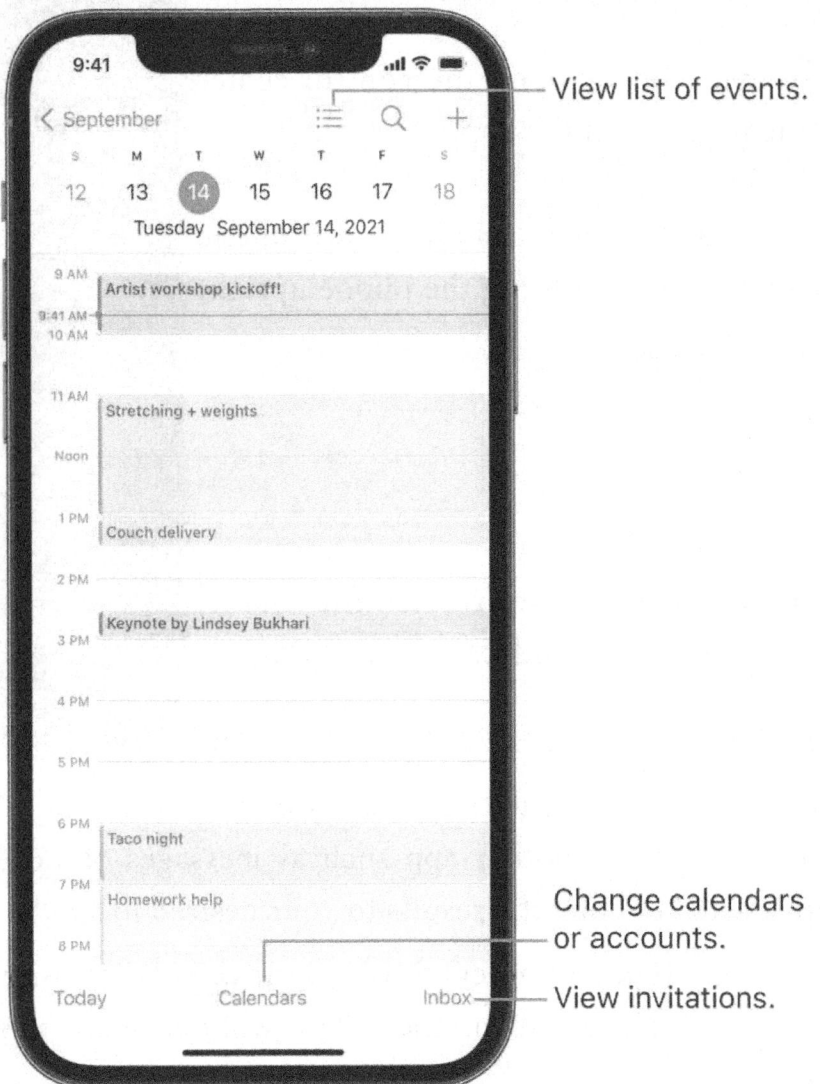

To change how you view your calendar on your iPhone, zoom in or zoom out in calendar apps to change the view, or, look for 🖥 at the top of the screen in the week and month view and tap it to change how your calendar will appear.

The Calendar app also lets you use more than one calendar at the same time. To add or remove other calendars:

Go to Settings ⚙ > Tap "Calendar" > Tap "Alternative Calendars" and choose any of the given calendars to use alongside the default calendar.

ADD EVENTS & ALERT ON CALENDAR

You can add events with alerts so you never miss an appointment, meeting, or party.

- Tap "Calendar" 28 > Open "day view" > Tap + at the top-right corner.

- Enter details of the event such as start and end time, repeat, or travel time.

- If you want to set an alert for the event, tap "Alert" and choose the time to receive the alert such as "At the time of event" or "15 minutes before" the event.

- To add an attachment such as photos or files to calendars, tap "Add Attachment," browse the file that you want to attach, tap the desired file, and then tap "Done."

You can also share your event with other apple users including your family members, friends, or co-workers. To add people to your event:

- Go to "Calendar" 28 > Find and open the already created event or create a new one > Tap "Invitees" > Add a family member or a friend to invite them to your event.

You can even edit the already added events. To change the details of already added events:

- Go to "Calendar" 28 > Find and open the event.

- Tap "Edit" at the top-right corner of the screen.

- You can see and update all the details of that event.

To delete an event:

- Go to "Calendar" 28 > Find and open the event.

- Tap "Edit" at the top-right corner of the screen.

- Scroll down to the bottom and tap "Delete Event."

USE CALENDARS WITH ICLOUD

iCloud keeps your events updated across all your IOS devices with your Apple ID. You can add or edit an event on one device and it'll sync the event on all your devices. It also keeps your events and details private, secured, and backed up.
To use Calendars with iCloud:
Go to Settings ⚙ > Tap "Your Name" appearing on the top of your screen > Tap "iCloud" > Enable "Calendar" so your iPhone can sync and show your events across all your IOS devices.

CAMERA

Your iPhone has one of the best quality cameras out there. It captures your moment in an instant using a variety of lenses and modes that lets you capture photos and videos in many different ways. Learn about your iPhone camera here and put it to practice to take the best shot of your life's precious moments.

BASIC CONTROLS & MODES ON CAMERA

The iPhone can switch between different modes to give you the best experience of your surroundings on your screen. Here are all the basics for your Camera app  and what picture mode to use so you can capture your moments in the best way possible.

Tap  on your home screen to open the camera. If your iPhone is locked, simply swipe left on the lock screen to instantly open the camera to take photos and videos. At the bottom of the screen, you'll see the capture button in the center, your recently captured photos are on the left, and on the right, you can see the  button, tap it to switch between the selfie camera & rear camera.

Just above your capture button, you can see camera modes. You can either tap any mode or swipe your finger left or right to switch between the available modes on your camera. Following are features of every mode:

Photo – This mode simply take photos without any effects and opens up when you tap the camera icon.

Videos – It simply records a video without any specialized effects.

Slo-mo – Adds a slow-motion effect to your videos to make them more enjoyable.

Time-lapse – A video mode that speeds up your recorded video.

Pano – The mode captures panoramic scenes or when you need to capture a wider landscape.

Portrait – Helps you capture professional photos by applying depth-of-field to your photos.

Cinematic – A portrait mode for your videos that applies depth-of-field to your videos.

Square – capture photos in square ratio. You can also choose your desired ratio by taping ⊙ at top of the screen, and then choosing from the given option i.e. 4:3, 16:9, and square.

To zoom in and out on your photos and videos, use the pinch gesture on the object. Alternatively, you can see the zoom buttons just above the modes. Tap the zoom between 0.5x – 3x range to zoom in and out. Tap and hold the toggles to zoom more precisely between the given range.

You'll see additional controls on the top of your camera screen. Tap these options to control and set the settings for flashlight, live photos, timer and filters on your photos.

Tap the "Shutter" to take the photo or record a video. You can also take photos by pressing the volume up or volume down button.

TAKE PORTRAIT PHOTOS & RECORD CINEMATIC VIDEOS

Portrait photos and cinematic videos create a beautiful effect by taking your personal photography to the next level. These modes create photos and videos with your desired object sharp, in focus, and with the background blurred to make your content more cinematic.

To take the best shot with portrait mode, open the camera app 📷 and choose "Portrait Mode." Portrait mode gives you a variety of effects to choose from.

Tap and drag the ⬡ to the left to choose the following option available in portrait mode photography:

- Natural Light: Captures photos in their natural light exposure

- Studio Light: Offers an additional color and sharpness in your photos making them brighter and more lit up.

- Contour Light: Most efficient to capture dramatic photos with high and low lights casting on objects.

- Stage Light: Your object such as your face or your pet is lit up against a deep black background. Stage light effect has a further two types including light-mono and high-key light mono that offers pictures in black and white effect or grayscale effects. Choose the one that makes your photo look best.

The light effects on portrait mode are adjustable. To set the lighting effects in portrait, tap ⬡ at the top of your camera screen and drag the slider to adjust the lighting effects for your photo.

Change the intensity of the portrait mode to only blur backgrounds as much as you need. You can even change the focus on captured photos:

- Choose the portrait mode in the camera app and bring the object in focus.

- Look for ⓕ at the top-right corner and tap it. Use the slider to adjust the focus.

- Drag the focus-slider to increase or decrease the blur intensity of the background.

- Once the focus is all set, tap "Shutter" to take a portrait picture.

To change the focus on already captured photos, go to the Photos app 🌸 ⸴ Open the desired photo > Tap "Edit" > Tap "Portrait" to turn the effect on and off or adjust the focus on your captured photos.

The cinematic mode in the video offers a variety of options to help you record high-quality personal videos with professional effects.

To record a cinematic video on your iPhone:

- Open the Camera app and choose "Cinematic Mode."

- Turn your phone sideways in landscape orientation and then tap to reveal the following options

f   Just like the portrait mode in photos, you can adjust the focus on video by clicking focus and dragging the slider.

⚡   Turn the flashlight on & off or select "Auto" to turn it on and off automatically depending on external light.

1x   Tap 1x button to switch between the telephoto and wide-angle to capture fewer or more objects in one frame.

⊕   Control the exposure to your videos. Use the slider to make your videos dark or bright

- Once your frame is set for video, Tap ● button to record the video. Tap it again to stop the recording.

VIEW YOUR PHOTOS & VIDEOS

All your photos and videos are saved in the Photo app 🌸 You can view your recently taken photos and videos, directly from the camera app or Photo app.

To view your photos & videos directly from your camera app, tap the photo in the lower-left corner of the camera app. It will open your recently taken photos and videos on your iPhone. Swipe through the photos and videos to view your recently taken shots. Tap "All Photos" at the top right corner to view your photos in the Photo app.

CLOCK

The clock app 🕐 is a tool from the iPhone which you can use not only as a stopwatch, alarm or timer, but for productivity and tracking sleep cycles.

MANAGE YOUR ALARMS

You can set, change or delete any alarm in clock apps by following these simple steps:

• Open the Clock app 🕐 and tap "Alarm" from the bar showing at the bottom of your screen.

• Tap ➕ at the top-right corner of the screen to add an alarm.

• On the next screen, set the time, alert, or frequency of the alarm from the given options.

• Tap "Save" to set your alarm.

• To turn the saved alarm on and off, simply use the toggle button in front of the added alarm in the list.

To change the time settings for any of your already added alarms:

• Tap "Edit" on the top left corner of your screen in Clock > Alarm.

• Tap the alarm that you want to edit.

• Make the desired changes and then tap "Save" to apply the changes.

You can also delete your added alarms from the list:

• Tap "Edit" on the top left corner of your screen in Clock > Alarm.

• Tap ➖ button and then tap "Delete" to remove the alarm from your list.

• Tap "Done" at the top-left corner when you are done.

MONITOR YOUR SLEEP CYCLE

One of the most beneficial features that the Clock app offers is to monitor your sleep cycle with the help of the Health app on your iPhone. The sleep cycle sets your bedtime and wake time and also monitors your activity on your phone to determine how many hours of sleep you are actually getting.

Go to the Health app to set your sleep cycle. Once you've set it up in your Health app, you can see and change your wake up and bedtimes to help your phone remind you of your bedtime and wake you up when you want to.

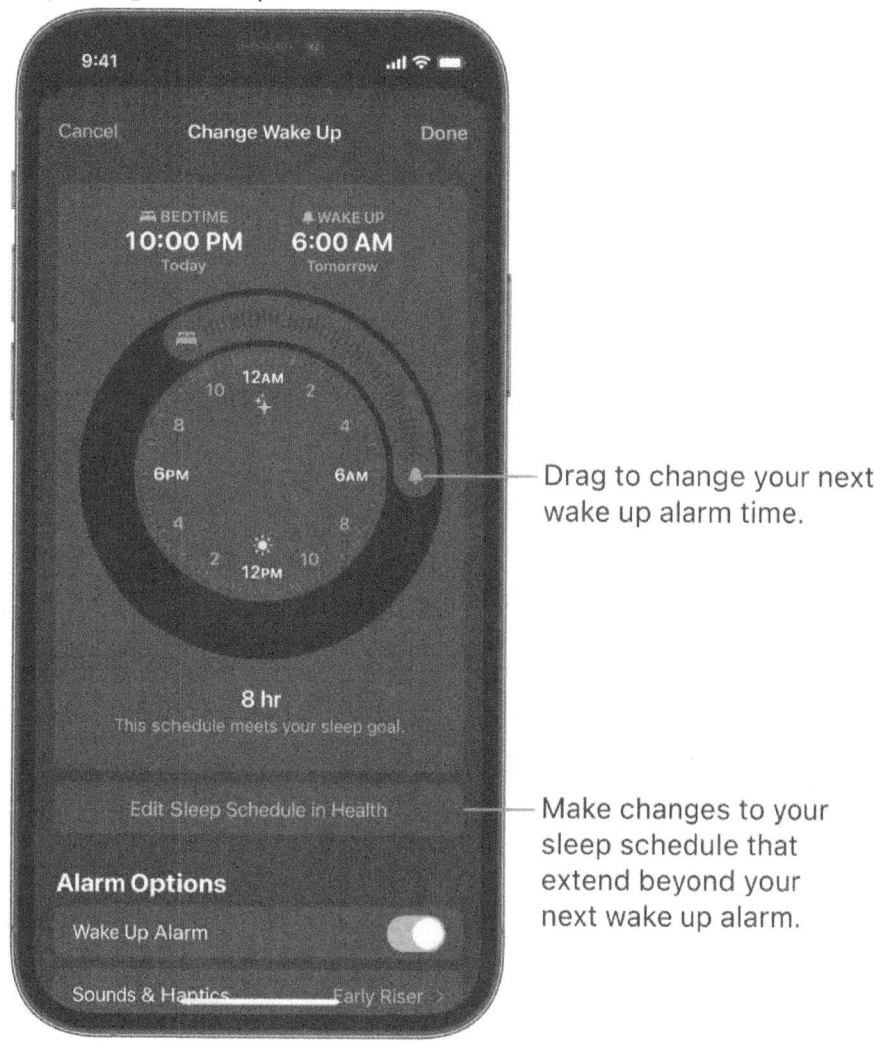

Drag to change your next wake up alarm time.

Make changes to your sleep schedule that extend beyond your next wake up alarm.

Once you set up your sleep goals in the Health app, your sleep cycle clock will appear on the top of your alarm list. Tap "Change" to edit your wake-up and bedtime or skip any alarm for the next day.

After taping "Change," your screen will give you the option shown in the above picture. Drag the slider around the clock to set your new wake-up time or bedtime. 🔔 is your wake-up time on your clock and 🛏 will be your bedtime. As you drag both, you can see your overall sleep hours just below the slider. In "Alarm Options," you can choose whether to ring the wakeup alarm, snooze, and settings related to "Sounds & Haptics."

WORLD CLOCK, STOPWATCH & TIMER

Other than alarm and sleep schedules, you can add and see world clocks to keep track of time around the world, and use a stopwatch or timer for personal tasks.

- To add, see, and delete the time from different cities around the world:
- Go to the Clock app 🕐 > "World Clock."
- Tap ➕ at the top-right corner, then search or select the cities that you want to add.
- Tap the desired city name to add it to your world clock list.
- Tap "Edit" to rearrange the list of added cities or tap ➖ and then "Delete" to remove the city from your list.

Use the stopwatch feature to record your time for a certain task. Go to the stopwatch and tap "Start." If you wish to take a timelapse in-between, tap the "Lap" button on the left side and your laps will appear in the list below. To stop and rest, simply tap the "Stop" button and then tap "Reset" to bring your stopwatch back to zero.

Timer is your digital countdown for a period of time that you set. Tap "Timer" and then set the time that you want to start a countdown for. Tap "Pause" to temporarily stop your timer or tap "Cancel" to stop and reset your timer. You can also choose the alert tone for your iPhone to play when your timer will hit zero on the clock.

*The timer is something you can easily use with Siri for tasks that come up during the day like when you're cooking pasta. Simply say "Her Siri, start the timer" or press the side button and say "Start timer" to get it going.

COMPASS

Compass app gives you directions, coordinates, and elevation of your current location. Tap the Compass app 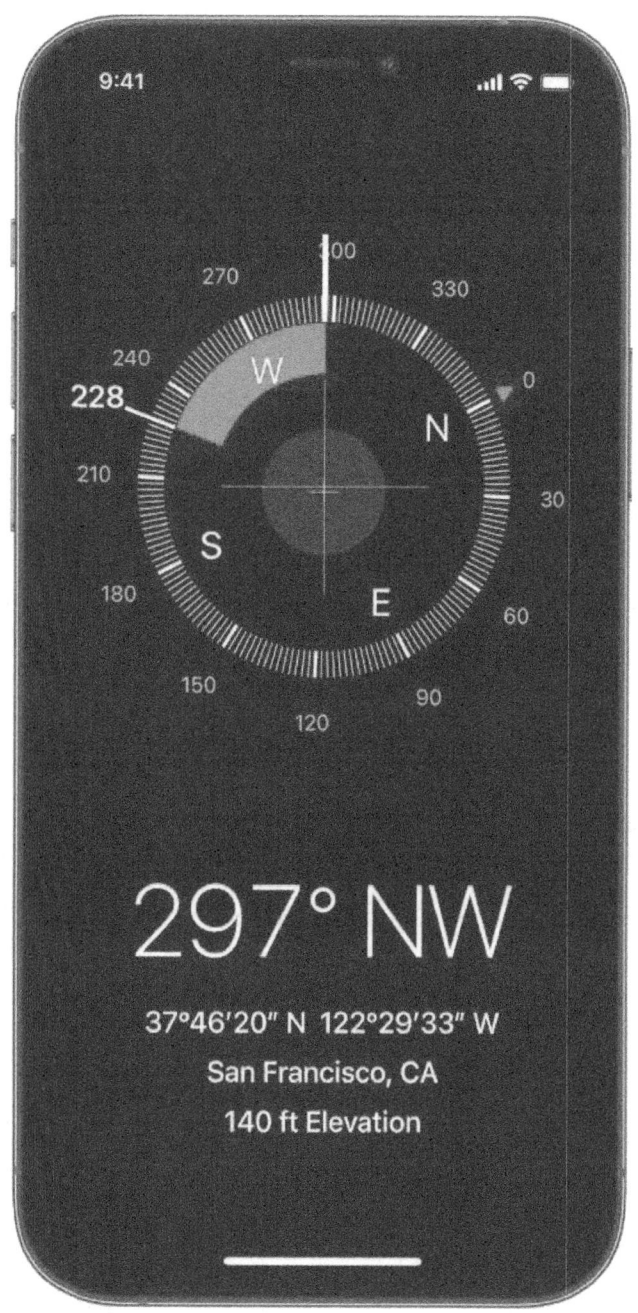 and your iPhone will show all the information about your location on your screen.

The Compass app can also help you stay in one direction. Tap the dial to set it for any specific direction. Every time you change direction it will show a red band to indicate how off you are from your set course.

You can see the location of your current coordinates on Maps by simply taping the coordinates below the campus.

CONTACT

The Contact app ⊡ keeps all the information about you and your contact private, secure, and backed up. You can add the numbers, emails, and home or business addresses of all your contacts in one place and access them instantly through the app.

ADD OR UPDATE CONTACTS & OTHER INFORMATION

You can save contact and all their relevant information at one place which makes it easy to access. The Contact app on your iPhone makes it convenient to search and access any desired contact and their information with just a few taps.

To add a contacts details:

- Go to the Contact app ⊡.

- Enter contact information such as name, number, email or other fields. You can also add photos to your contact. Tap the photo icon at top of the contact detail to add.

- To add any fields for more than one contact number, email or address, tap ＋ and then choose labels or create a custom label.

- Tap "Done" at the top-right corner to save the contact.

To access and update any contact from your saved contact list:

Go to the Contact app and tap any contact to see the saved information (you can use the search bar to find your desired contact by clicking the magnifying glass) and then tap to open the contact.

On this screen, you can see all the information related

[Phone screen showing contact card]

9:41

< Search   Edit

Edwina Greenaway
default: ⊡ Primary >

message call FaceTime mail pay

mobile
(780) 246-0687

home
e_greenaway@icloud.com

home
5005 Fulton Road
Edmonton AB T6A 3S9
Canada

birthday
June 1, 1986

Notes

Set the preferred line for phone calls and SMS/MMS messages (Dual SIM only).

Send a message, call, FaceTime, mail, or pay.

188

to your contact. You can also use the quick task buttons just below your contact photo i.e. Message, Call, FaceTime, Mail and Pay. Tap any of them to quickly contact or pay (through Apply pay).

To update any information to your contact:

- Tap "Edit" at the top-right corner of your screen to update any information related to your contact.
- Tap ⊕ or ⊖ to delete or add any information about your contact.
- Tap "Done" when you are finished updating your contact.

The iPhone also creates your own contact card and saves it in the contact app which is called "My Card." The information can be shared and used to Autofill any forms on the internet. For example, iPhone will autofill your name, contact number, email, and address when you are trying to fill in the information on an online store or website to make a purchase.

To add "My Card" on your iPhone:

- Tap "My Card" at the top of your contact list.
- Enter all your contact information including numbers, email, address, or any other fields.
- Tap "Done" to save the card.

If you don't see "My Card" at top of your contact app:

- Tap ＋ and fill in all the information. It will create a new contact with all your information.
- To make it "My Card," go to Settings ⚙ > Tap "Contacts" > Tap "My Info."
- Choose the contact that you just saved with all your information. The iPhone will create a "My Card" with the provided information.

USE ICLOUD TO KEEP YOUR CONTACTS SECURE, BACKED UP, & SYNCED

You can use iCloud to save your contacts. iPhone will upload all the contacts on your iCloud so you never have to worry about your contacts even if you change your phone or have lost it.

To set iCloud as your default account for all your contacts:

- Go to Settings ⚙ > Tap "Your Name" at top of the settings list.

- Tap "iCloud"

- Turn on the contact toggle so your iPhone can upload and sync your contacts across all your devices.

FACETIME

FaceTime ▢ supports both audio and video calls with your contacts. It even lets you share your screen and content with your friends and family while staying on the call. You can watch movies, share music, photos, web pages, and many other things, while getting a real-time response or reaction to your shared content.

To set up FaceTime, go to Settings ⚙ Tap "FaceTime," and then turn the FaceTime button on. In settings, you can change other settings which include notification settings, your Caller ID, and how you want people to contact you on your FaceTime i.e. by your Apple ID or Phone number.

MAKE OR RECEIVE CALLS USING FACETIME

Receiving or making a FaceTime call to your contact is as easy as making a regular call. You can make individual or group video and audio calls using your phone number or Apple ID. All you need is your iPhone and working Internet connection.

To make a call:

- Tap FaceTime ▢ and then tap "New FaceTime" on your screen.

- ⊕ you are using FaceTime for the first time, tap any contact from suggestions or tap to add a contact to make a FaceTime call.

- Once you make the call, it will appear on your list of recent calls in the FaceTime app. If you want to make a call to the same contact then tap 📞 o ▢◁ to make the call from your recent FaceTime call log.

- You can also start a FaceTime call through the Message app. In messages, open the messages with your contact and then tap ▢◁ and choose whether you want to make an audio call or a video call.

190

The following image shows the controls on your screen for the current call:

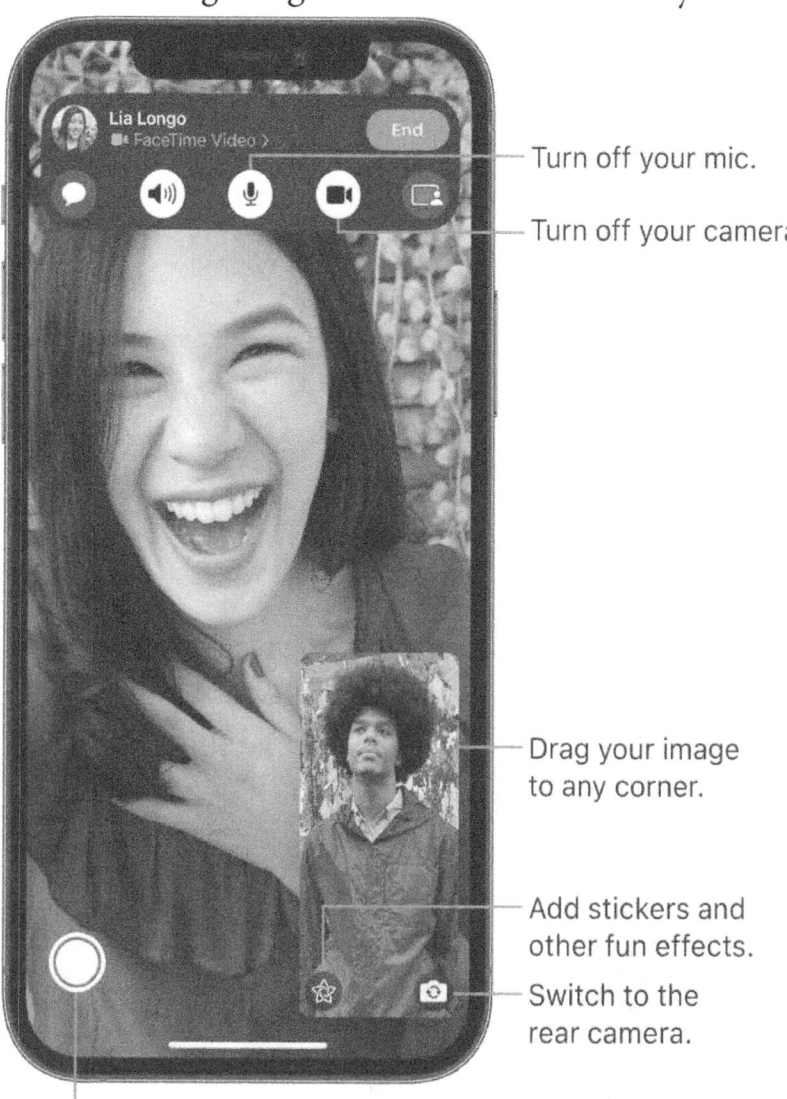

Turn off your mic.

Turn off your camera.

Drag your image to any corner.

Add stickers and other fun effects.

Switch to the rear camera.

Take a Live Photo.

To make a group call with your friends or family members:

• Tap FaceTime and then Tap "New FaceTime" on your screen.

• Tap to add a contact. Add all the contacts that you want to make a group call with. You can add up to 32 participants in a single group call.

• Tap or to make an audio or video group call.

In a group call, all of your participants will show up

as tiles on your screen.

When a participant speaks, the tile of the active participant will become more prominent on your screen to let you know who is currently speaking. If the number of participants can't fit the screen, a few of them will appear on your screen while the rest will show in a row at the bottom of your call screen. To find a participant, swipe through the row and you'll be able to see all your participants.

Receiving a FaceTime is similar to receiving a normal call on your iPhone. Tap "Answer" to receive the call or "Decline" by tapping the red button on your screen. There are also options to decline the call and set a reminder for a call back, or send the caller a message from the available quick message templates.

Set up a reminder to return the call later.

Send the caller a text message.

ADD MEMOJI, FILTER, TEXT, STICKER & OTHER AFFECT TO VIDEO CALLS

FaceTime makes your video calls more fun and enjoyable by offering video call effects. You can add text, stickers, memojis, and other fun effects to your video call. Your participants can also see your added effects and will also be able to add effects themselves that you can see on your screen.

PORTRAIT MODE

FaceTime supports portrait modes for your video calls too. You can blur your call background to make it more like a photo or video with the focus on you.

To add portrait mode effect to your calls, tap your tile on screen while you are in the call and then tap ⬚ to turn the portrait mode on and off during your call.

Tap ⬚ to switch to the rear camera to show the caller your surroundings. Tap it again to switch your camera back to the front. To add more exciting filters to your call, tap ✦ on your tile and then tap the following options to add:

Turn Portrait mode off or on.

MEMOJI

The iPhone uses the Face ID camera to make your emojis come alive. A memoji is a character from your emojis but with all the actions and expressions live from your face movements. You can use Memoji in the Message app and FaceTime.

To add Memoji to your FaceTime call:

- Tap your tile and then tap ✦ for more options.
- Tap 🧑 to reveal all the characters that you can use as your memoji. Tap your favorite character and it will appear as you face in a video call on FaceTime.

FILTERS

Filters change your appearance on camera by adding different colors and effects to your video during a FaceTime call.

To apply filters and change them during your call:

- Tap your tile and then tap ✦ for more options.

- Tap ⬤ and then simply tap the filter that you want to apply to your video call.

TEXT LABELS

Text labels are simply the text typed by you that appear on the call. Once you've typed the desired text in the given placeholder, you can place it on your screen anywhere you want. Your participant can do the same and it will appear on both of your screens.

To add text labels on your calls:

- Tap your tile and then tap ⊛ for more options.
- Tap **Aa** to see and choose the text label option showing up on your screen.
- Type the text in your selected label. To move it on the screen, tap outside of the text box or placeholder and then move the text with your fingers.
- If you wish to remove your text, tap your text label and then ⊗ to remove it from the screen.

SHAPES

FaceTime has different shapes to offer that you can use in your video for different purposes.

To add shapes:

- Tap your tile and then tap ⊛ for more options.
- Tap ▨ to see and choose any shape that you like to add to your video.
- To remove the shape, first, tap the shape and then tap.

STICKERS

You can add Memoji stickers or Emoji stickers just like a text label or shape. You can add it anywhere on your screen.

To add a Memoji or Emoji sticker:

- Tap your tile and then tap ⊛ for more options.

194

- Tap  to add an emoji sticker on the screen or tap 👶 to add a memoji sticker.
- Tap and drag the sticker on the screen to place it anywhere you want.
- Tap the sticker and then tap ✕ to remove it from your screen.

SHARE SCREEN OR VIDEOS & MUSIC USING SHAREPLAY

Sharing your photos, albums, plans, projects & many other things with your friends and families has become more advanced in iPhones & IOS devices. Through screen sharing, you can show your friends your content and get their reactions and opinion in real-time. It makes your call more fun and interactive.

To share the screen during your video call, tap the screen once to show all the video call controls on the screen if they are hidden, and then tap 🔲 and choose "Share My Screen." After a countdown from three, your screen will be shared with everyone on the call. You can open your gallery to show photos & albums, open safari to share any web pages, or other apps from your home screen to share with your participants.

SHAREPLAY

While screen sharing gives you the experience of sharing your photo albums, webpages, and other content, SharePlay allows you to watch movies and listen to music together. The movies, videos, and other content shared via SharePlay will have video and audio synced across all the participants' screens.

To use SharePlay during your call, open the streaming app that supports the feature such as Apple TV , Music app 🎵 or any other app downloaded from the App Store and support SharePlay. Play the content on your screen and tap "Play for Everyone." The option will only appear when the app supports the SharePlay feature.

After sharing the screen, every participant can see music and video controls on their screen which let them pause, play forward, or rewind the content on the screen. If a single participant uses any control on their screen, it will also apply to the other screens too. For example, if one participant pauses the movie or music, it will pause it on the other participants' devices all at once so your content remains synced.

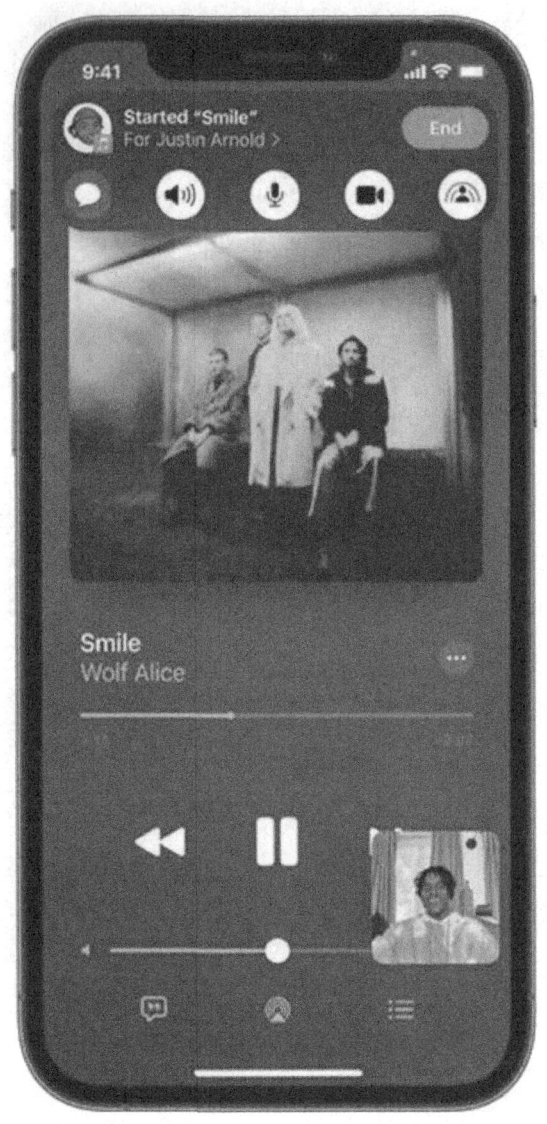
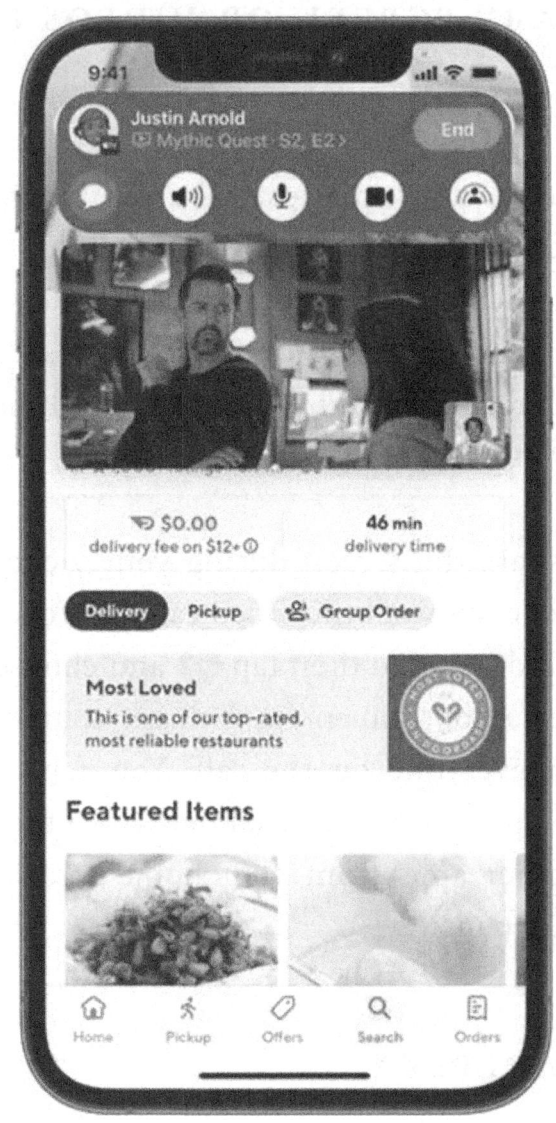

To use SharePlay in some apps, you and the other participant may need to buy the subscription. SharePlay can also be restricted by region, so if you're not able to access the SharePlay feature, check the availability by visiting the Apple website (the feature isn't available across all the countries).

FILES

The Files app ⬜ creates different folders and offers cloud storage to keep your documents and other data on the iCloud while updating them across all your IOS devices with your Apple ID. You can access and share all your files in one place using the Files app.

The Files app also lets you connect your external drives (USB, SD card, or other storage devices) directly to your IOS device.

ICLOUD DRIVE

You need to turn on the "iCloud Drive" feature from settings so your phone can access your data via iCloud and keep it updated across all the devices. To set up iCloud Drive:

Go to Settings ⚙ > Tap "Your Name" > Tap "iCloud" and then turn the "iCloud Drive" option on to store and share files using cloud storage.

You can use iCloud Drive to organize, modify and even share your documents and data. Within the Files app, you'll see different options that you can use to access and share data.

Open the Files app ⬜ and then tap "Browse" on the top-left corner of your screen. Here you can see the following available options:

• On My iPhone – Here you can see all the data on your iPhone in different apps. You have to give iCloud permission to access the data in these apps. To grant the permission, go to Settings ⚙ > Tap "Your Name" > Tap "iCloud" and scroll down to see all the apps that iCloud can access. Turn these apps on to access their data in the Files app.

• iCloud Drive – The drive stores & syncs your files across all your devices with your Apple ID. You can organize, edit, & share your files and folder directly from the app. In iCloud Drive, tap ••• to select multiple files and folders or do the following:

Organize: Sort your files & folder by their name, size, date, kind, or change how your data appears in iCloud drive i.e. in a grid or list form.

Add Folders: Tap "New Folder" to create a new folder to store and organize files according to your needs.

Scan Document: Tap "Scan Document" if you have any document that you wish to scan and upload, edit or share. To open the scanned document or any document that has already been added to your drive, tap ⬝⬝⬝ to edit and share it, or tap Ⓐ to sign or markup your document. Tap ⬆ to share it via messages or other supported apps.

ACCESS YOUR EXTERNAL STORAGES OR SERVERS IN FILES

File apps also support the feature to connect your external storage devices such as SD cards, USB drives, and other cloud storage such as Google Drive or DropBox. You can even connect to the online Servers directly through your iPhone.

Go to Files app 📁 > Tap "Browse" > Tap ⬝⬝⬝ to reveal more options and then tap "Connect to Server." On the next screen, choose whether you are joining as a "Guest" or "Registered User." Provide your user name and password to connect as a "Registered User." To disconnect your iPhone from the joined server, go to the "Browse" screen in the File app and tap ⏏ showing in front of your server name.

For cloud storage other than iCloud such as Google Drive, download the app from the App Store and set them up by signing in. Go to the Files app and then "Browse," tap "More Locations" from the list, and then enable all your external cloud storage to let them appear in your Files app.

External storages like SD cards, USB drives, or external hard drives need USB to lightning adaptors that you can get from the nearest Apple Store. Plug your external storage into the USB side of the adaptor and plug the lightning side into the iPhone port. Open the Files app and go to "Browse." You'll be able to see and access your external drive here.

FIND MY

Find My app 🔵 helps you see the location of your devices that are signed in with your Apple ID and also the location of your friends and family members that you add to your app using their Apple IDs or phone numbers. You can find your lost devices, lock them, play sound, and do other functions that enhance the security of all your IOS devices.

To set up Find My, go to Settings ⚙ > Tap "Your Name" > Tap "Find My" 🔵 and turn the feature on.

FRIENDS & FAMILY LOCATION

To add friends and family members to your Find My list, make sure that your location services are on and your phone has the permission to share your location with them as well. You will not be able to see the location of others if your location sharing feature is off. To share location with others, first, go to Find My 🔵 > 🔵 "Me" from the row at bottom of your screen > Turn on "Share My Location." You'll be able to add and see the location of other people now. To add people to your Find My list:

- Go to Find My 🔵 > Tap "People" at the bottom-left corner of your screen > Tap "Share My Location." It will send the person a location-sharing request. Once they accept your request, both of you will be able to see each other's locations.

- To stop sharing location with any person, tap "Person's Name" from the list and then tap stop sharing. Tap "Stop Sharing Location" again on your screen to confirm.

- To remove a person from your list, tap "Person's Name" then tap "Remove." Tap "Remove" again to confirm and it will remove the person from your list.

TRACK YOUR DEVICES & ITEMS

Find My keeps track of all your devices signed in with your Apple ID and other accessories connected with these devices (Airpods, Airtags & other third-party items). Go to Find My and tap "Devices" at the bottom to see all your devices signed in with Apple ID and accessories connected with them. Tap ✚ to add a new device to your list.

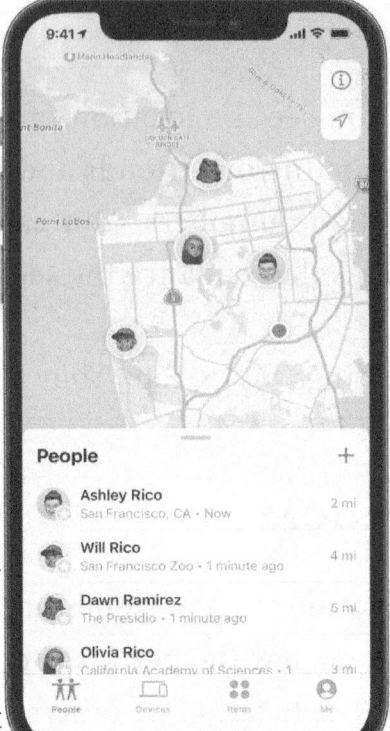
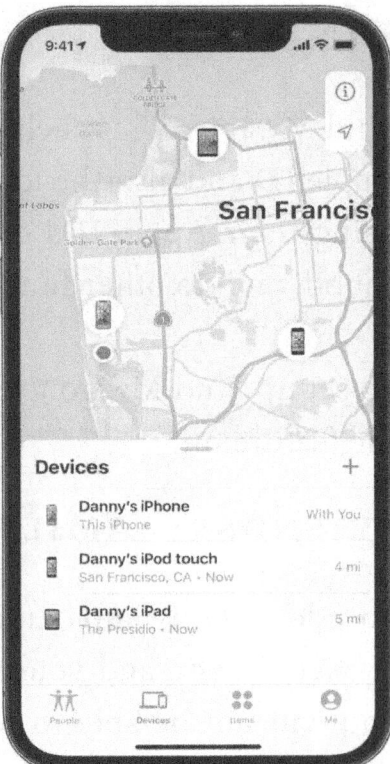

Tap any of the devices from the list to show its Find My options. You can see the directions to your device or tap "Direction" to open "follow your device" on Maps. If your device is nearby and you can't find it, tap "Play Sound." Your device will play a sound so you can listen and find your device. The feature comes in handy when you have more than one device or other accessories like AirPods and Apple Watch connected to your Apple ID. Turn on the "Notifications" feature so you can be notified every time your devices get separated from you. This will remind you to take your accessories with you when you are leaving work and have forgotten them.

If you've lost your device, you can tap "Mark As Lost" and enable different options to help Find My secure and find your device. This feature will leave a message on your device with your contact information or lock them so no one can access them without your permission.

The "Items" category at the bottom includes your other stuff like keys, wallets, purses, or any other item marked with an Airtag connected with your iPhone. You can access precise locations and there are other available options to secure your devices.

HEALTH

Track your every activity to improve your health right from your iPhone. The Health app ♥ records your activity data throughout your day and saves it on your iCloud. It can track the steps you've taken, floors you've climbed, and other exercises you've completed (which can be recorded automically, manually, or imported from your Apple Watch).

CREATE YOUR PROFILE & MEDICAL ID

To set up your profile & Medical ID in the Health app, open the app and tap your profile icon in the top-right corner of your screen. Tap "Health Details" and add all the relevant information for your general health.

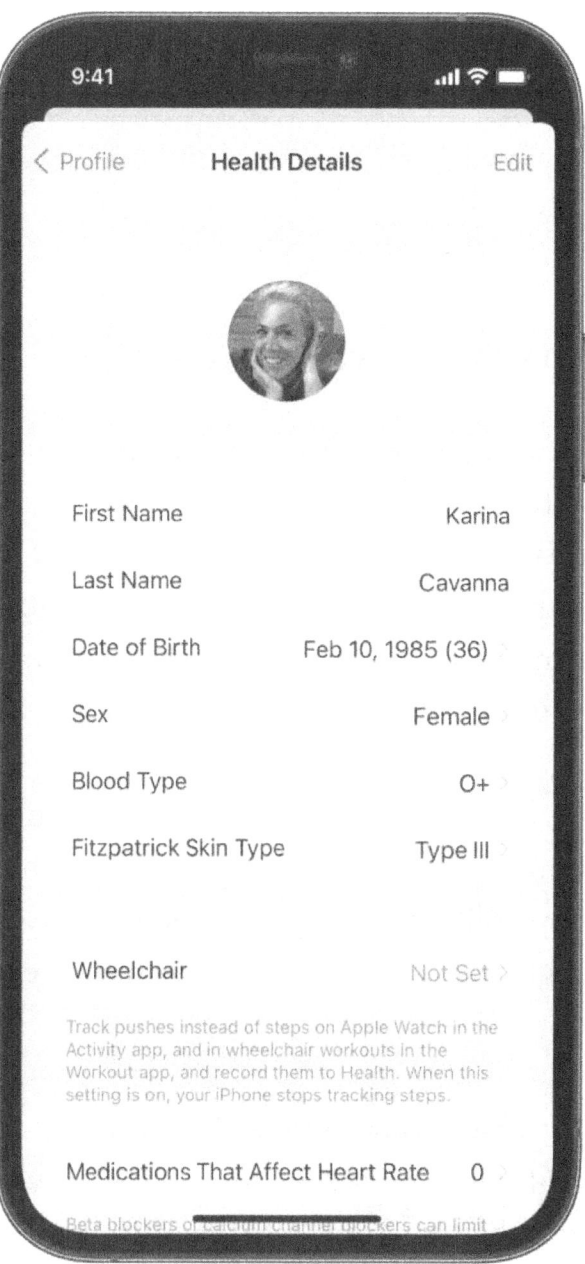

Your Medical ID keeps track of your body measurement or any other health conditions. A Medical ID can be accessed on the lock screen in case of an emergency. It helps 1st responders to get all basic information about your existing medical conditions like allergies, strokes, or any other information that can help them give you early medical attention. Go to the Health app, tap your profile and then tap "Medical ID" to view or update your personalized medical ID.

Note: For a first responder to see your Medical ID, they need to go to the passcode screen by swiping bottom to top and then tap "Emergency" on the bottom-left corner of the screen. Then on the dialer screen, they tap "Medical ID" to show all the information.

MONITOR YOUR ACTIVITY

Health app shows an easy-to-read and easy to access activity summary. The summary shows a list of different categories like walking, workouts, energy burned, and many others. Under each category, you can see a quick highlight of how much of an activity you have carried out throughout the day.

Open the Health app and tap "Summary" at the bottom of your screen to see these highlights. Tap Edit to see, add or remove any of the activity highlights shown in the list on the next screen.

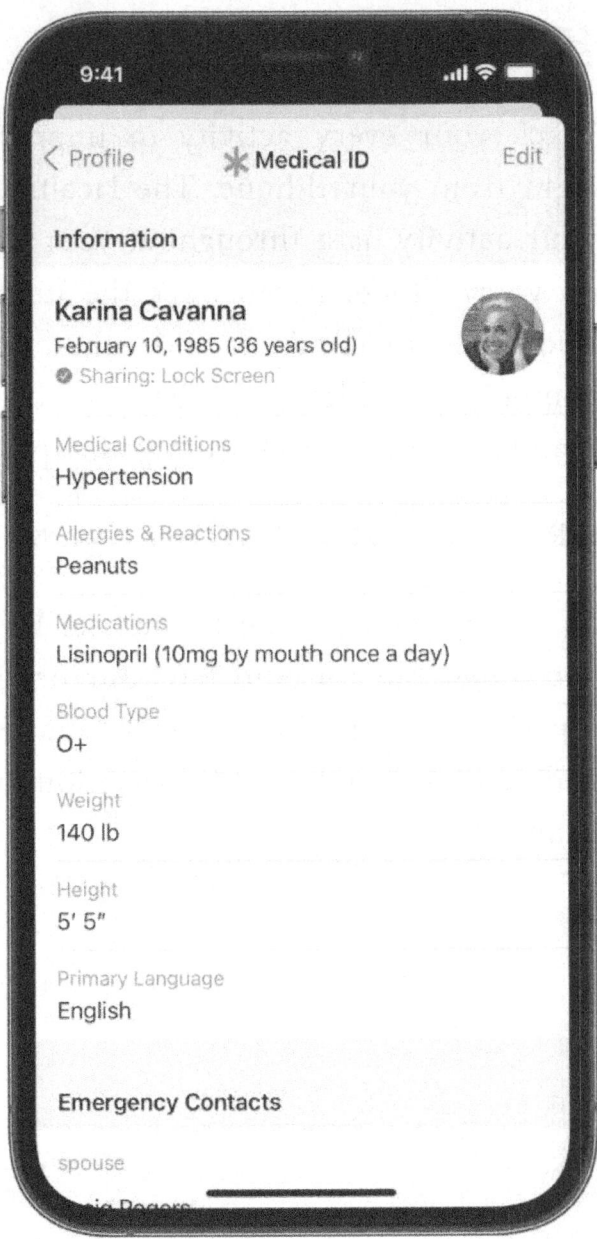

In case your phone has missed any important highlight from your daily activity, you can add it manually by taping the activity category and then tapping "Add Data" in the top right corner of your screen.

The Health app help you stay active and healthy by showing you all your health trends and suggesting you more activities. To see all your health trends and detailed information about any of the health categories, tap "Browse" at the bottom of your screen and tap any activity to show details. For example, if you wish to know how much of the cardio activity you've performed throughout a day, week, month, or even year, tap Mobility to see all your data.

ITUNES STORE

iTunes ⭐ is a store for all your favorite music, movies, and TV shows. You can purchase and download all your music shows in the app. Once purchased and downloaded, you can access it anytime on your iPhone.

Open the iTunes Store app and browse by the categories on your screen. Tap Music, Movies, or TV Shows to explore more under each category. In addition to these categories, you can tap "Charts" to see trending content, "Search" to find any specific content of your choice, and tap More for recommendations and suggestions based on your previous purchases.

To purchase in the store, tap the price of any music track, movie, or TV show and proceed with the payment. If you see ↓ instead of the price, it means you have already purchased it and you just have to download it.

Apart from Music, Movies, and TV shows, you can also download and purchase new notification tunes including incoming call ringtones, text tones, and other alert tunes. To buy new tones for your notification, tap "More" and then tap "Tones" to explore all of them. Go to "Search" to find the tone that you are looking for. If it's paid, tap the price to purchase it.

MANAGE & SEE ALL YOUR PURCHASE ON THE ITUNES STORE

In the iTunes Store, tap "More" and then go to "Purchase." You'll see all your purchases made on your iTunes Store on your device. You can also see the information of when and how your account was billed for the purchase, receive an email receipt of your purchase, or report any problem for purchases you've made in previously.

In "Purchase," you'll see all the content that you've purchased so far with your Apple ID in the iTunes store. So, if you wish to download any old purchase, tap ↓ to download the content back to your phone.

MAIL

You can send and receive your emails directly from your iPhone using the Mail app ✉. The iPhone offers different tools in the Mail app to write and send professional & personal emails of any kind. While writing your email in the Mail app, you can attach photos and videos, use different text sizes, fonts, styles, bullet points, and more to create engaging emails.

To set up your Mail app, open the app and then choose which account you want to set up from the given list. For example, if you have a Gmail account that you want to sign in with, tap Google and then enter your login information to set up the Mail app. If you wish to add multiple accounts then go to Settings ⚙ > tap "Mail" > Tap "Accounts" and then choose "Add Account." Choose your option and provide login information to set up your new account in the Mail app.

In the image below are the controls on the mail app to check the inbox for new emails, compose and send new emails to someone, or organize them.

COMPOSE OR REPLY TO YOUR

EMAILS

You can write new emails or respond to your received emails in your Mail app. Open the app, and do the following:

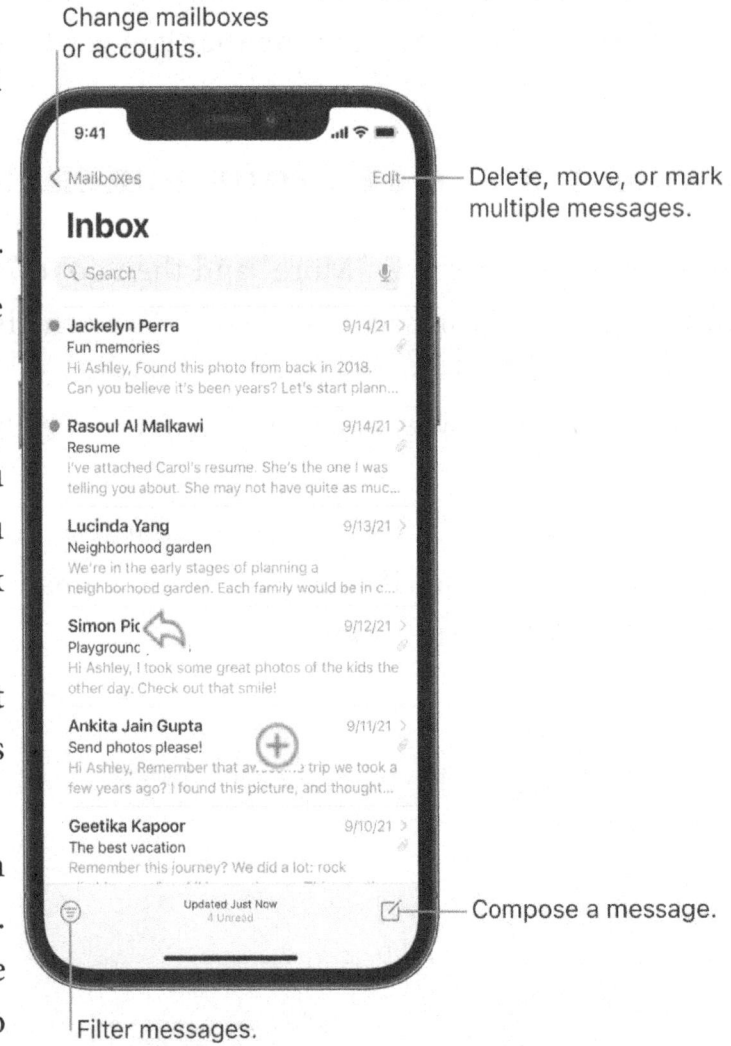

- Tap ✎ to write a new email. If you want to write a reply to an email that you just received, tap the email in your inbox and then tap   to write a reply.

- Type your recipient email address at the top or tap   to add an email address from your contacts.

- Enter any recipients in Cc to whom you want to send a copy of the email. In Bcc you can send copies to multiple recipients without revealing them to other recipients.

- Type your subject and then type your email. Once done writing, tap ⬆ to send your email.

You can change the formatting of text, add bullet points, add attachments, and much more while composing an email to make it more professional or engaging. Tap the place in the email where you want to add attachments or make changes and then tap ‹ in the format bar located right above your keyboard to reveal more options

- Tap 🖼 to add photos or videos from your gallery to your email. Tap any photo or video to insert it into your new email.

- Tap 📷 to take and add new pictures and videos to your email.

- For text formatting and styles, tap Aa and then choose any font, style, or color of your text. You can also add bullet points and numbering lists to your email. To change the formatting of already typed text, select your text and then tap Aa to choose your styles, color, or fonts.

- Tap 📄 to add a PDF or other files and documents. Choose any document from the given location and then tap to insert it into your email. To scan a new document tap and scan the document. After scanning, you can crop the document, add filters, or do other changes before you finally attach it to your email.

- Add drawings to your email by tapping Ⓐ and then start drawing. Tap "Done" and then tap "Insert Drawing" to add it to the email or tap "Save to Files" to save it for later. Tap "Discard Changes" to delete it.

MANAGE YOUR MAILBOXES

Mail app supports multiple inboxes for your emails. It helps the user to organize emails and even multiple accounts using a single app. Your mailboxes are categories and can receive and organize different emails so you can easily read and reply to them.

To manage your mailboxes, tap ‹ on the top-left corner of your screen in the mail app. Once you are on the mailboxes screen, tap "Edit" at the top-right corner of your screen. Tap any of the Inboxes to add it your mailboxes or tap and hold the ≡ to move the mailbox up or below its position in the list. Tap "Done" to finish organizing your mailboxes.

MAPS

Use the Maps app 🗺 to explore the places around you. Maps can help you find directions to your favorite restaurants, malls, and other places in your surrounding. You can find out about new places that you are planning to go to by seeing reviews left by people who have already visited and shared their experiences.

Your iPhone may need your permission to use your location, if you don't allow it you will not be able to use Maps on your phone. To allow the location services, Go to Settings ⚙ > Tap "Privacy" > Tap "Location Services" and turn them on. To allow Maps the location permission, scroll down the list under "Location Services" and then tap Maps. Set the access from the given options there.

You can see the following controls on your Maps screen:

- Tap ◁ to see your current location in the center of your map with north on the top of your screen. ➤ shows your current location without north on the top of your screen. Tap ⬆ to lock north to the top of your screen.

- You can also choose different types of maps used for different kinds of travel. To view and choose other types of maps, tap the button just below your current location button and then choose a map from the options shown on your screen. These types are Exploring 📖 , Driving 🚗 , Public Transport 🚆 and Satellite 🌐 .

- Tap 2D or 3D to change how you view your maps. 3D maps can help you know the floors of buildings and identify any flyovers and bridges on your route.

FIND DIRECTION TO PLACES

To find & get directions to new places, go to the search bar and type the place name e.g. type the name of the gym or restaurant that you want the directions to. If you don't know your surroundings, Maps can even show you different places around you. To explore your surroundings, open Maps 🗺 and tap the search bar. You'll see different categories under the search bar. Type the name of the restaurant, store, or any other place that you want to get the directions to. You can also tap any of the categories in the "Nearby" section to see more options to visit.

By tapping the name of the place you're interested in, the information about the place such as description, address, and contact information will pop up. You can also see reviews left by other people about the place. Tap the "Direction Button" to set a route to your new destination. The app can provide more than one route for your destination and suggest the shortest and fastest possible route. To switch between these routes, tap the alternative route showing on your screen.

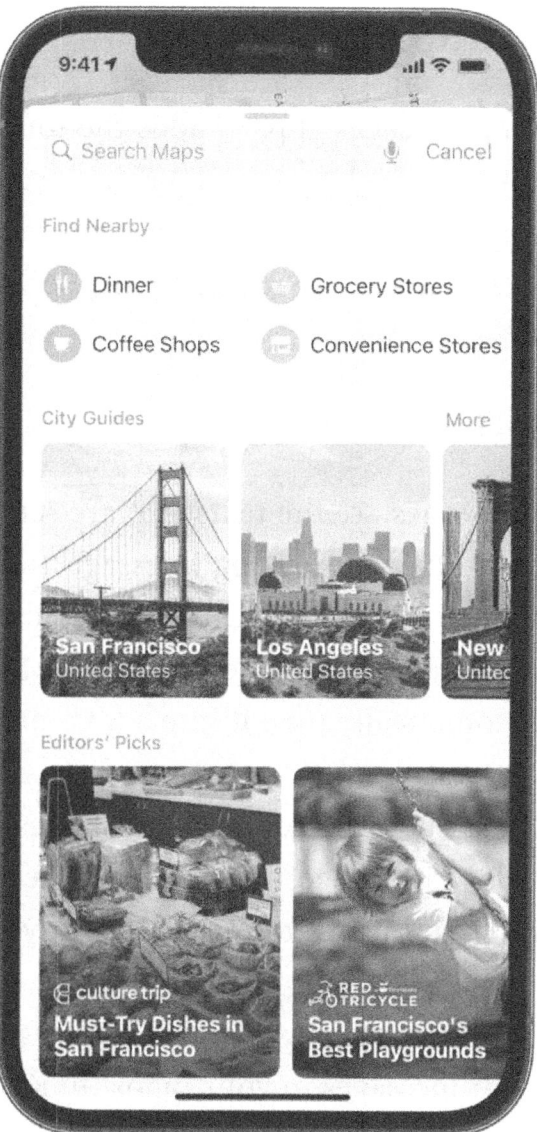

PIN A PLACE

You can drop a pin in Maps to set a route to your destination. A pin helps you mark any location on Maps that you can follow the directions to, or, you can share this location with others.

To pin a location on your Maps:

- Find your destination or place by searching it up or scrolling map around your location.

- Tap and hold the location on your screen to drop a pin.

- After dropping the pin, you can move the pin to change location or make it more precise by zooming in. To add it to your favorites on maps, or tap ••• to reveal more options (including sharing it with your contacts).

BOOK A RIDE TO YOUR DESTINATION

Maps work with different online ride-booking apps so you can book a ride to a destination right from your Maps. Exploring and booking rides can help you plan better and also save you time on your trips too.

To book a ride in Maps, you must download the compatible ride-booking apps (i.e. Uber or Didi) on your iPhone from the App Store. The Maps app has suggestions for you depending on which is the cheapest. Go to Maps and search or tap your destination on the screen, tap "Direction," and then tap 🧍 to book a ride.

MESSAGES

The Messages app ⬭ adds the touch of fun effects, photos and video sharing, to make your conventional texting more enjoyable and productive at the same time. It's supported by Apple Pay so you can send or receive money with your contacts and tt also works with apps like Maps or other third-party location apps to share locations with your friends and family in an instant.

IMESSAGES

iMessages are the texts that are sent from iPhone user to iPhone user. Your message bubbles turn blue when using iMessage and stay green when you text someone who doesn't have an iPhone. iMessage can be sent and received over Wi-Fi connections or cellular connections. If you are sending someone an iMessage and don't have an Internet connection, iPhone will automatically turn it into a text message.

To set up iMessages go to Settings ⚙ > Tap "Messages" and then turn "iMessages" on. Just below iMessage, tap "Send & Receive" to choose whether you want to send and receive messages using your email ID or your phone number.

Your text messages and iMessages are be stored on the iCloud. iPhones keeps the copies of your messages in your inbox on iCloud and updates them when you sign in to a new device.

Go to Settings ⚙ > tap "Your Name" > tap "iCloud" and then scroll down until you see "Messages" and turn it on.

START A CONVERSATION

To start a conversation with your contacts, open the Messages app and then tap ☑ the top-right of your screen. Tap "Edit" to select multiple conversations to delete, or pin any conversation in your Messages app.

Type the contact name that you want to start a conversation with or tap ⊕ to add it from your contact list. Type your message in the message bar and then tap ⬆ to send your message. If it's blue it means that you are sending an iMessage. If it's green, it indicates that you are sending a text message.

You can also start a FaceTime call from your conversation in the Messages app. While you are in conversation with a contact, tap ⬚◁ at the top-right of your conversation and then choose if you want to make an audio or video call.

ADD BUBBLE & SCREEN EFFECTS TO YOUR MESSAGE

You can send messages with effects that apply to your message bubble or message screen. The feature works only when you are sending iMessage from one iPhone to another. You and your recipient both can send and receive these effects. Once you receive a message with effects, it will auto-play the applied effect on the message. Tap "Replay" just below the message to play effects applied to the messages in your conversation.

To apply Bubbles or Screen effects, type your message and then tap & hold the ⬆ button. You'll see different effects that you can choose from. Tap "Bubble" on the top of the screen to show all the effects that you can apply to your message bubble. Tap "Screen" to see effects that can be applied to your message screen.

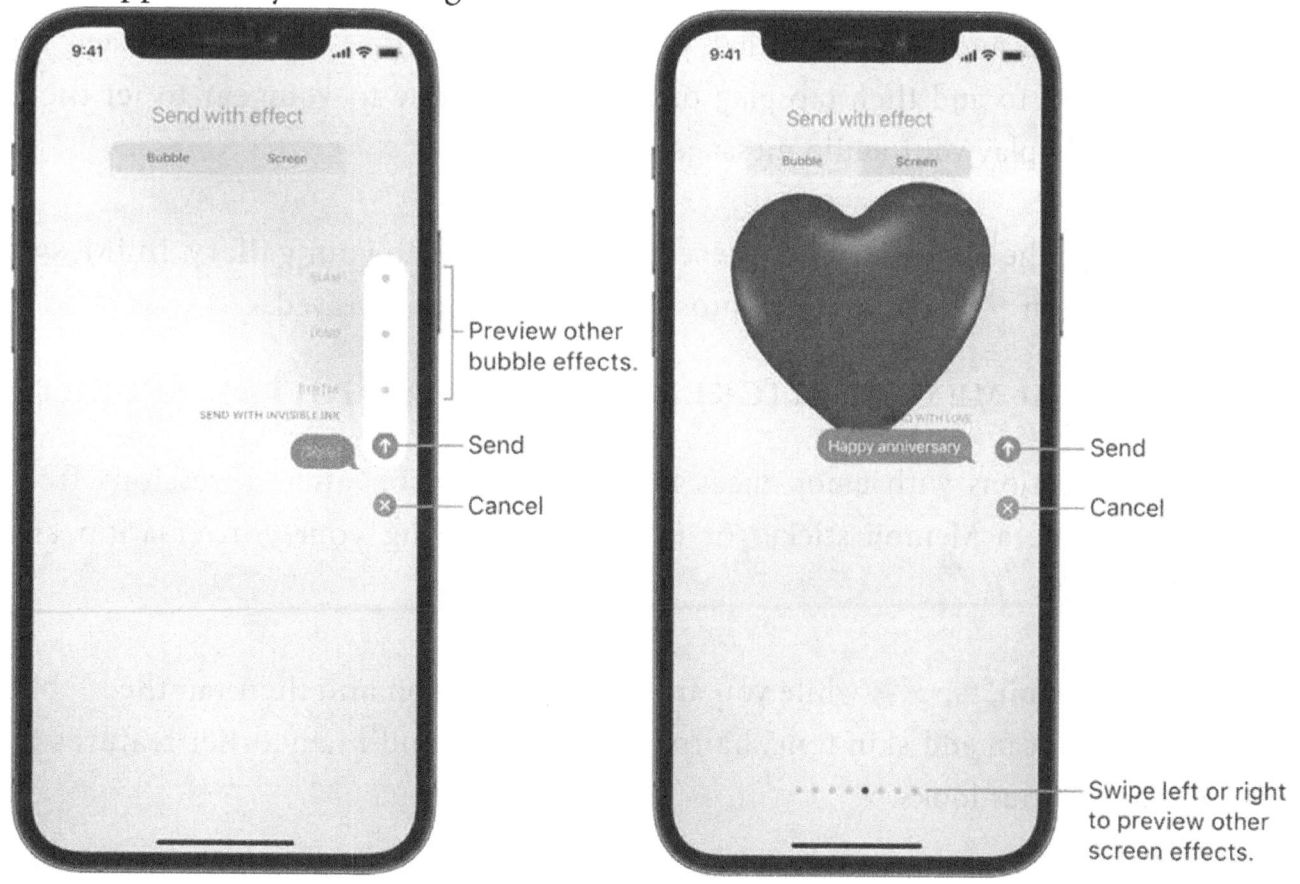

SEND PHOTOS, VIDEOS & AUDIO MESSAGES

iMessages can send and receive photos, videos, and audio messages using an active internet connection.

To send photos, videos, or audio messages to your recipient, tap the bar just above your keyboard:

- Tap 📷 to capture a new photo or video to add it to your conversation. Choose the photo or video mode and then tap the capture button to take a photos or record a video. Tap the send button at the lower-left corner to send or tap "Edit," "Effects," or "Markup" to edit or add filters to your picture and videos before sending.

- Tap 🌸 to add photos or videos from your iPhone gallery. Choose a photo or video and then tap ⬆ to send it to your contact. To edit, add markups or effects to your photo or video, tap it again.

- Tap 🔘 to record your audio message for your recipient. After you've recorded your message, you can tap ▶ to listen to your audio message before sending it. If your message is ready to send then tap ⬆ . If you want to record it again then tap ⊗ and record it again.

To listen to an audio message that you've received, either tap the message that you want to listen to and then tap play or raise your phone to your ear to let the iPhone automatically play your audio message.

You can save the photos & videos received in iMessage to your gallery. In iMessage, tap the save button ⬇ next to the photos or videos sent or received.

CREATE & SEND MEMOJI STICKERS, VIDEOS & DIGITAL EFFECTS

Memojis are animations with emoji faces but with live-action and expressions from your face. You can create a Memoji sticker or even videos during your conversation and then instantly send them.

To create your Memoji, tap 🐵 while you are in a conversation and then tap the ⊕ button to create memoji. You can add skin tone, hairstyle, facial hair and many other features to make the memoji match your looks.

Tap "Done" on the top-right corner of your screen to add your memoji to your collections. Your created memoji are added to collections and remain available to use in other conversations too. To send memoji stickers to another conversation, tap 😊 and then tap memoji that you want to send.

To record a live video of yourself with memoji, tap 😊 just above your keyboard. Choose the character that you want to use as your face in the video and then tap ⚪ to record your message with your facial expressions. Tap ⬆ to send the recorded memoji as your face or tap 🗑 to cancel and record again.

Tap 🔘 to create and send digital stickers. Here you can create different shapes and effects to send in your chat. On the right side of your digital stickers screen, you can choose the color of your sticker, and on the right side, tap the video button to add these effects to your newly captured photos or videos.

To use built-in shapes and effects, use the following gestures to send them in your conversation:

• Tap with one finger to create a color burst on your screen.

• Tap & hold with one finger to create a fireball of your selected color.

• Tap with two fingers to send a kiss effect.

• Tap and hold with three fingers to send a heart, drag your three fingers down to when the heart appears on your screen to send a heartbreak digital effects.

You can also draw your own unique shapes on the screen and send them.

MUSIC

Apple Music 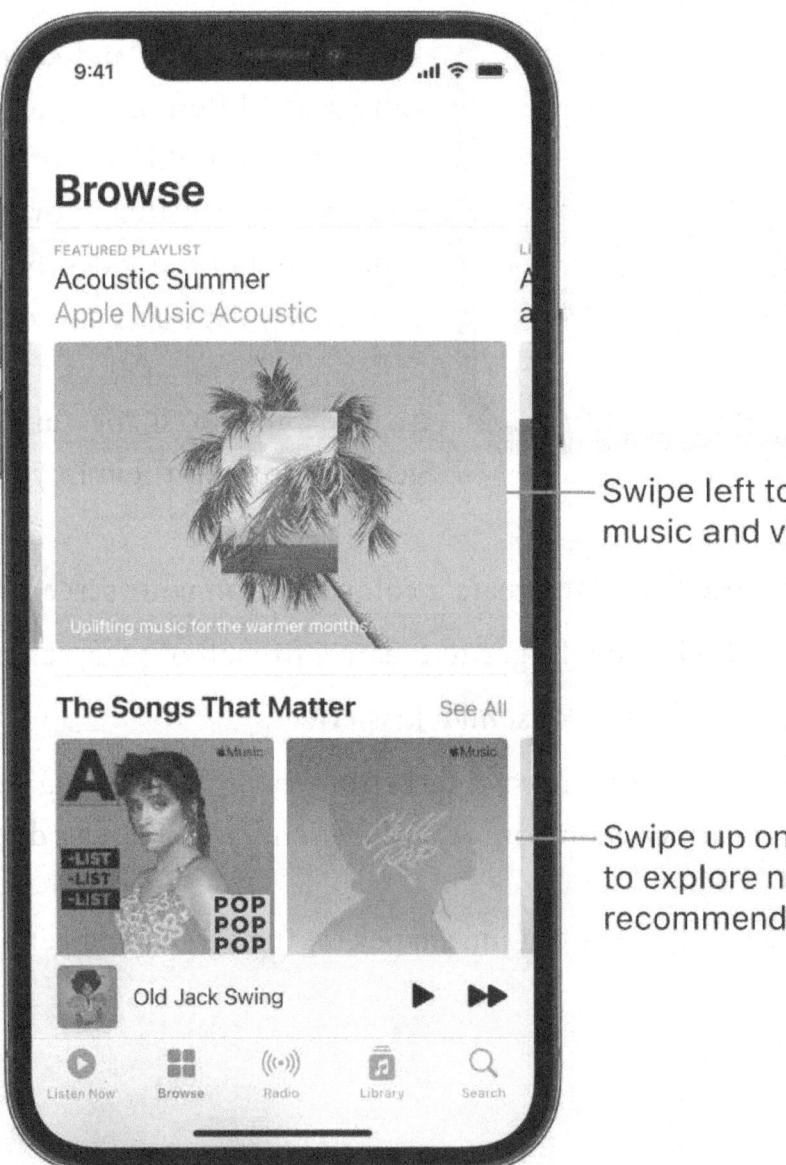 offers the latest songs from artists across the world. You can stream music online, download it to your iPhone or listen to different radios in the Music app. Millions of ad-free songs are just a few clicks away from you.

SUBSCRIBE TO APPLE MUSIC

To enjoy your favorite music on your iPhone, you need an active subscription to Apple Music. Open your Music app to subscribe to Apple Music. You can see the subscription plans and instructions when you open your Music app for the first time on your iPhone. Go to Setting > tap "Music" and then tap subscriptions to see the plans and subscribe.

You can also download your music directly from the iTunes Store and listen to it in the Music app. Go to the iTunes Store and search for your favorite music. You can buy your music, stream it or download it to your device and listen to it offline.

To manage your Apple Music subscription, Go to the Music app > tap "Your Profile" at the top-right corner of your screen > tap "Manage Subscriptions" to change or cancel your Apple Music plan.

After subscribing, you are set to explore your favorite music. Tap "Browse" at the bottom of your screen in the Music app to find and download new music genres.

Swipe left to see featured music and videos.

Swipe up on the screen to explore new and recommended music.

212

CONTROLS ON YOUR MUSIC APP

To listen to your purchased and downloaded music on your iPhone, tap "Library" from the bar at bottom of your screen.

In the library, tap any category to find a song or artist from music stored on your iPhone. You can also create your own personalized playlists and queues to play music to your moods.

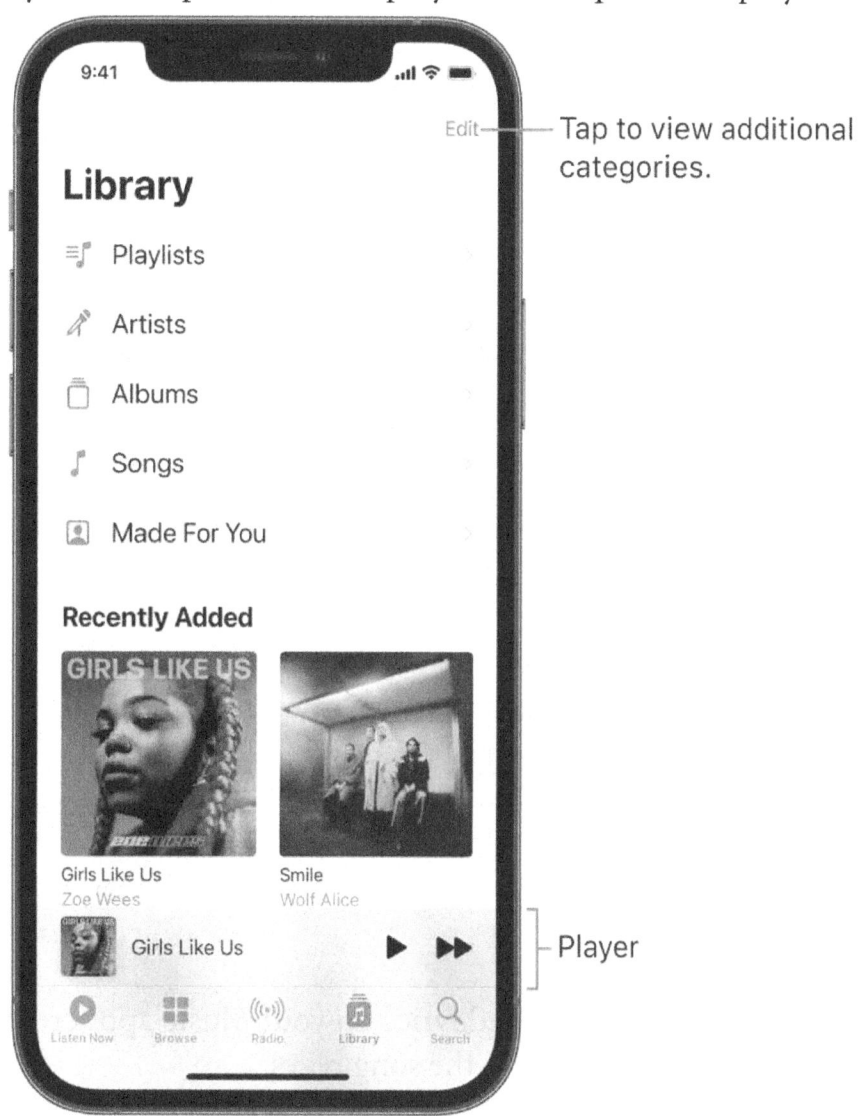

Tap any of the songs in your music library and then use the following controlson the next page in your Music app:

 Tap it to play the recent song on your player.

 Pause the music that you are listening to.

 Tap once to play the next song on the playlist or queue. Tap and hold to fast-forward your current song.

 Tap once to return to the current song's beginning then tap again to play previous song. Tap and hold to rewind a song.

 While in a queue, tap it once to repeat the song at the end of the queue and tap it again to repeat a single track.

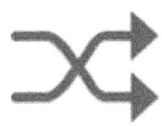 Open queue and then tap the shuffle button to let the song play in a random order in your player.

 Tap it to minimize your player in the Music app.

 It shows time-synced lyrics on your Music app screen as the song plays.

 Listen and stream music on Bluetooth & AirPlay devices connected to your phone.

 Tap the button to see and organize songs in the queue.

To control volume and duration for your music manually, you can use the sliders on the screen. You can also choose how your music sound on your iPhone's speakers. iPhone gives you a different option to make your music sound the best. Go to Settings 🌐 > tap "Music" and then choose "EQ." Change it to your what best suits your preferred music.

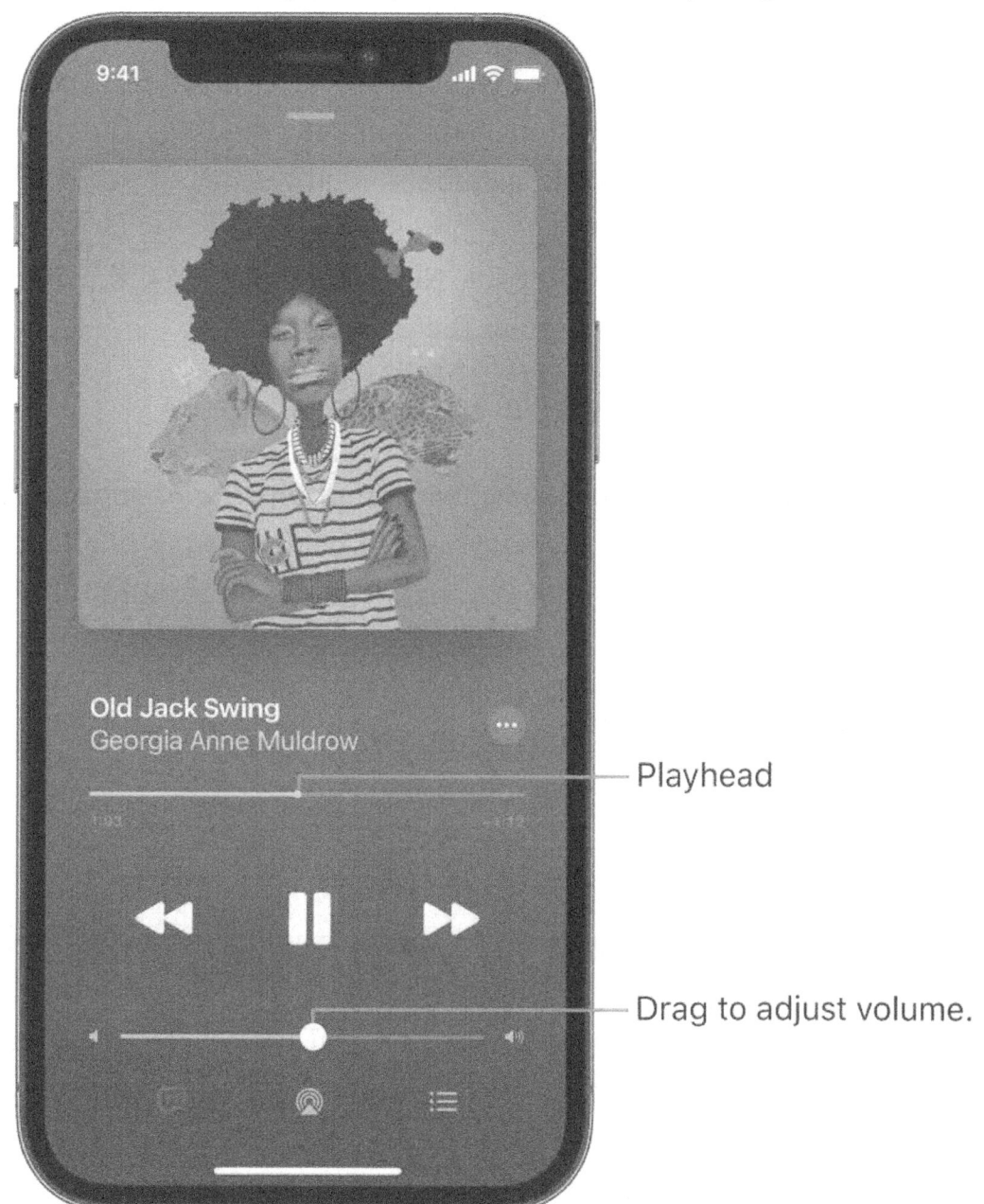

LISTEN TO RADIO ON MUSIC APP

Music app offers to play different radio stations without a subscription. You can listen to your local radio frequency or any of your favorite stations from your iPhone.

Go to the Music app and then tap "Radio" from the bar. Choose a station or go to the search bar to type the name or frequency of the station that you want to hear. Tap your desired station to play on your iPhone.

NEWS

The News app N gets all the updates and stories on the topics that you follow from the world's most popular and credible sources. It collects and curates stories both in your app and on your home screen using the widget to keep you updated on events and topics that interest you the most. The app makes suggestions based on your reading. The more you read the better it understands and suggests interesting content.

You can even subscribe to Apple News+ in your News app to access the most popular magazines, newspapers, and top publishers around the world.

GET STARTED & PERSONALIZE YOUR NEWSFEED

Open the News app to get started. All your news stories from topics and sources will appear on your app's screen. To follow your favorite sources and channels, tap "Following" at the bottom of the screen and then tap ⊕ in front of the channel that you want to follow.

If you want to discover new channels or search for any specific channel, go to the "Discover" section, look for any channel that interests you, and then tap ⊕ to follow the channel. Tap "Search" if you want to find a channel and then follow it.

To unfollow any topic, channel, or publication, go to "Following" and then swipe left on the topic, channel, or publication name that you want to unfollow and then tap "Unfollow."

To manage notifications for the topics and channels that you follow, go to Settings ⚙ tap "News," then tap "Restrict Stories in Today" and confirm the choices to manage notifications about stories.

APPLE NEWS+

Apple News+ offers premium stories and content in the News app. Here you can access premium publishers, magazines, and news stories from paid sources on different topics.

To subscribe to Apple News+, open the News app and then tap any magazine or paid channel that you want to subscribe to. Tap the "Subscription" button showing in that magazine, channel, or publication. Follow the on-screen instructions to subscribe to your selected publisher or magazine. With Apple News+ you download your stories on your iPhone to read them later.

To cancel your subscription, go to "Following" and then swipe to the bottom. Tap "Subscription" and then tap and follow the on-screen instruction to cancel any subscription in your Apple News+.

The News app also offers audio news that you can listen to on the go. It helps you stay updated if you are short on time for reading your stories and headlines. Tap ⬤ and then browse any story that you want to hear. Tap the story that you want to hear, and the app will start to play the story. Use the audio control in the to control the volume, speed, and other features related to your audio stories being played on your iPhone.

NOTES

From noting down your grocery list to keeping your private information safe, the 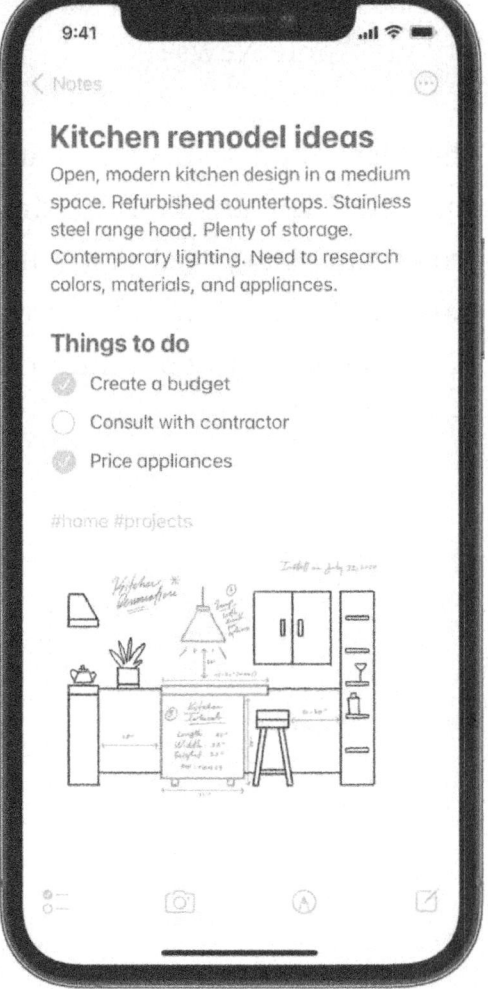 Notes app offers a variety of ways to note down your information and also keep it safe and updated with the help of your iCloud.

`CREATE NEW NOTES

To create a new note in the app, open the Notes, tap [icon] at the bottom of your screen and type your new notes. To do formatting, styling, or adding attachments, do the following:

- Tap [icon] to add tables in your notes. Touch any cell to start writing content in it. To delete or add columns and rows in your table, tap the selection handle to add or delete columns and rows. To delete the whole table, tap any cell and then tap to reveal more options. Here you can copy, delete, share or convert the table into simple text.

- Tap [icon] to add a checklist to record and organize your items in notes. You can add or remove items in the list and mark them checked. After checking the items on the list, you can sort them manually or automatically. To automatically sort the checked items in your list, go to Settings [icon] > Tap "Notes," then tap "Sort Checked Items" and turn on "Automatically."

- Tap Aa to add titles, headings, subheadings, or other formatting including bullet points and styling features in your notes. To format your already typed text, select the text and then tap Aa to do the formatting you want.

- Tap [icon] and then choose whether you want to take a new photo, choose one from the gallery or scan a document to add. You can scan and add text right from a document in your notes app. Tap [icon] and then bring the text to the camera. Tap [icon] when it appears on the camera screen to add text to your notes.

- Tap [icon] to draw and add sketches, shapes, or other drawings to your notes. On the drawing screen, you can tap and use different tools such as colors, markers, pencils, and rulers to make your drawing more precise and eye-catching.

Once you have finished, tap "Done" at the top-right corner to save the notes. You can also lock your private notes to make them more secure. While editing the note, tap ⋯ and then tap lock. The iPhone may ask you to set the password for notes. Go to Settings 🌐 Tap "Notes" and then tap "Password" to set a new password for your private notes.

ORGANIZE YOUR NOTES USING TAGS & SMART FOLDERS

The Notes app can create and organize your notes using folders, tags, and quick search options to help you organize and find them within a few taps.

Open the Notes and tap 📁 at the bottom-left corner under the folder list and then choose between "New Folder" or "New Smart Folder." A smart folder recognizes the tags you type during your notes and automatically adds them to your smart folder created for the tag.

To add a tag to your notes, simply type "#" and then type your tags (such as work, personal, etc.) without the space between word and "#." The notes app will turn it yellow and add it to the Tags section under the folders list. To delete or edit any tag, go to the notes and tap the tag to remove it or retype it to a new one.

Tap "Edit" at the top-right corner to sort your folder in your preferred way.

USE NOTES WITH ICLOUD

To keep your notes backed up and synced across multiple IOS devices, go to Settings 🌐 > Tap "Your Name" > Tap "iCloud," and then turn on the notes.

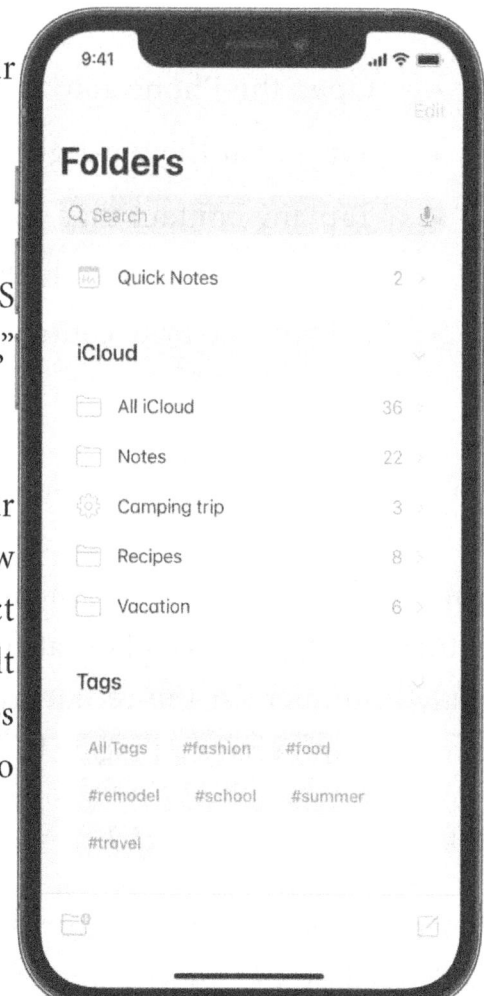

You have the option to use different accounts, such as your Google account, to back up your notes. To do this, follow these steps: Go to Settings 🌐 , tap on "Notes," then select "Accounts." Choose your preferred account as the default option for storing your notes. If you want to save your notes exclusively on your iPhone without uploading them to iCloud, enable the "On My iPhone" account.

219

PHONE

Phone app 📞 manages your call logs, voicemails, contacts, and allows you to make a call. To call a contact from your phone book use the dialer in the Phone app. You can also save a new number to contacts directly from your dialer.

MAKE A CALL OR SAVE THE CONTACT

- Open the Phone app. Tap "Keypad" from the bar at bottom of your screen.

- Dial the number that you want to call and then tap 📞 button to make a call.

- Tap ⊗ to erase the number from your screen if you've made any mistakes.

- If you want to save the phone number to your contact, tap "Add Number" which appears just below the phone number when you dial it.

- Tap 📞 to end the call.

To make a call or message a contact quicky from your phone app, add them to your favorite list. To do that:

- Open the Phone app 📞 and tap Favorites at the bottom left corner of your screen.

- Tap + at the top-right corner. It will open your contact list.

- Tap any contact that you want to add to your favorites. Choose if you want to add a shortcut for a message, an audio call, or a video call.

- All your favorite contacts will be added to the list in "Favorites" which you can access quickly in the Phone app.

To call back contacts or redial the last number, go to the Phone app, tap "Recent" from the bar at bottom of the screen and then tap the number that you want to redial. You can see your call log for all your incoming and outgoing calls with time and dates. To see more information such as call duration or other options, tap ⓘ in front of your contact or recently dialed number. In the recent call log, tap "Edit" at the top-right corner to remove a single contact from your call log or to clear the entire log.

RECEIVING A CALL

For an incoming call on your iPhone, you can receive, decline, or silence it. If your phone is locked, slide the answer button to answer the call or press the side button or volume up or low button once to silence it. To decline the call while your phone is locked, press the side button twice.

If your phone is unlocked, the incoming call will show in one of two ways. If you're on the home screen you'll see the call screen with all the options. If you're in another app, your call will show in the banner form at top of your screen.

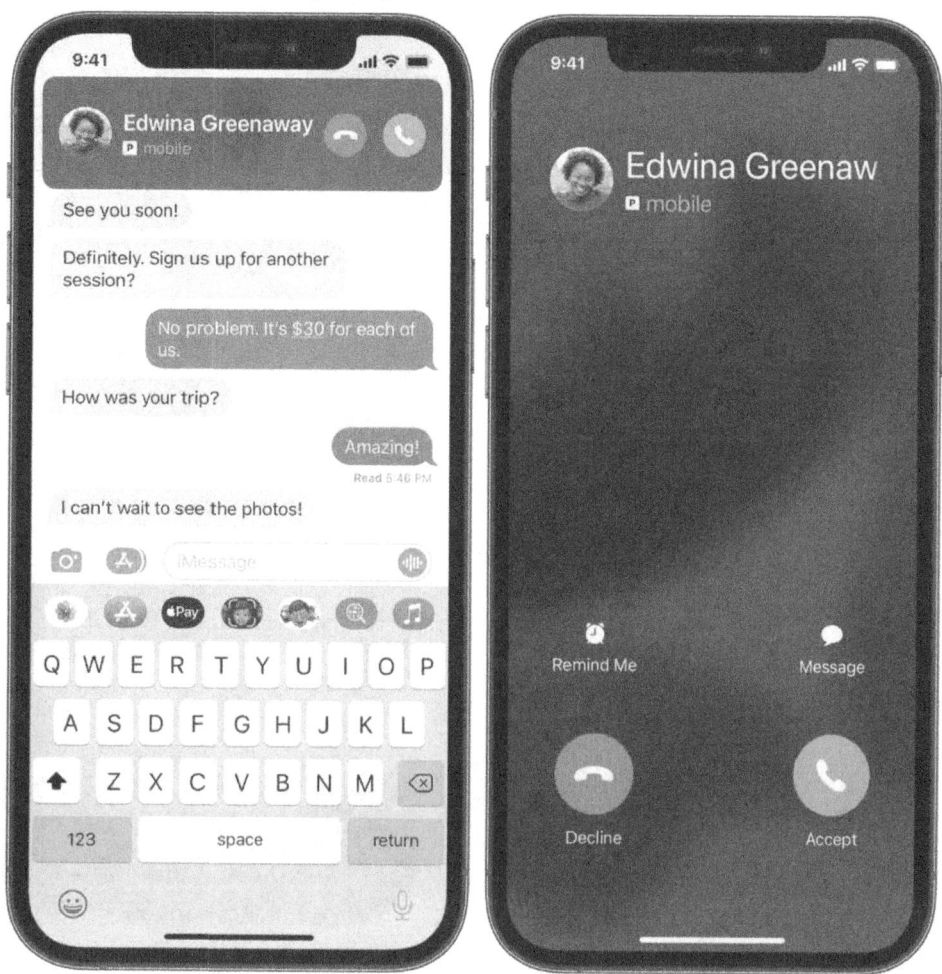

Tap or to receive to decline the call. On the call screen tap "Message" to send a message and decline the call at the same time. Tap "Remind Me" to set a reminder for a callback. Pressing any of the two will decline the call.

While on the call, you can use different controls to do the following:

Tap "Mute" to turn your mic off during the call. Your caller won't be able to hear your voice.

Tap "speaker," to choose how you want to hear your call i.e. from an earpiece, speaker, or any other Bluetooth accessories connected to your phone.

Tap "add call" and then dial any number to make a conference call **isa**or tap "FaceTime" to convert your audio call into FaceTime audio or video call

Tap "contacts" to add a person from your contacts in a conference call.

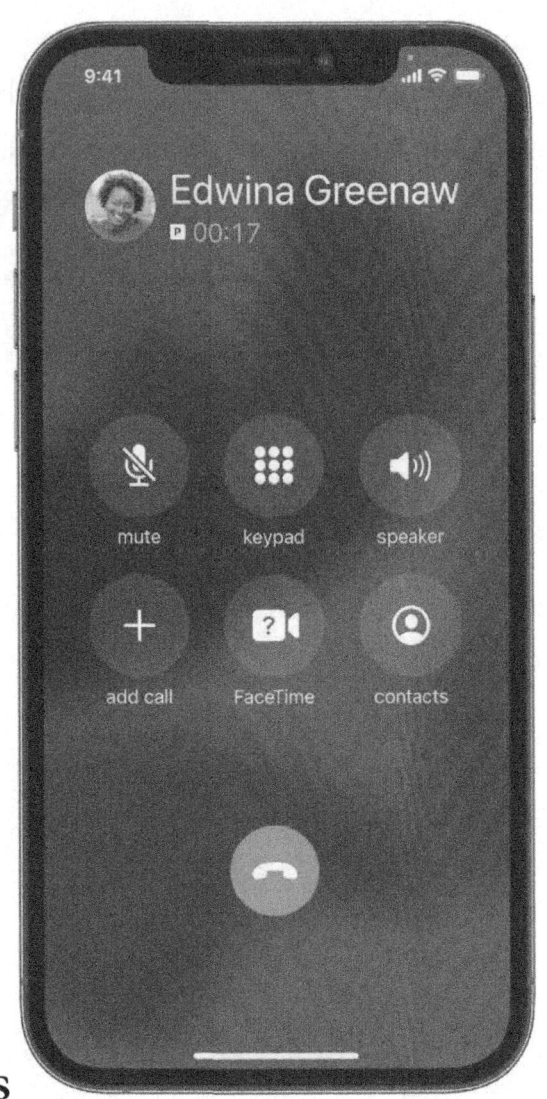

SET UP OR CHECK YOUR VOICEMAILS

Open the Phone app and tap "Voicemail" from the bar at the bottom. You'll be asked to set up your "Voicemail" the first time you open the voicemail section. Follow the instructions to set up your voicemail and password.

After finishing the setup, your voicemail will appear in the Phone app under "Voicemail." To listen to your voicemail, go to the Phone app and tap "Voicemail," tap ▶ to play your voicemail, or tap ⬆ or 🗑 to share or delete any of your voicemail messages.

PHOTOS

The Photos app  keeps all your captured photos and videos organized in one place. In the app you can view, share or edit your photos and videos in simple ways.

VIEW YOUR PHOTOS & VIDEOS

The Photos app views your photos and videos by organizing them in different sections. You can view and switch between these sections by using the navigation bar at the bottom of your screen.

Tap to navigate Photos.

Library – Keeps your photos organized by days, months, and years. Tap "All Photos" to view every photo on your iPhone.

For You – Featured photos from your library as well as photos shared with you via iCloud and iMessage. You can also see sharing suggestions where you can easily send and receive photos with friends & family members using iCloud.

Albums – View and organize your photos and videos using different albums. You can create and share albums with other users using iCloud. Go to albums and tap ╋ to add new albums.

Search – Use the search bar to find a photo using keywords like places, people, dates, or any other information related to your photos.

Tap any photo to open it. To zoom in and out either use your fingers to pinch out or double-tap to zoom in and out of your photo. While viewing an individual photo, use the sliding bar at the bottom of your screen to slide between other photos.

Swipe to browse through your photos.

SHARE, EDIT, OR DELETE YOUR PHOTOS

To go back to the previous view of the photo library, tap ⟨ or tap and drag your opened photo down. Tap "Edit" to add filters, adjust color, or do any other editing on your photos.

Tap ⬆ to see sharing and other options including the "Hide" option. From the share sheet, tap "Hide" to remove the photo from the list and add it to the hidden album. To view hidden photos, tap "Album," scroll down to the bottom, and tap "Hidden" to view all your hidden photos.

Tap ⓘ to view additional information about your photo including what time the photo was taken, the location it was taken, people in photos, camera lens information, and file size.

To add photos to your "Favorite" album so you can easily find and see them, tap the "Heart" on the bottom. To view your favorite photos, go to albums and tap the "Favorite" album. All your favorite photos will appear here.

Tap 🗑 to delete the photo. Your deleted photos will be moved to "Recently Deleted" under your Albums. Your photos will stay in "Recently Deleted" for 30 days before they'll be permanently removed from your iPhone. To recover any deleted photos, go to "Recently Deleted" > tap "Select" and then select the photo and videos that you want to recover. Choose whether to recover your photos or videos or delete them permanently from your phone.

USE PHOTOS WITH ICLOUD

Turn on the iCloud photo to back up, share, and sync your photos across multiple IOS devices. You can access your photos and videos from any device signed in with your Apple ID.

Go to Settings ⚙ > Tap "Your Name" and then tap iCloud > Turn on "iCloud Photos." Choose "Optimize iPhone Storage" to keep the original quality and resolution of photos and videos on the iCloud and a low-quality copy on your iPhone gallery to help you save space on your phone. Alternatively tap "Download and Keep Originals" to keep the original quality and resolution of your photos and videos both on the iPhone and iCloud.
Turn on "My Photo Stream" & "Shared Album" to upload and stream your photos across all your IOS devices or with other people. You can see the shared albums and stream photos in "Albums" on your Photos app 🌸 .

PODCAST

Discover your favorite podcasts from different categories on the Apple Podcast app 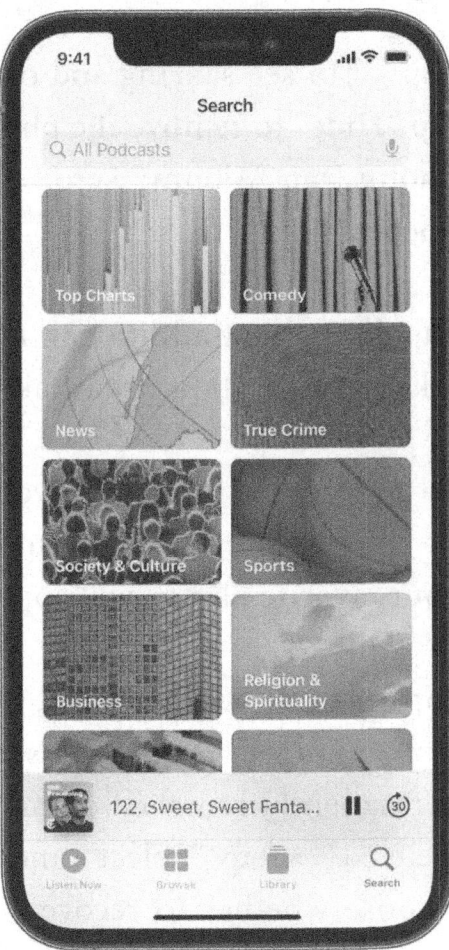. Use the Podcast app to follow audio shows, download new episodes, and listen to them on the go.

FIND & FOLLOW SHOWS ON PODCAST

To look for new shows to follow, open the Podcast app and tap "Browse" at bottom of your screen to see suggestions of trending and top chart shows in the podcast. To find shows related to different categories such as sports, science, technology, or other topics, tap the "Search" button at bottom of your screen.

Tap any of the categories to see more related shows and then tap the show that you want to follow. Use the search bar to find any specific shows by name.

- Tap the show and then tap ➕ to follow the show.

- Tap ⬤⬤⬤ to control notifications, downloads, and other options related to your podcast. If you would like to download a show, tap ⬤⬤⬤ and then tap "Settings," scroll to the bottom and turn "Automatic Download" on.

- To manage notifications for all the shows that you follow on the Podcast, tap 👤 and then tap "Notification." Turn notifications on or off for shows that you follow.

LISTEN & ORGANIZE YOUR SHOWS

Tap "Library" to listen and organize all the shows that you follow on your podcast app. In the Library section tap any of the following:

- Tap "Shows" to see all your followed podcast shows.

- "Saved" is where your all saved episodes from different shows will appear. To save any episode of the show, tap  to save an episode from any show.

- "Downloaded" will keep the downloaded episodes of your show so you can listen to them later.

- To see the newest episodes from the shows, tap "Latest Episodes."

Tap "Listen Now" to see and play a podcast that you were listening to previously or to see recently played episodes from all your shows.

Use the controls on the podcast player to control your listening. You can play/pause, forward/rewind, control volume and speed at which you listen to your podcast, or listen to your podcast using connected Bluetooth devices. Tap ••• to see more options such as download or what to play next.

REMINDERS

Use the Reminder app 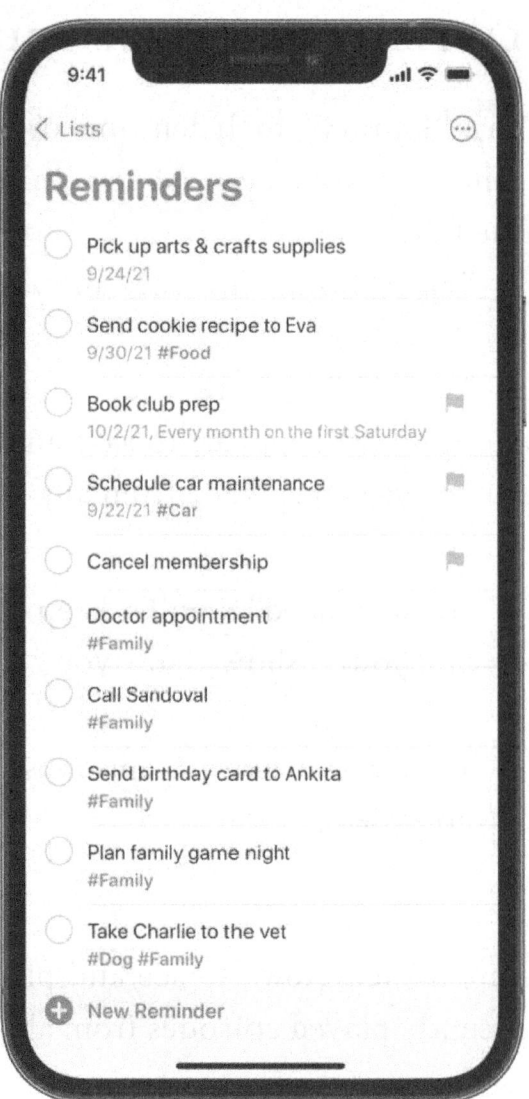 to create reminders for tasks or to-do lists to help you stay productive and attentive to what's most important. You can create reminders with time, location or even add attachments for your tasks or to-do lists.

ADD REMINDERS

Open the reminders app and tap "Add list" to start a new list of reminders. Name the list such as work or grocery and begin creating tasks or to-do lists. Tap your newly created list then tap "New Reminder" to add a new reminder to your list.

To directly add a new reminder, tap "New Reminder" on the bottom-left corner of your screen in your Reminder app .

A new reminder will appear when you tap "New Reminder," type the reminder text and use the bar just above the keyboard to add additional details and alerts to your reminder:

- Tap ⊞ to set a date and time for your reminder.
- Tap ◁ to add a location for your reminder to alert you about your task. When the iPhone enters your input location, the Reminder app will remind you about your added task or to-do list.
- Tap ⚑ to flag an important reminder so you can easily find the important ones from your list.
- Tap # to add tags to your reminder.
- Tap ⟐ to add photos from the library or take a new one. Choose "Scan a Document" to instantly scan and attach any important documents to your reminder.

MARK COMPLETE, EDIT, OR DELETE YOUR REMINDERS

To update information or edit times of your reminder, tap the reminder from your list and then tap ⓘ and do the following:

- Add URL's & Notes to your reminder.

- Add subtasks to help you remember smaller tasks as well.

- Set priorities by choosing from high, medium, or low. It will help you prioritize your tasks especially when you have a long list.

- Tap "List" to move the reminder from one list to another.

You can update other information such as time, date, or location for your reminder too.

To mark a task as completed, go back to your list and tap the empty circle next to your reminder. It will turn blue indicating that the task has been completed. Reminders that are marked completed will be hidden from your list. To see all the completed tasks from your list, tap ⋯ at the top-right corner of the screen and then tap "Show Completed." Tap "Clear" to delete all the completed tasks.

You can also delete reminders from your list. Go to your reminder list, tap and swipe left on the reminder that you wish to delete, and then tap the "Delete" button to remove it from the list.

SAFARI

The Safari app  is the default browser on iPhones. You can visit websites, open and preview shared links, fill out forms and more. Safari also works with iCloud to sync your webpages and visit history across all your devices.

To visit a website or search a keyword on Safari, open the app and type your website or keyword in the search bar.

To control webpages and manage tabs on Safari, use the following controls:

Add or Remove Tabs: If you have multiple web pages opened on different tabs, tap to see and manage all your opened webpages and tabs.

Enter a web address or search term, or quickly access your Favorites.

• Tap and slide the tabs to the left of the screen to delete it or tap ╋ at the bottom-left corner to add new ones.

• To open a Private Tab, tap ⬜ and then tap ⌄ at the bottom. Tap "Private" to open the private tab. A private tab does not record your web activity including your logins, passwords, and history

Share or Save A Webpage: Tap ⬆ to share the link with your contacts, apps or do the following.

230

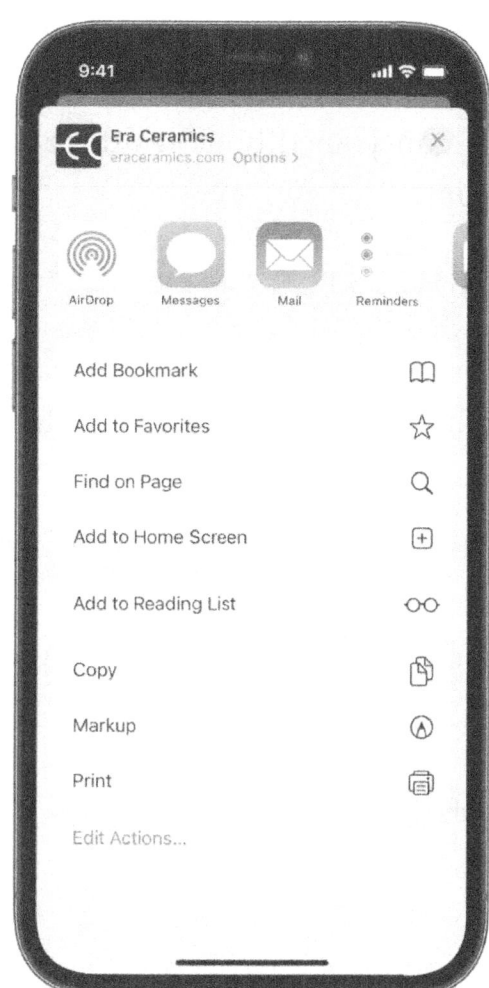

Add Bookmark or Favorite a link to save & quickly access them quickly from your Safari start page.

Tap "Find on Page" to search any keyword on a webpage.

To add webpage shortcut directly to your home screen, tap "Add to Home Screen". The link will appear on your home screen, place it anywhere with your apps for quick access.

Create your own reading list to add web pages. You can see your reading list on the Safari start page.

Manage Your History, Reading List & Favorites: Tap and choose any one of the three:
History – Keeps track of all web pages that you visited. Safari shows your browser history sorted by time.
Reading List – You can save any article or webpage to the reading list and then access it later in Safari. Reading list can save and download your web pages for you to read or see content offline.
Favorite – All the web pages added to your favorites will appear here.
Web Pages Layout & Reading Mode: To change the web page layout including the position of the search bar, tap AA and do the following:
Change the size of the web page that you are visiting
Move the search bar to top or bottom or Go to Settings ⚙ > Tap "Safari" and choose tabs, now select "Tab Bar" or "Single Tab"
Open the web page reading mode to remove any distractions when you are reading blogs or long articles
You can see other options such as website settings, toolbar options, and many others.

STOCKS

Keep an eye on market activities using your Stocks app on your iPhone. Add stocks to your watchlist and get stats, charts, and news at your fingertips.

ADD OR REMOVE COMPANIES TO YOUR WATCHLIST

You can instantly view changes in companies' stock prices, increase or decrease in percentages, and their market values. To add stocks, funds, or any index to your watchlist:

- Open the Stocks app and go to the search bar. Enter the companies stock name, symbol, fund, or index and tap search.

- Tap your desired stock from the search result and then tap "Add" or "Add to Watchlist."

If you want to remove any company or stock from your watch list:

- Go to the Stocks app and open your watchlist.

- Swipe the stock to the left of your screen and then tap to remove it from the watchlist, or go to your watchlist, tap and then tap next to the stock that you want to remove, tap remove the stock

- To rearrange your watchlist, tap > tap "Edit," and then tap & hold to move the stock to a new position.

VIEW STOCK ACTIVITY FROM YOUR WATCHLIST

To see data of the stock added to your watchlist, open your watchlist and tap the stock that you to pull up the charts, performance and news.

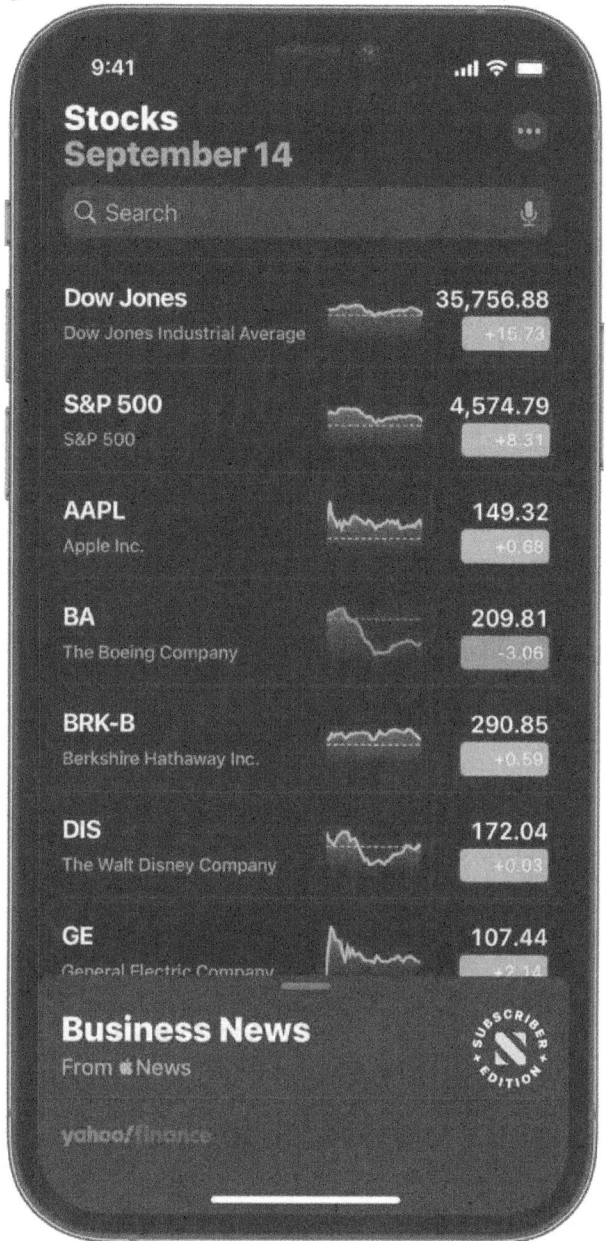

The Stock app provides extensive data on how the stock is performing aided with interactive charts that offer performance trends for the specific stocks. To see the stock performance data on the chart with respect to date and time, do the following:

- Tap and hold with one finger at any point on the chart to see the performance of the stock at a certain time.
- Tap and hold with two fingers at any point on the chart to see the value of the stock at a given time.

To see additional data such as highs and lows, Beta, and EPS, swipe the data showing just below the charts.

READ & HEAR NEWS STORIES ABOUT YOUR STOCKS

Stocks work with the integration of Apple News to bring you news about the companies added to your watchlist. You can read stories about the company's activities or recent events which help you better understand and predict the upcoming trends of the market.

To read stories about your stock in Apple News, go to the watchlist and tap your desired stock. Scroll to the bottom and you'll see all the stories related to the company or stock that you added.

TIPS

The Tips app 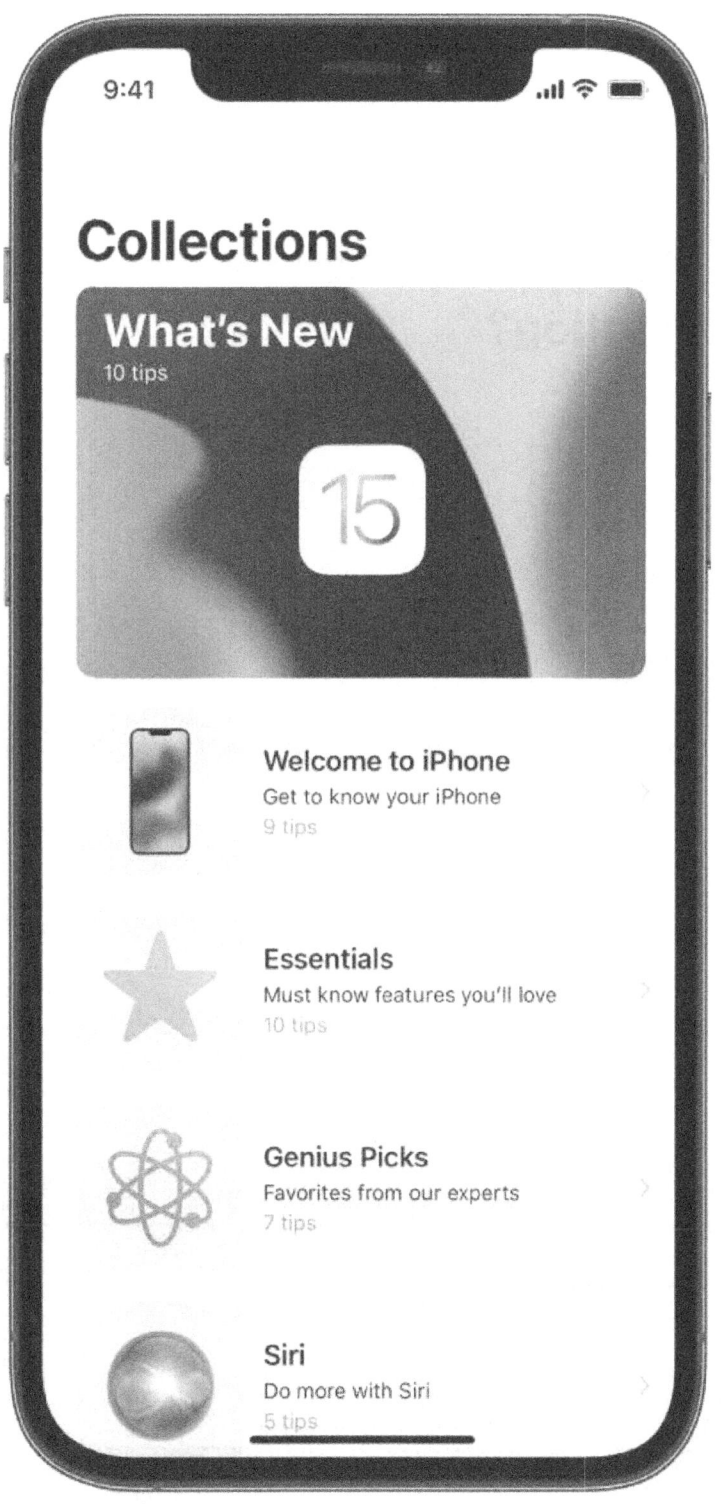 gives you a variety of tips on how to use your iPhone more easily using gestures and shortcuts. Tips about different apps and gestures are sorted into categories. Tap any of the categories to see different tips and gestures instructions.

The Tips app is constantly adding newer tips. To get the notification every time a new tip arrives, Go to Settings > Tap "Notification > Choose "Tips" from the list and then choose the options on how you want to receive the notification from the app.

TRANSLATE

The Translate app  help users communicate in different languages using their iPhone. You can translate both text and voice while talking to someone in another language or use your camera to detect and translate the text you see.

TRANSLATE TEXT & VOICE TO DIFFERENT LANGUAGE

Open the Translate app and tap the language names you want your text and voice to be translated in. To translate the text, tap "Enter text" and then tap "go" on your keyboard.

If you want to translate your voice, then tap  and speak into the mic. The translate app will convert your phrase or words into text and show the translation on your screen.

You can do the following with your translation:

- Play an audio translation of your text. To do so, tap ▶
- Add the most used translations to favorites for quick easy access later on. Tap ☆ to do so.
- Find out the meaning and definition of a single word. Tap 📖 and then tap the word.

TRANSLATE IN CONVERSATION MODE

In "Conversation Mode," the translate app shows all translations, both from text or speech, in conversation bubbles. Both parties can listen or read the translated text and audio and see the whole conversation on the screen.

Tap "Conversation" from the bar at the bottom of your screen to start a conversation. Set the two languages that you want the translation in. Once it's set, tap   and speak in one of the languages. Translate will detect your language and automatically translate it into the other one. You can use additional controls in conversation mode for better communication:

- Tap 🔲 to do conversation in "Side-by-Side" or "Face-to-Face" mode. If the person is sitting next to you, choose "Face-to-Face" mode so you can both use different speech buttons   to speak without having to disrupt the conversation.
- Tap ••• and then enable the following options:
  - Tap "Auto Translation" to let the Translate app

237

automatically detect and listen to which person is speaking.

- Enable "Detect Language" to automatically find the language of the speaker if you do not know it already.

- Turn on "Play Translation" so your iPhone can play the translated language automatically to listeners.

You can use the Translate app without the internet by downloading the language to your iPhone. Go to Settings ⚙ > tap "Translate" > tap "Downloaded Language" and then tap ⊙ next to the language you want to use for the offline mode.

TRANSLATE IN-APP, PHOTOS TEXT, OR USE CAMERA

Translate also works with other apps to do in-app translations of any text. While using another app:

- Select the text that you want to translate and then tap "Translate."

- If you don't see "Translate," tap ▶ to see more options related to your selected text, and then tap "Translate."

For in-app translations of the text, you can replace the original text with translated text, copy the translation, change language, add translation to favorites to access later, or open the translation of the text in the translate app.

To translate text in photos:

- Open the photo in your photo library.

- If the photo has text in it, the iPhone will show a lens icon 📝 on it. Tap it.

- Select the text in the photo and then tap "Translate."

You can translate text by bringing it directly to your camera app:

- Open the camera app and bring the text in your camera frame.

- The iPhone will show 📝 on your screen when it detects the text.

- Select the text and then tap "Translate."

APPLE TV

Apple TV  is a streaming service from Apple. You can watch TV shows, movies, sports and other streaming services connected to Apple TV on your iPhone. In the Apple TV app you can rent and pre-order shows and movies, download them on your device or play them on other devices (Macs, iPads, Apple TV, or other smart TVs that support the Apple TV app).

SUBSCRIBE TO APPLE TV+ & OTHER CHANNELS

Apple TV+ offers various premium channels including Paramount+ and other entertainment channels directly to your iPhone. You need to subscribe to your favorite channels for an ad-free entertainment experience.

To subscribe to channels on your Apple TV app:

- Go to the Apple TV app > Tap "Watch Now" and then scroll down until you see channels.
- Tap the channel that you want to subscribe to.
- Tap the "Subscription button" to see further details such as a free trial and instructions for the subscription.

Go to the "Original" section in the Apple TV app to access and subscribe to Apple TV+ original shows, movies, and other content. You can watch on-demand content from your iPhone and other IOS devices. To do so:

- Go to Apple TV and tap "Originals."
- Tap the "Subscription Button" to see details and instructions for the subscription.

MANAGE YOUR SUBSCRIPTIONS ON THE APPLE TV APP

You can change or cancel your subscriptions for Apple TV+ or all the channels that you have subscribed to.

- In the Apple TV app, tap "Watch Now."
- Tap your profile icon at the top-right corner of the screen.
- Tap "Manage Subscriptions." Here you can see & manage all your subscriptions.

DISCOVER, SEARCH & STREAM YOUR CONTENT

Open the Apple TV app and go to "Watch Now" to get recommendations from Apple TV. Apple TV curates content on your screen based on your watch history on the app. The more you watch the more relative the recommendations will become. You can also discover and watch content from different channels. Go to the channel row to see what's new and trending on the channels.

Tap "Search" to find exactly what you are looking for. You can search content either by name or by categories (sports, thriller, comedy, etc). Type your keyword in the search and then tap any movie or show to see more details or play it on your app.

Apple TV+ originals and other shows and movies from Apple production will play on the Apple TV app. If your want to watch content from other streaming apps, the app will automatically lead you to the streaming app where you can watch that content.

- Tap the "Title" of the show or movie that you want to watch.
- Tap "Play" if the show or movie is available on Apple TV or Apple TV+.
- If you want to see it on other streaming apps, scroll down to "How to watch" and then tap any of the streaming apps that you want to watch it on.

To save and download titles on your device for later, tap ↓ . You can access your downloaded content in "Library" in the Apple TV app tv.

PURCHASE, RENT, OR PRE-ORDER YOUR FAVORITE CONTENT

With an Apple TV+ subscription, you also get to enjoy services like buying, renting, or pre-ordering your favorite shows and movies in the app. Tap "Store" and choose the item that you want and then choose any of the following:

Buy – Buy any movie or show and it will be yours to keep on your Apple TV app.

Rent – Your item will be rented to you for the next 30 days. After you play it, you have 48 hours to watch it before it's deleted. You can play as many times as you want within the 48 hours.

Pre-Order – You will be automatically billed for the movie or show that you pre-order. Turn on the automatic download if you want your content to be downloaded once it's out.

VOICE MEMO

Take audio notes, record your music practices, save voice memos, or more all from your iPhone using the Voice Memo app ⬛ You can record, edit, and share your recording with your contacts and keep them backed up using iCloud.

To enable Voice Memos on iCloud, go to Settings ⬤ Tap "Your Name" and then turn "Voice Memo" on.

RECORD NEW VOICE MEMOS

To start a recording, open the Voice Memo app on your iPhone:

- Tap ⬤ the recording will start after the iPhone plays the start tone.
- Tap ⬤ to stop the recording. The recording will stop after the stop tone.

To mute the start and stop tone on your recording, use the volume up and down button. Lower the volume using the volume down button. Go all the way down to mute. Raise the volume to unmute.

Use the additional controls to record the audio to your needs. If you wish to record your audio in parts, review it, or record it then do the following:

- Tap ⬤ to start the recording.
- Tap ⏸ to pause the recording and then tap "Resume" when you are ready to record the audio again.
- To review your recording before saving it, tap ▶
- Tap "Done" to save your recording when you are finished.

Voice Memo continues recording in the background while using other apps and only stops when audio is played from.

PLAYBACK & ORGANIZE YOUR MEMOS

Your saved recordings will appear on the list in the Voice Memo ⬛ app. Open the app and then tap the recording that you want to play.

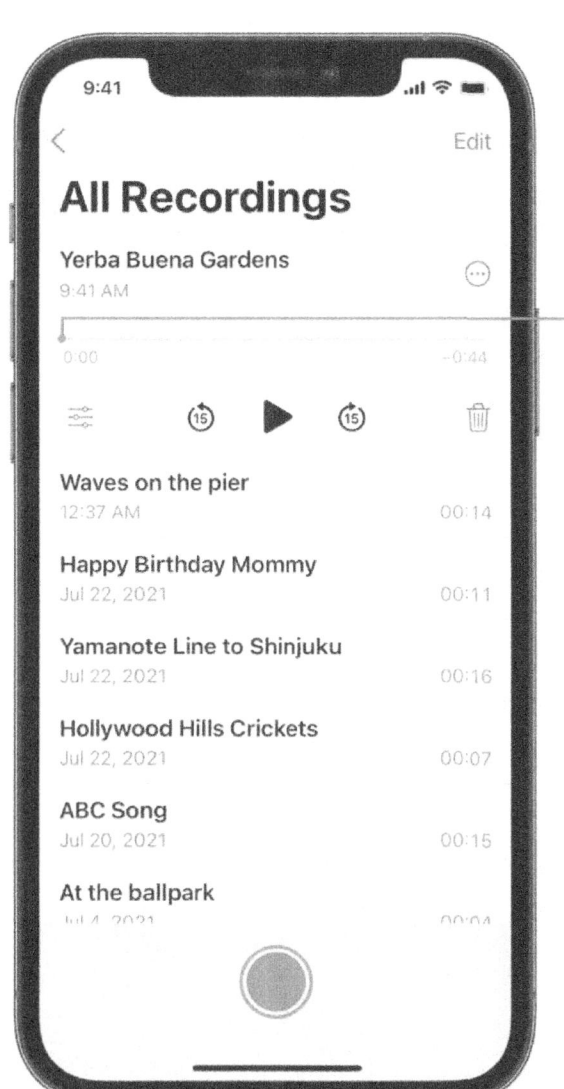

Drag to go to a specific place in the recording.

Use the following controls to play a recording:

- Tap ▶ to play the recording.
- Tap ❚❚ to pause the recording.
- Tap ⟲15 to rewind the playback by 15 seconds.
- Tap 15⟳ to skip forward the playback by 15 seconds.

For additional options tap ☰ and then do any of the following:

Control Playback Speed	Drag the slider towards 🐢 to slow the playback speed and towards 🐰 for faster playback.
Skip Over Silence	Tap "Skip Silence" to turn on the feature. Memo app will analyze the recording and automatically skip the silence in your audio.
Enhance Your Recordings	The feature reduces background noise and echos in your recording. Tap to turn it on.

Tap ✖ and then tap ▶ to apply and play the recording with your applied options. To turn off all your playback options, tap ☰ and then choose "Reset."

ADD RECORDINGS TO FAVORITES OR CREATE FOLDERS

Organize the voice memos in folders or add them to favorites to quickly find a specific recording. To make the search option easier, rename your recordings to your needs. Tap any of the recordings and then tap its name and type a new one to replace the previous one.

To add recordings to your favorites folder, tap the recording, then tap ⋯, and then tap ♡

To create a new folder and move recordings:

- Tap "Edit" at the top-right corner of your recoding list.
- Select the recordings from the list and then tap "Move."
- Tap 📁 to create new folders. Type the folder name and then tap the folder to move recordings to the new folder.

To see all the folders in your Voice Memo app, tap ＜ at the top-left corner above the list. To organize the folders, tap "Edit" on the top-right corner above the folders then:

- Tap ⊖ and then tap 🗑 delete the entire folder.
- Tap and drag ☰ to reorder your folder list.
- Tap "Done" when finished.

EDIT, RE-RECORD OR DELETE RECORDINGS

Open the recording list, tap the recording and then tap ⋯, then "Edit Recording".
Tap ⊐ to trim the recording.

- Tap "Trim" to keep the part within the yellow frame and delete the rest.
- Tap "Delete" to erase the part within the yellow frame and keep the rest.
- To review the changes, tap ▶ and then tap "Save" to keep the changes made to your recording.
- To record a part in your recording, tap the recording from the list and then tap ⋯, tap "Edit Recording" and then:

- Position the playhead on the part which you want to re-record. Tap and hold the waveform and then drag it left or right to position the playhead.

- Tap "Replace" to record. Tap ❚❚ to pause and resume your new recording.
- Tap ▶ to review your changes
- Tap "Done" to save your replaced recordings.

To delete recordings:

- Tap the recording that you want to delete and then tap 🗑
- To delete more than one recording, tap "Edit" at the top-right corner above the list. Select the recording that you want to delete and then tap "Delete."

Deleted recordings will move to "Recently Deleted" where they stay for the next 30 days before being automatically deleted permanently.

Drag the yellow trim handles on the waveform to select a section of the recording.

WALLET

The Wallet app 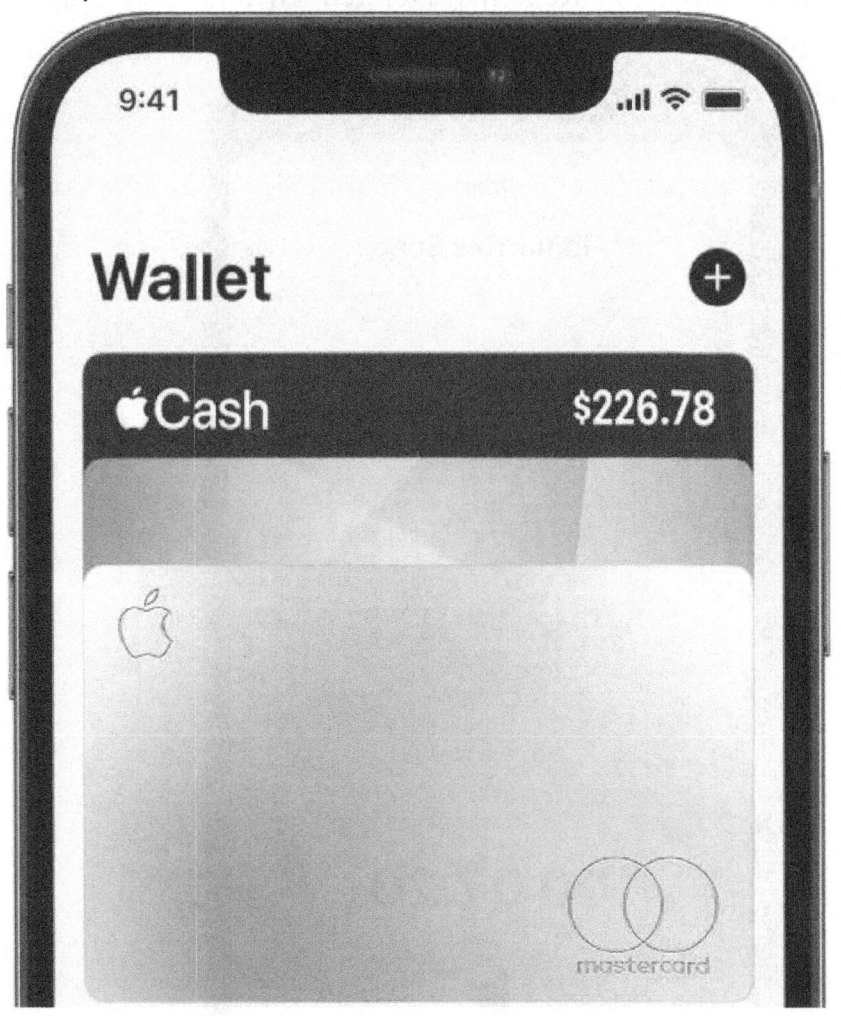 saves you the hassle of carrying all your cards, IDs, passes, and more. All your cards and IDs can be stored on your phone and are one tap away for you to access when it's time to use them.

SAVE YOUR CREDIT & DEBIT CARD

Open the Wallet app and then tap ➕ . Follow the on-screen instruction to add your new card.

- You can take a photo of your card by positioning the card to fit in the frame on your screen.

- You can manually enter card number of the card.

You may need to provide verification to your bank or card issuer in order to set up the Wallet app on your iPhone. Your first card will be set as your default payment method. To change your default payment method in the app, simply tap and drag the card and bring it to the front of the stack on your Wallet app screen.

246

USE APPLE PAY TO MAKE PAYMENTS

To use Apple Pay or Cards in your Wallet app to make a payment:

- Press the side button twice. Your default card on the Wallet app will appear on your screen (tap the card if you want to make payment with another card in your Wallet app).

- Authenticate with your Face ID or passcode.

- Bring your iPhone's top near contactless POS machine.

- Hold your iPhone near it until you see "Done" on your screen.

You can make these payments only at places where you see the following signs:

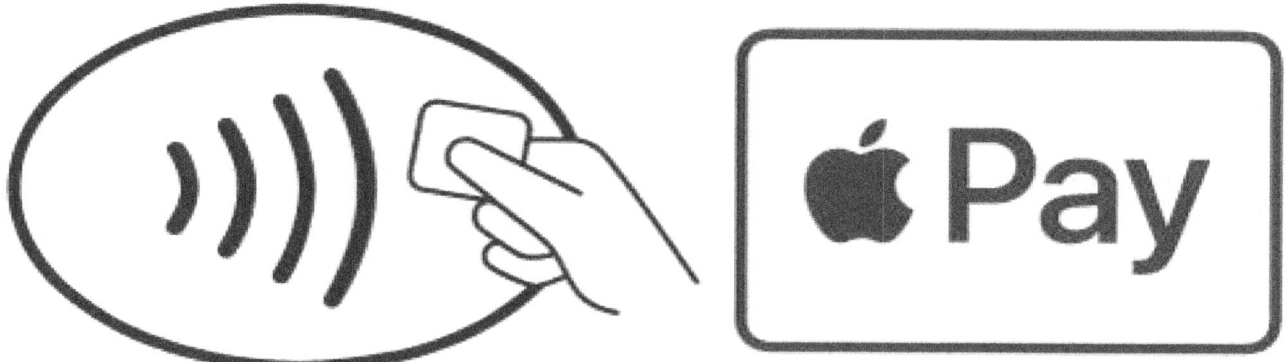

To use your payment methods when shopping from an app or on a website:

- Choose "Apple Pay" at the checkout.

- Confirm details of your order i.e. billing details, shipping address, and contact information.

- Double press the side button and authenticate the payment with your passcode or face ID.

247

APPLE CASH

The money sent or received within your Message app goes to your Apple Cash account on your Wallet app. You can use Apple Cash for shopping where Apple Pay is accepted or send it directly to your bank account.

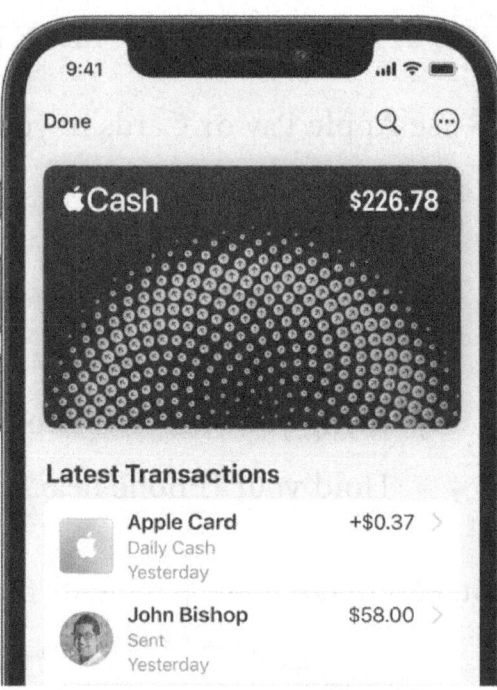

To enable Apple Cash, go to Settings ⚙ > Tap "Wallet & Apple Pay" > Turn on "Apple Cash." You can now send and receive money in Messages.

To access and manage your "Apple Cash" account, go to the Wallet app 📧 > Tap "Apple Cash," and you will be able to see all your transactions made using "Apple Cash".
Tap ⋯ to see other options related to your Apple Cash cards such as adding more money, transferring the Apple Cash to your bank account, or updating your bank account information.

ADDING YOUR APPLE CARD TO THE WALLET APP

You can apply for your Apple Card directly from your Wallet app. To apply for your Apple Card, tap ➕ and then tap "Apply for Apple Card." Make sure to:

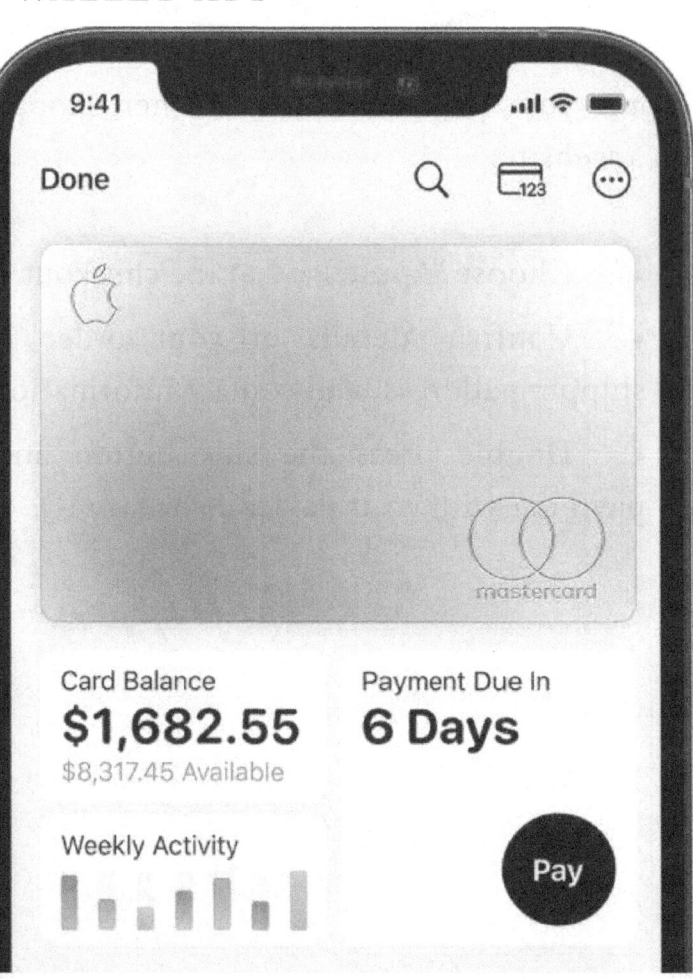

- Provide all your information asked on your screen.

- Agree to all terms and conditions to proceed.

- Review and choose Apple Card offers shown on your screen. Accept the offer that suits your need.

You can see your Apple Card number to use it where Apple Pay is not supported. Tap  to see your card's information (i.e. Card Number, expiration date, CVV)

To review your transactions and statement, go to the Wallet app and tap your "Apple Card." To view your transaction history for a specific period, search any of your previous transactions or get a weekly, monthly, or yearly statement.

ADD DIGITAL KEYS TO YOUR WALLET APP

The iPhone uses Near Field Communication (NFC) technology to store your keys and present them on your screen whenever you need them. You can add keys to your car, home, or hotel to your phone for easy access and also to prevent them from unexpected loss.

NFC technology senses when you're near your car, home lock, or hotel room, presenting your card to the lock screen for quick access. Hold the top of your iPhone near your car, home, or hotel lock and it will automatically unlock them. You can also access your card through your Apple Watch.

In the case of a car and hotel room, you may need to download the app provided by the car manufacturer and your hotel. To add keys to your home, use the Apple Home app and then access them in your Wallet app.

ADD YOUR STUDENT IDS

The apps with your student ID communicate with the Wallet app on your iPhone. Open the app that is provided by your educational institution, sign in and add your Student ID. Your Student ID card will also appear in your Wallet app. You can access it anytime on your lock screen.

Turn "Express Mode" on to access your card without having to authenticate without Face ID or a passcode. Bring the top of your iPhone near the reader and the iPhone will automatically show your relative card on the screen.

To authenticate your cards and payment through your Student ID, turn "Express Mode" off. You'll have to use Face ID or passcode every time you access your ID.

ADD YOUR PASSES & COUPONS

The Wallet app also saves your tickets, boarding passes, coupons, and many other digital passes, organizing them according to how you use them. The Wallet app will automatically ask you whether you want to save your pass or not when you make a purchase using your Apple Pay. Alternatively you can add these passes from other apps such as third-party Wallet enabled apps, Messages, Mail, Safari, AirDrop, or scan a barcode on your passes. To add them manually using QR codes, open the camera and position your pass on your screen. iPhone will scan and add your pass to your Wallet.

Access these cards within your Wallet app or bring the top of your iPhone near the contactless reader and the pass will appear on the screen. You may need to authenticate with a Face ID or passcode.

WEATHER

In Weather app you can check the weather for your location as well as other locations. You can see hourly forecast or forecasts for the next ten days to plan your days accordingly.

CHECK YOUR LOCAL WEATHER

When you open the Weather app on your iPhone, it will show you the weather report for your current location.

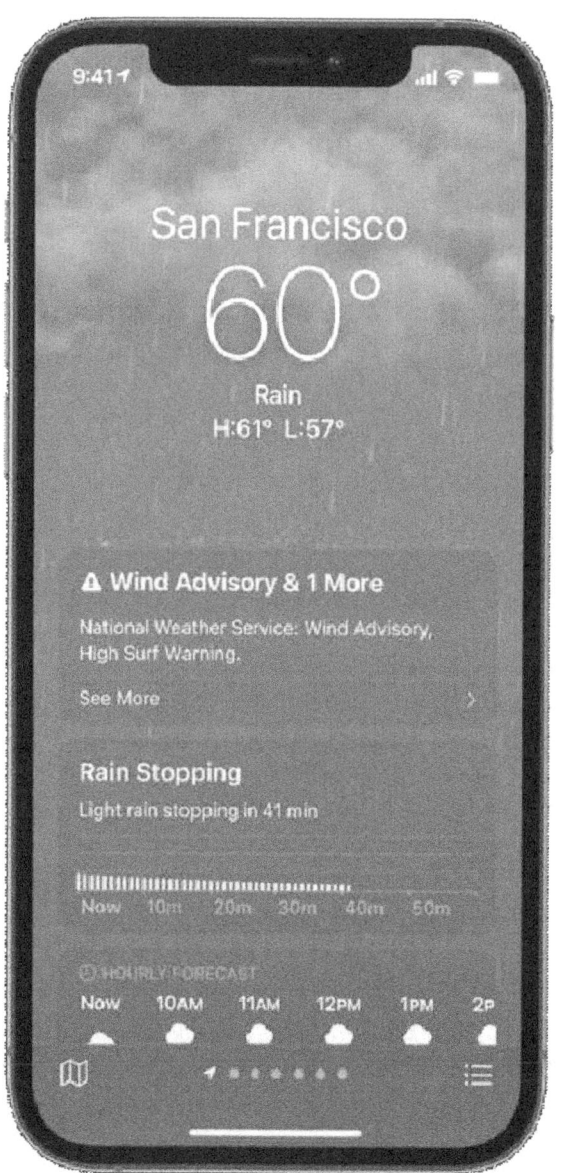

Here you can see the following information about the weather condition of your location:

- See hourly forecasts just below the temperature. Swipe the hours to see more hourly forecasts.

- Swipe up to see the forecast for the next ten days.

- View weather around your area on the map.

- Check the air quality of your location.

- Scroll to the bottom of your screen to see information like sunset, sunrise, wind speed and direction, and UV Index.

ADD & MANAGE MORE LOCATIONS TO THE WEATHER APP

Add a new location and check the weather at any moment in your weather app. Tap ⋮☰ at the bottom corner to go to your weather list and do the following:

- Tap the "Search Bar" at the top and then type the name of the city that you want to add. Tap the name of the city when it appears in the search result.

- Tap "Add" on the top-left corner to add it to your weather list.

To delete a city from your weather list:

- Go to the weather list and swipe left on the city that you want to remove from the list and then tap 🗑. Alternatively, tap ⚫⚫⚫ at the top-right corner of the list and then tap "Edit list" and then remove the city

To reorder your added location.

- Tap ⚫⚫⚫ in your weather list.

- Tap and then drag the city to a new location in the list.

CONTROL NOTIFICATION, TEMPERATURE UNITS & MORE

In the weather list, tap ⚫⚫⚫ to see more options and then choose any of the following:

- Tap "Edit list" to manage locations on your weather lists.

• Tap "Notification" to receive notifications for rain, snow, sleet, or any other severe weather condition. To enable weather notification, you need to enable the location service for the Weather app. Go to Settings ⚙ > tap "Privacy" > tap "Location Service" and then tap "Weather." Change the option to "Always" to receive notifications according to your current location.

• Choose between "Celsius" & "Fahrenheit" to view your temperature in any of the two units.

• Tap "Report an Issue" if you find the weather information is not accurate on your phone.

GET WEATHER CONDITIONS USING MAPS

Weather maps provide the weather condition of your location and the area around you.

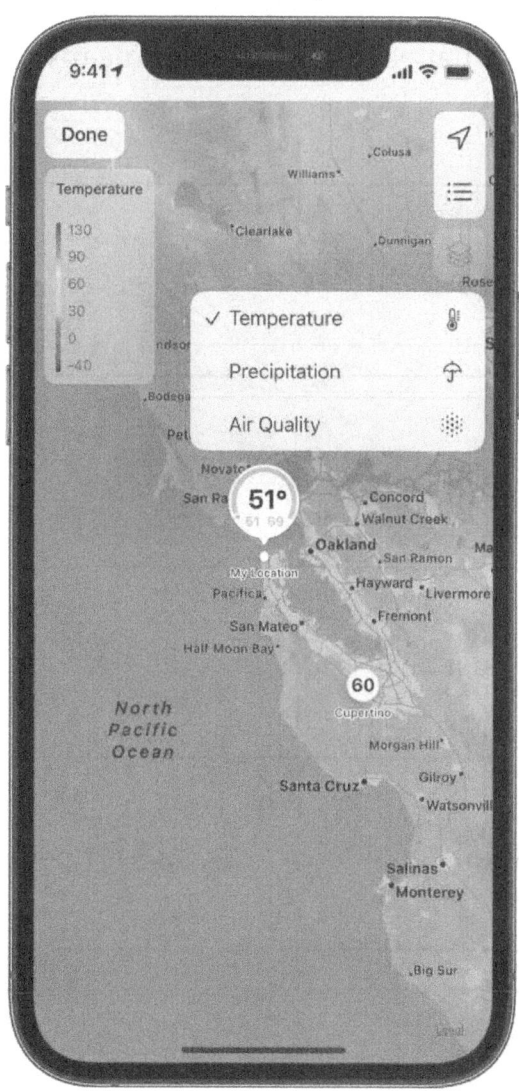

To use weather maps, open a weather location from your list, tap 🗺 at the bottom left corner of your screen and then do the following:

- Switch between any of the three maps view i.e. Air quality, Precipitation, and Temperature.

- Zoom in and out by pinching on the screen or tap and hold with one finger to move the map around your location.

- When moving maps, tap ⟁ to return to your current location. Tap and hold a location on the weather map to reveal additional options such as adding it to your list or viewing its weather forecast and more.

- Tap ⋮≡ to see another location on the map from your list.

- Tap "Done" at the top-left corner to hide the weather map view.

READ THE WEATHER ICONS

Every weather icon indicates a specific weather condition. You can read weather by simply looking at these icons and here's what each one of them means.

	Sunrise		Sunset
	Clear		Partly Cloudy
	Dust		Haze
	Smoke		Fog
	Windy		Cloudy

	Thunderstorm		Showers
	Heavy Showers		Drizzel
	Hail/Mixed Rain		Tornado
	Snow		Scattered Storm
	Sleet/Heavy Snow		Blowing Snow
	Frigid Temps		Cloudy
	Clear		

Update, Backup, Restore & Reset Your iPhone

Apple provides regular updates to your IOS so your iPhone in tip top condition working like it's brand new. Software updates can contain major or minor changes depending on the version. You can update your iPhone manually and set it to "Automatic Update" which allows your phone to download and install new software as it comes out.

UPDATE MANUALLY

To update your iPhone manually, go to Settings ⚙ > tap "General" and then tap Software Update. If there are no new updates, your screen will show the message that your phone is up to date and there are no further actions required.

If you see new updates on the screen, tap "Download and Install." Your iPhone will automatically download and ask to install new updates. After the download is complete, your phone will ask you permission to update. Give permission to update your software or do it later.

AUTOMATIC UPDATE

Go to Settings ⚙ > tap "General" and then tap Software Update > tap "Automatic Update" and then choose the following:

• Turn on "Download iOS Updates." Your iPhone will only download the update and not install it.

• Turn on "Install iOS Updates." Your iPhone will download and install the new updates.

You will receive a notification before the installation of the download updates. The iPhone will download and install updates at night when it is connected to a power source and Wi-Fi.

BACKUP YOUR DATA

To back up your data, go to Settings ⚙ > tap "Your Name" > tap "iCloud" and then turn on "iCloud Backup." Your iPhone will start the backup when it's charging and connected to Wi-Fi.

To backup manually, tap "Back Up Now" just below the "iCloud Backup" toggle. Your phone must be connected to a Wi-Fi network.

RESTORE YOUR DATA

Your Data can be restored on a newly erased iPhone or if you've recently switched to a new iPhone. To restore data on your new iPhone, turn it on, choose language and region, and then:

- Tap "Set Up Manually."
- Tap "Restore from iCloud Backup."
- Follow the on-screen instructions to restore your data.

RESET IPHONE

iPhone can be reset in different ways. You can erase your all data, reset the home screen layout or keyboard, and other settings back to what they were on your new iPhone.

Go to Settings ⚙ > tap "General", Scroll down and then tap "Transfer or Reset iPhone".

Apple gives its users free cloud storage to transfer all their data to a new device using iCloud. Even if your data exceeds your current storage plan, tap "Get Started" to get free iCloud storage for the next 21 days to transfer your data to a new iPhone.

Tap "Reset" and then choose any of the following to take action:

Reset All Settings: It will reset your iPhone Network, Keyboard, Location, and all other settings back to the new iPhone. Your Apple Cards will also be removed. Your media or other data will not be deleted.

Reset Network Setting: Resets your device name, remov trusted devices, and websites from Safari.

Reset Keyboard Dictionary: The words that you added as shortcuts in your keyboard will all be deleted.

Reset Home Screen Layout: Brings all the apps to their position as they were on your new iPhone.

Reset Location & Privacy: Turns all location services to their default settings.

ERASE ALL CONTENT & SETTINGS

Tap "Erase All Content & Settings" to remove all the data and media from your iPhone. You'll be asked to provide verification to erase your iPhone. You can sign in with your Apple ID or passcode to give authentication to erase your iPhone.

Dear Apple Pro! I hope you are enjoying exploring the world of Apple devices thus far! Your feedback means a lot to me and it can be a valuable gift to fellow readers who are considering this guide. Writing a review on Amazon is a simple yet incredibly helpful way to pay it forward. Scan this QR code to take you straight there!

Your words have the power to inspire confidence in others, just as I've aimed to do with this book. Whether you found the content insightful, the instructions clear, or if you have any suggestions for improvement (I WILL incorporate it into following books), your review will be appreciated.

By sharing your thoughts, you not only assist other seniors in making an informed choice but also support the author (that's me!). Your review provides insights that can guide prospective readers, making their journey with the Apple products more enjoyable and stress-free.

Thank you for considering this request. Your words can make a big difference, and together, we can make the Apple world even more accessible and enjoyable for everyone, everywhere!

Thank you,
Jason Brown

Apple Watch for Seniors

A Simple Step By Step Guide For Beginners

Jason Brown

Apps & Icons

Activity	Alarms	App Store
Audiobooks	Blood Oxygen	Calculator
Calendar	Camera Remote	Compass
Contacts	Cycle Tracking	ECG
Find Devices	Find Items	Heart Rate
Home	Mail	Maps
Medications	Memoji	Messages
Mindfulness	Music	Find Friends
Noise	Now Playing	Stopwatch
Photos	Podcasts	Voice Memos
Remote	Settings	Weather
Sleep	Stocks	Shortcuts
Timers	Tips	News
Walkie-Talkie	Wallet	Phone
Workout	World Clock	Reminders

Status icon	What it means
●	You have an unread notification. Swipe down on the watch face to read it.
⚡	Apple Watch is charging.
⚡	Apple Watch battery is low.
○	Low Power Mode is on.
🔒	Apple Watch is locked. Tap to enter the passcode and unlock.
💧	Water Lock is on, and the screen doesn't respond to taps. Press and hold the Digital Crown to unlock.
🌙	Do Not Disturb is turned on. Calls and alerts won't sound or light up the screen, but alarms are still in effect.
👤	Personal Focus is turned on.
🪪	Work Focus is turned on.
🛏	Sleep Focus is turned on.
✈️	Airplane mode is turned on. Wireless is turned off but non-wireless features are still available.
🎭	Theater mode is turned on. Apple Watch is silenced and its display won't light up when you raise your wrist.
🏃	You have a workout in progress. To end the workout, see End and review your workout.
✖	Apple Watch with cellular has lost the connection to a cellular network. See Use your Apple Watch with a cellular network.

Status icon	What it means
	Apple Watch is connected to its paired iPhone.
	An app on Apple Watch is using location services.
	Apple Watch is connected to a known Wi-Fi network.
	There's wireless activity or an active process happening.
	The microphone is on.
	Apple Watch is connected to a cellular network. The number of green bars indicates signal strength.
	You've made yourself available to be reached on Walkie-Talkie. Tap the icon to open the Walkie-Talkie app.

SETTING UP YOUR iWATCH

Introducing Your Apple Watch

Say hello to the Apple Watch, the adaptable wearable partner that can inspire you to enhance your activity levels, monitor vital health details, maintain connections with your loved ones, and offer numerous other capabilities, whether paired with your iPhone or used independently.

This manual is designed to unveil the multitude of incredible features that the Apple Watch has to offer, especially with watchOS 9.4.

Apple Watch gestures

You use several basic gestures to interact with Apple Watch.

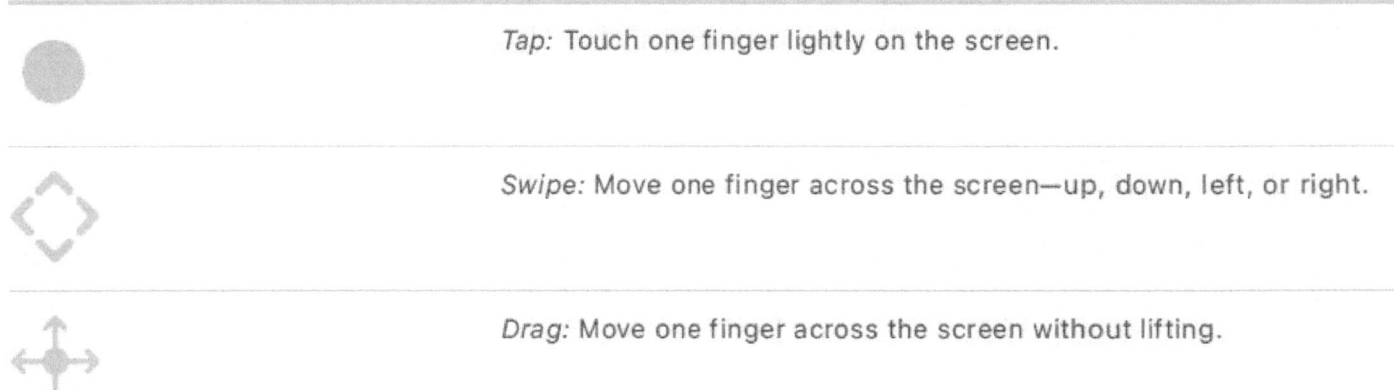

Tap: Touch one finger lightly on the screen.

Swipe: Move one finger across the screen—up, down, left, or right.

Drag: Move one finger across the screen without lifting.

Setting Up and Connecting Your Apple Watch with iPhone

To utilize your Apple Watch with watchOS 9, it's essential to establish a connection between your watch and an iPhone 8 or a later model running iOS 16 or newer. During this process, both your iPhone and Apple Watch's setup assistants collaborate to facilitate the pairing and configuration of your watch.

Note: If you encounter visibility challenges with either your Apple Watch or iPhone, you can utilize VoiceOver or Zoom to assist you, even during the initial setup. Refer to the "Set up Apple Watch using VoiceOver or Zoom" guide for further details.

SETTING UP, PAIRING, AND CONFIGURING YOUR APPLE WATCH

1. Place your Apple Watch on your wrist. Adjust the band or select an appropriate band size to ensure a snug and comfortable fit.

2. To power on your Apple Watch, press and hold the side button until the Apple logo appears.

3. Bring your iPhone in close proximity to your Apple Watch. Wait for the Apple Watch pairing screen to display on your iPhone's screen, then tap "Continue."

Alternatively, you can launch the Apple Watch app on your iPhone and tap "Pair New Watch."

4. Choose the "Set Up for Myself" option.

5. As prompted, position your iPhone in such a way that your Apple Watch is visible within the viewfinder of the Apple Watch app. This action will establish a connection between the two devices.

6. Select "Set Up Apple Watch," and then follow the step-by-step instructions provided on both your iPhone and Apple Watch to complete the setup process.

ALL APPLE WATCHES BUTTONS AND LAYOUTS

Apple Watch Series 8

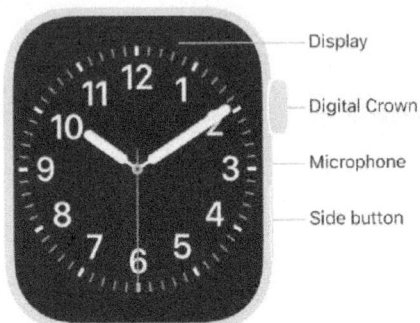

- Display
- Digital Crown
- Microphone
- Side button

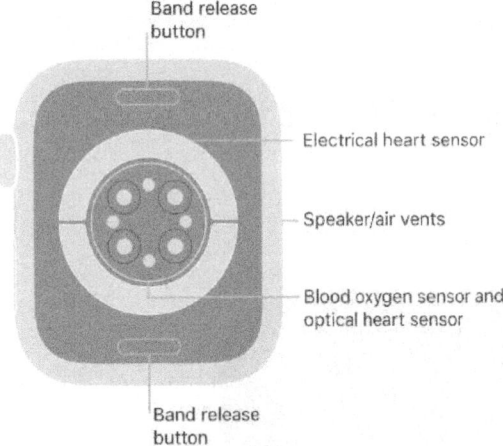

- Band release button
- Electrical heart sensor
- Speaker/air vents
- Blood oxygen sensor and optical heart sensor
- Band release button

Apple Watch Series 7

- Display
- Digital Crown
- Microphone
- Side button

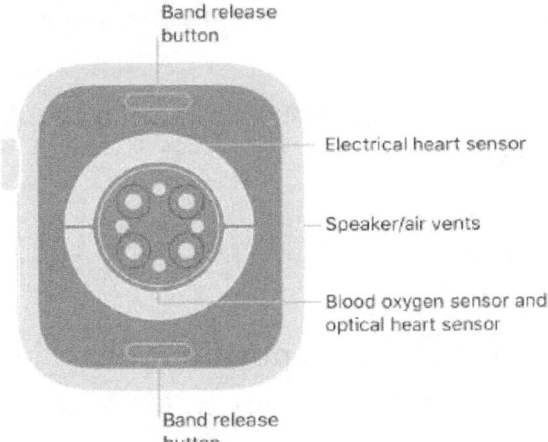

- Band release button
- Electrical heart sensor
- Speaker/air vents
- Blood oxygen sensor and optical heart sensor
- Band release button

Apple Watch Series 6

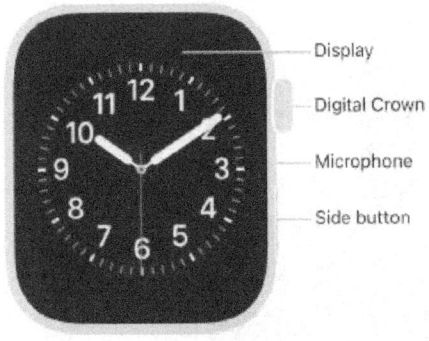

- Display
- Digital Crown
- Microphone
- Side button

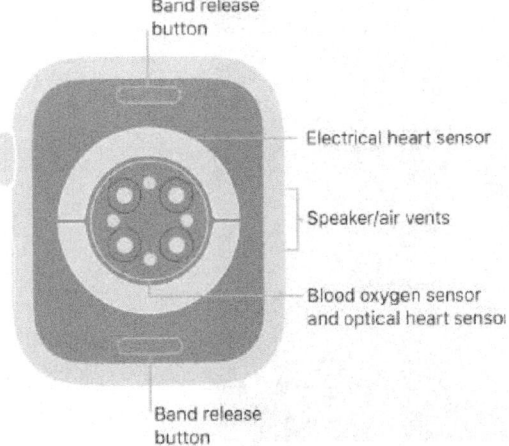

- Band release button
- Electrical heart sensor
- Speaker/air vents
- Blood oxygen sensor and optical heart sensor
- Band release button

Apple Watch SE (2nd Generation)

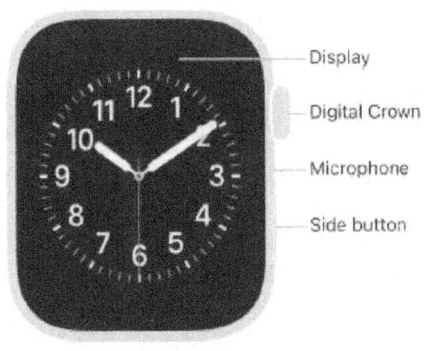

- Display
- Digital Crown
- Microphone
- Side button

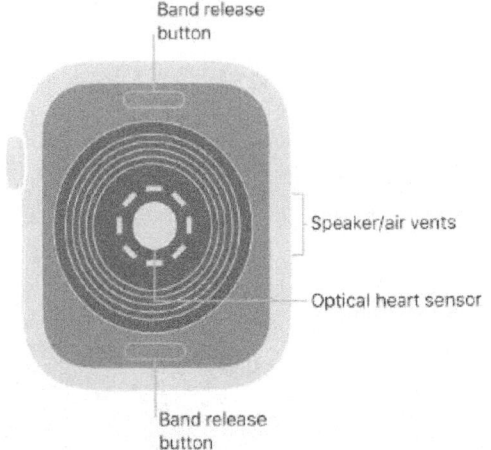

- Band release button
- Speaker/air vents
- Optical heart sensor
- Band release button

APPLE WATCH SE

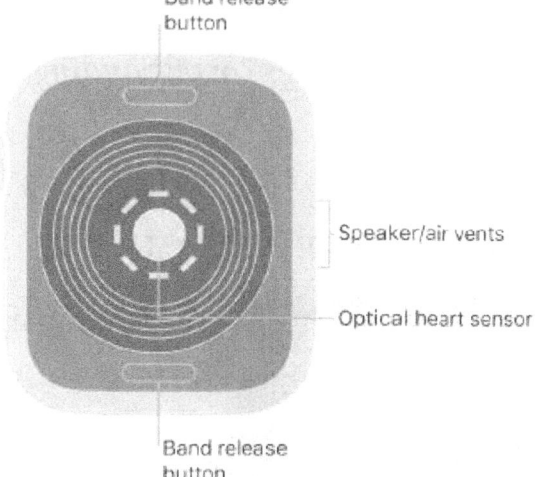

Display

Digital Crown

Microphone

Side button

Band release
button

Speaker/air vents

Optical heart sensor

Band release
button

APPLE WATCH SERIES 4 AND SERIES 5

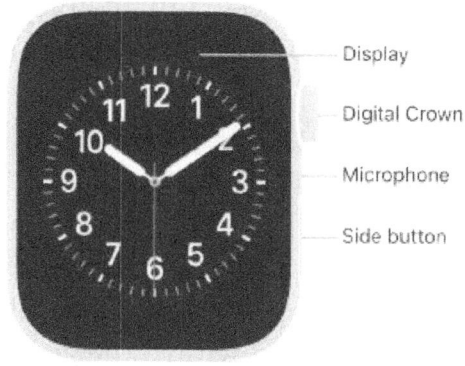

Display

Digital Crown

Microphone

Side button

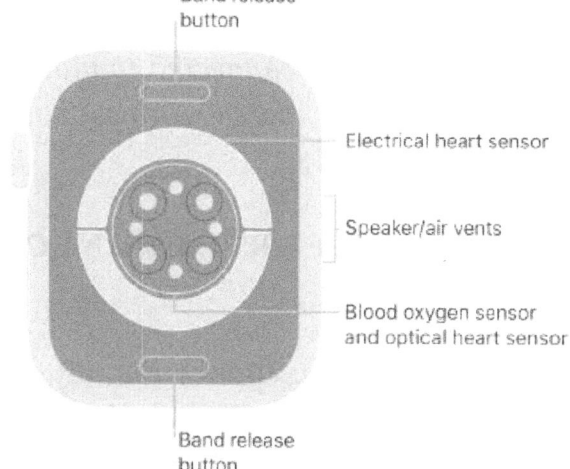

Band release
button

Electrical heart sensor

Speaker/air vents

Blood oxygen sensor
and optical heart sensor

Band release
button

THE APPLE WATCH APPLICATION

Utilize the Apple Watch application on your iPhone to personalize watch faces, configure settings and notifications, set up the Dock, install applications, and perform various other tasks. If you're interested in acquiring additional applications from the App Store, refer to the "Get more apps" section for detailed guidance.

ACCESSING THE APPLE WATCH APPLICATION

1. On your iPhone's home screen, tap the icon of the Apple Watch application.
2. Select "My Watch" within the application to access and modify the settings associated with your Apple Watch.

If your iPhone is connected to more than one Apple Watch, the settings corresponding to your active Apple Watch will be displayed.

EXPLORING FURTHER INFORMATION ABOUT APPLE WATCH

In the Apple Watch application, the "Discover" tab offers links to valuable Apple Watch tips, an informative overview of your device, and this user guide. All of this content is conveniently accessible on your iPhone.

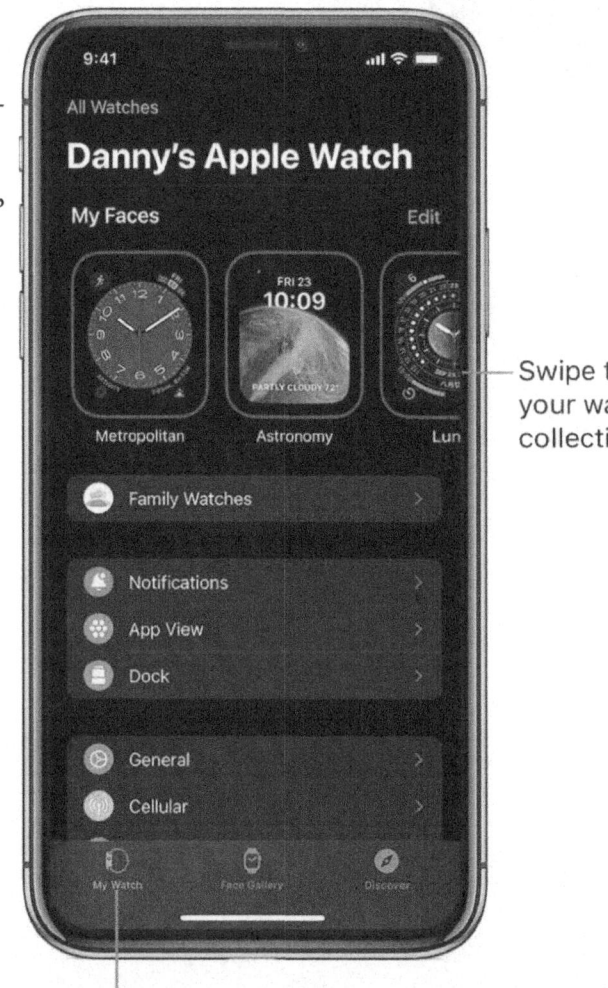

Swipe to see your watch face collection.

Settings for Apple Watch.

268

CHARGING YOUR APPLE WATCH

SETTING UP THE CHARGER

1. Place your charger or charging cable on a level surface in a well-ventilated area.
   - The Apple Watch Magnetic Fast Charger to USB-C Cable (included with Apple Watch Series 7 and Apple Watch Series 8) or the Apple Watch Magnetic Charging Cable (for other models) is provided with your Apple Watch.
   - Optionally, you can also utilize accessories like the MagSafe Duo Charger or Apple Watch Magnetic Charging Dock (available separately).

2. Connect the charging cable to the power adapter (available separately).

3. Plug the power adapter into an electrical outlet.

INITIATING APPLE WATCH CHARGING

1. Gently position the Apple Watch Magnetic Fast Charger to USB-C Cable (included with Apple Watch Series 7 or later) or the Apple Watch Magnetic Charging Cable (included with earlier models) onto the back of your Apple Watch.

   Note: The concave end of the charging cable will magnetically attach to the back of your Apple Watch, ensuring proper alignment.

2. Your Apple Watch will emit a chime to indicate the commencement of charging (unless it is in silent mode). Simultaneously, a charging symbol ⚡ will be displayed on the watch face.
   - The symbol appears in red when your Apple Watch requires power, transitioning to green when charging is active.
   - If your Apple Watch is in Low Power Mode, the charging symbol will be yellow.

CHARGING PLACEMENT OPTIONS

- You can charge your Apple Watch with its band open in a flat orientation or on its side.
- If using the Apple Watch Magnetic Charging Dock or MagSafe Duo Charger, simply place your Apple Watch on the dock.

LOW BATTERY INDICATION

In situations where your battery level is significantly low, you might see an image of the Apple Watch Magnetic Fast Charger to USB-C Cable or Apple Watch Magnetic Charging

Cable, accompanied by a low battery symbol ⚡ on the screen.

Here is a guide on where to place all chargers for each Apple Watch.

Apple Watch Series 8

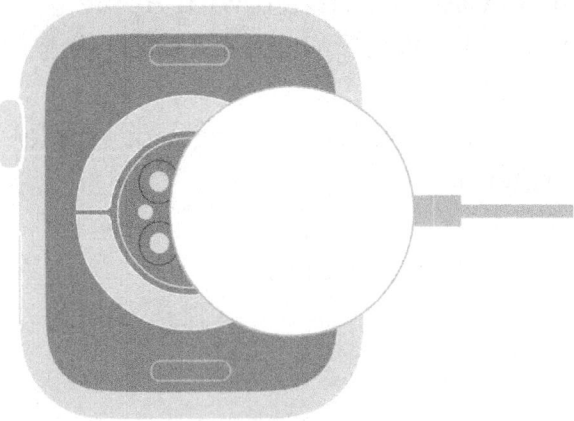

Apple Watch SE (2nd Generation)

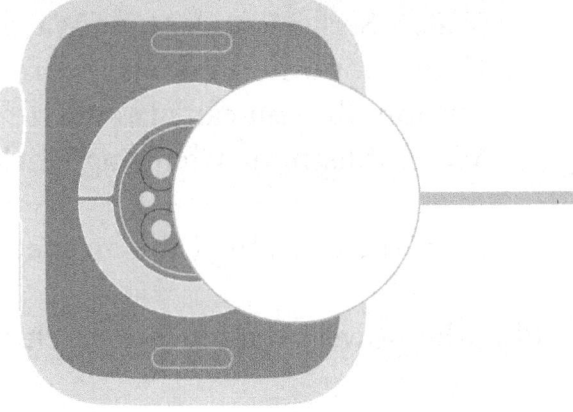

Apple Watch Series 7

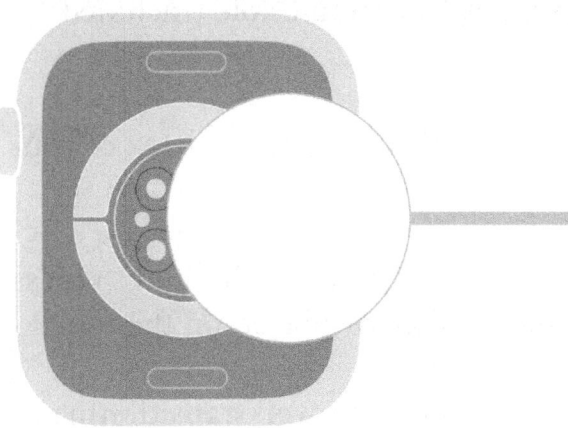

Apple Watch Series 6

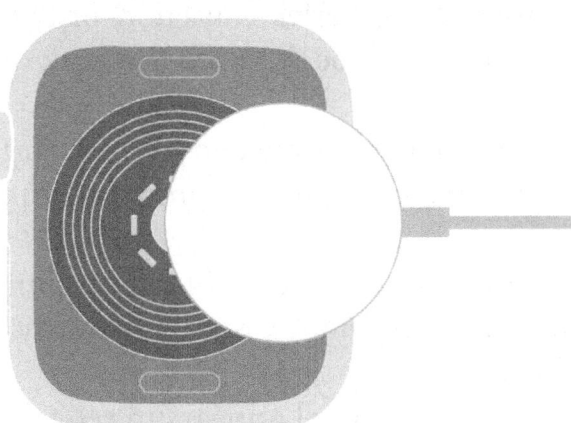

Apple Watch SE

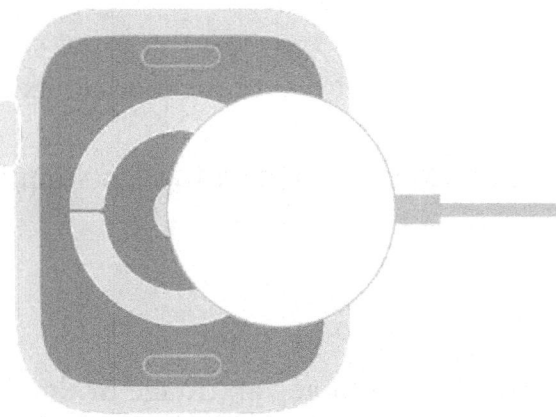

Apple Watch Series 4 & 5

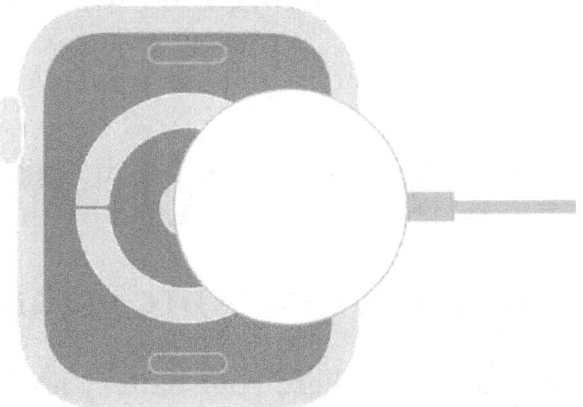

CHECK REMAINING POWER

To see remaining power, touch and hold the bottom of the screen, then swipe up to open Control Center. To more quickly check the remaining power, add a battery complication to the watch face.

View the percentage of remaining battery life.

CONSERVING BATTERY POWER

To extend your battery life, consider activating Low Power Mode. Enabling this feature will result in the deactivation of the Always On Display, background measurements of heart rate and blood oxygen levels, as well as heart rate notifications.

Some notifications might be delayed, emergency alerts could be delayed, and specific cellular and Wi-Fi connections may be restricted. Cellular functionality will remain inactive until you explicitly need it, such as when streaming music or sending messages.

Note: Keep in mind that Low Power Mode will automatically deactivate once your battery reaches 80% charge.

1. Touch and hold the bottom of the screen, then swipe up to open Control Center.
2. Tap the battery percentage, then turn on Low Power Mode.
3. To confirm your choice, scroll down, then tap Turn On Low Power Mode.
You can tap Turn On For, then choose On for 1 Day, On for 2 Days, or On for 3 Days.

Tip: If you've connected battery-powered devices like AirPods to your Apple Watch via Bluetooth, you'll find their remaining charge displayed on this screen. When the battery level descends to 10 percent or lower, your Apple Watch will notify you and present the option to enable Low Power Mode.

For comprehensive insights into Low Power Mode, refer to the Apple Support article titled "Use Low Power Mode on your Apple Watch."

Tip: To uncover strategies for optimizing battery longevity, explore the guide on "Maximizing Battery Life and Lifespan" available on the official Apple website.

RETURN TO REGULAR POWER MODE

1. Press and hold the lower portion of the screen, and then swipe upwards to unveil the Control Center.
2. Tap the battery percentage and deactivate Low Power Mode.

Monitoring Time Since Last Charge:

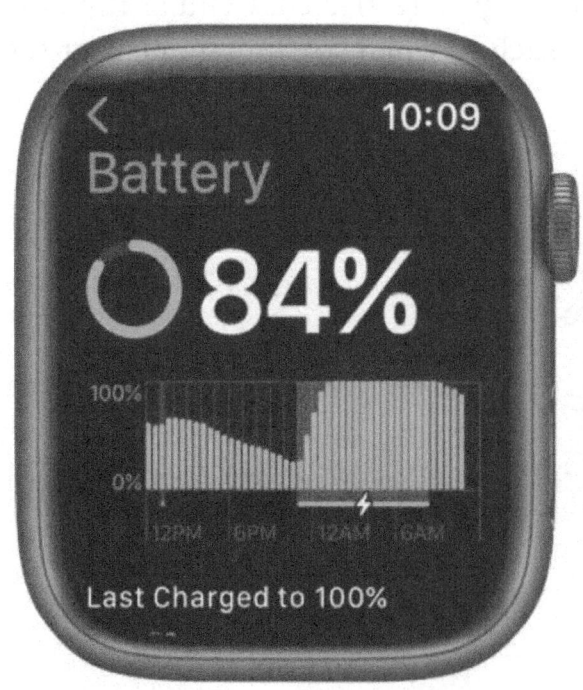

ACCESSING BATTERY INFORMATION

1. Launch the Settings app on your Apple Watch.
2. Select "Battery."

On the Battery screen, you'll find details such as the remaining battery percentage, a graphical representation illustrating recent battery charge history, and specifics regarding the time of the last charge.

CHECKING BATTERY HEALTH

You have the ability to determine your Apple Watch battery's capacity relative to its original state when new.

1. Open the Settings app on your Apple Watch.
2. Tap "Battery," and then navigate to "Battery Health."

Should your Apple Watch's battery capacity experience significant decline, the device will provide alerts, indicating that it may be time to explore available service options.

PREVENTING BACKGROUND APP REFRESH

When transitioning to a new app, the previous app doesn't remain actively open or occupy system resources. However, it might still refresh, checking for updates and new content in the background. Background app refresh activity can contribute to power consumption. To optimize your battery life, you can disable this feature.

1. Access the Settings app on your Apple Watch.
2. Navigate to "General," then select "Background App Refresh."

You can choose to deactivate "Background App Refresh" entirely, preventing all apps from refreshing, or customize the setting by scrolling down and turning off refresh for specific apps.

Note: Apps featuring complications on the current watch face will continue to refresh, even if their background app refresh setting is turned off.

TURN ON AND WAKE APPLE WATCH

POWERING ON AND OFF YOUR APPLE WATCH

Power On:
To activate your Apple Watch, hold down the side button until the Apple logo becomes visible (a brief black screen may appear before this).
The watch face will be displayed once your Apple Watch is turned on.

Power Off:
Typically, you'll keep your Apple Watch operational at all times. However, if you wish to power it off, follow these steps:

1. Press and hold the side button until the sliders emerge.
2. Tap the icon  positioned at the upper right corner.
3. Slide the Power Off slider to the right.

When your Apple Watch is powered off, you can press and hold the Digital Crown to view the current time.

ALWAYS ON

Enabling Always On Display Mode

For compatible Apple Watch models, the Always On feature ensures that your watch face and the current time remain visible even when your wrist is not raised. The moment you lift your wrist, your Apple Watch seamlessly resumes full functionality.

Note: When your Apple Watch is operating in Low Power Mode, the Always On Display is deactivated. To view the watch face, a simple tap on the display is sufficient.

Always On Display is accessible on Apple Watch Series 5, Apple Watch Series 6, Apple Watch Series 7, and Apple Watch Series 8.

Here's how you can configure Always On Display

1. Access the Settings app on your Apple Watch.
2. Choose "Display & Brightness," then select "Always On."
3. Activate Always On by toggling the switch. Additionally, you can fine-tune the following options:
  • Show Complication Data: Select the complications that will display data when your wrist is down.
  • Show Notifications: Choose which notifications will be visible while your wrist is down.
  • Show Apps: Decide which apps will remain visible when your wrist is down.

Waking the Apple Watch Display

By default, there are several ways to awaken your Apple Watch display:
  • Raising your wrist will initiate the display, and it will return to sleep mode when you lower your wrist.
  • Tapping the display or pressing the Digital Crown will have the same effect.
  • Rotating the Digital Crown in an upward motion will also wake the display.

If you prefer that your Apple Watch does not wake when you raise your wrist or turn the Digital Crown, follow these steps:
1. Launch the Settings app on your Apple Watch.
2. Navigate to "Display & Brightness."

3. Disable "Wake on Wrist Raise" and "Wake On Crown Rotation."

ADJUSTING CLOCK FACE RETURN DURATION

Modify the time it takes for your Apple Watch to revert to the clock face after exiting an app:
1. Launch the Settings app ⚙️ on your Apple Watch.
2. Navigate to "General," and select "Return to Clock." Scroll down and pick the timing preference for your Apple Watch's return to the clock face:
   - Always
   - After 2 minutes
   - After 1 hour
3. Alternatively, press the Digital Crown to swiftly return to the clock face.

By default, the chosen setting applies to all apps. However, personalized times can be set for individual apps. To do this:
1. Tap an app on the same screen.
2. Select "Custom," and then pick the desired time duration.

RESUMING PREVIOUS ACTIVITY

For specific apps like Audiobooks, Maps, Mindfulness, Music, Now Playing, Podcasts, Stopwatch, Timers, Voice Memos, Walkie-Talkie, and Workout, you can configure your Apple Watch to return you to your last activity upon waking from sleep.
1. Access the Settings app ⚙️ on your Apple Watch.
2. Go to "General," and choose "Return to Clock." Scroll down, tap the app you're interested in, and activate "Return to App."

To return to the clock face, simply halt the current activity within the app (e.g., pause a podcast, conclude a route in Maps, or cancel a timer).

For further control, you can also manage these settings through the Apple Watch app on your iPhone:
1. Open the Apple Watch app.
2. Tap "My Watch," proceed to "General," and then select "Return to Clock."

PROLONGING DISPLAY DURATION

Extend the time the display remains active upon tapping to wake your Apple Watch:
1. Launch the Settings app ⚙️ on your Apple Watch.
2. Choose "Display & Brightness," then select "Wake Duration." Opt for "Wake for 70 Seconds."

LOCKING AND UNLOCKING YOUR APPLE WATCH

Unlocking Your Apple Watch

There are two primary methods for unlocking your Apple Watch: manual entry of the passcode or setting it to unlock automatically when your iPhone is unlocked.

• Manually Enter Passcode: To unlock your Apple Watch, wake it and then input the watch passcode.

• Unlock with iPhone: You can configure your Apple Watch to unlock automatically when you unlock your paired iPhone. To do this:
  1. Open the Apple Watch app on your iPhone.
  2. Tap "My Watch," proceed to "Passcode," and enable "Unlock with iPhone."

Please note that your iPhone must be within a standard Bluetooth range (approximately 33 feet or 10 meters) of your Apple Watch to facilitate automatic unlocking.

CHANGE YOUR PASSCODE

Modifying Your Apple Watch Passcode
If you wish to alter the passcode you initially established Apple Watch, adhere to these instructions:

1. Access the Settings app ⚙ on your Apple Watch.
2. Tap "Passcode," then select "Change Passcode." Follow complete the process.

Alternatively, you can do this through the Apple Watch app on your iPhone:
1. Launch the Apple Watch app 🅞.
2. Tap "My Watch," navigate to "Passcode," and choose "Change Passcode." Follow the on-screen prompts to complete the procedure.

Disabling the Passcode
If you wish to deactivate your passcode, follow these steps:
1. Tap the Settings app ⚙ on your Apple Watch.
2. Tap "Passcode," then select "Turn Passcode Off."

You can also achieve this via the Apple Watch app on your iPhone:
1. Open the Apple Watch app 🔲.
2. Tap "My Watch," navigate to "Passcode," and choose "Turn Passcode Off."

Note: If you disable your passcode will render Apple Pay unavailable on your Apple Watch.

AUTOMATIC LOCKING MECHANISM

By default, your Apple Watch will lock automatically when it's not being worn. To adjust the wrist detection setting, proceed as follows:
1. Launch the Settings app on your Apple Watch ⚙️.
2. Tap "Passcode," then toggle the "Wrist Detection" option on or off.

Switching off wrist detection will impact the following Apple Watch functions:
• When authorizing an Apple Pay payment using your Apple Watch, you'll be prompted to input your passcode after double-clicking the side button.
• Certain Activity measurements won't be accessible.
• Heart rate tracking and notifications will be deactivated.
• The automatic locking and unlocking feature will be disabled.
• Even if a significant impact fall is detected, Apple Watch won't automatically initiate an emergency call.

FORGET YOUR PASSCODE

If you happen to forget your passcode, the solution involves erasing your Apple Watch. You can accomplish this through the following methods:

• Unpairing and Pairing: Detach your Apple Watch from your iPhone to wipe out both watch settings and the passcode. Subsequently, you can re-establish the pairing.

• Resetting and Pairing: Another option is to reset your Apple Watch and then pair it anew with your iPhone.

ERASE APPLE WATCH AFTER MULTIPLE UNLOCK ATTEMPTS

To safeguard your data in situations where your watch is lost or stolen, you can configure your Apple Watch to erase its content after 10 consecutive, incorrect passcode attempts.

1. Access the Settings app on your Apple Watch ⚙️.
2. Tap "Passcode," then activate the "Erase Data" feature.

ADJUSTING LANGUAGE AND ORIENTATION ON APPLE WATCH

LANGUAGE OR REGION SELECTION

If you've configured your iPhone to support multiple languages, you can opt for the language displayed on your Apple Watch.

1. Access the Apple Watch app 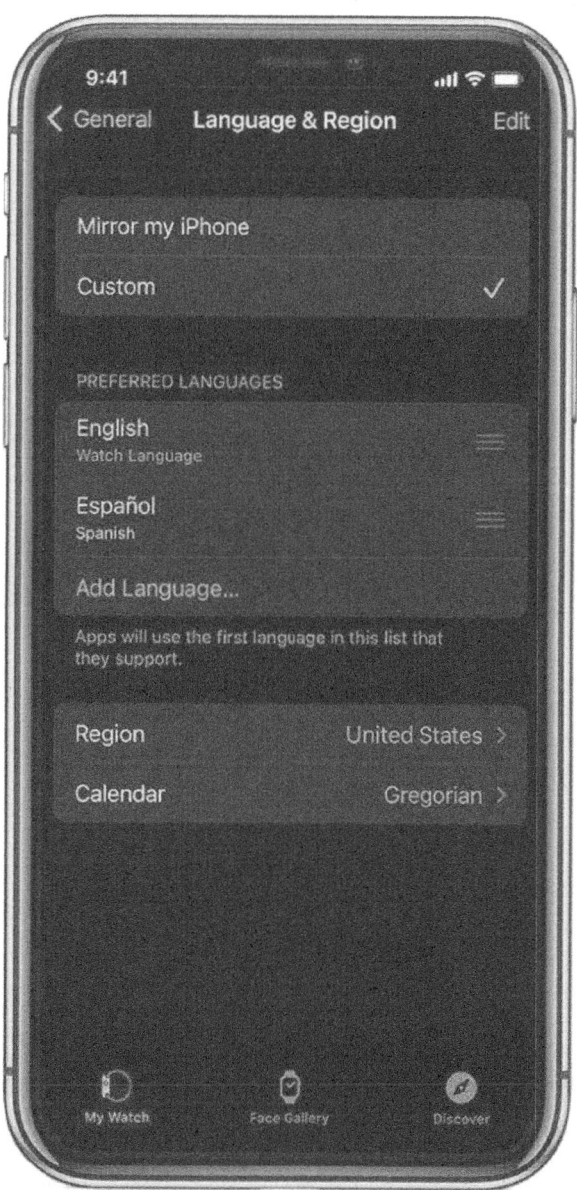 your iPhone.

2. Tap "My Watch," navigate to "General" > "Language & Region," then tap "Custom" and select your preferred language.

CHANGING WRIST OR DIGITAL CROWN PLACEMENT

If you wish to transfer your Apple Watch to your opposite wrist or prefer to have the Digital Crown positioned on the opposite side, you can modify your orientation settings. This ensures that raising your wrist triggers your Apple Watch and that turning the Digital Crown corresponds to your preferred direction.

1. Launch the Settings app  on your Apple Watch.
2. Navigate to "General" > "Orientation."

Alternatively, you can do this by using the Apple Watch app on your iPhone. Access "My Watch," proceed to "General," and select "Watch Orientation."

REMOVE, CHANGE, AND FASTEN APPLE WATCH BANDS

Ensure you choose a band that matches your Apple Watch case size. Bands meant for Apple Watch (1st generation) or Apple Watch Series 1, 2, and 3 can be used with Apple Watch Series 4, 5, SE, 6, 7, SE (2nd Gen), and 8, as long as their sizes are compatible. Bands for 38mm, 40mm, and 41mm cases are interchangeable, while those for 42mm, 44mm, and 45mm cases are also interchangeable.

Most bands created for Apple Watch Series 4, 5, SE, 6, 7, SE (2nd Gen), and 8 are suitable for prior watch versions. The Solo Loop and Braided Solo Loop bands are tailored for Apple Watch Series 4, 5, SE, 6, 7, SE (2nd Gen), and 8. Bands designed for early Apple Watch models are also compatible with Apple Watch Series 4, 5, SE, 6, 7, SE (2nd Gen), and 8.

DETACH AND REPLACE BANDS

1. Depress the band release button on your Apple Watch.
2. Glide the band to the side to detach it, then slide the new band into place.

Avoid applying excessive force when inserting a band. If you encounter difficulty while removing or inserting a band, press the band release button once more.

SECURE THE BAND

To ensure the best functionality, it's important for your Apple Watch to fit snugly on your wrist.

The underside of your Apple Watch requires contact with your skin to facilitate features like wrist detection, haptic notifications, and heart rate tracking. Wearing your Apple Watch with the correct fit—neither overly tight nor too loose, with some space for ventilation—enhances your comfort and enables the sensors to perform their tasks effectively. Furthermore, the sensors function optimally when the watch is worn on the top side of your wrist.

APPS ON YOUR iWATCH

OPEN APPS ON APPLE WATCH

Access Apps Easily
The Home Screen provides access to all your Apple Watch apps, while the Dock offers swift entry to your most frequently used ones. You have the option to include up to 10 preferred apps in the Dock for convenient access.

Opt for Grid or List Display
Customize how your apps are shown on the Home Screen by selecting between grid and list views. Here's how:
1. Press and hold on the Home Screen.
2. Select either Grid View or List View.

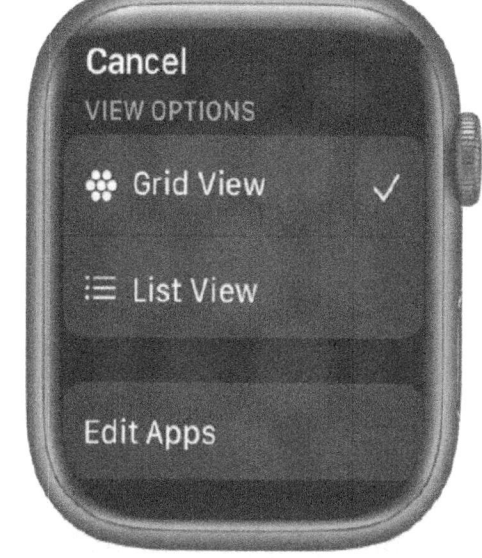

OPEN APPS FROM THE HOME SCREEN

Depending on your view, you will have different methods to access Apps.

In grid view: Tap the app icon. If you're on the Home Screen, turning the Digital Crown opens the app at the center of the display.

From the watch face, press to see the Home Screen.

Tap to open an app.

• In list view: Rotate the Digital Crown and tap an app.

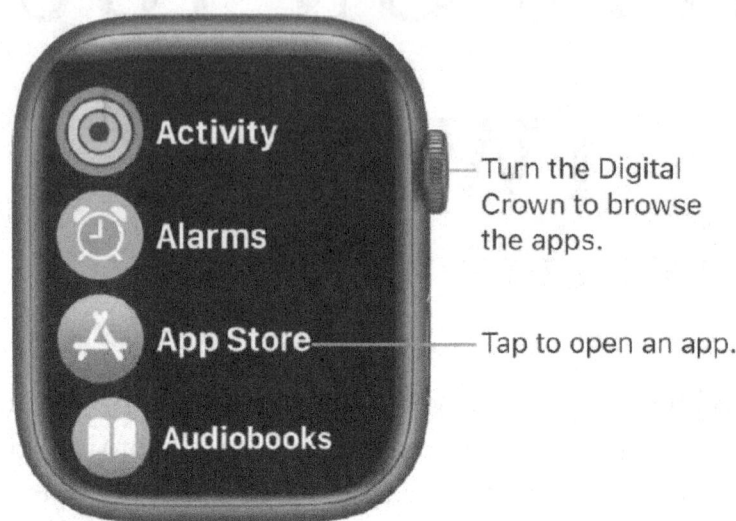

Turn the Digital Crown to browse the apps.

Tap to open an app.

RETURNING TO THE HOME SCREEN

After using an app, press the Digital Crown once. To switch to the watch face (or in grid view, tap the Home Screen), press it again.
Swift App Switching
To swiftly access your most recently used app while in another app or viewing the watch face, double-click the Digital Crown.

ARRANGE APPS ON APPLE WATCH

Adjusting app placement in grid view is simple:
1. Press the Digital Crown on your Apple Watch to reach the Home Screen.
If you're in list view, hold the Home Screen and select Grid View.
Alternatively, open the Settings app on your Apple Watch, access App View, then opt for Grid View.
2. Long-press an app and choose Edit Apps.
3. Move the app to your preferred spot.
4. Conclude the process by pressing the Digital Crown.

Touch and hold an app, then drag to a new location.

REMOVE AN APP FROM APPLE WATCH

To remove an app from your Apple Watch, follow these steps:
- On the Home Screen, touch and hold.
- Tap Edit Apps and select the X next to the app's name.
- The app will be removed from your watch but remains on your paired iPhone, unless you delete it there as well.

In list view, you can also swipe the app left, then tap to remove it from your watch. Note that if you remove an app from your iPhone, it will also be deleted from your Apple Watch.

TO ADJUST APP SETTINGS

1. Launch the Apple Watch app on your iPhone.
2. Tap My Watch, then scroll to the installed apps.
3. Tap an app to modify its settings.
Keep in mind that restrictions you set on your iPhone can impact your Apple Watch, such as disabling the Camera app.

CHECK APP STORAGE

- Open the Settings app on your Apple Watch.
- Navigate to General > Storage.

Alternatively, you can access this information through the Apple Watch app on your iPhone under General > Storage.

ADDING APPS TO YOUR APPLE WATCH

Your Apple Watch comes with various pre-installed apps for communication, health, fitness, and time management. You also have the option to install third-party apps from your iPhone or download new apps from the App Store directly on your Apple Watch. All your apps are accessible from the Home Screen.

TO GET MORE APPS FROM THE APP STORE ON YOUR APPLE WATCH

1. Open the App Store app on your watch.
2. Turn the Digital Crown to explore featured apps.
   - Tap a category or "See All" below a collection to discover more apps.
3. To get a free app, tap "Get." To purchase an app, tap the price.

If you see a cloud icon instead of a price, you've already acquired the app and can download it again without any charge. Note that some apps may require the iOS version on your iPhone as well.

For specific apps, use the search field at the top of the screen, or type using Scribble (available on Apple Watch Series 7 and Apple Watch Series 8). You can also explore popular app categories by selecting a category.

Keep in mind:
- When using cellular data on your Apple Watch, be aware of potential data charges.

- Scribble, a feature that lets you write on the screen, is available on Apple Watch Series 7 and Apple Watch Series 8, accessible by swiping up and tapping Scribble.

- Note that the availability of Scribble may vary depending on language settings.

INSTALL APPS FROM YOUR IPHONE

Your Apple Watch can automatically install apps from your iPhone if there's a corresponding watchOS app available. These apps will appear on your Home Screen. However, if you prefer more control over which apps are installed, follow these steps:

1. Open the Apple Watch app on your iPhone.
2. Tap "My Watch," then select "General."
3. Turn off "Automatic App Install."
4. Scroll down to "Available Apps" on the same page.
5. Tap "Install" next to the apps you want to have on your Apple Watch.

This way, you can ensure that only the apps you specifically choose are installed on your Apple Watch, giving you a more tailored and organized experience.

APPS

Use Apple's default apps & In-app features for entertainment, connectivity & productivity.

ACTIVITY APP

Stay Active with Apple Watch
Keep track of your daily activity with the Activity app ◎ on your Apple Watch. This app helps you monitor your movement throughout the day and encourages you to achieve your fitness goals. It tracks your standing frequency, movement, and exercise minutes. You'll notice three rings in various colors that sum up your progress. The objective is to minimize sitting, increase movement, and accomplish each ring's goal every day.

Your activity records are also stored in the Fitness app on your iPhone. After tracking at least six months of activity, you can view trend data for active calories, exercise minutes, stand hours, distance walked, cardio fitness, walking pace, and more. In the Fitness app, tap "Summary" and then navigate to "Trends" to see how your activity compares to your average.

START YOUR FITNESS JOURNEY

When setting up your Apple Watch, you'll be prompted to configure the Activity app. If you decide not to at that moment, you can do it later when you open the Activity app for the first time.

1. Open the Activity app ⊚ on your Apple Watch.
2. Swipe left to read about Move, Exercise, and Stand, then tap "Get Started."
3. Use the Digital Crown to input your sex, age, height, weight, and wheelchair usage.
4. Select your activity level and get moving toward a healthier you.

MONITOR YOUR PROGRESS

You can easily track your progress by opening the Activity app on your Apple Watch whenever you want.

The Activity app showcases three rings:
- The **red** Move ring illustrates active calories burned.
- The **green** Exercise ring highlights the minutes of brisk activity completed.
- The **blue** Stand ring indicates how frequently you stood and moved for at least one minute per hour.

If you've told the specified that you use a wheelchair, the blue Stand ring changes to the Roll ring, which tracks how often you rolled for at least one minute per hour.

By turning the Digital Crown, you can view your current totals. Continue scrolling to access a graph of your progress, your total steps, overall distance, workouts, and flights climbed. If a ring overlaps, you've surpassed your goal. Turn the Digital Crown and tap "Weekly Summary" to assess your performance for the week.

VIEW YOUR WEEKLY SUMMARY

1. Open the Activity app ⊚ on your Apple Watch.
2. Scroll to the bottom of the screen using the Digital Crown, then tap "Weekly Summary."

This summary includes your week's totals for calories, average calories, steps, distance, flights climbed, and active time.

ADJUST YOUR GOALS

If you feel that your activity goals are either too demanding or not challenging enough, you can modify them.

1. Open the Activity app ⊚ on your Apple Watch.

2. Scroll to the bottom of the screen using the Digital Crown, then tap "Change Goals."
3. Adjust a goal by tapping ⊖ or ⊕, then proceed by tapping "Next."

Each Monday, you receive notifications about the previous week's achievements and can tailor your goals for the upcoming week. Your Apple Watch recommends goals based on your past performance.

REVIEW YOUR ACTIVITY HISTORY

1. Open the Fitness app on your iPhone and tap "Summary."
2. Within the Activity section, tap ▦ and select a date to review your activity for that day.

Check Your Trends & Track Your Progress Over Time

The Fitness app on your iPhone offers valuable insight into your progress over time through the Trends section, which provides daily trend data for active calories, exercise minutes, stand hours, walking distance, stand minutes, cardio fitness, walking pace, and running pace. Trends compare your activity over the past 90 days with the previous 365 days.

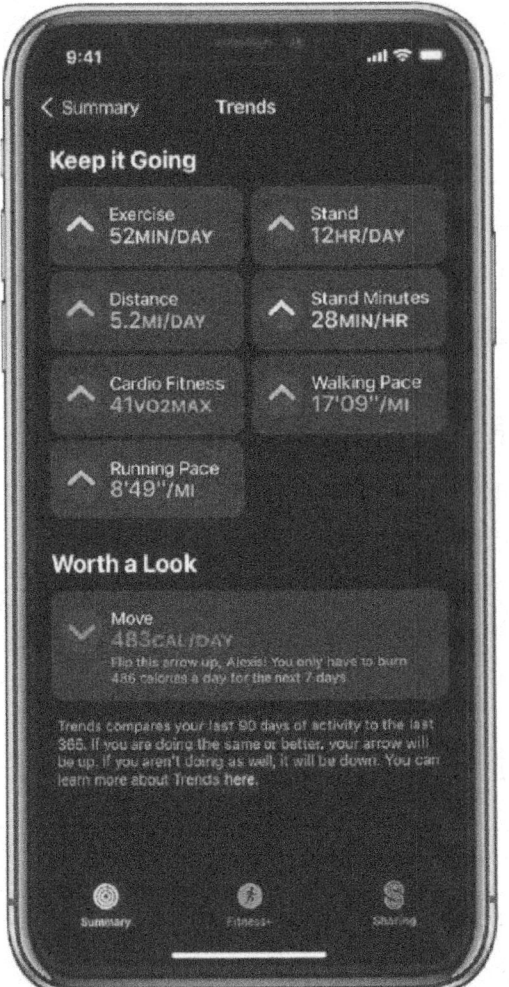

To assess your trend and make improvements, follow these simple steps:
1. Launch the Fitness app on your iPhone and tap "Summary."
2. Swipe up to access the trends section.
3. If you're interested in reversing a trend, tap "Show More."
4. To review the history of a specific trend, tap on it.

When the Trend arrow for a specific metric points upward, it indicates that your fitness levels are being maintained or improved. Conversely, if the arrow points downward, your 90-day average for that metric is declining. To inspire you to reverse the trend, you'll receive coaching tips, such as "Walk an extra quarter of a mile a day."

View Your Achievements

Your Apple Watch rewards you with various awards for achieving personal records, maintaining streaks, and reaching significant milestones. To access your collection of awards, which includes Activity Competition awards and awards you're currently working towards, follow these steps:

1. Open the Activity app ⊚ on your Apple Watch.
2. Swipe left twice to reach the Awards screen.
3. Scroll down to view your awards. Tap an award to get more information about it.

Alternatively, you can access your awards through the Fitness app on your iPhone. Simply tap the Summary tab and swipe up to find Awards at the bottom of the screen.

For details on participating in competitions with friends, refer to "Compete with your friends."

MANAGE ACTIVITY REMINDERS

Activity reminders can be invaluable in helping you meet your goals. Your Apple Watch keeps you informed about your progress and alerts you if you're lagging behind your activity targets. To customize which reminders and alerts you want to receive, use these instructions:

1. Open the Settings app ⚙ on your Apple Watch.
2. Tap on "Activity," then configure your desired notifications.

You can also make these adjustments through the Apple Watch app on your iPhone. Open "My Watch," then tap "Activity."

PAUSE DAILY COACHING

If you prefer to temporarily deactivate activity reminders, follow these steps:

1. Open the Settings app ⚙ on your Apple Watch.
2. Tap "Activity," then toggle off "Daily Coaching."

You can also manage this setting via the Apple Watch app on your iPhone by navigating to "My Watch," tapping "Activity," and turning off "Daily Coaching."

ALARMS APP

SETTING ALARMS

Creating an alarm on your Apple Watch is a simple way to receive sound or vibration notifications at specific times. Here's how you can do it:

1. Use Siri : Command Siri by saying something like, "Set a repeating alarm for 6 a.m."

2. Manually Set an Alarm:
   a. Open the Alarms app ⏰ on your Apple Watch.
   b. Tap "Add Alarm."
   c. Choose between AM or PM, then select the desired hours and minutes. Note that this step isn't necessary when using the 24-hour time format.
   d. Adjust the time by turning the Digital Crown, then tap ✓.
   e. To activate or deactivate the alarm, tap the corresponding switch. Alternatively, tap the alarm time to customize options such as repeat, label, and snooze settings.

Note: If you prefer an alarm that silently vibrates your wrist without sound, enable silent mode.

AVOID THE SNOOZE BUTTON

When an alarm goes off, tapping the Snooze button grants you a few extra minutes before the alarm resounds. If you'd like to remove the snooze option, follow these steps:

1. Launch the Alarms app ⏰ on your Apple Watch.
2. Tap the alarm from the list of alarms, then switch off Snooze.

MANAGING ALARMS

Removing or adjusting alarms on your Apple Watch is easy. Follow these steps to handle your alarms effectively:

Deleting an Alarm:
1. Launch the Alarms app 🕐 on your Apple Watch.
2. Tap the alarm from the list.
3. Scroll down and tap "Delete."

Skipping a Wake-Up Alarm:
If you have a wake-up alarm as part of your sleep schedule, you can skip it for that evening:
1. Open the Alarms app 🕐 on your Apple Watch.
2. Tap the wake-up alarm listed under Sleep | Wake Up.
3. Choose "Skip for Tonight."

SYNCING ALARMS BETWEEN IPHONE AND APPLE WATCH

You can have the same alarms on both your iPhone and Apple Watch for consistent reminders:
1. Set the alarm on your iPhone.
2. Open the Apple Watch app ⌚ on your iPhone.
3. Tap "My Watch," then tap "Clock," and enable "Push Alerts from iPhone."

With these steps, you can effectively manage your alarms on both your Apple Watch and iPhone. Your Apple Watch will alert you when alarms go off, allowing you to snooze or dismiss them directly from your watch. Please note that your iPhone won't alert you when alarms on your Apple Watch are triggered.

AUDIOBOOK

Listening to audiobooks on your Apple Watch is simple. Follow these steps to add and play audiobooks:

ADDING AUDIOBOOKS

1. Launch the Apple Watch app  on your iPhone.
2. Tap "My Watch," then choose "Audiobooks."
3. Select "Add Audiobook" and pick the audiobooks you want to sync with your Apple Watch.

AUDIOBOOK STORAGE AND SYNC

• Your currently playing audiobook and the one listed below "Want to Read" will sync to your Apple Watch if there's space available.
• Up to five hours from each audiobook you add will also be downloaded to your watch when space permits.
• Audiobooks sync to your watch when it's connected to power.

PLAYING AUDIOBOOKS

1. Connect your Bluetooth headphones or speakers to your Apple Watch.
2. Open the Audiobooks app on your watch.
3. Scroll through the artwork using the Digital Crown.
4. Tap an audiobook to start playing it.

You can easily add and enjoy your favorite audiobooks on your Apple Watch. Remember that only audiobooks from Apple Books can be synced to your watch.

Playing and Controlling Audiobooks from your library

You can easily play and control your audiobooks on your Apple Watch. Here's how:

Streaming Audiobooks from Library:

1. Ensure your Apple Watch is near your iPhone or connected to Wi-Fi/cellular network (for cellular models).
2. Open the Audiobooks app  on your Apple Watch.
3. Tap "Library" and select an audiobook to start playing it.

Using Siri to Play Audiobooks

You can use Siri to start playing an audiobook. Just say, "Play the audiobook 'In the Time of the Butterflies.'"

Controlling Playback

- Adjust the volume by turning the Digital Crown.
- Use playback controls to pause, resume, skip forward, or go back.

▶	Play the audiobook.
❚❚	Pause playback.
⟳15	Skip ahead 15 seconds.
⟲15	Skip back 15 seconds.
1x	Playback speed. Options include 1x, 1 1/4x, 1 1/2x, 1 3/4x, 2x, and 3/4x.
☰	Choose a track or chapter.

BLOOD OXYGEN

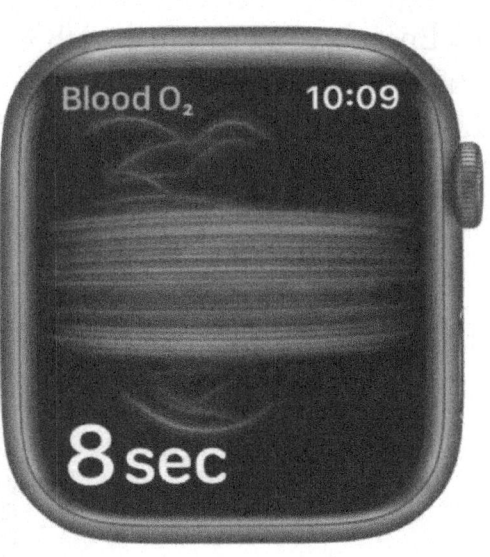

Measuring Blood Oxygen Levels with Apple Watch

You can use the Blood Oxygen app on your Apple Watch Series 6 or later to measure the percentage of oxygen that your red blood cells carry from your lungs to the rest of your body. This measurement can provide insights into your overall health and well-being. Keep in mind that the Blood Oxygen app's measurements are not meant for medical use and may not be available in all regions.

SETTING UP BLOOD OXYGEN MEASUREMENTS

1. Open the Settings app on your Apple Watch.
2. Tap "Blood Oxygen" and toggle on "Blood Oxygen Measurements."

DISABLING BACKGROUND MEASUREMENTS IN SPECIFIC MODES

When using Sleep Focus or theater mode, you might want to turn off background blood oxygen measurements to avoid distraction from the bright red light that shines against your wrist.
1. 1. Open the Settings app on your Apple Watch.
2. 2. Tap "Blood Oxygen" and toggle off "In Sleep Focus" and "In Theater Mode."

The Blood Oxygen app on your Apple Watch can periodically measure your blood oxygen level throughout the day if you have background measurements turned on. Additionally, you can manually take an on-demand measurement whenever you want.

STEPS TO TAKE AN ON-DEMAND BLOOD OXYGEN MEASUREMENT

1. Open the Blood Oxygen app on your Apple Watch.
2. Place your arm on a table or your lap, ensuring your wrist is flat and the Apple Watch display is facing upward.
3. Tap "Start" and hold your arm very still during the 15-second countdown.
4. Once the measurement is complete, you'll receive the results. Tap "Done."

VIEWING YOUR BLOOD OXYGEN MEASUREMENTS HISTORY

1. Open the Health app on your iPhone.
2. Tap "Browse," then go to "Respiratory" and select "Blood Oxygen."

CALCULATOR

Using the Calculator App on Your Apple Watch

The Calculator app on your Apple Watch allows you to perform basic arithmetic calculations and provides quick tools for calculating tips and splitting bills.

QUICK CALCULATION

1. Open the Calculator app  your Apple Watch.
2. Tap the numbers and operators to perform calculations and get results.

CALCULATING TIPS AND SPLITTING BILLS

1. Open the Calculator app on your Apple Watch.
2. Input the total amount of the bill.
3. Tap the "Tip" option.
4. Use the Digital Crown to select the desired tip percentage.
5. Tap "People" and use the Digital Crown to enter the number of individuals sharing the bill.

You will see the calculated tip amount, the overall total including the tip, and the individual amount each person needs to contribute if the bill is divided equally.

You can also utilize Siri to perform calculations by speaking your query aloud, such as "What's 73 times 9?" or "What's 18 percent of 225?"

The Calculator app on your Apple Watch offers quick and convenient tools for performing calculations, calculating tips, and splitting bills among friends or family.

CALENDAR

Checking and Managing Your Calendar on Apple Watch

The Calendar app on your Apple Watch allows you to access and manage your scheduled events, both in the near future and further ahead. Here's how you can use the Calendar app on your Apple Watch:

VIEW CALENDAR EVENTS

1. Open the Calendar app 7 on your Apple Watch or tap the date or an event on the watch face.
2. Turn the Digital Crown to scroll through your upcoming events.
3. Tap an event to view its details, including time, location, invitation status, and notes.
   - To return to the next event, tap the "<" symbol in the top-left corner.

CALENDAR DISPLAY RANGE

The Calendar app 7 on your Apple Watch displays events from the past six weeks and up to two years into the future in List and Day view.
The app can show events from all calendars on your iPhone or only the ones you choose. You can configure this setup on your iPhone using the Calendar app settings.

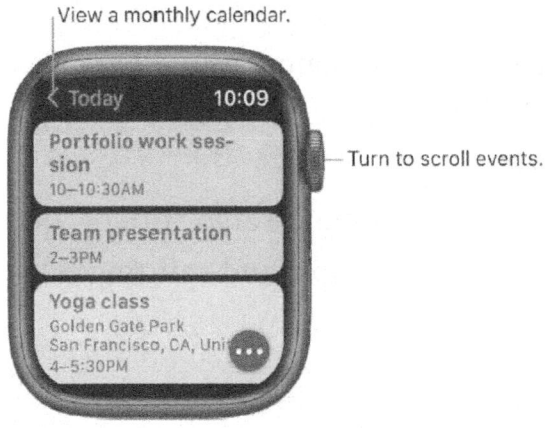

View a monthly calendar.

Turn to scroll events.

SIRI INTEGRATION

You can also use Siri to interact with your calendar events. For example, you can ask Siri, "What's my next event?" to get information about your upcoming schedule.

SWITCHING BETWEEN WEEKLY AND MONTHLY VIEWS

The Calendar app on your Apple Watch offers different viewing options to help you easily navigate through your events and appointments. Here's how you can change the way you view your calendar:

1. 1. Open the Calendar app on your Apple Watch.
2. 2. Tap the icon that looks like four small squares ().
3. 3. Choose from the available viewing options:
    - - Up Next: Displays your upcoming events for the week.
    - - Day: Shows events specifically for the current day.
    - - List: Presents a comprehensive list of all your events from the past two weeks to the next two years.

Navigating Within Views
- - In Day view: Swipe left or right to move to different days.
- - In List view or Up Next view: Turn the Digital Crown to navigate through your events.

RETURNING TO CURRENT DAY AND TIME:

To quickly jump back to the current day and time, tap the current time displayed in the top-right corner of the screen.

VIEWING WEEKS AND MONTHS:

While in Day or List view, you can also access week and month views.
- To show the current week: Tap the "<" symbol in the top-left corner.
- To view a different week: Swipe left or right.
- To select a specific week's events: Tap a day on the weekly calendar.
- To show the current month while viewing the current week: Tap the "<" symbol in the top-left corner.
- To view a different month: Turn the Digital Crown.
- To choose a week in the monthly calendar: Tap the desired week.

MANAGING EVENTS ON APPLE WATCH

The Calendar app on your Apple Watch allows you to effortlessly manage your events, create new ones, respond to invitations, and even get directions to event locations. Here's how you can perform various tasks related to events:

Adding an Event
Events you create on your iPhone's Calendar app are automatically synced to your Apple Watch.
1.   1. Use Siri: Say a command like "Create a calendar event titled Meeting with John for tomorrow at 2 p.m."
2.   2. Use the Calendar app on Apple Watch
•   - While in Up Next, Day, or List view, tap the "Add Event" button ().
•   - Fill in event details such as title, description, date, time, invitees, and choose the calendar.
        - Tap "Add" to create the event.

Deleting or Changing an Event
• Tap the event, then tap "Delete" and confirm the deletion.
• For recurring events, you can choose to delete just the selected instance or all future occurrences.
• To make changes to an event, use the Calendar app on your iPhone.

RESPONDING TO CALENDAR INVITATIONS

• If you see the invitation notification immediately, tap "Accept," "Decline," or "Maybe" at the bottom.
• If you come across the notification later, tap it in your notifications list, then respond.
• If you're in the Calendar app, simply tap the event to respond.

Contacting an event organizer
In the event details, tap the organizer's name, then use the available communication options like phone, message, email, or Walkie-Talkie.

Getting Directions to an Event Location if an event includes a location:
1. Open the Calendar app 7 on your Apple Watch.
2. Tap the event, then tap the address.
3. Your Apple Watch can provide directions to the event's location.

CAMERA REMOTE

Your Apple Watch can serve as a handy tool for capturing photos remotely and setting up the perfect shot. Whether you want to take a picture from a distance, adjust the frame, or set a timer, your Apple Watch can assist you. Here's how you can utilize the Camera Remote and Timer features.

Choose options.

Take a photo.

USING CAMERA REMOTE

Camera Remote  allows you to control your iPhone's camera using your Apple Watch.

Ensure that your Apple Watch is within Bluetooth range of your iPhone (approximately 33 feet or 10 meters).

To initiate the Camera Remote function
1. Open the Camera Remote app on your Apple Watch.
2. Position your iPhone for the desired shot, using your Apple Watch as a viewfinder.
3. Utilize the Digital Crown to zoom in or out.
4. Adjust exposure by tapping the key area of the shot on your Apple Watch's preview.
5. When ready, tap the Shutter button on your Apple Watch to capture the photo.
   - The photo is saved in your iPhone's Photos app, but you can review it on your Apple Watch.

REVIEWING PHOTOS ON APPLE WATCH

After capturing a photo using Camera Remote, you can review it directly on your Apple Watch:

- Tap the thumbnail in the bottom left to view the photo.
- Swipe left or right to navigate through other photos.
- Turn the Digital Crown to zoom in further.
- Drag on a zoomed photo to pan.
- Double-tap a photo to fill the screen.
- Tap the screen to show or hide the Close button and shot count.

Tap Close when you're done reviewing.

USING TIMER

The Timer feature helps you set a delay for taking a photo, allowing you to get ready for the shot.

To set a timer:
1. Open the Camera Remote app 📷 on your Apple Watch.
2. Tap •••, then customize the timer's settings, camera, flash, Live Photo, and HDR options.

These features can help capture the perfect shot using your iPhone's camera while using your Apple Watch as a remote control while ensuring you're included in your photos even when you're behind the lens.

COMPASS

Using the Compass App ⚊ on Apple Watch
The Compass app on Apple Watch provides you with information about your direction, location, and elevation.

Note: If you're using Apple Watch SE or Apple Watch Series 5 or later, you can take advantage of additional features like Compass Waypoints and Backtrack for navigation.

VIEWING BEARINGS, ELEVATION, INCLINE, AND COORDINATES

- The center of the watch face displays your bearing.
- Scroll the Digital Crown to reveal information about incline, elevation, and coordinates on the inner compass ring.
- Further scrolling shows waypoints' locations if you've created any.
- To access a list view for details, tap at the top left.

Adding, Editing, and Clearing Bearings:

Open the Compass app ⚊ on your Apple Watch.

To add a bearing
- Tap ☰, scroll down, and choose Bearing.
- Use the Digital Crown to set the bearing, then tap Done.

To edit a bearing:
- Tap ☰, scroll down, and select Bearing.
- Adjust the bearing using the Digital Crown, then tap Done.

To clear a bearing:
- Tap ☰, scroll down, and tap Clear Bearing, then tap Done.

TO USE TRUE NORTH INSTEAD OF MAGNETIC NORTH

Open the Settings app ⚙ on your Apple Watch.

Tap Compass, then turn on Use True North.

You can also select a grid system, such as DMS, decimal degrees, MGRS/USNG, or UTM, through the Compass settings screen.

CREATING AND VIEWING COMPASS WAYPOINTS

If you have an Apple Watch SE or Apple Watch Series 6 with watchOS 9 or later, you can utilize Compass Waypoints in the Compass app. Compass Waypoints allow you to mark your current location and determine the distance and direction to each waypoint you set up.

Here's how to use Compass Waypoints:

1. Open the Compass app 🧭 on your Apple Watch.
2. Tap the 📍 symbol to add a new waypoint.
3. Provide details for the waypoint, such as a label, color, or symbol (like car or home). Once you're done, tap Done.
4. To view a Compass Waypoint:
   - Tap on any of the three Compass screens.
   - Use the Digital Crown to select the desired waypoint.
   - Tap Select.
     The screen will display the distance and direction to the waypoint, for instance, "3.7 miles to your left."
5. You can tap the bottom of the screen to see the waypoint on a map, complete with its coordinates.
6. If you need to edit information about a waypoint, tap ✏️ on the waypoint screen.

FIND YOUR WAY BACK

On your Apple Watch SE or Apple Watch Series 6, equipped with watchOS 9 or newer, you can utilize the Compass app to help you retrace your route and navigate back to your starting point, particularly when you're in unfamiliar areas.

Please note that the Backtrack feature is designed for use in remote environments—such as locations far from your usual places like home or work—and in areas with limited Wi-Fi coverage.

Here's how to retrace your steps using the Compass app:

1. Open the Compass app ⊼ on your Apple Watch.
2. Tap 👣, and then press Start to initiate the recording of your route.
3. When you wish to retrace your steps, tap ⏸ and choose Retrace Steps. The compass will guide you towards your original starting point.
4. Follow the path displayed on the compass to navigate back to where you initially activated Backtrack.
5. Once you've reached your original starting point, you can conclude the process by tapping 👣 and selecting Delete Steps.

The Backtrack feature can be a handy tool when you need to navigate back to your original location, offering a sense of security and guidance when exploring unfamiliar surroundings.left corner of the camera app. It will open your recently taken photos and videos on your iPhone. Swipe through the photos and videos to view your recently taken shots. Tap "All Photos" at the top right corner to view your photos in the Photo app.

CONTACTS

Within the Contacts app  you can efficiently manage, edit, and share your contacts, ensuring seamless communication across your devices linked to the same Apple ID. Here's how to navigate and make the most of this app on your Apple Watch

VIEW AND INTERACT WITH CONTACTS

1. Open the Contacts app on your Apple Watch.
2. Use the Digital Crown to scroll through your contacts list.
3. Tap a contact to access detailed information and any accompanying notes.

EFFORTLESS COMMUNICATION

You can easily initiate various forms of communication directly from the Contacts app.

1. Open the Contacts app on your Apple Watch.
2. Scroll through your contacts using the Digital Crown.
3. Select a contact, then choose from the following options:
- Tap to view the contact's phone numbers. Tap a number to make a call.
- Tap to access existing message threads or start a new one.
- Tap to compose an email.
- Tap to send an invitation for Walkie-Talkie or, if they've already accepted and enabled Walkie-Talkie, start a conversation.

CREATING A NEW CONTACT

1. Open the Contacts app on your Apple Watch.
2. Swipe downwards, then tap New Contact.
3. Enter the contact's name and, if relevant, company information.
4. Include a phone number, email address, and physical address as needed, then tap Done.

SHARING, EDITING, OR REMOVING CONTACTS

1. Open the Contacts app ![icon] on your Apple Watch.
2. Scroll through your list of contacts using the Digital Crown.
3. Choose a contact, scroll down, and then tap Share Contact, Edit, or Delete Contact, depending on your intention.

CYCLE TRACKING

Stay Informed with Cycle Tracking

With the Cycle Tracking app 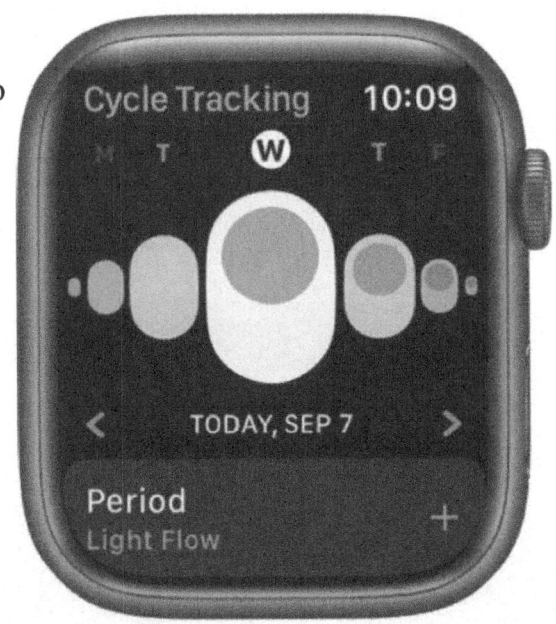, managing your menstrual cycle becomes effortless. You can easily log crucial details such as flow information and symptoms like headaches or cramps. This app uses the logged data to predict the start of your next period or fertile window, sending you timely alerts. Plus, when you pair this information with heart rate data, the Cycle Tracking app's predictions become even more accurate. If you wear an Apple Watch Series 8 during sleep, the app can utilize wrist temperature for enhanced period predictions and retrospective ovulation estimates.

SAFEGUARDING YOUR PRIVACY

The Health app ensures your data remains secure and empowers you to control what information you share. Your privacy is a top priority, and the Health app is built with that principle in mind.

SETTING UP CYCLE TRACKING

1. Open the Health app ♥ on your iPhone.
2. Tap Browse located at the lower right, bringing up the Health Categories screen.
3. Find and tap on Cycle Tracking.
4. Initiate the process by tapping Get Started, then follow the onscreen instructions to configure notifications and other preferences.

TRACK YOUR MENSTRUAL CYCLE WITH APPLE WATCH

1. Launch the Cycle Tracking app on your iPhone.
2. Utilize the available buttons and selection options to details, such as flow level and symptoms.

ECG

Apple Watch Series 4 or a newer model, can utilize the built-in electrical heart rate sensor and the ECG app 〰 to perform an electrocardiogram. This feature allows you to monitor your heart's electrical activity and gain insights into your cardiac health.

Please note that the ECG app requires your iPhone to be updated to at least iPhone 8 or a later version of iOS, and your Apple Watch needs to be running the latest version of watchOS. It's important to know that the ECG app is not available on Apple Watch SE and might not be accessible in all regions.

TO RECORD AN ECG

1. Open the Health app ♥ on your iPhone. Follow the onscreen instructions to set up the ECG feature. If you don't see a setup prompt, access the Health app, tap Browse at the bottom right, then navigate to Heart > Electrocardiogram (ECG).
2. On your Apple Watch, launch the ECG app.
3. Find a comfortable position by resting your arm on a table or in your lap.
4. Use the hand opposite your watch and place your finger on the Digital Crown. Wait as your Apple Watch records the ECG. It's important to note that during the session, you don't need to press the Digital Crown.

This simple process allows you to perform an ECG conveniently and gain valuable insights into your heart's electrical activity.

After the recording is complete, you will receive a classification of the recorded ECG. To further enhance the details, you have the option to tap "Add Symptoms" and select any relevant symptoms you may be experiencing. Once you've chosen your symptoms, tap "Save" to include these notes, and then tap "Done" to complete the process.

To review your ECG results on your iPhone, open the Health app ♥, tap "Browse" at the bottom right, and then navigate to "Heart" > "Electrocardiograms (ECG)."

USE FIND PEOPLE, DEVICES, AND ITEMS

Discover the whereabouts of your loved ones with your Apple Watch

The Find People app  provides a convenient means to locate and stay connected with people who hold significance in your life. By utilizing this app, you can find the location of individuals who share their location with you. As long as your friends and family members use iPhone, iPad, iPod touch, Apple Watch SE, or Apple Watch Series 4 or later, they will appear on a map, enabling you to swiftly pinpoint their positions. You also have the option to set up notifications that inform you when your acquaintances arrive at or depart from specific places.

ADD SOMEONE TO YOUR CIRCLE

1. Launch the Find People app on your Apple Watch.
2. Scroll down and tap "Share My Location."
3. Choose a contact using either Dictation, Contacts, or Keypad.
4. Pick an email address or phone number associated with that contact.
5. Determine the duration for which you wish to share your location—be it an hour, until the day's end, or indefinitely.

Upon your sharing of your location, your chosen contact will receive a notification regarding the same. They are then free to opt for sharing their own location in return. Once your contact agrees to share their location with you, you can conveniently track their whereabouts either through a list or on a map, accessible via the Find My app on iPhone, iPad, iPod touch, Mac, or the Find People app on Apple Watch.

If you wish to cease sharing your location with a particular contact, access the Find People screen, tap the name of the contact, and then select "Stop Sharing."

To stop the sharing of your location with everyone, navigate to the Settings app on your Apple Watch. From there, proceed to Privacy & Security > Location Services, and deactivate "Share My Location."

DISCOVER THE WHEREABOUTS OF FRIENDS

Access the Find People app  on your Apple Watch. This will display a list of your friends, each accompanied by their approximate location and the distance from your current position. Employ the Digital Crown to extend your view to more friends.
To pinpoint the exact location of a specific friend on a map, along with an approximate address, tap their name.
When you're ready to return to the list of friends, tap the "<" icon positioned in the top-left corner of the screen.

Alternatively, you can engage Siri by saying, "Where is Julie?"

NOTIFY A FRIEND ABOUT YOUR MOVEMENTS

1. Launch the Find People app on your Apple Watch.
2. Choose the friend you wish to notify, scroll down, and tap "Notify [name of friend]."
3. Activate "Notify [name of friend]" on the following screen. You will then be prompted to decide whether you want to notify your friend when you depart from your location or when you arrive at their location.

RECEIVE NOTIFICATIONS ABOUT YOUR FRIEND'S LOCATION

1. Open the Find People app on your Apple Watch.
2. Select the friend of interest, scroll down, and tap "Notify Me."
3. Turn on "Notify Me," and then make the choice to receive notifications when your friend leaves their current location or when they reach your specified location.
4.
5.

MONITOR YOUR HEART RATE USING APPLE WATCH

Checking your heart rate offers valuable insights into your overall well-being. Apple Watch provides various ways to keep track of your heart rate, whether during workouts, daily activities, Breathe sessions, or whenever you wish.

Note: Ensure both your wrist and Apple Watch are dry and clean to avoid inaccurate readings due to water and sweat.

VIEW YOUR HEART RATE

To observe your current heart rate, resting rate, and walking average rate, access the Heart Rate app on your Apple Watch.

CONTINUAL MONITORING

Your Apple Watch consistently measures your heart rate as long as you are wearing it.

Review Heart Rate Trends

Launch the Heart Rate app ♡ on your Apple Watch.
Tap on "Current," "Resting Heart Rate," or "Walking Average" to display your heart rate data across the day.

For a broader perspective on your heart rate data over a longer timeframe, open the Health app on your iPhone. Navigate to "Browse," tap on "Heart," and choose the desired time frame—hour, day, week, month, or year.

Activate Heart Rate Monitoring

By default, Apple Watch tracks your heart rate during various activities like using the Heart Rate app, workouts, Breathe sessions, and Reflect sessions. If you have previously disabled heart rate tracking, you can enable it again.
1. Access the Settings app ⚙ on your Apple Watch.
2. Go to "Privacy & Security" and tap on "Health."
3. Select "Heart Rate" and toggle on "Heart Rate."

You can also do this by opening the Apple Watch app on your iPhone, selecting "My Watch," tapping on "Privacy," and then enabling "Heart Rate."

Please remember: For functions such as wrist detection, haptic notifications, blood oxygen level readings (exclusive to Apple Watch Series 6, Apple Watch Series 7, and Apple Watch Series 8), and heart rate monitoring, your Apple Watch's back needs to be in contact with your skin. A comfortable fit—neither too tight nor too loose—ensures optimal functionality while keeping you at ease.

HEART HEALTH WITH APPLE WATCH

Your Apple Watch can serve as a vigilant guardian for your heart health, notifying you of any irregularities. Here are some ways it can keep you informed:

Heart Rate Notifications

Your Apple Watch can send alerts if your heart rate stays above or below a chosen threshold after you've been inactive for at least 10 minutes. You can activate these notifications when you first open the Heart Rate app or later.

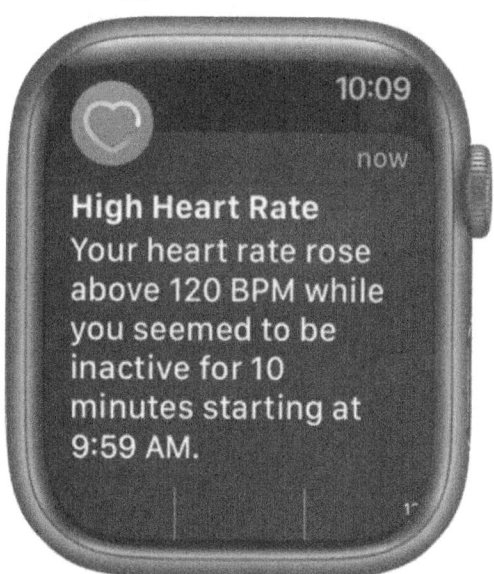

Irregular Heart Rhythm Notifications:
For regions where available, your watch can notify you if it detects an irregular heart rhythm that may indicate atrial fibrillation (AFib). If you've already been diagnosed with AFib, the watch can help you track your heart's arrhythmia frequency and monitor lifestyle factors that influence it.

Enable Notifications
- High or Low Heart Rate Notifications:
  - - Access Settings on your Apple Watch, tap on "Heart," then set a heart rate threshold.
  - - Alternatively, use the Apple Watch app on your iPhone, navigate to My Watch >

Heart, and set the threshold.

Irregular Heart Rhythm Notifications
- Open Settings on your Apple Watch, tap "Heart," and turn on Irregular Rhythm Notifications.
- Or, on your iPhone's Apple Watch app, go to My Watch > Heart and activate Irregular Rhythm.

AFib History Display

For people who live with AFib, the Health app on your iPhone can provide a history of your AFib occurrences. You'll receive weekly notifications estimating the time spent in AFib during the previous calendar week if you've worn your watch adequately.

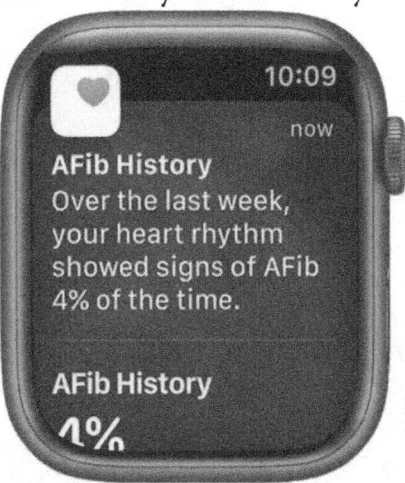

Cardio Fitness Notifications

Your Apple Watch can estimate your cardio fitness based on heart rate data during outdoor activities. It sends notifications if your cardio fitness level falls into the "Low" range, and every four months thereafter if it remains low.

Enable Notifications

Cardio Fitness Notifications

- In Settings on your Apple Watch, tap "Heart," then activate Cardio Fitness Notifications.

Alternatively, use the Apple Watch app on your iPhone, navigate to My Watch > Heart, and enable Cardio Fitness Notifications.

HOME

Your Apple Watch empowers you to control your smart home efficiently through the Home app. This app lets you command HomeKit-enabled accessories, including lights, locks, thermostats, and more, all with enhanced security. You can also make use of Intercom messages on supported devices and view video streams from HomeKit Secure Video cameras. With your Apple Watch, your home controls are conveniently accessible on your wrist.

GETTING STARTED

1. Set up your home using the Home app 🏠 on your iPhone.
2. Define rooms, add HomeKit-enabled accessories, and create scenes.

Accessories, scenes, and rooms added on your iPhone are automatically available on your Apple Watch.

VIEWING HOME STATUS

The Home app 🏠 on your Apple Watch displays the current status of accessories you're using. For example, you can see the temperature from your thermostat or whether your front door is locked. Simply tap a button to control the accessory or access more details.

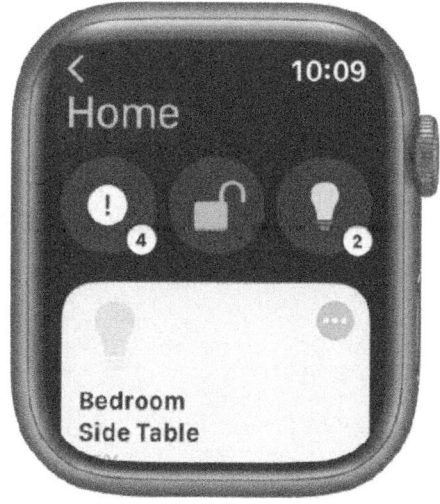

CONTROLLING ACCESSORIES AND SCENES

1. Open the Home app 🏠 on your Apple Watch.
2. At the top of the screen, you'll find relevant scenes and accessories for that moment.
3. To control an accessory or scene, tap ⚫⚫⚫.

- For accessories like lights, tap ⚫⚫⚫ to turn on/off or adjust settings.
- Swipe left to access additional controls, like brightness or color adjustments.
- To control favorites or accessories in a room, tap the favourites or room, then tap an accessory or tap ⚫⚫⚫ to adjust the settings.
- To view a camera's video stream, tap Cameras and select a camera.

RUNNING SCENES

You can activate pre-defined scenes by opening the Home app on your Apple Watch and tapping the desired scene.

MANAGING MULTIPLE HOMES

- If you have multiple homes set up, you can switch between them on your Apple Watch.
- Open the Home app 🏠 on your Apple Watch.
- If the Home Screen is displayed, tap a home.
- If a specific home is visible, tap "<" and then select a different home.

*Note: T*he Home app allows seamless control of your smart home, including managing HomeKit-enabled accessories and scenes, right from your Apple Watch.

MAIL

Effortless Mail Management on Your Apple Watch

Stay on top of your emails with the convenience of your Apple Watch. You can read and respond to messages using various methods, making communication seamless.

READ MAIL NOTIFICATIONS

- When a new mail arrives, just raise your wrist to read the notification.
- Swipe down from the top or tap "Dismiss" to clear the notification.
- If you miss a notification, swipe down on the watch face later to see unread notifications.
- Manage email notifications by going to the Apple Watch app on your iPhone, then navigating to Mail > Custom.

READ MAIL IN THE MAIL APP

1. Open the Mail app  on your Apple Watch.
2. Use the Digital Crown to scroll through the message list.
3. Tap a message to read it.
4. To jump to the top of a lengthy message, turn the Digital Crown or tap the top of the screen.

Messages are formatted for Apple Watch viewing, maintaining most text styles. Tap website links in Mail to view web-formatted content optimized for Apple Watch. Double-tap to zoom in on content.

Note: Website links may not be available in all regions.

SWITCH TO IPHONE

To read a message on your iPhone
1. Wake your iPhone.
2. On iPhones with Face ID, swipe up and pause to open the App Switcher. (On iPhones with a Home button, double-click the Home button to access the App Switcher.)
3. Tap the bottom button to open the Mail app.

COMPOSE AND REPLY TO MAIL

Create a Message:
1. Open the Mail app ✉ on your Apple Watch.
2. Use the Digital Crown to scroll to the top and tap "New Message."
3. Add a recipient by tapping "Add Contact," select the account to send from by tapping "From," create a subject by tapping "Add Subject," and then tap "Create Message."
- If you've set up multiple languages, tap "Language," choose a language, then tap the "Create Message" field.

COMPOSE AND REPLY METHODS

- Reply using the QWERTY and QuickPath keyboard (Apple Watch Series 7 and 8, select languages).
- Use dictation 🎤, Scribble 👆, emoji 😀, or prepared responses.
- If needed, switch to your iPhone to type a response.

REPLY TO A MESSAGE IN THE MAIL APP

1. Open the Mail app ✉ on your Apple Watch.
2. Scroll to the bottom of the message you want to reply to.
3. Tap "Reply."
   - If there are multiple recipients, tap "Reply All."
   - Tap "Add Message," and then proceed with the following methods to reply on the next page.

SMART REPLIES

1. To send a smart reply, scroll to view a list of useful phrases. Simply tap one to send it.
2. Customize smart replies by opening the Apple Watch app on your iPhone.
3. Navigate to My Watch > Mail > Default Replies > Add reply.
4. Reorder or delete default replies by tapping "Edit" and dragging or tapping the delete icon ⊖.
5. If the available smart replies aren't in the language you need, scroll down, tap "Languages," and choose a language.

Note: The available languages are those enabled on your iPhone via Settings > General > Keyboard > Keyboards.

COMPOSE YOUR OWN REPLY

- Tap the "Add Message" field to compose a personalized reply.

REPLY ON IPHONE

1. If you prefer to respond on your iPhone:
2. Wake your iPhone and open the App Switcher.
   - On iPhones with Face ID, swipe up from the bottom edge and pause.
   - On iPhones with a Home button, double-click the Home button.

3. Tap the button at the bottom of the screen to open the email in the Mail app on your iPhone.

MAPS

Discover and Navigate with Ease Using Apple Watch's Maps App

Your Apple Watch is equipped with a Maps app  that lets you explore your surroundings and find your way with ease.

DISCOVER PLACES WITH SIRI

- Use Siri for quick queries like:
- "Where am I?"
- "Find coffee near me."

SEARCH ON THE MAP

1. Open the Maps app on your Apple Watch.
2. Tap "Search," then use voice dictation, scribble, or the QWERTY and QuickPath keyboard (available on Apple Watch Series 7 and Series 8, and not in all languages).
3. On Apple Watch Series 7 and Series 8, access Scribble by swiping up from the bottom of the screen and tapping "Scribble."

FIND NEARBY SERVICES

1. Open the Maps app on your Apple Watch.
2. Tap the ≡, then select a category like Restaurants or Parking.
3. Choose a result to view details, and scroll using the Digital Crown.
4. Tap "<" in the top-left corner to go back to the list of results.

EXPLORE GUIDES

1. Open the Maps app on your iPhone.
2. Tap the search field, swipe up, and:
   - Tap a cover below City Guides or Guides We Love.
   - Tap "Explore Guides" to browse and tap a guide cover.
   - Tap an entry below Browse by Publisher, then tap a cover.
3. Swipe up, tap ╋ next to a location's name, and choose a guide or tap "New Guide."
4. On your Apple Watch, scroll down and tap the guide to view its locations.

VIEW AND SEARCH YOUR CURRENT LOCATION

1. Open the Maps app  on your Apple Watch.
2. Tap "Location" to see your current location.
3. To search around your location, tap the magnifying glass icon and tap ••• "Search Here."
   - Tap "Transit Map" to view nearby transit options.

INTERACT WITH THE MAP

- Pan the map: Drag with one finger.
- Zoom in or out: Turn the Digital Crown.
- Double-tap to zoom in on a location.
- Return to your current location: Tap ⌐ at the bottom right.

PLAN ROUTES AND GET DIRECTIONS

- Open the Maps app on your Apple Watch.
- Scroll to Favorites, Guides, or Recents, and tap an entry for directions.
- Select a mode for driving, walking, transit, or cycling directions.
- Choose an alternate route, adjust preferences, and see route details.
- Tap a route to start navigation and see an overview with turns and distances.

EXPLORING LANDMARKS AND MARKED LOCATIONS

1. Tap the marker on the map for the chosen spot.
2. Use the Digital Crown to view details.
3. Tap "<" at the top left to go back to the map.

*Note: T*o call the location, tap its phone number. For iPhone access, use the App Switcher. (Swipe up from the bottom edge for Face ID iPhones or double-click the Home button for iPhones with a Home button.) Tap the button at the screen's bottom to open Phone.

PLACING, ADJUSTING, AND REMOVING PINS

- Place a pin: Press and hold on the map, wait for the pin to drop, then release.
  - To drop a pin at your current spot, tap the blue dot, then "Mark My Location."
- Adjust a pin: Press and hold to move it or place a new pin.
- Remove a pin: Tap it, see address info, scroll with the Digital Crown, then tap "Remove Marker."

ACCESSING RECENT LOCATIONS

1. Open Maps app  on your Apple Watch.
2. Scroll down, tap a location under "Recents."
   - "Recents" may include recently viewed guides from your iPhone.

GETTING DIRECTIONS

ASK SIRI

- "Directions to the nearest gas station?"
- "Get directions home."
- "How far to the airport?"

Note: Drop a pin on the map to estimate an address, then tap the pin to view address info.

FETCHING DIRECTIONS

1. Launch the Maps app 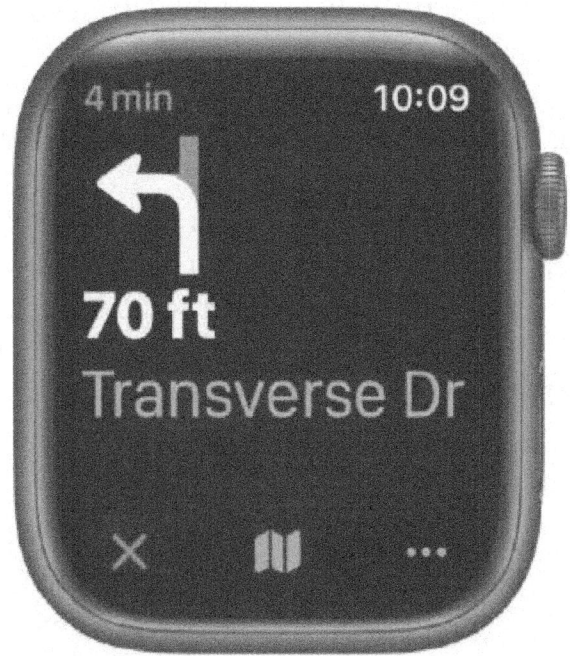 on your Apple Watch.
2. Scroll to Favorites, Guides, or Recents.
3. Tap an entry for driving, walking, transit, or cycling directions.
4. Choose a mode, see suggested routes, and tap a route for an overview.
   - Find your estimated arrival time at the top left. Tap it to check arrival time.

Note: When selecting Cycling, see elevation changes on the route overview. Tap ●●● to learn about road types—bike paths, main roads, or walking-required roads.

MEDICATIONS

Take charge of your medications, vitamins, and supplements through the Health app on your iPhone. The Medications app 💊 on your Apple Watch allows you to monitor and log your medications, along with setting up reminders.

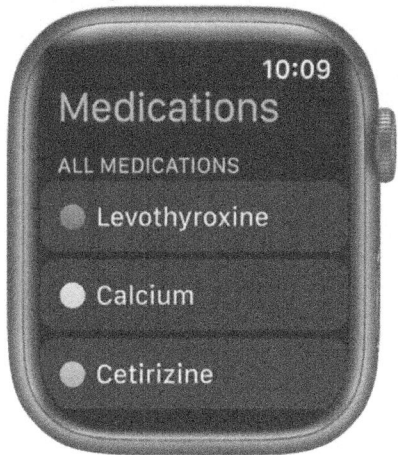

Note: The Medications feature should never replace professional medical advice. While additional info might be on your medication labels, it's vital to consult your healthcare provider before making any health-related choices.

CREATING A MEDICATION SCHEDULE ON IPHONE

1. Launch the Health app on your iPhone, tap Browse at the bottom right, and then tap Medications.
2. Choose to Add Medication (if you're starting your list) or Add a Medication (if you're adding more).
3. Identify your medication using these options:

Type the name: Tap the search field, type the name, and tap Add.

- For U.S. users, suggestions appear while you type, and you can pick one or finish typing and add.

Use the camera Option 📷
Tap next to the search field and follow onscreen instructions.
If there's no match, tap Search by Name, then type it as above.

Follow onscreen instructions to create a visual identifier, set a schedule, and understand potential interactions.

LOGGING YOUR MEDICATIONS

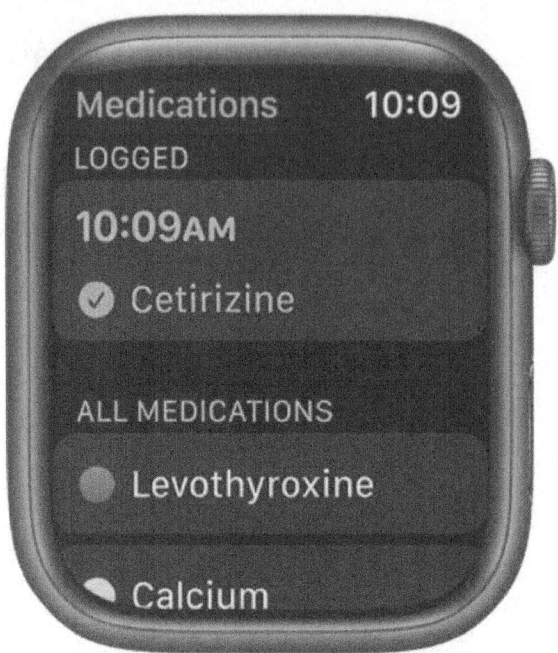

Your Apple Watch reminds you to take medications as per your schedule in the Health app
💜 on iPhone.

Follow these steps to log them:
1. Tap a notification if it prompts you to log your medications, or open the Medications
   app on your Apple Watch.
2. Tap the current medication schedule, e.g., morning medications.
3. Tap Log All as Taken.
   • This records dosage, units taken, and the time. To log individual medications, scroll
     down, tap a medication under Your Medications, and then tap Log.
   • The medication name and time logged will be visible under Logged.

To update a logged medication, tap it, select Taken or Skipped, and then tap Done.

You can view your log and medication history on your iPhone's Health app under Browse
and Medications.

MEMOJI

Unleash your creativity with the Memoji app , where you can craft your own unique Memoji persona. Customize features like skin tone, freckles, hairstyle, facial traits, glasses, headwear, and more. Multiple Memojis can be designed to reflect various moods.

CRAFTING A MEMOJI

1. Open the Memoji app on your Apple Watch.
2. If it's your first time using the Memoji app, tap Get Started.
   - If you've previously made a Memoji, scroll down, and tap ⊕ to create a new one.
3. Tap each feature and use the Digital Crown to select your desired options. Watch your Memoji come to life as you add details like hairstyle and eyewear.
4. Tap Done to add your new Memoji to the collection.
5. The Memojis you create can be used as stickers in Messages.

For another Memoji, tap ⊕ and then add features.

EDITING MEMOJI AND MORE

Open the Memoji app on your Apple Watch, tap a Memoji, and explore these options

- Edit a Memoji: Tap features like eyes and headwear, then turn the Digital Crown to choose a variation.
- Craft a Memoji watch face: Scroll down and tap Create Watch Face.
  Swipe left on your watch face to discover your new Memoji watch face. This face is also included in your watch face collection on the Apple Watch app on your iPhone.
- Duplicate a Memoji: Scroll down and tap Duplicate.
- Delete a Memoji: Scroll down and tap Delete.

MESSAGES

Stay connected by reading incoming text messages directly on your Apple Watch. Respond using the QWERTY and QuickPath keyboard (only available on Apple Watch Series 7 and Apple Watch Series 8 in certain languages), dictation, Scribble, prepared responses, or switch to your iPhone for longer replies.

STEPS TO READ A MESSAGE

1. Feel a tap or hear an alert sound indicating a new message? Raise your Apple Watch to read it.
2. Turn the Digital Crown to scroll through the message content.
3. Tap the top of the screen to swiftly navigate to the message's beginning.

Note: Web links within messages are tappable for viewing web-formatted content, and double-tap to zoom in. If the message is from a while ago, touch and hold the top of the screen, swipe down to see the message notification, then tap to read. To mark the message as read, scroll down and tap Dismiss. To dismiss the notification without marking it as read, press the Digital Crown.

DETERMINING SENT TIMES

To check when messages were sent, swipe left on a message within a conversation in the Messages conversation list.

MUTING OR DELETING CONVERSATIONS

- Mute a conversation: Swipe left on a conversation in the Messages conversation list and tap 🔕.
- Delete a conversation: Swipe left on a conversation in the Messages conversation list and tap 🗑.

ACCESSING PHOTOS, AUDIO, MUSIC, AND VIDEO

Messages can include multimedia content. Follow these steps to access them on your Apple Watch

- Photo: Tap a photo to view, double-tap to enlarge, and drag to navigate. Tap < in the top-left corner to return. To share, tap the photo, then select the sharing option ⬆. To save it, scroll down and tap Save Image or Create Watch Face.

- Audio Clip: Tap the clip to listen. Tap Keep to retain it for longer. It remains for 30 days, but you can adjust this on your iPhone's settings.
- Music: Tap a song, album, or playlist to play it in the Music app (Apple Music subscription required).
- Video: Tap a video to play it fullscreen. Control playback with taps and swipes. Save videos by opening the message on your iPhone.

MANAGING MESSAGE NOTIFICATIONS

1. Open the Apple Watch app on your iPhone.
2. Tap My Watch, then Messages.
3. Customize notification options under Custom to determine how you're notified when receiving messages.

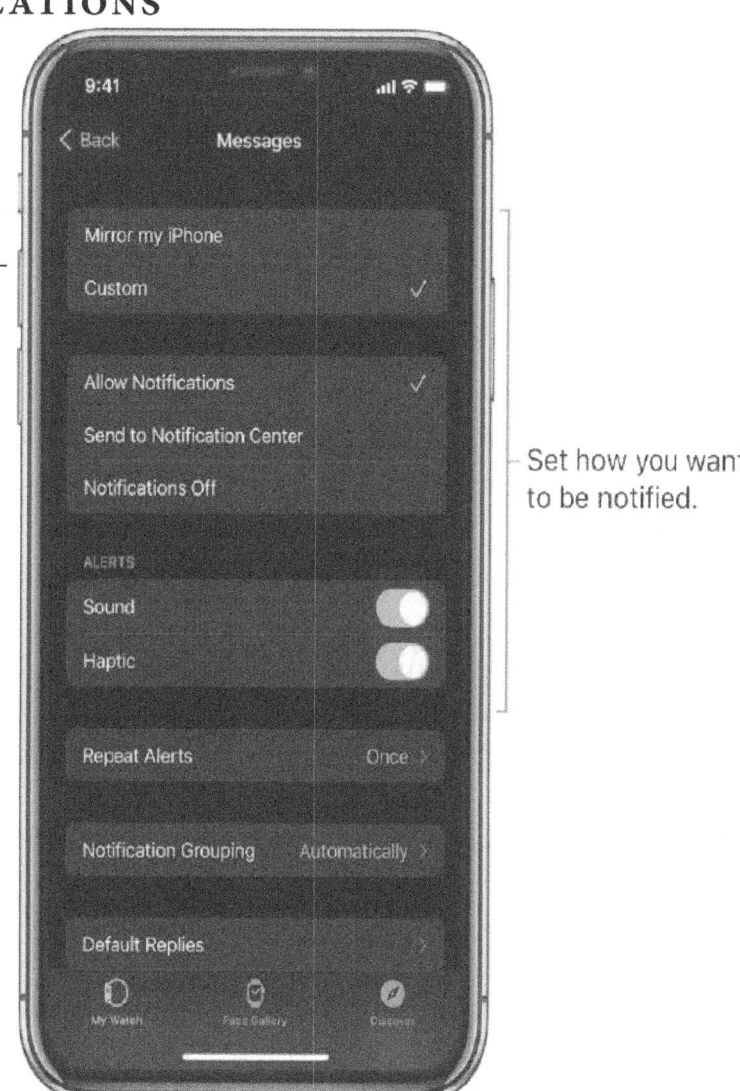

Set how you want to be notified.

Note that certain Focus settings might affect message notifications.

SENDING MESSAGES FROM YOUR APPLE WATCH

Stay in touch effortlessly by composing and sending messages from your Apple Watch. Not only can you include text, but you can also add images, emoji 😊, Memoji stickers 🧑, audio clips 🎤, and even send money through Apple Pay 💵Cash or share your location.

CREATING A MESSAGE

1. Launch the Messages app on your Apple Watch.
2. Scroll to the top and tap New Message.
3. Add a contact by tapping Add Contact or selecting from recent conversations. Alternatively, you can:
   - Use the search field or dictate a phone number 🎤 .
   - Choose from your entire list of contacts 👤 .
   - Manually enter a phone number ⌨ .
4. Tap Create Message.
5. If you use multiple languages on your Apple Watch, select a language if needed.

COMPOSING A TEXT MESSAGE

Composing a message is simple. After creating a message, tap the Create Message field and use any of the following methods to compose your message:

- Utilize Scribble: Write your message with your finger. Edit using the Digital Crown and use predictive text.
- Dictate text: Tap the microphone icon 🎤 , speak your message, and tap Done. Punctuation can also be dictated.
- Use the QWERTY and QuickPath keyboard: (Available on Apple Watch Series 7 and Apple Watch Series 8, but not in all languages) Enter characters or swipe with QuickPath to form words.
- Include emoji 😄: Access frequently used or browse categories to find the right emoji.
- Use your iPhone keyboard: If your paired iPhone is nearby, you can use its keyboard to compose messages.

SENDING VARIOUS TYPES OF MESSAGES FROM YOUR APPLE WATCH

Diversify your messaging style by choosing from a range of options without needing to type a single character. Once you've created your message, explore these alternatives:

SMART REPLY

Swipe to view a collection of convenient phrases that you can use. Tap one to select, then tap Send.

To customize these options, go to the Apple Watch app on your iPhone, select My Watch, navigate to Messages > Default Replies, and tap Add Reply. For further personalization, you can tap Edit to reorder or delete phrases by tappying ⊖ .

If the smart replies are not in your desired language, scroll down, select Languages, and choose the appropriate language. These languages align with those enabled on your iPhone under Settings > General > Keyboard > Keyboards.

MEMOJI STICKER

Tap 🔤, navigate through the Memoji Stickers collection, choose a variation, and then tap 🔘 Send.

STICKER

Tap 🔤, tap 🔘, scroll to the bottom, and then tap More Stickers. Select a sticker and tap Send. For creating new stickers or viewing your full collection, utilize the Messages app on your iPhone.

GIF

Tap 🔤, tap 🔍, select a GIF, and then tap Send. If you need a specific GIF, enter a search term in the Search field, tap a resulting GIF, and then tap Send.

AUDIO CLIP

Tap 🔤, tap 〰️, record your mess
age, tap Done, and then tap Send.

USING APPLE CASH FOR TRANSACTIONS

1. While in a conversation, tap 🔤 next to the iMessage field.
2. Tap ⬤Cash.
3. Adjust the amount using the Digital Crown, then tap Send.
4. Double-click the side button to send the payment.

Note: Availability of Apple Cash varies by region.

SHARE YOUR LOCATION

To send someone a map showing your current location, scroll down, then tap Send Location.

On your paired iPhone, make sure Share My Location is turned on in Settings  > [your name] > Find My > Share My Location. Or, on your Apple Watch with cellular, open the Settings app , go to Privacy > Location Services, then turn on Share My Location.

Share your location in a message.

Messages screen showing a map of the sender's location.

CONTACT THE PERSON YOU'RE MESSAGING

1. While viewing a conversation, scroll down.
2. Tap Details, then tap 📞 , 📞 , ✉️ , or 🔘 .

Scroll down and tap Share Contact to share the contact with others.

RESPONDING TO MESSAGES ON YOUR APPLE WATCH

Replying to a Message

Scroll down using the Digital Crown to reach the bottom of the message, and then select your preferred method of reply.

You can also use Tapbacks for quick responses—press and hold a specific message in the conversation, then choose a Tapback option like thumbs-up or heart.

Direct Reply to a Specific Message

In a group conversation, you can provide a direct response to a particular message to maintain organized conversations.

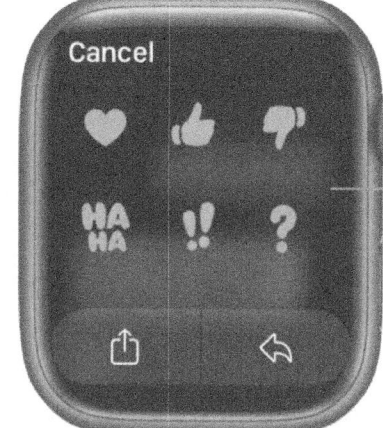

Double-tap a message, then tap to choose a Tapback.

1. Within a Messages conversation, hold your finger on a specific message you wish to reply to.
2. Tap ↩.
3. Craft your response and tap Send.
   The message you send will only be visible to the recipient of your response.

Sharing Messages with Others

1. In a Messages conversation, touch and hold a specific message Tap ↑.
2. Choose recipients you frequently exchange messages with, or select Messages or Mail.
3. If you opt for Messages or Mail, add contacts and include a subject if sending an email.
4. Tap Send.

MINDFULNESS

Utilize your Apple Watch to embrace mindfulness through the Mindfulness app ✸. This app encourages you to allocate a few minutes each day for focusing, centering, and connecting with your breath. Additionally, with an Apple Fitness+ subscription, you can access guided meditations directly on your Apple Watch.

STARTING A REFLECT OR BREATHE SESSION

Begin your mindfulness journey by opening the Mindfulness app ✸ on your Apple Watch, and then follow these steps:

- For Reflect: Tap Reflect, read the theme, concentrate your attention, and tap Begin.
- For Breathe: Tap Breathe, slowly inhale as the animation expands, and exhale as it contracts.

To conclude a session before its completion, swipe to the right and tap End.

ADJUSTING SESSION DURATION

Customize your mindfulness experience by setting the session duration:

1. Open the Mindfulness app on your Apple Watch.

2. Tap , choose Duration, and then select a duration from one to five minutes.

FINE-TUNING MINDFULNESS SETTINGS

Tailor your mindfulness practice with these setting adjustments:
1. Open the Settings app  on your Apple Watch.
2. Tap Mindfulness, and then make the following adjustments
   - Reminders: Turn Start of Day and End of Day reminders on or off; add extra reminders as needed.
   - Weekly Summary: Toggle Weekly Summary on or off.
   - Mute Reminders: Activate "Mute for today."
   - Breath Rate: Adjust the breaths per minute by tapping Breath Rate.
   - Haptics Settings: Tap Haptics, and choose None, Minimal, or Prominent.
   - New Meditations: Enable Add New Meditations to Watch to download fresh meditations when your watch is charging. Completed meditations are automatically removed.

You can also adjust these settings via the Apple Watch app on your iPhone by navigating to My Watch > Mindfulness.

MONITORING HEART RATE DURING SESSIONS

After completing a Reflect or Breathe session, your heart rate is displayed on the Summary screen. For a more detailed review, access your heart rate information later by launching the Health app on your iPhone, tapping Browse, then Heart > Heart Rate. Swipe up and tap Breathe.

USING THE BREATHE WATCH FACE

Quickly access mindfulness sessions by adding the Breathe watch face:

1. On your current watch face, press and hold the display.
2. Swipe left until you reach the end, then tap the New button (+).
3. Rotate the Digital Crown to select Breathe, and tap Add.
4. Tap the watch face to open the Mindfulness app.

SUBSCRIPTION MINDFULNESS

Enjoy Guided Meditations with Your Apple Watch

If you're an Apple Fitness+ subscriber, you can indulge in guided meditations through your Apple Watch while it's paired with AirPods, Bluetooth headphones, or speakers. Please note that Apple Fitness+ availability varies by country and region.

STARTING A GUIDED MEDITATION

To begin your soothing meditation experience, follow these straightforward steps

1. Launch the Mindfulness app on your Apple Watch.
2. Tap Fitness+ Audio Meditations.
3. Scroll through the meditation options to find one that resonates with you.
    *   Details like the theme, trainer, and duration of the meditation are displayed towards the bottom of each episode.
4. Tap (i) to access more information about the meditation, add it to your library, or play its playlist in the Music app .
5. Choose a meditation to initiate the session.
    *   During the meditation, Apple Watch will show the elapsed time and your current heart rate.

To pause or conclude a guided meditation, swipe right while the meditation is playing, then tap Pause or End. If you wish to start a workout while continuing with the meditation, tap Workout and select a suitable workout.

REVIEWING COMPLETED MEDITATIONS

1. Once you've finished a meditation, it's stored in My Library. To access this collection, you can use your Apple Watch or the Fitness app on your iPhone.
2. Open the Mindfulness app on your Apple Watch.
3. Tap Fitness+ Audio Meditations.
    *   Scroll to the bottom of the screen and tap My Library to view the meditations you've enjoyed.
4. Tap (i) to gather more insights about a meditation, download it, remove it from your library, or play its playlist in the Music app.

Opt for a meditation to replay it whenever you like.

You can also explore your library across your iPhone, iPad, or Apple TV. Just open the Fitness app on your device (access Fitness+ on iPhone) and navigate to My Library.

MUSIC

Manage Your Music Collection on Apple Watch

ADD MUSIC TO APPLE WATCH

By adding music to your Apple Watch, you ensure that you can enjoy your favorite tunes wherever you are, even without your iPhone by your side. Here's how you can do it.

USING YOUR IPHONE

- Open the Apple Watch app 🎵 on your iPhone.
- Tap "My Watch" and then select "Music."
- Under "Playlists & Albums," tap "Add Music."
- Choose the specific albums and playlists you'd like to sync with your Apple Watch.

USING YOUR APPLE WATCH

- If you're an Apple Music subscriber, you can directly add music using your Apple Watch.
- Open the Music app 🎵 on your watch.
- Tap "Listen Now" or "Search" and navigate to the music you want to add.
- Select a playlist or album, then tap ••• the "Add to Library" option.
- A confirmation message will let you know the item has been added.

Keep in mind that music you've recently listened to will automatically be added if you're an Apple Music subscriber. If you haven't played anything, Apple Music's recommendations will be added.

ADD A WORKOUT PLAYLIST

For those workout sessions, you can set up a playlist that plays automatically when you start a workout using the Workout app on your Apple Watch. Here's how:

USING YOUR IPHONE

- Open the Apple Watch app 🎵 on your iPhone.
- Tap "My Watch," then select "Workout."
- Under "Workout Playlist," choose a playlist to associate with your workouts.

REMOVE MUSIC FROM APPLE WATCH

If you need to free up space or simply want to tidy up your music collection on your Apple Watch, you can remove music as needed:

USING YOUR IPHONE

- Open the Apple Watch app 🎵 on your iPhone.
- Tap "My Watch," then select "Music."
- For music you've added, tap Edit, then tap ➖ to reove the items you want.
- To remove automatically added music, toggle off "Recent Music" or other auto-added options.

USING YOUR APPLE WATCH

- If you're an Apple Music subscriber, you can remove music directly from your watch.
- Open the Music app 🎵 on your watch.
- Navigate to "Library," then "Downloaded," and select "Playlists" or "Albums."
- Swipe left on a playlist or album, tap ••• then tap Remove, then confirm by tapping "Delete."

Remember that songs or playlists removed from your Apple Watch will also be removed from other devices using the same Apple ID. To check how much music is stored on your Apple Watch, go to settings ⚙️ > "General" > "Storage" on your watch or "General" > "Storage" in the Apple Watch app on your iPhone.

PLAYING MUSIC ON YOUR APPLE WATCH

The Music app 🎵 on your Apple Watch lets you easily choose and play music. Whether you want to listen to songs stored on your watch, control music on your iPhone, or stream from Apple Music or Apple Music Voice (subscription required), you can do it all. Here's how.

USING SIRI

You can ask Siri to play specific songs, albums, or playlists for you. Just say things like:

- "Play 'enough for you' by Olivia Rodrigo."
- "Play more songs from this album."
- "Play my workout playlist."
- "Play Apple Music Country."
- "Play cool jazz."
- "Play the dinner party playlist."
- "Play a playlist to help me relax."
- "Play more like this."

PLAYING MUSIC

Once your Apple Watch is connected to Bluetooth headphones or speakers, follow these steps to play music using the Music app :

PLAY MUSIC ON APPLE WATCH

- Open the Music app on your Apple Watch.
- Turn the Digital Crown to browse through album artwork.
- Tap a playlist or album to start playing it.
- Use the Apple Watch app on your iPhone to manage which songs are available on your Apple Watch.

PLAY MUSIC FROM YOUR IPHONE (NO BLUETOOTH PAIRING REQUIRED)

- Scroll to the top of the screen on your Apple Watch.
- Tap "On iPhone."
- Select a playlist, artist, album, or song to play from your iPhone's music library.

PLAY MUSIC FROM YOUR MUSIC LIBRARY

- Open the Music app on your Apple Watch.
- Tap "Library."
- Choose a playlist, artist, album, or song to play.
- For music already downloaded to your watch, tap "Downloaded" and select the music.

REQUEST MUSIC FROM APPLE MUSIC

- If you're an Apple Music or Apple Music Voice subscriber, you can ask for specific music by raising your wrist.
- Request an artist, album, song, genre, or part of a song lyric.

PERSONALIZED MUSIC

As an Apple Music subscriber, you can enjoy music personalized for you:

1. Open the Music app  on your Apple Watch.
2. Scroll to the top and tap "Listen Now."
3. Explore playlists and albums curated based on your preferences.
4. Tap a category, then an album or playlist, and tap the play button ▶.

MANAGING THE QUEUE

When playing music, you can manage the queue of upcoming songs:

1. Open the Music app  on your Apple Watch.
2. Start playing an album or playlist, then tap the queue icon ☰.
3. Tap a track in the queue to play it.

Auto Play adds similar music to the queue's end. To disable Auto Play, tap the ∞ option.

To add songs of your choice to the queue, swipe left on a song, playlist, or album; tap the ••• icon, then select "Play Next" or "Play Last." Remember, turning off Auto Play on one device won't affect other devices using your Apple ID.

CONTROLLING PLAYBACK AND MORE WITH MUSIC ON YOUR APPLE WATCH

ADJUSTING VOLUME

Turn the Digital Crown to control the volume. You can use these controls to manage music playback on both your Apple Watch and iPhone:

- Play the current song.
- Pause playback.

- Skip to the next song.
- Double-tap to skip to the previous song or to return to the beginning of the current song.

▶	Play the current song.
❚❚	Pause playback.
▶▶	Skip to the next song.
◀◀	Skip to the beginning of the song; double-tap to skip to the previous song.

SHUFFLE AND REPEAT

You can shuffle albums, songs, and artists from the Music screen:
- Tap an album, artist, or playlist.
- Tap the shuffle icon ⤨ to shuffle the content.

You can also control shuffle and repeat from the playback screen:
- While music is playing, tap the three dots •••.
- Choose ⤨ or ⤻ to customize your listening experience.
Tap the "Repeat" ⤻ icon twice to repeat a song.

USING MUSIC ON APPLE WATCH

You can interact with your music library on Apple Watch:
- While music is playing, tap the three dots ••• on the Now Playing screen for more options.
- Swipe left on a song, playlist, or album in Listen Now and Library, then tap the ••• icon for more choices.
- Tap ＋ to add items to your library from these options.

SHARING MUSIC

If you're an Apple Music subscriber, you can share playlists, albums, and songs:
1. Open the Music app 🎵 on your Apple Watch.
2. Choose where you want to start (On iPhone, Listen Now, or Library).
3. Tap Playlists, Albums, or Songs.
4. Swipe left on a playlist, album, or song.
5. Tap the ••• icon, then select "Share [Playlist, Album, Song]."
6. Choose a sharing method.
You can also share a song directly from the Now Playing screen by tapping the ••• icon and selecting "Share Song." For songs from radio stations, choose "Share Station."

CELLULAR CONNECTION SETTINGS

To listen to music over cellular, follow these steps:

1. On your iPhone, go to Settings  > Music.
2. Turn on Cellular Data.
3. Tap Audio Quality > Cellular Streaming, then choose a quality setting. Note that higher quality settings use more data.

LISTENING TO RADIO ON APPLE WATCH

The Music app 🎵 on your Apple Watch offers a variety of radio options, including Apple Music 1, Apple Music Hits, Apple Music Country, and broadcast radio stations:

LISTENING TO APPLE MUSIC RADIO

- Open the Music app 🎵 on your Apple Watch.
- Tap Radio, then select Apple Music 1, Apple Music Hits, or Apple Music Country.

LISTENING TO FEATURED OR GENRE STATIONS

- Open the Music app 🎵 on your Apple Watch.
- Tap Radio, and use the Digital Crown to browse stations and genres crafted by music experts.
- Tap a genre to explore its stations, and select a station to start listening.

LISTENING TO BROADCAST RADIO

You can enjoy broadcast radio stations on your Apple Watch by asking Siri. For example, say "Play Wild 94.9" or "Tune in to ESPN Radio." You can use station names, call signs, frequencies, or nicknames.

Please note that some features may not be available in the Apple Music Voice Plan. For more details, refer to the Apple Support article on Apple Music Voice. Also, broadcast radio availability varies by country or region.

NEWS

Reading News Stories on Your Apple Watch

The News app  on your Apple Watch keeps you informed about current events by presenting news stories tailored to your interests.

WAYS TO ACCESS NEWS STORIES

- Open the News app  directly on your Apple Watch.
- Tap the News complication on a watch face.
- Tap a news item on the Siri watch face.
- Tap a notification from the News app.

READING A NEWS STORY

1. Open the News app  on your Apple Watch.
2. Use the Digital Crown to scroll through the story summary.
3. If you wish to read the full story on your iPhone, iPad, or Mac, scroll to the bottom of the summary and tap "Save for Later."

READING STORIES ON OTHER DEVICES

- iPhone: Open the News app  on your iPhone, tap "Following," then "Saved Stories." Locate and tap the story.
- iPad: Open the News app  on your iPad, tap "Saved Stories" in the sidebar, then select the story.
- Mac: Open the News app  on your Mac, click "Saved Stories" in the sidebar, and click the story.

CUSTOMIZING NEWS FEEDS

To read stories only from the channels you follow, you can restrict stories in Today
1. Open the Settings app ⚙ on your iPhone.
2. Tap "News," then turn on "Restrict Stories in Today."

Please be aware that restricting stories limits the variety of content in Today and other feeds. If you follow only one channel, your feed will consist mainly of stories from that channel. This setting removes Top Stories and Trending Stories.

NAVIGATING NEWS STORIES

1. Open the News app 🅽 on your Apple Watch.
2. Swipe left to move to the next available story.
3. Swipe right to return to the previous story.

If you're reading the summary, tap "Next Story" at the bottom to proceed.

OPENING STORIES ON IPHONE

To open news stories on your iPhone from your Apple Watch

1. Open the News app 🅽 on your Apple Watch.
2. Wake your iPhone and access the App Switcher (swipe up from the bottom edge or double-click the Home button on iPhones with Face ID).
3. Tap the button that appears at the bottom of the screen to open the News app on your iPhone.

NOISE

Measuring Environmental Noise with Your Apple Watch

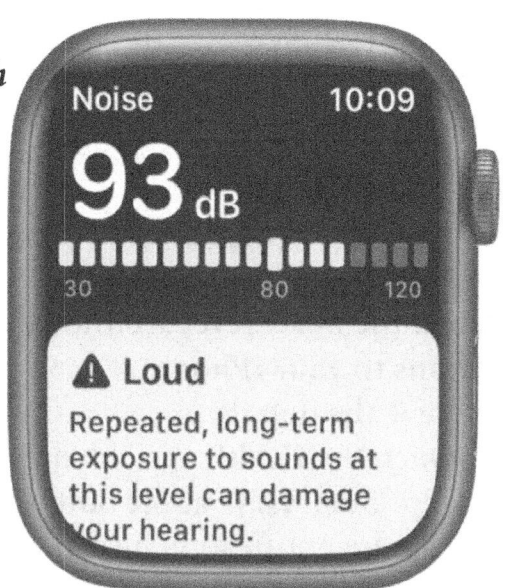

USING THE NOISE APP

The Noise app on your Apple Watch gauges the surrounding sound levels by utilizing the microphone and monitoring duration. It can alert you with a wrist tap when noise reaches a level that could impact your hearing.

Please note that the Noise app employs the microphone solely for measuring sound levels; no sounds are recorded or stored for this purpose.

TO CONFIGURE THE NOISE APP

1. Open the Noise app 🦻 on your Apple Watch.
2. Tap "Enable" to activate monitoring.
3. For future environmental noise measurements, access the Noise app 🦻 or use the Noise complication.

RECEIVING NOISE NOTIFICATIONS

1. Open the Settings app ⚙ on your Apple Watch.
2. Navigate to Noise > Noise Notifications and select your preferred setting.
You can also adjust this in the Apple Watch app on your iPhone under My Watch > Noise > Noise Threshold.

DISABLING NOISE MEASUREMENT

1. Open the Settings app ⚙ on your Apple Watch.
2. Go to Noise > Environmental Sound Measurements and switch off "Measure Sounds."
You can also adjust this in the Apple Watch app on your iPhone under My Watch > Noise, then toggle off "Environmental Sound Measurements."

ENVIRONMENTAL NOISE MONITORING

When you pair your Apple Watch with your iPhone and set up the Noise app 🎧 on your watch, the data on environmental sound levels is automatically transmitted to the Health app on your iPhone (requires watchOS 6 or later).

VIEWING NOISE NOTIFICATIONS DETAILS

When the noise level around you might impact your hearing, Apple Watch sends notifications to your iPhone.
To view the details:
1. Open the Health app 💜 on your iPhone.
2. Tap "Summary" at the bottom left.
3. Tap the notification near the top of the screen, then select "Show More Data."

TRACKING EXPOSURE OVER TIME

To observe your exposure to environmental noise levels:
1. Open the Health app 💜 on your iPhone.
2. Tap "Browse" at the bottom right, then choose "Hearing."
3. Tap "Environmental Sound Levels" and utilize the following options:

- Tabs at the top display exposure levels over different periods.
- Tap the information icon ⓘ to learn about sound level classifications.
- Swipe the graph to adjust the displayed time span.
- Touch and hold the graph to view details about a specific moment.
- Tap "Show More Data" for average exposure details.
- Tap "Exposure" below the graph to see a line indicating average exposure.
- Tap "Show More Data," then "Range" to view the high and low range of noise levels.

NOW PLAYING

CONTROL AUDIO PLAYBACK

Now Playing empowers you to manage audio playback on Apple Watch, iPhone, and other connected devices.

ACCESS NOW PLAYING

You can access Now Playing through various methods
- Open the Now Playing app ▶ on your Apple Watch.
- Press the side button and tap "Now Playing" in the Dock (it's the first item).
- Tap the Now Playing complication if you've added it to your watch face.

CONTROL MUSIC, PODCASTS, OR AUDIOBOOKS ON IPHONE

1. Launch the Music 🎵, Podcasts 🎙, or audiobook 📖 app on your iPhone and begin playing a song, podcast, or audiobook.
2. Open Now Playing ▶ on your Apple Watch to utilize controls like play, pause, and more.
3. Use the Digital Crown to adjust the volume.

USING NOW PLAYING WITH DIFFERENT DEVICES

If multiple devices can play audio, such as an Apple Watch, iPhone, and HomePod

- The top-left corner displays the name of the device you're currently controlling.
- Tap "<" to reveal a list of available devices and choose one to control it.

PHONE

ANSWER A CALL

- Lift your wrist to view the caller's information.
- To send the call to voicemail, tap the red "Decline" button.
- To answer on your Apple Watch, tap "Answer" and utilize the built-in microphone and speaker or a paired Bluetooth device.
- If you prefer to answer with your iPhone or send a text message instead, tap ••• and choose an option.
- If you select "Answer on iPhone," the call is put on hold, and the caller hears a repeated sound until you answer on your iPhone.

    If you can't find your iPhone, touch and hold the ••• bottom of the screen, swipe up, then tap ((☐)) on your Apple Watch.

DURING THE CALL

- Switch the call from your Apple Watch to your iPhone by unlocking your iPhone and tapping the green button or bar.
- Adjust the call volume by turning the Digital Crown. You can also tap 🎤 to mute your end of the call.
- Enter digits using the keypad if needed by tapping ●●●, then selecting "Keypad."
- Switch the call's audio to another device by tapping ●●●, then choosing a device.
- During a FaceTime Audio call, adjust the volume, mute the call with 🎤, or choose an audio destination.

LISTENING TO VOICEMAIL

If you receive voicemail, you'll get a notification. Tap the Play button to listen to it. You can also listen later by opening the Phone app 📞 on your Apple Watch and tapping "Voicemail."

ON THE VOICEMAIL SCREEN, YOU CAN:

- Adjust volume using the Digital Crown.
- Start and stop playback.
- Skip ahead or back five seconds.
- Call back the voicemail sender.
- Delete the voicemail.

MAKING PHONE CALLS

You can easily make phone calls using voice commands or manually.

- Ask Siri to call someone or dial a specific number.
- Open the Phone app 📞 on your Apple Watch, tap "Contacts," choose a contact, and tap the phone button.
- Dial a number directly by tapping "Keypad," entering the number, and tapping .
- For recent contacts or favorites, tap "Recents" or "Favorites" respectively.

MAKING CALLS OVER WI-FI ON APPLE WATCH

If your cellular provider supports Wi-Fi calling, you can use your Apple Watch to make and receive calls over Wi-Fi instead of relying on the cellular network. This is particularly useful when your paired iPhone isn't accessible or powered off. Your Apple Watch must be within range of a Wi-Fi network that your iPhone has previously connected to.

SETTING UP WI-FI CALLING

1. On your iPhone, navigate to Settings ⚙ > Phone.
2. Tap "Wi-Fi Calling" and enable both "Wi-Fi Calling on This iPhone" and "Add Wi-Fi Calling for Other Devices."
3. Open the Phone app 📞 on your Apple Watch.
4. Choose a contact and tap 📞.
5. Select the desired phone number or FaceTime address for the call.

IMPORTANT NOTE ON EMERGENCY CALLS

While you can make emergency calls over Wi-Fi, it's recommended to use your iPhone over a cellular connection whenever possible for more accurate location information. If needed, you can temporarily disconnect your Apple Watch from Wi-Fi to ensure you're using your iPhone for emergency calls.

VIEWING CALL INFORMATION ON APPLE WATCH

While engaged in a call on your iPhone, you can access call details on your Apple Watch using the Phone app 📞. You can also end the call from your Apple Watch, especially useful when you're using earphones or a headset.

USING DUAL SIM IPHONE WITH APPLE WATCH

If you have a Dual SIM iPhone with multiple cellular plans, you can also use multiple lines on your Apple Watch with cellular capabilities. Here's how:

1. Set up your first plan during initial watch setup.
2. To add a second plan, open the Apple Watch app on your iPhone, go to My Watch > Cellular > Set Up Cellular or Add a New Plan.
3. Follow the steps to select the additional plan for your Apple Watch.

SWITCHING BETWEEN PLANS

1. On your Apple Watch, navigate to Settings ⚙ > Cellular.
2. Choose the desired plan for your watch to use.

RECEIVING CALLS AND MESSAGES WITH MULTIPLE PLANS

- When your Apple Watch is connected to your iPhone, you can receive calls and messages from both plans. The watch indicates which line received the notification.
- If your Apple Watch is connected to cellular and your iPhone isn't nearby, calls and messages come through based on the line you've chosen in the Apple Watch app.

PHOTOS

Managing Photos on Apple Watch

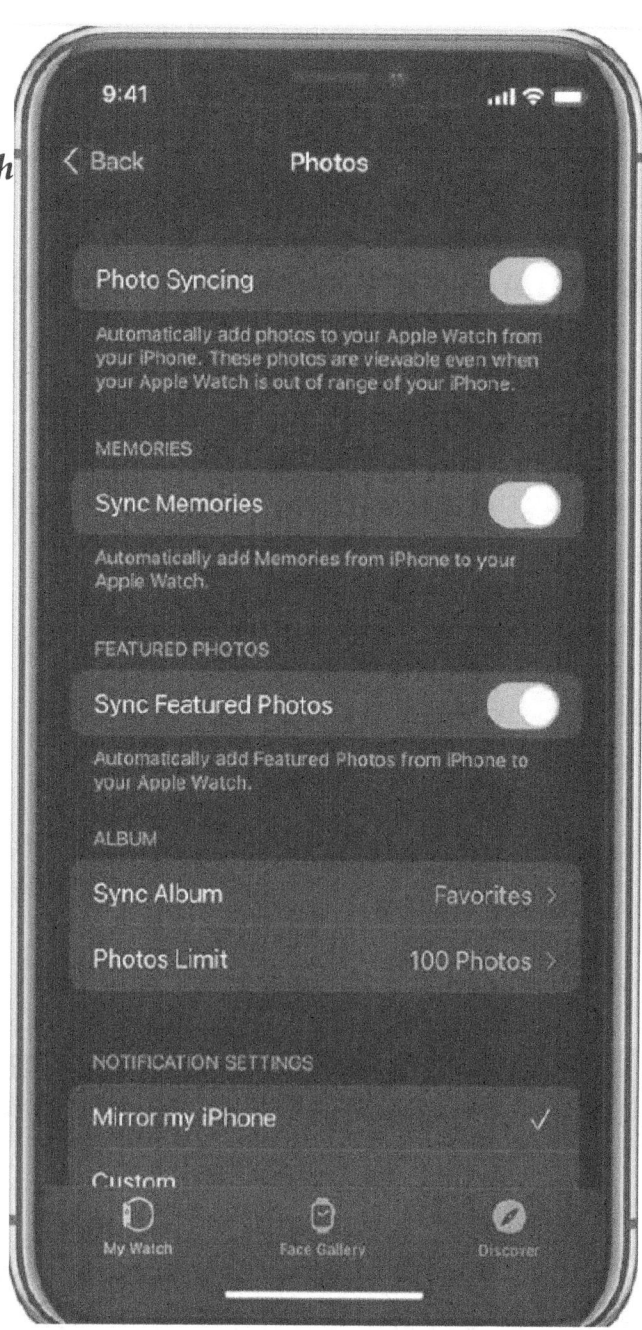

CHOOSING PHOTO ALBUMS AND

STORAGE

The Photos app on your Apple Watch enables you to enjoy photos from your chosen iPhone album, highlighted photos, and Memories.

SELECTING THE ALBUM TO DISPLAY

Initially, your Apple Watch showcases photos from your Favorites album—pictures you've marked as favorites. However, you can modify this setting.

1. Open the Apple Watch app on your iPhone.

2. Navigate to My Watch > Photos > Sync Album, and then select your preferred album.

REMOVING PHOTOS FROM APPLE WATCH

To delete a photo from your Apple Watch, access the Photos app on your iPhone, and delete the picture from the synced album.

DISPLAYING FEATURED PHOTOS AND MEMORIES

Your Apple Watch can automatically sync featured photos and Memories from your iPhone's photo library.

1. Launch the Apple Watch app on your iPhone.
2. Access My Watch > Photos, and enable Sync Memories and Sync Featured Photos.

PAUSING PHOTO SYNCING

If you want to stop your iPhone from syncing Memories, featured photos, or photos from a chosen album, follow these steps:

1. Open the Apple Watch app on your iPhone.
2. Go to My Watch > Photos, and turn off Photo Syncing.

MANAGING PHOTO STORAGE

The quantity of photos stored on your Apple Watch depends on available space. To allocate space for other content, you can limit the number of photos stored.

1. Open the Apple Watch app on your iPhone.
2. Visit My Watch > Photos > Photos Limit.

TO VIEW THE NUMBER OF PHOTOS ON YOUR APPLE WATCH

- On your Apple Watch: Go to General > About in the Settings app ⚙ .
- On your iPhone: Access General > About in the Apple Watch app.

TAKING SCREENSHOTS ON APPLE WATCH

1. On your Apple Watch, navigate to Settings ⚙ > General > Screenshots, and tap Enable Screenshots.
2. To capture a screenshot, simultaneously press the Digital Crown and the side button. Screenshots are saved in your iPhone's Photos app for later viewing.

VIEWING PHOTOS AND MEMORIES ON APPLE WATCH

Exploring Photos in the Photos App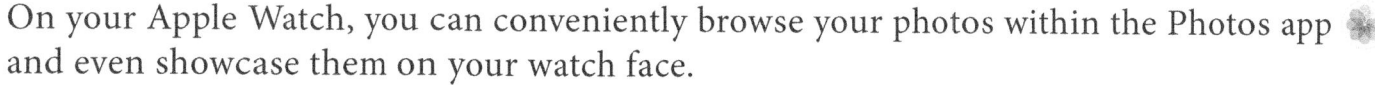

On your Apple Watch, you can conveniently browse your photos within the Photos app 🌸 and even showcase them on your watch face.

Tap to view a photo.

BROWSING PHOTOS

Open the Photos app 🌸 on your Apple Watch and use the following steps to navigate through your photos.

1. Tap on a memory, Featured Photos, or an album that you've synced to your Apple Watch.
2. Tap on a specific photo to open and view it.
3. Swipe left or right to navigate between different photos.
   - Use the Digital Crown to zoom in or out on a photo, and drag to move around within a photo.
   - Zoom out completely to see the entire album of photos.

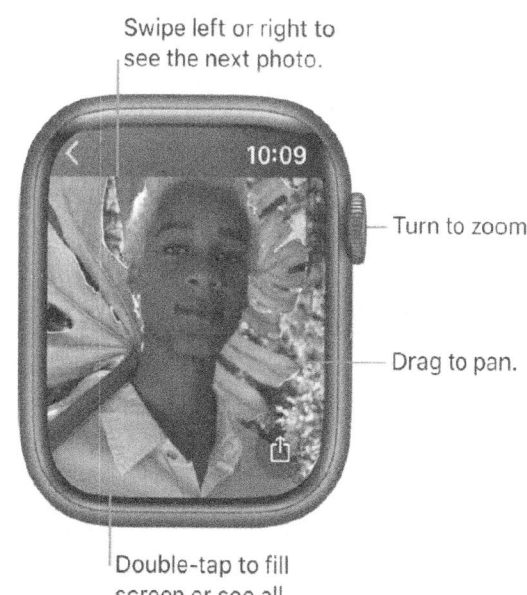

Swipe left or right to see the next photo.

Turn to zoom.

Drag to pan.

Double-tap to fill screen or see all.

VIEWING MEMORIES ON WATCH FACES

Aside from checking out Memories in the Photos app ❀ , you can also enjoy them on the Siri and Photos watch faces.

- To see a recent memory on the Siri watch face, select the Siri watch face and tap on a memory.
- To view photos from Memories on the Photos watch face, access the Apple Watch app on your iPhone, go to Face Gallery, choose the Photos watch face, and select Dynamic.

  - The Dynamic watch face will showcase images from your recent Memories, updating with new ones.

VIEWING LIVE PHOTOS

Find the Live Photo ◉ in the bottom-left corner of a picture. To experience a Live Photo, touch and hold the photo.

SHARING PHOTOS

While viewing a photo in the Photos app on your Apple Watch, tap on ⬆, then pick a sharing option that suits you.

CREATING A PHOTO WATCH FACE

While viewing a photo within the Photos app ❀ on your Apple Watch, tap on ⬆, scroll down, and then tap Create Face. If you prefer, you can also generate a Kaleidoscope watch face inspired by the photo, or include a new Photos watch face using the Apple Watch app on your iPhone. To learn more, explore the Customize the Watch Face section.

Note: For added convenience, you can efficiently design a watch face on your iPhone. Launch the Photos app on your iPhone, select a photo, tap on , swipe up, click on Create Watch Face, and decide whether to create a Portraits, Photos, or Kaleidoscope watch face.

PODCASTS

Listening to Podcasts on Apple Watch:

ADDING PODCASTS TO APPLE WATCH

By adding podcasts to your Apple Watch, you can enjoy them even when your iPhone is not around. You can achieve this via the Apple Watch app on your iPhone or directly on your Apple Watch.

USING YOUR IPHONE

When you follow podcasts and create stations in the Podcasts app on your iPhone, recent episodes from those shows can be downloaded to your Apple Watch when it's connected to a power source. Refer to the iPhone User Guide for details on following podcasts and creating stations.

1. Launch the Apple Watch app on your iPhone.
2. Go to My Watch, tap Podcasts, and then take any of the following actions:

- To add episodes from stations: Under Add Episodes From, tap Up Next, Saved, or a specific station, and then choose the number of episodes to download to your Apple Watch.
- To add episodes from podcasts you follow: Under Shows, select Add Shows, tap next to the desired shows, and tap Done.

Your Apple Watch will automatically add three episodes of each show when connected to power. You can modify this by tapping on a show and selecting your preferred number of episodes.

FOLLOWING AND UNFOLLOWING PODCASTS WITH APPLE WATCH

1. Open the Podcasts app 🎙️ on your Apple Watch.
2. Try the following:
   - Tap Listen Now, tap You Might Like, choose a show, and tap Follow.
   - Tap Search, enter the podcast name, select the show, and tap Follow.
3. Tap on ●●●, then set the number of episodes to download when your Apple Watch connects to power.

To unfollow a show, tap Library, choose the show, tap ↓, and then select Unfollow Show.

ACCESSING DOWNLOADED PODCASTS

1. Open the Podcasts app 🎙️ on your Apple Watch.
2. Tap Library, and then tap Downloaded.

LISTENING TO PODCASTS

You can enjoy podcasts stored on your Apple Watch or stream them from your iPhone.

1. Connect Bluetooth headphones or speakers to your Apple Watch.
2. Proceed with the following options:
   - Scroll through the artwork and tap a podcast to play it.
   - Tap Library, tap Downloaded, and select a podcast to play it.
   - Tap On iPhone, choose a category, locate an episode, and tap to play it.

STREAMING PODCASTS

If your Apple Watch is near your iPhone or connected to Wi-Fi or cellular (for compatible models), you can stream podcasts.

Open the Podcasts app 🎙️ on your Apple Watch and do the following:
- Stream from your library: Tap Library, choose a show, tap See All, and then tap an episode.
- Explore suggested podcasts: Tap Listen Now, scroll down, tap a category, and select an episode.
- Search for a podcast: Tap Search, enter the podcast name, tap Search, select a result, and tap an episode.

USING SIRI TO PLAY PODCASTS

Activate Siri and say something like "Hey Siri, play the podcast [Podcast Name]." Siri will play the latest episode of the requested podcast.

MANAGING PLAYBACK

You can control playback directly on your Apple Watch

- Adjust volume using the Digital Crown.
- Play, pause, skip forward 30 seconds, skip back 15 seconds.
- Change playback speed (1x, 1 1/2x, 2x, and 1/2x).
- Choose an episode from the currently playing podcast.

View more episodes.

Change playback speed.

Choose playback option

▶	Play the current podcast.
‖	Pause playback.
⟳30	Skip ahead 30 seconds.
⟲15	Skip back 15 seconds.
1x	Playback speed. Options include 1x, 1 1/2x, 2x, and 1/2x.
☰	Choose an episode of the currently playing podcast.

CUSTOMIZING PODCAST SETTINGS

You can customize Podcasts settings on your Apple Watch:

1. Open the Settings app ⚙ on your Apple Watch.
2. Tap Podcasts and adjust settings like Up Next, Saved, Continuous Playback, Skip buttons interval, and more.

REMINDERS

Your Apple Watch keeps you updated on reminders you set up in the Reminders app on your Apple Watch, iPhone, and other Apple devices where you're signed in with your Apple ID. If you want to know how to set up the Reminders app on your iPhone, consult the iPhone User Guide.

VIEWING AND MANAGING REMINDERS

1. Open the Reminders app on your Apple Watch.
2. Tap a list to access it.
3. To mark a reminder as completed, tap on the left side of an item, or tap the reminder and then tap Mark as Completed.
4. Use the < in the top-left corner to return to the list view.
5. To see completed reminders, tap a list, choose View Options, and tap Show Completed.
   - To view all completed reminders, tap the All list, select View Options, and tap Show Completed.
   - To adjust the order of your lists, open the Reminders app on your iPhone, tap Edit, and then drag the list to a new location.

SHARING AND COLLABORATING ON LISTS

You can collaborate with others who use iCloud by sharing a list. Shared lists indicate who a reminder is assigned to. On your Apple Watch, you can join a shared list, but you can't create a shared list from the watch. For more details on shared reminder lists, refer to the iPhone User Guide.

Turn to see more lists.

Tap to view the items.

RESPONDING TO REMINDER NOTIFICATIONS

- If you receive a reminder notification: Tap the notification, swipe (or turn the Digital crown to scroll) the reminder, then tap Mark as Completed or choose a reminder time.
- If you notice the notification later: Locate it in your list of notifications, and then respond accordingly.

CREATING REMINDERS

- Use Siri: Speak a command like "Remind me to pick up my dry cleaning at 5 PM." You can also utilize Siri to create a list directly on your Apple Watch.
- Use the Reminders app: Scroll to the bottom of any list, and tap Add Reminder.

DELETING AND EDITING REMINDERS

1. Open the Reminders app 🅜 on your Apple Watch.
2. Access a list, then either swipe left on the reminder and tap 🗑, or tap the reminder, scroll down, and tap Delete.

EDITING A REMINDER

You can edit reminders on your self-set Apple Watch

1. Open the Reminders app 🅜 on your Apple Watch.
2. Access a list, tap a Reminder, tap Edit, and then perform any of the following actions:

- Change the reminder's name using the keyboard options available (QWERTY, QuickPath, Scribble, or emoji). Note: QuickPath is only available on Apple Watch Series 7 and Apple Watch Series 8.
- Add a note.
- Set a date and time, with options to repeat the reminder.
- Include a tag or create a new one.
- Add a location-based reminder, for example, when arriving home or connecting to a Bluetooth-enabled car.
- Flag the reminder.
- Select a priority level.
- Assign the reminder to a different list.

REMOTE

CONTROLLING MUSIC ON A MAC OR PC

Utilize the Remote app on your Apple Watch to manage music playback on a computer within the same Wi-Fi network.

ADDING A MUSIC LIBRARY

1. Open the Remote app ▶ on your Apple Watch.
2. Tap Add Device.
   - If you're using the Music app on macOS 10.15 or later: Launch Apple Music and select your device from the list displayed alongside your library.
   - If you're using iTunes on your Mac or PC: Click the Remote button located near the top left of the iTunes window.
3. Enter the displayed 4-digit code on your Apple Watch.

PLAYBACK CONTROL FROM APPLE WATCH

You can control playback in the following ways:
- Utilize playback controls available in the Remote app ▶.
- Adjust volume using the Digital Crown.
- Tap 🔊, then choose an audio output.

SELECTING A MEDIA LIBRARY

- If you've added multiple libraries: Choose the desired one when opening the Remote app ▶ on your Apple Watch.
- If music is already playing: Tap < at the top left of the playback controls and then select the library.

REMOVING A MEDIA LIBRARY

1. Open the Remote app ▶ on your Apple Watch.
2. Long-press a device.
3. Once the device icon starts jiggling, tap X to remove it, then tap Remove.

APPLE TV CONTROL WITH APPLE WATCH

Your Apple Watch can function as a remote for an Apple TV when both are connected to the same Wi-Fi network.

PAIRING APPLE WATCH WITH APPLE TV

If your iPhone has never joined the Apple TV's Wi-Fi network, follow these steps:
1. Open the Remote app  on your Apple Watch.
2. Tap your Apple TV. If it's not listed, tap Add Device.
3. On the Apple TV, navigate to Settings > Remotes and Devices > Remote App and Devices, and choose Apple Watch.
4. Enter the passcode displayed on your Apple Watch.
    • Once the pairing icon appears next to your Apple Watch, it's ready to control the Apple TV.

USING APPLE WATCH TO CONTROL APPLE TV

Ensure the Apple TV is awake and follow these steps:
1. Open the Remote app on your Apple Watch.
2. Select your Apple TV and swipe in various directions to navigate the menu.
3. Tap to select the highlighted item.
4. Use the Play/Pause button to pause or resume playback.
5. Press the Menu button to return or hold it to access the main menu.

To initiate the screen saver, move to the top-left corner of the Apple TV's Home Screen and tap the Menu button.

Control another device.

10:09

SELECT

Swipe to move through Apple TV menu options; tap to select.

Tap to go back or touch and hold to return to main menu.

UNPAIRING AND REMOVING APPLE TV

1. On the Apple TV, navigate to Settings > Remotes and Devices > Remote App and Devices.
2. Choose your Apple Watch under Remote App, then select Unpair Device.
3. Open the Remote app on your Apple Watch and tap Remove when the "lost connection" message appears.

SLEEP

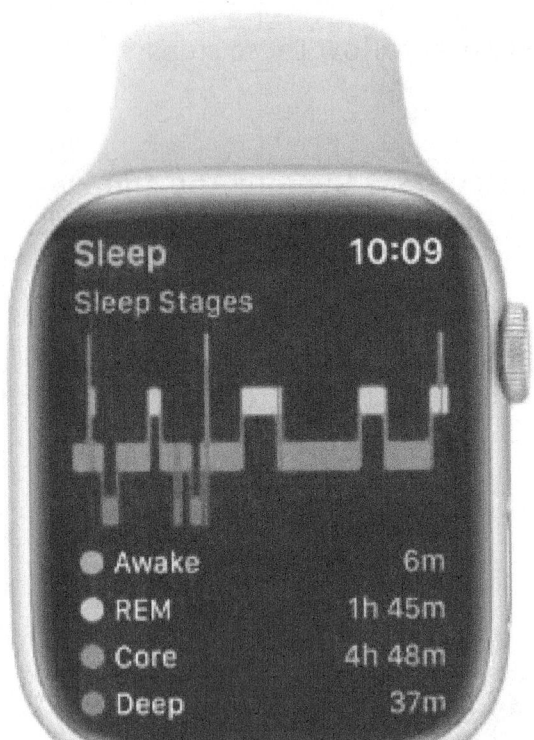

SLEEP TRACKING WITH APPLE WATCH

The Sleep app  on Apple Watch empowers you to establish bedtime routines that aid in achieving your sleep targets. Don your watch before sleep, and it will estimate the duration spent in various sleep stages: REM, Core, and Deep. It can also provide insights into when you might have awakened. Upon waking up, access the Sleep app to view your sleep duration and trends across the last 14 days.

BATTERY CHARGE ALERT

When your Apple Watch charge drops below 30 percent before bedtime, a reminder will prompt you to recharge it. In the morning, simply check the greeting to assess the remaining battery charge.

SLEEP SCHEDULING

Apple Watch tracks your sleep as per the customized sleep schedule you establish. You can also manually activate Sleep Focus to minimize disturbances before and after sleep. To garner sleep data, Apple Watch must track your sleep for a **minimum of four hours** each night.

MULTIPLE SCHEDULES OPTION

You can create various schedules, tailored for different days. Each schedule allows for the following settings:

- Set a sleep goal (desired sleep hours)
- Determine bedtime and wake-up time
- Choose an alarm sound for waking up
- Specify when to activate Sleep Focus (limiting pre-sleep distractions)
- Enable sleep tracking, which utilizes your movement to detect sleep during sleep hours with active Sleep Focus

DISABLING SLEEP FOCUS

Press and hold the Digital Crown to unlock your device and swipe up to open Control Center. Tap 🛏 to disable Sleep Focus.

ENABLING SLEEP ON APPLE WATCH

1. Launch the Sleep app 🛏 on your Apple Watch.
2. Follow the on-screen instructions.

Alternatively, you can access the Health app 💙 on your iPhone, tap Browse, select Sleep, and then tap Get Started under Set Up Sleep.

ADJUSTING OR DISABLING WAKE-UP ALARM

1. Open the Sleep app 🛏 on your Apple Watch.
2. Tap your existing wake-up time.
3. To modify the wake-up time, turn the Digital Crown to set a new time and tap ✅ .

If you wish to disable the wake-up alarm, turn off Alarm. Alternatively, you can use the Health app on your iPhone, tap Browse, choose Sleep, and tap Edit under Your Schedule to make adjustments.

These changes only change the forthcoming wake-up alarm; your regular schedule resumes afterward.

ALTERNATE DISABLING METHOD

You can also turn off the next wake-up alarm within the Alarms app . Locate the alarm under Sleep | Wake up, tap it, and then select Skip for Tonight.

ADJUSTING OR ADDING A SLEEP SCHEDULE:

CHANGE OR ADD A SLEEP SCHEDULE

1. Launch the Sleep app 🛏 on your Apple Watch.
2. Tap Full Schedule, and proceed with one of the following actions:
   - To modify an existing sleep schedule, tap the current schedule.
   - To introduce a new sleep schedule, tap Add Schedule.
   - For altering sleep goal, tap Sleep Goal, and specify your desired sleep duration.
   - To adjust Wind Down time, tap Wind Down, and define how long Sleep Focus should activate before bedtime. Sleep Focus darkens the watch display and activates Do Not Disturb to minimize distractions prior to sleep.
3. There are extra customizations including:
   - Set Days for the Schedule: Access your schedule, tap Active On, select days, and tap <.
   - Adjust Wake Time and Bedtime: Within your schedule, tap Wake Up or Bedtime, use the Digital Crown to set new times, and tap ✓.
   - Set Alarm Options: In your schedule, control Alarm by toggling it on or off and selecting Sound & Haptics to choose an alarm sound.
   - Remove or Cancel a Schedule: To eliminate an existing schedule, tap your schedule and tap Delete Schedule at the bottom. To cancel creating a new one, tap Cancel at the top.

MODIFYING SLEEP SETTINGS

1. Access the Settings app ⚙ on your Apple Watch.
2. Tap Sleep, and proceed to customize the following settings:
   - Turn On at Wind Down: If you'd rather manage Sleep Focus manually in Control Center, disable this option.
   - Sleep Screen: Simplify the Apple Watch display and iPhone Lock Screen during Sleep Focus to minimize distractions.
   - Show Time: Display the date and time on your Apple Watch and iPhone during Sleep Focus.
1. Toggle Sleep Tracking and Charging Reminders on or off.
   - When Sleep Tracking is enabled, Apple Watch records sleep data in the Health app on your iPhone.
   - Activating Charging Reminders results in reminders to charge your watch before Wind Down time and notifications when your watch is fully charged.

REVIEWING SLEEP HISTORY

1. Launch the Sleep app  on your Apple Watch.
2. Scroll down to view the previous night's sleep duration, time spent in sleep stages, and a 14-day sleep average.

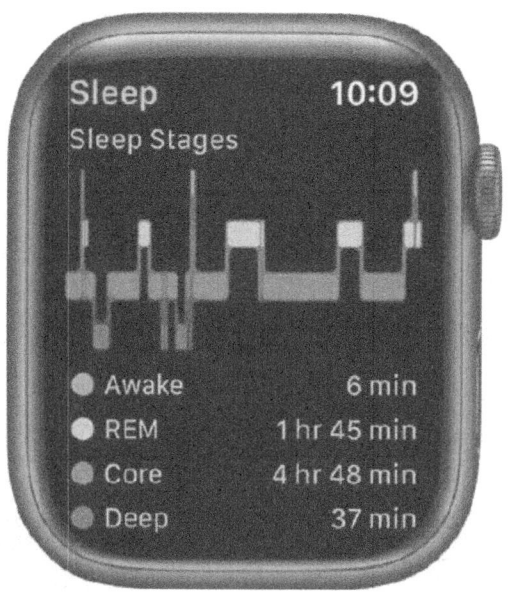

EVALUATING RESPIRATORY RATE:

Use your Apple Watch to monitor your breathing rate during sleep, which can provide valuable health insights.

1. Open the Health app on your iPhone, tap Browse, then tap Respiratory.
2. Select Respiratory Rate and tap Show More Respiratory Rate Data to view your sleep-related breathing patterns.

MONITORING WRIST TEMPERATURE WITH APPLE WATCH SERIES 8

Wear your Apple Watch Series 8 during sleep to track changes in wrist temperature, aiding well-being assessment.

1. Ensure Track Sleep with Apple Watch is enabled.
2. To establish a baseline, activate Sleep Focus and wear your watch while sleeping.
   - Wrist temperature data becomes available after about five nights.

REVIEWING WRIST TEMPERATURE

1. Open the Health app 💜 on your iPhone, tap Browse.
2. Navigate to Body Measurements and tap Wrist Temperature.
3. Tap a chart point for detailed sample information.

DEACTIVATING WRIST TEMPERATURE TRACKING

1. Open the Apple Watch app on your iPhone.
2. Tap My Watch, proceed to Privacy, and toggle off Wrist Temperature.

STOCKS

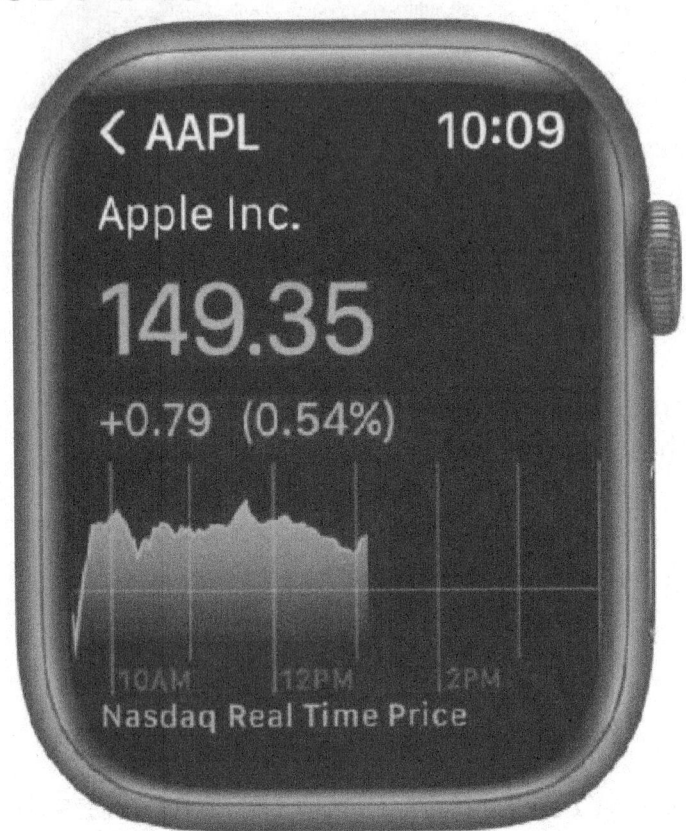

MONITORING STOCKS WITH THE STOCKS APP

Utilize the Stocks app 📈 on your Apple Watch to access information about stocks you follow on your iPhone. For comprehensive guidance on using the Stocks app on your iPhone, refer to the iPhone User Guide.

USING SIRI FOR STOCK INFORMATION

You can also obtain stock information via Siri. For instance, ask Siri questions like: "What was today's closing price for Apple stock?"

ADDING AND REMOVING STOCKS

Manage your tracked stocks directly from your Apple Watch. Follow these steps within the Stocks app 📈 on your watch:

- To add a stock: Scroll to the bottom, tap Add Stock. Input the stock name using text entry, Scribble (available on Apple Watch Series 7 and 8), or dictation. Confirm the selection.
- To remove a stock: Swipe left on the stock you wish to remove, then tap X. For rearranging stock order, tap and hold a stock, and drag it to the desired position.
- Rearranging stocks on one device automatically applies changes to the other.

VIEWING STOCK DATA

1. Launch the Stocks app  on your Apple Watch.
2. Tap a stock to access its data.
3. To return to the stock list, tap <, or use the Digital Crown to navigate to the next stock in the list.

SELECTING STOCKS FOR SIRI WATCH FACE

1. Open the Settings app on your Apple Watch.
2. Navigate to Stocks > Selected Stock, and make a selection.

CUSTOMIZING DATA METRICS

Tailor the data metrics displayed in the Stocks app, complications, and the Siri watch face by following these steps:

- To modify the data metric in the Stocks app: Open the Stocks app on your Apple Watch, tap Viewing, and choose Points, Market Cap, or Percentage.
- For changing the data metric on Stocks complications and the Siri watch face: In the Settings app on your Apple Watch, tap Stocks > Data Metric, and select a metric. You can also adjust this setting via the Apple Watch app on your iPhone.

SWITCHING TO STOCKS ON IPHONE

1. Access the Stocks app on your Apple Watch.
2. On your iPhone, access the App Switcher by swiping up from the bottom edge and pausing (Face ID devices) or double-clicking the Home button (Home button devices).
3. Tap the displayed button at the bottom of the screen to open the Stocks app on your iPhone.

STOPWATCH

PRECISELY TIME EVENTS WITH EASE

Effortlessly time events with Apple Watch's accuracy. It can track entire events up to 11 hours and 55 minutes, recording lap or split times. Results can be presented as a list, a graph, or displayed live on your watch face. The Chronograph and Chronograph Pro watch faces include the built-in stopwatch feature.

OPENING AND SELECTING A STOPWATCH

1. Open the Stopwatch app  on your Apple Watch, or tap the stopwatch directly on your watch face (if it's added or you're using the Chronograph or Chronograph Pro watch face).
2. Choose from Analog, Digital, Graph, or Hybrid formats on the Stopwatch screen.
3. To switch to a different format while viewing the stopwatch, tap < and select your preferred format.

STARTING, STOPPING, AND RESETTING THE STOPWATCH

Open the Stopwatch app 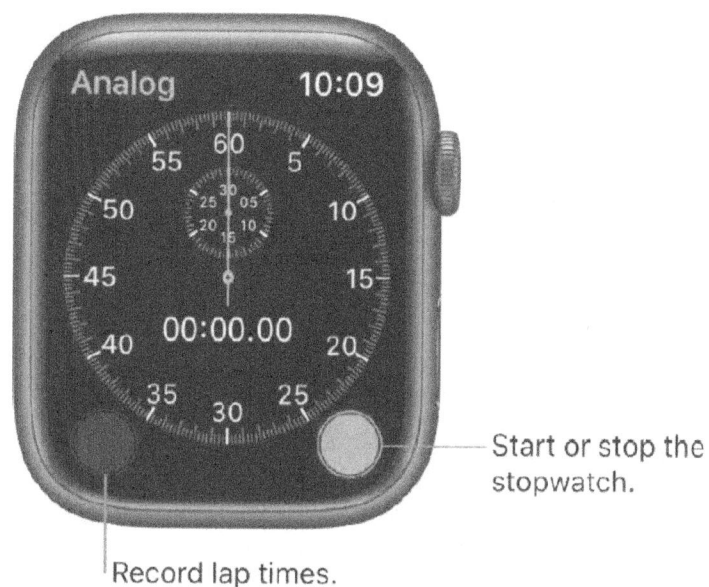 on your Apple Watch, pick a format, and perform these actions:

- To start timing: Tap the Start button (usually green on the analog stopwatch).
- To record a lap time: Tap the Lap button (typically white on the analog stopwatch).
- To finalize the time: Tap the Stop button (usually red on the analog stopwatch).
- To reset the stopwatch: If the stopwatch is stopped, tap the Reset button (typically white on the analog stopwatch).

Start or stop the stopwatch.

Record lap times.

CONTINUOUS TIMING

Even if you switch back to the watch face or access other apps, the stopwatch will continue running in the background.

REVIEWING AND ANALYZING RESULTS

After timing an event, you can review the results on the same display you used for timing. Alternatively, you can switch displays to examine your lap times. Fastest and slowest laps are indicated with green and red markers. If the display shows a list of lap times, use the Digital Crown to scroll through them.

TIMERS

Apple Watch's Timers app helps you manage time effectively. You can establish multiple timers, each capable of tracking time for up to 24 hours.

USING SIRI FOR TIMERS

Simply ask Siri to set a timer. For instance, say "Set a timer for 20 minutes."

QUICK TIMER SETUP

1. Open the Timers app 🕐 on your Apple Watch.
2. To swiftly start a timer, tap a predefined duration (like 1, 3, or 5 minutes) or select a timer from your recent ones below Recents.
   - For a custom timer, swipe down and tap Custom.
   - When one timer ends, you can quickly restart a timer with the same duration by tapping 🔄.

PAUSING AND ENDING TIMERS

1. When a timer is running, access the Timers app on your Apple Watch.
2. Tap ▮▮ to pause, tap ▶ to resume, or tap ✕ to conclude the timer.

CREATING A PERSONALIZED TIMER

1. Open the Timers app 🕐 on your Apple Watch.
2. Scroll up and tap Custom.
3. Adjust hours, minutes, or seconds using the Digital Crown.
4. Tap Start to initiate the custom timer.

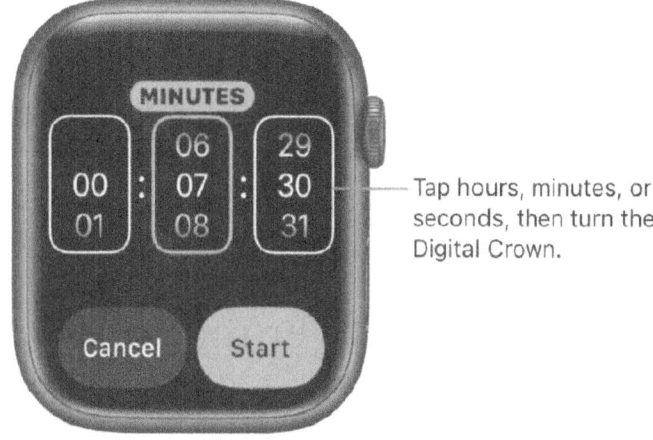

Tap hours, minutes, or seconds, then turn the Digital Crown.

MANAGING MULTIPLE TIMERS

1. Access the Timers app 🕐 on your Apple Watch.
2. Create and initiate a timer.
   • Use Siri to label timers, such as "Pizza." Just say, "Set a 12-minute pizza timer."
3. Return to the Timers screen by tapping <, then set up additional timers.
   • All ongoing timers are displayed on the Timers screen. Pause with a tap and resume with .
   • To delete a running or paused timer, swipe left and tap X.

FAVORITE TIMERS

1. Open the Timers app 🕐 on your Apple Watch.
2. Swipe left on a recent timer, then tap ⭐.
   • The timer becomes a favorite and is listed under the Favorites section.

VOICE MEMOS

Recording and Playing Voice Memos on Apple Watch

Utilize the Voice Memos app  on your Apple Watch to conveniently record personal notes and thoughts.

RECORDING A VOICE MEMO

1. Open the Voice Memos app on your Apple Watch.
2. Tap the record button to commence recording.
3. Tap the stop button to conclude the recording.

LISTENING TO A VOICE MEMO

1. Access the Voice Memos app on your Apple Watch.
2. Tap on a recording displayed on the Voice Memos screen.
3. To initiate playback, tap the play button   .

EDITING AND DELETING RECORDINGS

1. Open the Voice Memos app on your Apple Watch.
2. Select a recording from the Voice Memos screen.
3. To modify the recording's name, tap , then choose Edit Name.
   - To delete the recording, tap ● ● ●, then select Delete.

SYNCING YOUR VOICE MEMOS

Voice memos you record on your Apple Watch are automatically synchronized with your other devices, including Mac, iPad, and iOS devices where you're signed in using the same Apple ID.

WALKIE TALKIE

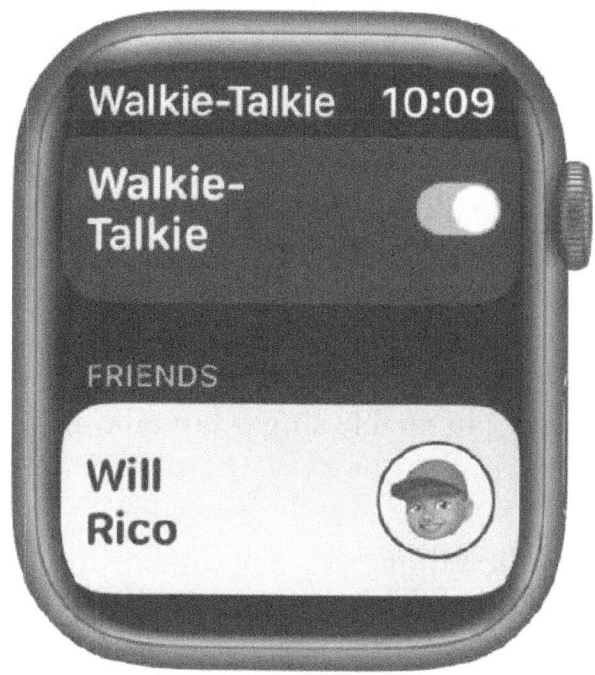

Experience the joy of communicating with another compatible Apple Watch user through the Walkie-Talkie feature. This simple and enjoyable method operates like a traditional walkie-talkie.

Press a button to talk, release to listen, and wait for the response. Both participants need connectivity, either via Bluetooth connection to an iPhone, Wi-Fi, or cellular. It's important to note that Walkie-Talkie might not be available in all regions.

INVITING A FRIEND

1. Launch the Walkie-Talkie app 🖲 on your Apple Watch for the first time.
2. Browse the list of contacts and tap a name to send an invitation.

After your friend accepts the invitation, you can initiate Walkie-Talkie conversations whenever both of you are available. To add more contacts, tap "Add Friends" on the Walkie-Talkie screen and select a contact.

ENGAGING IN A WALKIE-TALKIE CHAT

1. Open the Walkie-Talkie app on your Apple Watch.
2. Tap your friend's name.
3. Hold down the Talk button and speak.

If your friend is available, their Apple Watch will open the Walkie-Talkie app, allowing them to hear your message. Adjust your speaking volume using the Digital Crown.

TALKING WITH A SINGLE TAP

If pressing and holding the Talk button is challenging, you can enable single-tap talking.

1. Access the Settings app on your Apple Watch.
2. Tap Accessibility and turn on "Tap to Talk" below Walkie-Talkie.
Once enabled, tap once to talk and tap again to finish speaking. This setting can also be adjusted in the Apple Watch app on your iPhone under Accessibility.

MANAGING CONTACTS

To remove contacts

In the Walkie-Talkie app , swipe left on a contact and tap X.

SETTING YOURSELF AS UNAVAILABLE

1. Swipe up on the screen to open Control Center.
2. Scroll down and tap .

Alternatively, open the Walkie-Talkie app and scroll to the top of the screen, then turn off Walkie-Talkie. Activating theater mode also makes you unavailable for Walkie-Talkie.

WALLET & APPLE PAY

UNDERSTANDING WALLET ON APPLE WATCH

The Wallet app is designed to provide convenient access to your cards and passes in one location. Wallet can hold a variety of items, including:

- Apple Pay cards like Apple Card and Apple Cash (Refer to "Set up Apple Pay" for more details)
- Transit cards (Learn about using transit cards)
- Digital keys (See how to use digital keys)
- Driver's license or state ID (Discover using your driver's license or state ID)
- Employee badges (Accessing your workplace credentials)
- Student ID cards (Using contactless passes or student ID cards)
- Rewards cards, boarding passes, and event tickets (Using Wallet for passes)
- Vaccination records (Understanding COVID-19 vaccination cards)

APPLE PAY ON APPLE WATCH

Apple Pay ensures a simple, secure, and private payment method on your Apple Watch. By storing your cards in the Wallet app on your iPhone and adding them to your Apple Watch, you can leverage Apple Pay in various ways:

- Contactless payments and apps: Utilize credit, debit, and prepaid cards added to the Wallet app to make purchases at stores supporting contactless payments and within apps compatible with Apple Pay.

Upon setting up Apple Pay in the Apple Watch app on your iPhone, you're equipped for in-store purchases, even without your iPhone present. (Apple Pay availability varies by region.)

- Person-to-person payments: In watchOS 4 and later versions, you can seamlessly send and request money securely via Messages or Siri.
- Transit cards: Add transit cards, which appear at the top of your collection in the Wallet app , above your passes.

For up-to-date information regarding Apple Pay availability and participating card issuers, consult the Apple Support article titled "Apple Pay Participating Banks."

IMPORTANT CONSIDERATIONS

Note: Unpairing your Apple Watch or deactivating your passcode will result in the inability to use Apple Pay, and any cards stored in Wallet will be removed. If wrist detection is turned off, you'll need to enter your passcode each time you use Apple Pay.

SETTING UP APPLE PAY ON YOUR APPLE WATCH

ADDING A CARD VIA YOUR IPHONE

1. Launch the Apple Watch app on your iPhone.
2. Select "My Watch" and then tap on "Wallet & Apple Pay."
3. If you already possess cards on your other Apple devices or recently removed cards, tap "Add" next to the card you wish to include. Input the card's CVV.
4. For any other card, choose "Add Card" and proceed by following the onscreen prompts.

Please note that your card provider might require additional verification steps to confirm your identity.

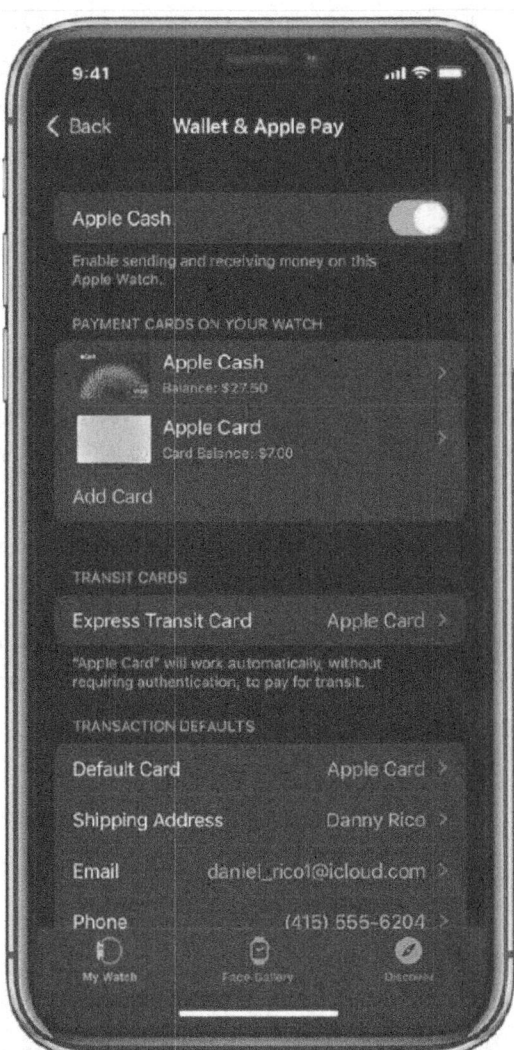

ADDING A CARD DIRECTLY ON APPLE

WATCH

You have the convenience of adding Apple Account, credit, debit, and transit cards directly on your Apple Watch.

1. Open the Wallet app 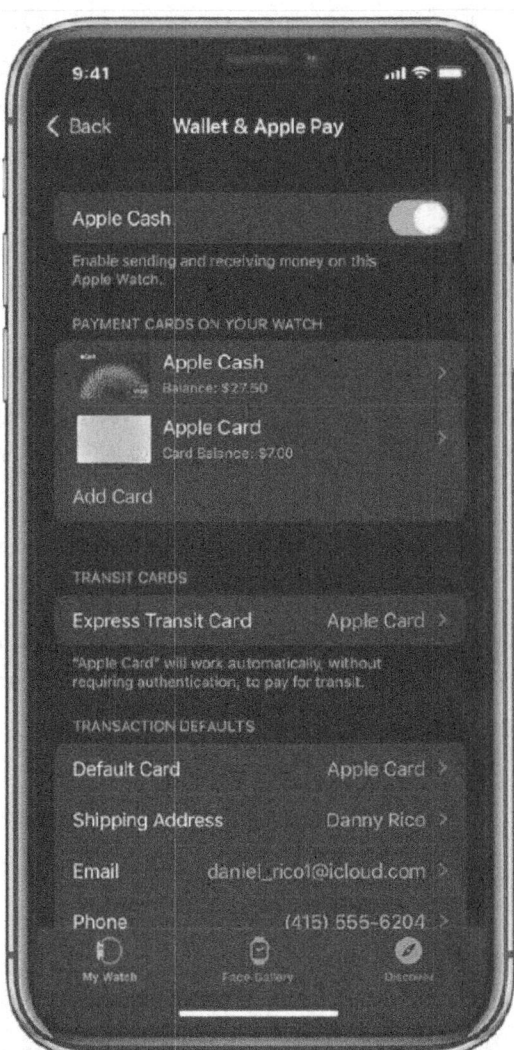 on your Apple Watch.
2. Scroll down to the bottom of the screen and tap "Add Card."

3. Select between Apple Account, Debit or Credit Card, or Transit Card, and then proceed by following the instructions displayed on the screen.

MANAGING APPLE PAY ON YOUR APPLE WATCH

SELECTING YOUR DEFAULT CARD

1. Access the Apple Watch app on your iPhone.
2. Tap "My Watch," followed by "Wallet & Apple Pay."
3. Tap "Default Card," and then choose the desired card.

REARRANGING PAYMENT CARDS

Open the Wallet app on your Apple Watch, press and hold a card, and drag it to a new position. For managed Apple Watches, this applies to both payment cards and passes.

REMOVING A CARD FROM APPLE PAY

1. Launch the Wallet app on your Apple Watch.
2. Select a card by tapping it.
3. Scroll down and tap "Remove."

You can also perform this action via the Apple Watch app on your iPhone by tapping "My Watch," "Wallet & Apple Pay," selecting the card, and then tapping "Remove Card."

FINDING THE DEVICE ACCOUNT NUMBER

When you make a payment using your Apple Watch, the Device Account Number is sent along with the payment. To find the last four digits of this number:

1. Open the Wallet app on your Apple Watch.
2. Tap a card to select it, then tap "Card Information."
Note: For Apple Card, you must enter your Apple Watch passcode before accessing card details. This can also be done via the Apple Watch app on your iPhone.

MODIFYING DEFAULT TRANSACTION DETAILS

You can customize your in-app transaction preferences, such as default card, shipping address, email, and phone number:

1. Launch the Apple Watch app on your iPhone.
2. Tap "My Watch," then "Wallet & Apple Pay."
3. Scroll down and tap "Transaction Defaults." Edit any desired item.

IN CASE OF LOST OR STOLEN APPLE WATCH

If your Apple Watch is lost or stolen, consider the following steps:

- Activate lost mode to halt the ability to pay from your Apple Watch.
- Sign in to appleid.apple.com with your Apple ID to remove the ability to pay using cards in Wallet. Under Devices, choose your device and click "Remove All" under Apple Pay.
- Contact your card issuers for further assistance.

MAKING PAYMENTS WITH APPLE WATCH

Paying in-store:
1. Double-click the side button.
2. Scroll and choose a card.
3. Hold your Apple Watch close to the contactless card reader, display facing it.

A gentle tap and beep indicate the payment was sent. A confirmation notification arrives in Notification Center.

MAKING IN-APP PURCHASES

1. While in an app on your Apple Watch, opt for the Apple Pay choice during checkout.
2. Review details and double-click the side button to pay.

SENDING, RECEIVING, AND REQUESTING MONEY WITH APPLE WATCH

Sending Money with Apple Cash

Apart from using Apple Cash for in-store purchases, you can effortlessly send money to friends and family. This can be done through messages or even Siri. Receiving and requesting money is just as straightforward.

Note: Apple Cash is limited to certain regions and supports iPhone SE and iPhone 6 models and later. For comprehensive information on Apple Pay and Apple Cash, refer to the iPhone User Guide.

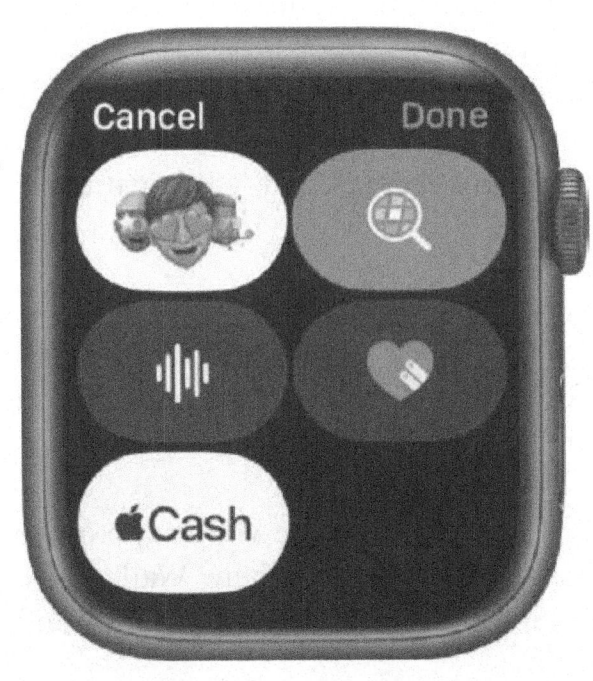

SENDING A PAYMENT FROM APPLE WATCH

Use Siri: Voice a command like "Send $25 to Claire." If you have multiple contacts named Claire, you'll be prompted to pick the intended one.

1. Launch the Messages app ⬤ on your Apple Watch.
2. Initiate a new conversation or select an existing one, then tap ⬤, followed by   .
3. Use the Digital Crown or plus/minus buttons to select a whole dollar amount. For fractional amounts (e.g., $10.95), tap the dollar value, then tap the amount after the decimal and adjust using the Digital Crown.
4. Confirm and send the payment by double-clicking the side button. Upon successful payment, a confirmation message appears.

The payment is initially debited from your Apple Cash balance. If this balance is insufficient, the remaining sum is drawn from your linked debit card.

CANCELING A PAYMENT

You can cancel a payment if the recipient hasn't accepted it yet.
1. Access the Wallet app ⬤ on your Apple Watch.
2. Choose a card by tapping it, then scroll through your transaction list.
3. Tap the pending transaction, and then tap "Cancel Payment."

This action can also be performed through the Apple Watch app on your iPhone: "My Watch" > "Wallet & Apple Pay" > Apple Cash card > "Transactions" > unpaid transaction > "Cancel Payment."

REQUESTING PAYMENT

You can initiate payment requests using Siri or messages.
- Via Siri: "Ask James to send me $30."
- Using Messages: Launch the Messages app ⬤ on your Apple Watch, start a new conversation or select an existing one, then tap ⬤, followed by ⬤Cash . Swipe left on the Send button, input the amount, and tap Request.

Upon your first usage of Apple Cash, you need to agree to the terms and conditions on your iPhone before accepting payments. Subsequent payments are automatically accepted, unless you prefer manual acceptance. To alter this setting, open Wallet on your iPhone, tap the Apple Cash card, tap ● ● ●, and then tap "Manually Accept Payments."

RESPONDING TO A PAYMENT REQUEST

1. Tap the Send button displayed in the payment request within Messages.
2. Change the amount by turning the Digital Crown or tapping on-screen buttons, if desired.
3. Send the payment by tapping Send and double-clicking the side button.

VIEWING TRANSACTION DETAILS

- In Messages: Open the Messages app ⬤ on your Apple Watch and tap on an Apple Pay essage to access a transaction summary.
- In Wallet: Launch the Wallet app ⬤ on your Apple Watch, tap a card, and scroll through the list of transactions. Tap a transaction for more information.

To review your complete Apple Cash transaction history on your iPhone, access the Apple Watch app, navigate to "My Watch," tap "Wallet & Apple Pay," select your Apple Cash card, tap "Transactions," and swipe to the bottom to request a transaction statement via email.

MANAGING APPLE CASH WITH APPLE WATCH (U.S. ONLY)

RECEIVING AND USING APPLE CASH

When you receive money through Apple Cash, the funds are added to your Apple Cash card within the Wallet. You can utilize Apple Cash immediately for transactions where you would typically use Apple Pay—whether in stores, apps, or online. Additionally, it's possible to transfer your Apple Cash balance to your bank account. If you're responsible for a family sharing group, you can set up Apple Cash Family for family members.

MANAGING APPLE CASH PAYMENT FEATURES

Navigate to the Apple Watch app on your iPhone, tap "My Watch," then select "Wallet & Apple Pay." Here, you can perform the following actions:

- Tap the Apple Cash card to initiate setup. If Apple Cash is already configured on another device, it will be ready for use on your Apple Watch.
- Enable or disable the Apple Cash card, as well as the ability to send and receive money, on this particular device.
- View your suggested PIN, which can also be accessed on your Apple Watch through the Wallet app   . Scroll down on your Apple Cash card and tap "Card Information." A PIN isn't necessary for Apple Cash, as payments are authenticated by Face ID, Touch ID, or a secure passcode. However, some terminals may still require a four-digit code to finalize a transaction.
- Check your Apple Cash balance by opening the Wallet app ⬤ on your Apple Watch

and selecting your Apple Cash card. Alternatively, double-click the side button and scroll to the Apple Cash card.

- Manage Apple Cash Family for family members under 18.

Please note that person-to-person payments with Apple Pay and Apple Cash are subject to regional availability.

Apple Cash and the sending and receiving of payments through Apple Pay are services offered by Green Dot Bank, an FDIC member.

ADDING AND USING PASSES IN WALLET ON APPLE WATCH

Leverage the Wallet app  on your Apple Watch to store and access your boarding passes, event tickets, coupons, student ID cards, and more conveniently. Passes that you have on your Wallet app on the iPhone are automatically synchronized to your Apple Watch. This allows you to utilize passes on your watch for actions such as flight check-ins, coupon redemptions, and access to certain areas.

CUSTOMIZING PASS OPTIONS

1. Open the Apple Watch app on your iPhone.
2. Tap "My Watch," then select "Wallet & Apple Pay."

ADDING A PASS

To include a pass, use any of the following methods:

- Follow the instructions received via email from the issuer.
- Utilize the pass issuer's dedicated app, if available.
- Tap "Add" in the notification.
- If you receive a pass via Messages, tap to add it.

USING A PASS

You can seamlessly employ various passes on your Apple Watch.

- When a pass notification appears on your Apple Watch, tap it to display the pass. If necessary, scroll to access the barcode.
- For barcode passes, double-click the side button, scroll to your pass, and present the barcode to the scanner. Alternatively, open the Wallet app on your Apple Watch, select the pass, and scan it.

ACCESSING PASS INFORMATION

To retrieve additional details about a pass—like flight departure and arrival times—perform these steps:

1. Open the Wallet app ⬤ on your Apple Watch.
2. Select a pass, scroll down, and tap "Pass Information."

USING CONTACTLESS PASSES AND

STUDENT ID CARDS

With a contactless pass or student ID card, you can present your Apple Watch to a contactless reader for verification.

- If a contactless pass notification appears, tap it. If not, double-click the side button and hold your Apple Watch close to the reader.
- For student ID cards on supported campuses, simply place your Apple Watch near the reader, with the display facing it, until your watch vibrates—there's no need to double-click the side button.

REORDERING AND REMOVING PASSES

On your Apple Watch, use the Wallet app ⬤ to rearrange transit, access, payment cards, and passes. Dragging a payment card to the top slot designates it as the default payment card.

On a managed Apple Watch, you can reorder all types of passes. To remove a pass, double-click the side button, select the pass, scroll down, and tap "Delete." Alternatively, open the Wallet app on your iPhone, tap the pass, tap , and choose "Remove Pass." Removing a pass on one device will also remove it from the other.

VIEWING EXPIRED PASSES

Expired passes are hidden to keep things organized on your Apple Watch. To see these passes:

1. Open the Wallet app ⬤ on your Apple Watch.
2. Scroll to the bottom and tap "View [number] Expired Passes."
3. Select a pass to view its details, and unhide, share, or delete it if needed.

To continuously display expired passes, open the Settings app ⚙ on your Apple Watch, tap "Wallet & Apple Pay," and turn off "Hide Expired Passes."

USING REWARDS CARDS ON APPLE WATCH

ADDING REWARDS CARDS

If you possess a rewards card from a merchant that supports this feature, you can conveniently include it in your Wallet and effortlessly present it to a contactless reader Cash transactions using your Apple Watch.

ADDING A REWARDS CARD TO APPLE WATCH

You can add a rewards card to Wallet through different methods:
- Email or Website Link: If you come across an "Add to Apple Wallet" link in an email or on a website, tap the link to add the rewards card.
- Notification: After using Apple Pay and providing your rewards card details, you might receive a notification on your iPhone prompting you to add the card as a rewards card. Tap the notification and select "Add."
- Message: Simply tap a rewards card sent to you in Messages.

USING A REWARDS CARD ON APPLE WATCH

When asked to provide your rewards information (and upon seeing the Apple Pay logo), follow these steps:
1. Double-click the side button on your Apple Watch.
2. Hold your watch a few centimeters away from the contactless reader, with the display facing the reader.

By default, your Apple Watch displays the rewards card, eliminating the need to scroll.

MAKING APPLE PAY PURCHASES ON MAC WITH APPLE WATCH

For websites supporting Apple Pay, you can initiate a purchase in Safari on your Mac and finalize the payment using your Apple Watch.
To authenticate payments on your Apple Watch, ensure that your iPhone and Mac share the same Apple ID for iCloud. Both your Mac and Apple Watch should also be in proximity and connected to Wi-Fi.

SHOPPING ON MAC AND PAYING WITH APPLE WATCH

1. While shopping online in Safari on your Mac, select the Apple Pay option during checkout.
2. Review payment, shipping, and billing details on your Mac. Make sure it indicates "Confirm with Apple Watch."
3. If the confirmation message appears, double-click the side button on your Apple Watch to complete the payment.

DISABLING APPLE PAY PAYMENTS ON MAC

By default, you can confirm Apple Pay transactions made on your Mac using your Apple Watch. You can do this by:

1. Open the Apple Watch app ⬛ on your iPhone.
2. Go to "My Watch," then "Wallet & Apple Pay."
3. Turn off "Allow Payments on Mac."

USING TRANSIT CARDS WITH APPLE WATCH

On your Apple Watch, you can utilize a transit card through Apple Pay to pay for fares where applicable. Refer to the Apple Support article "Ride transit with Apple Pay" for more details. Note that Apple Pay availability and features may vary by location.

If a preferred card is not required by a transit system, you can use a payment card in Wallet for transit payment without double-clicking the side button. To set up a card for Express Transit:

1. Open the Settings app ⚙ on your Apple Watch.
2. Navigate to "Wallet & Apple Pay," then select "Express Mode."
3. Choose the card you wish to use, enter your Apple Watch passcode, and follow the instructions for payment.

USING YOUR DRIVER'S LICENSE OR STATE ID IN WALLET ON IPHONE AND APPLE WATCH (U.S. ONLY)

ADDING YOUR LICENSE OR ID

You can securely and conveniently add your driver's license or state ID to the Wallet app on your iPhone and Apple Watch. This allows you to present your license or ID at specific TSA security checkpoints using either device. (Note that the license or ID must be issued by a participating state.)
Adding Your License or ID to iPhone and Apple Watch

1. Open the Wallet app ⬤ on your iPhone.
2. Tap the ➕ button   .
3. Choose "Driver's License" or "State ID" and then select your state.
- If your state isn't listed, it might not be participating yet.

382

4. Decide if you want to add the license or ID to your iPhone only or both iPhone and paired Apple Watch.
4. Follow the onscreen instructions to scan the front and back of your license or ID.

USING YOUR LICENSE OR ID ON APPLE WATCH

1. Hold your Apple Watch display near the identity reader.
2. Review the information to be shared.
3. Double-click the side button on your Apple Watch to present your license or ID.
- A checkmark appears when your license or ID is successfully presented.

To use your license or ID on your Apple Watch, you must unlock your iPhone using Face ID or Touch ID each time you put on your watch. Afterward, you can use the license or ID without further authentication until you remove the watch.

ACCESSING CAR, HOME, WORKPLACE, AND HOTEL KEYS IN WALLET

In the Wallet app on your Apple Watch, you can store keys for your car, home, and hotel room.

UNLOCKING AND STARTING YOUR CAR

With a compatible car and digital car key in Apple Wallet, you can unlock, lock, and start your car using your iPhone or Apple Watch (Series 6 and later). Ultra Wideband ensures that you can't lock your device in the car.

UNLOCKING YOUR HOME

For HomeKit-compatible smart locks, you can unlock your door using a home key in Apple Wallet on supported devices. Add a home key through the Home app on your iPhone.

ACCESSING YOUR WORKPLACE

If your workplace participates, add your corporate access badge to the Wallet app. To access badge-secured areas, hold your iPhone or Apple Watch near the reader.

UNLOCKING YOUR HOTEL ROOM

At participating hotels, add your room key to Apple Wallet using the hotel app, check in remotely, and use your iPhone or Apple Watch to unlock your room.

USING COVID-19 VACCINATION CARDS IN WALLET ON APPLE WATCH

With iOS 15 or newer, you have the option to securely download verifiable COVID-19 vaccination and lab records. These records are stored in the Health app on your iPhone. Once downloaded, it's easy to add the vaccination record to your Wallet app on iPhone. This record is then automatically synchronized with your Apple Watch (requires iOS 15.1 and watchOS 8.1 or later). This feature is supported by certain healthcare providers and authorities. You can then present your vaccination card stored in your Wallet app as proof of vaccination.

SHOWING YOUR VACCINATION CARD

To present your vaccination card using your Apple Watch, follow these steps:
1. Double-click the side button on your Apple Watch.
2. Scroll to locate your vaccination card.
3. Tap the card to open it and reveal the QR code.
4. Show the QR code to the reader as required. Depending on the situation, you might be asked to verify your identity by showing an official photo ID, like your driver's license.

REVIEWING YOUR CARD INFORMATION

If you need to review the information stored on your vaccination card, simply follow these steps:
1. Scroll down within the card details.
2. Tap "Pass Information" to access additional information.

WEATHER

CHECKING THE WEATHER

You can easily get weather updates on your Apple Watch using Siri. Just say something like, "What's tomorrow's forecast for Honolulu?"

Turn to see more weather information.

Tap to see temperature or precipitation forecast.

VIEWING WEATHER CONDITIONS

To check weather conditions, follow these steps:
1. Open the Weather app on your Apple Watch.
2. Tap on a city to see the current temperature and conditions for the day.
3. Tap the display to cycle through hourly forecasts for rain, conditions, or temperature.
4. Scroll down to view air quality, UV index, wind speed, humidity, visibility information, and a 10-day forecast.
5. Tap the "<" in the top-left corner to return to the list

ADDING A CITY

To add a new city to your weather list:
1. Open the Weather app on your Apple Watch.
2. Scroll to the bottom of the list and tap "Add City."
3. Enter the city name using Scribble, dictation, or type it directly (for Apple Watch Series 7 and 8).
4. Tap "Search" and select the city name from the results.

REMOVING A CITY

To remove a city from your list:
1. Open the Weather app 🌥.
2. Swipe the city you want to remove to the left, then tap "X."

CHANGING WEATHER METRICS

You can choose the metric displayed below each city:
1. Open the Weather app 🌥.
2. Tap "Viewing" at the top of the screen.
3. Choose "Conditions," "Precipitation," or "Temperature."

SETTING DEFAULT CITY

1. Open the Settings app ⚙ on your Apple Watch.
2. Go to "Weather," then tap "Default City."
3. Choose a city from the list you added on your iPhone or Apple Watch.

WEATHER ADVISORIES

If there's a significant weather event, you might receive a notification at the top of the Weather app. Tap "Learn More" to get further details about the event.

WORKOUT

USING THE WORKOUT APP

The Workout app 🏃 on your Apple Watch is a great tool to manage your workout sessions. It allows you to set specific goals like time, distance, or calories for your workouts. Your progress is tracked, and your results are summarized. You can also review your complete workout history using the Fitness app on your iPhone.

ENHANCEMENTS IN WATCHOS 9

On previous models, the workout app has some features listed through this guide, this will be detailed in the following page along with the Apple watchOS 9 new enhancements including:

- Heart Rate Zones: Monitor workout intensity with automatic or manually created Heart Rate Zones.
- New Workout Views: View important metrics like Activity rings, Heart Rate Zones, Running Power, Elevation, Splits, and segments by turning the Digital Crown.
- New Running Metrics: Running form metrics like Stride Length, Ground Contact Time, and Vertical Oscillation are available as metrics in Workout Views (for Apple Watch SE and Series 6 and later).
- Custom Workouts: Customize work and recovery intervals with alerts for pace, heart rate, cadence, and power.
- Multisport Workout: Easily switch between workouts like triathlons using auto-detection.
- Running Power: Measure your running effort in watts and maintain a sustainable level (for Apple Watch SE and Series 6 and later).
- Race Route: Race against your previous or best result in an Outdoor Run or Outdoor Cycle workout.
- Automatic Track Detection: When starting an Outdoor Run at a track, you're prompted to begin a Track workout with lane options and lap alerts.
- Swimming Enhancements: Pool Swim workouts now detect a kickboard stroke type and track efficiency with SWOLF score.

STARTING A WORKOUT

Tap to set workout goals.

Turn the Digital Crown to choose another workout.

TO START A WORKOUT ON

YOUR APPLE WATCH

1. Open the Workout app 🏃.
2. Turn the Digital Crown to choose your workout type.
3. Tap "Add Workout" at the bottom for special sessions.
4. Tap the desired workout and start.

You can also ask Siri to start a workout, like "Start a 30-minute run" or "Go for a 5-mile walk."

SETTING A PACE FOR OUTDOOR RUN:

You can set a target pace for an outdoor run:

1. Open the Workout app 🏃.
2. Choose "Outdoor Run" and tap●●●"Create Workout," then select "Pacer."
3. Adjust the distance and target time.

Your watch displays your average and current pace, and whether you're ahead or behind your chosen pace.

USING RACE ROUTE

For familiar routes, race against your previous or best time:

1. Open the Workout app 🏃.
2. Tap ●●● next to an Outdoor Run or Cycle.
3. Choose "Race Route," then select "Last" or "Personal Best."

Your watch shows your progress compared to the route and remaining distance.

COMBINING ACTIVITIES IN A SINGLE WORKOUT

1. Open the Workout app 🏃 on your Apple Watch.
2. Start your first workout, like an outdoor run.
3. When you want to switch to a different activity, such as an outdoor bike ride, swipe right, tap the ➕ icon, and choose the new workout.
4. Once you've finished all activities, swipe right and tap "End."
5. Use the Digital Crown to navigate through the results summary.
6. Scroll to the bottom and tap "Done" to save the workout.

Note: Built-in GPS allows accurate distance tracking during outdoor workouts, so you can leave your iPhone at home.

CREATING A MULTISPORT WORKOUT

With a Multisport workout, combine running, cycling, and swimming activities. Your Apple Watch detects switches between these activities.

1. Open the Workout app 🏃 on your Apple Watch.
2. Depending on if it's your first Multisport workout or not:
   - First Multisport workout: Tap the Multisport workout, then "Create Workout."
   - Subsequent workouts: Tap the ••• icon, then "Create Workout."
3. Add activities (e.g., Outdoor Run) by tapping "Add" for each.
4. Configure alerts and activity order by tapping each activity. Reorder activities by dragging.
5. Customize Workout Views for each activity.
6. Name the workout by tapping "Untitled" and entering a name.
7. Choose automatic/manual transitions between activities under "Transitions."
8. Save the Multisport workout by tapping "Create Workout."
9. To start a Multisport workout, open the app, scroll to the Multisport workout, tap the ➕ icon, and choose a workout.
10. To delete a Multisport workout, tap the Multisport workout tile, tap the 🚫 icon next to the workout, scroll down, tap "Delete Workout," then confirm "Delete."

ADJUSTING APPLE WATCH DURING A WORKOUT

While working out, make the most of your Apple Watch:
- Raise your wrist to view workout stats like time, pace, distance, calories burned, and heart rate. Turn the Digital Crown for more views.

- Pause and resume by pressing the side button and Digital Crown together or by swiping right and tapping "Pause" (except for swimming).
- Mark workout segments by double-tapping the display.
- Control music and volume by swiping left for the Now Playing screen.
- To enable or disable Voice Feedback, open Settings ⚙ on your Apple Watch, go to Workouts, then Voice Feedback.

AUTOMATIC TRACK WORKOUTS ON APPLE WATCH

With the newest update, your Apple Watch seamlessly recognizes when you're at a track. During an Outdoor Run workout, your watch suggests a start Tracking workout option.

STARTING A TRACK WORKOUT

1. Open the Workout app 🏃 on your Apple Watch.
2. Select "Outdoor Run."
   - If your watch detects that you're at a track, it prompts you to choose a lane.
3. Tap "Choose Lane," adjust your lane using the plus/minus buttons, then tap "Confirm."
4. If it's your first Track workout, select a measurement unit (Miles or Meters), then confirm.

To modify the measurement unit later, navigate to the Settings app ⚙ then Workout > Units of Measure, and choose a unit under Track Workouts.
Your Apple Watch informs you if you leave or arrive at a track mid-workout, ensuring accurate tracking.

ENABLING LAP ALERTS

Receive alerts displaying distance, time, and pace for each track lap:
1. Tap ••• next to "Outdoor Run," then tap 🖊 next to any goal.
2. Tap "Alerts," turn the Digital Crown upwards, select "Track Lap," and enable "Lap Alert."

LANE ADJUSTMENT DURING A WORKOUT

If you change lanes during your workout:
Swipe right on the watch face, tap "Lane," and enter the new lane.

ENDING AND REVIEWING YOUR WORKOUT

When you achieve your goal, a tone and vibration signal completion. If you wish to continue, your Apple Watch continues gathering data until you stop it.
1. Swipe right, then tap "End."
2. Use the Digital Crown to navigate the results summary, then tap "Done" at the bottom.

Note: The heart rate sensor remains active for three minutes post-workout to measure recovery.*

WORKOUT REVIEW

1. Open the Health app 🩷 on your iPhone.
2. Tap "Summary," then select a workout.

The summary includes workout specifics, splits, heart rate, and route. Tap "Show More" next to each item for detailed information.

For route tracking, enable it during initial setup or later in:
- Apple Watch: Settings app ⚙> Privacy > Location Services > Apple Watch Workout > While Using the App.
- iPhone: Settings > Privacy > Location Services > Apple Watch Workout > While Using the App.

Note: To view a specific workout type, tap "Show More" beside Workouts, select the type, and to return to all workouts, tap the workout name and "All Workouts."

CUSTOMIZE YOUR WORKOUTS ON APPLE WATCH

ADJUSTING WORKOUT GOALS

Personalize your workouts on Apple Watch to match your fitness aspirations. Tailor time, calorie, and distance targets, incorporate warmup and cooldown periods, and include work and recovery intervals.

MODIFYING GOALS

In watchOS 9, customizing existing workouts and crafting your desired workout is easy:
1. Open the Workout app 🏃 your Apple Watch.
2. Scroll to your chosen workout.
3. Tap ●●●, then select "Create Workout."
4. Opt for a goal like Calories, Distance, or Time; set a value; and tap "Done."
5. Start the edited workout by tapping the adjusted goal.
6. You can also tap < to save the edited workout and begin later.

To remove edited goals from a workout, scroll to the workout, tap ●●●, tap 🖊 next to the goal, scroll down, tap "Delete Workout," and confirm deletion.

ADDING INTERVALS

Tailor your workouts with warmup, work, recovery, and cooldown intervals:
1. Open the Workout app 🏃 on your Apple Watch.
2. Choose your desired workout.
3. Tap ●●●, scroll to the bottom, and tap "Create Workout."
4. Opt for "Custom," and perform the following:
   - Add a warmup: Tap Warmup, select Time, Distance, or Open, and add a heart rate alert if desired.
   - Incorporate work and recovery intervals: Tap Add, tap Work or Recovery, and choose Time, Distance, or Open. You can include multiple intervals.
   - Add a cooldown: Tap Cooldown, choose Time, Distance, or Open. With "Open," you can include a heart rate alert.
   - Name the workout: Tap "Untitled" below Custom Title and enter a name.
   Note:For stationary workouts like Elliptical or Pilates, Distance isn't available.

5. Tap "Create Workout." This button is active if a work or recovery interval is added.
6.
To remove warmup or cooldown periods, tap ●●● next to the workout, tap 🖊 within the Custom tile, tap Warmup or Cooldown, and tap "Skip." For work or recovery intervals, tap the interval, then tap "Delete Interval."

Custom workouts apply to all workout types except Multisport, Pool Swim, and Open Water Swim.

ADDING ALERTS

Receive various alerts during workouts, such as heart rate alerts:
1. Open the Workout app 🏃 on your Apple Watch.
2. Choose the workout.
3. Tap ●●●, tap the edit button for a tile, and tap "Alerts."
4. Opt for an alert, configure it, and these added alerts apply to future instances of that workout.

VIEWING HEART RATE ZONES

In watchOS 9, monitor your cardio-focused workout intensity by viewing Heart Rate Zone data on your Apple Watch. Heart Rate Zones are calculated from your health data, showing effort levels from light to challenging.

VIEWING ZONES DURING A WORKOUT

1. Open the Workout app 🏃 on your Apple Watch.
2. Begin a cardio-focused workout, like an outdoor run.
3. Scroll to the Heart Rate Zone workout view using the Digital Crown.

The display showcases your Heart Rate Zone, heart rate, time in the current zone, and average heart rate.

REVIEWING ZONE DATA

1. Open the Fitness app ♥ on your iPhone.
2. Select a workout and tap Show More next to Heart Rate.
A graph illustrates the time spent in each zone.

EDITING ZONES

While Heart Rate Zones are usually calculated from health data, you can manually adjust them:
1. Open the Settings app ⚙ on your Apple Watch.
2. Navigate to Workout > Heart Rate Zones.
3. Choose Manual, select a zone (2, 3, or 4), and input upper and lower limits.

Alternatively, use the Apple Watch app on your iPhone. Tap My Watch, go to Workout > Heart Rate Zones, opt for Manual, select a zone, and input limits.
Viewing and Customizing Workout Metrics on Apple Watch:

TRACKING YOUR PROGRESS

Apple Watch provides valuable metrics such as active calories, heart rate, and distance during workouts to help you monitor your performance. Each workout type displays default metrics relevant to the activity, which you can personalize.

SWITCHING VIEWS

During a workout, simply turn the Digital Crown to cycle through different workout views.

PERSONALIZING VIEWS

The workout views depend on your chosen activity. Cardio-focused workouts feature more default views, but you can customize some of them to match your workout preferences.

1. Open the Workout app 🏃 on your Apple Watch.
2. Scroll to your selected workout.
3. Tap •••, tap 🖊 within any tile, then tap "Workout Views."
4. Choose "Edit Views," browse through the workout views, and tap "Include" next to the metrics you want to appear.
5. For the first two workout views, select metrics by tapping 🖊 in the Metric 1 or Metric 2 set, and choosing a different metric.

ENHANCING YOUR RUNNING METRICS

In watchOS 9, Apple Watch offers insights into your running form and power:
- Vertical oscillation: Vertical movement with each step, measured in cm.
- Ground contact time: Time foot is on the ground while running, measured in ms.
- Stride length: Distance per step, measured in meters.
- Running power: Output of work while running, measured in watts.

OUTDOOR RUN METRICS

The Outdoor Run workout presents various metrics:
- Metric 1: Current heart rate, rolling mile, average pace, distance
- Metric 2: Running cadence, stride length, ground contact time, vertical oscillation
- Heart Rate Zones: Current heart rate, time in zone, average heart rate
- Split: Split number, split pace, split distance, current heart rate
- Segment: Segment number, segment pace, segment distance, current heart rate
- Elevation: Elevation profile, elevation gained, current elevation
- Power: Power profile, current power, average power
- Activity rings: Move, exercise & stand.

SWIM EFFICIENTLY

In watchOS 9, Pool Swim workouts feature kickboard detection and SWOLF scores, combining stroke count with time for one pool length.

STARTING A SWIM WORKOUT

1. Open the Workout app 🏃 on your Apple Watch.
2. Choose Open Water Swim or Pool Swim.

Pause or resume your swim by pressing the Digital Crown and side button together. Water Lock engages when swimming to prevent accidental interactions. After swimming, press and hold the Digital Crown to unlock the screen and clear any water from the speaker.

VIEWING SWIM SUMMARY

Unlock your Apple Watch and tap End to see your swim workout summary. It tracks sets, rest periods, stroke types, and total distance. Set paces are visible in your iPhone's workout summary.

CLEARING WATER MANUALLY

1. Swipe up on the screen to open Control Center, then tap 💧.
2. Hold the Digital Crown to clear water from the speaker after swimming.

USING GYM EQUIPMENT WITH APPLE WATCH

Apple Watch can sync data with compatible cardio equipment like treadmills, ellipticals, and indoor bikes, providing accurate workout insights.
Pairing Your Watch

Follow these steps to pair your Apple Watch with gym equipment:
1. Check for compatibility—look for "Connects to Apple Watch" on the equipment.
2. Ensure your watch detects gym equipment: Open Settings ⚙ on your Apple Watch, tap Workout, and enable Detect Gym Equipment.
3. Hold your Apple Watch close to the contactless reader on the equipment with the display facing it. A tap and beep indicate successful pairing.

STARTING AND ENDING A WORKOUT

Begin by pressing "Start" on the equipment and end by pressing "Stop." Workout data integrates into the Activity app on your Apple Watch and the Fitness app on your iPhone.

UPDATING YOUR PROFILE

For accurate calculations, update your height, weight, sex, age, and wheelchair status:
1. Open the Apple Watch app ⬛ on your iPhone.
2. Go to My Watch, select Health > Health Details, and tap Edit.
3. Adjust Height or Weight as needed.

CALIBRATING FOR ACCURACY

Your Apple Watch uses your profile and GPS for accurate metrics. If you run with your iWatch, the 🏃 app calibrates your stride for distance accuracy.

CHANGING MEASUREMENT UNITS

Adjust the Workout app's measurement units to your preference:
1. Open Settings ⚙ on your Apple Watch.
2. Tap Workout, scroll down, and tap Units of Measure to change energy, pool length, cycling, walking, and running units.

AUTO-PAUSE AND MANUAL PAUSING

Enable Auto-Pause for outdoor running and cycling workouts to pause and resume automatically. Manually pause using the side button and Digital Crown.

WORKOUT REMINDERS

Receive prompts to start the Workout app during activities like walking, running, and swimming:
1. Open Settings ⚙ on your Apple Watch.
2. Tap Workout, and adjust Start and End Workout Reminder settings.

CONSERVING POWER

Prolong battery life during workouts by activating Low Power Mode:
1. Open Settings ⚙ on your Apple Watch.
2. Tap Workout, and enable Low Power Mode.

During workouts, Low Power Mode conserves energy by turning off certain features. To further save battery life, turn off GPS and Heart Rate Readings.

WORLD CLOCK

Apple Watch's World Clock feature lets you view time across various cities.

Turn to scroll through cities.

ADDING AND REMOVING CITIES

Here's how to add and remove cities in World Clock:

1. Open World Clock 🌐 on your Apple Watch.
2. Tap Add City.
3. Enter the city name using Scribble or dictation (available on Apple Watch Series 7 and 8).
4. Tap the city name to add it. To remove a city, swipe left and tap X.

Cities added on your iPhone appear on your Apple Watch too.

CHECKING TIME IN OTHER CITIES

1. Open World Clock 🌐 on your Apple Watch.
2. Use the Digital Crown or swipe to scroll through the list.
3. Tap a city to see additional info like sunrise and sunset times.
4. Tap < or swipe right to return to the city list.

You can also add a World Clock complication to your watch face for quick access.

CHANGING CITY ABBREVIATIONS

To alter city abbreviations on your Apple Watch

1. Open the Apple Watch app 🔲 on your iPhone.
2. Go to My Watch, then Clock > City Abbreviations.
3. Change an abbreviation by tapping a city.

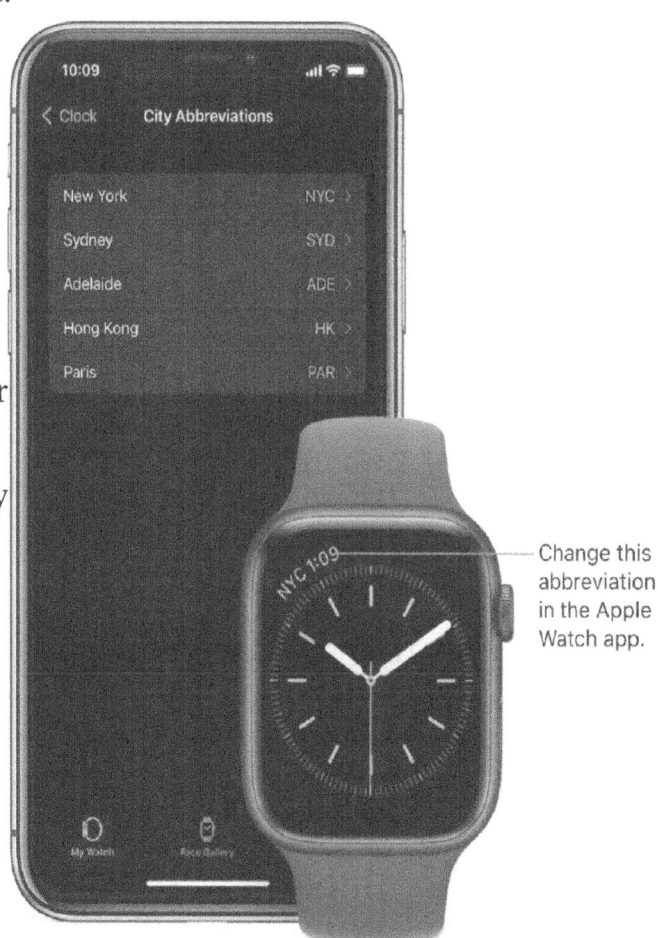

Change this abbreviation in the Apple Watch app.

UPDATE, BACKUP, RESTORE & RESET YOUR IWATCH

Apple provides regular updates to your IOS so your iPhone in tip top condition working like it's brand new. Software updates can contain major or minor changes depending on the version. You can update your iPhone manually and set it to "Automatic Update" which allows your phone to download and install new software as it comes out.

Digital Crown

Side button

RECOVER APPLE WATCH

If your Apple Watch displays an animation of a watch and iPhone brought together, follow these steps:

1. Position your iPhone close to your Apple Watch.
   Ensure your iPhone is running iOS 15.4 or later, connected to Wi-Fi with Bluetooth on, and unlocked.
2. Place your Apple Watch on its charger.
3. Double-click the side button on your Apple Watch, then follow the prompts on the iPhone.

RESTORE APPLE WATCH FROM BACKUP

Your Apple Watch automatically backs up to your paired iPhone, allowing restoration from a backup. These backups are included in your iPhone's backup—whether to iCloud, Mac, or PC. iCloud backups can't be directly viewed.

BACKUP AND RESTORATIO

- Backup: When paired with an iPhone, Apple Watch content continuously backs up to the iPhone. Unpairing devices initiates a backup. For details, see "Back up your Apple Watch" on Apple Support.
- Restore from Backup: Pairing your Apple Watch with the same iPhone or getting a new Apple Watch lets you choose "Restore from Backup" and select a stored backup on your

iPhone.

Managed family member's Apple Watch backs up to their iCloud account while connected to power and Wi-Fi. To disable iCloud backups, navigate to Settings > [account name] > iCloud > iCloud Backups on the managed watch, then disable iCloud Backups.

UPDATING APPLE WATCH SOFTWARE

Easily update your Apple Watch software via the Apple Watch app on your iPhone.

CHECK AND INSTALL UPDATES

1. Open the Apple Watch app on your iPhone.
2. Access My Watch, go to General > Software Update, and if available, tap Download and Install.

Alternatively, go to Settings app on your Apple Watch, then navigate to General > Software Update.

FORGOT APPLE WATCH PASSCODE

If your Apple Watch is disabled due to forgotten or repeatedly incorrect passcodes, use the Apple Watch app on your iPhone to re-enter the passcode. If still forgotten, reset your Apple Watch and set it up again.

Important: If Erase Data is enabled, after 10 unsuccessful attempts, your Apple Watch data is erased.

Dear Apple Pro!
I hope you have
enjoyed exploring
the world of Apple
devices. Your feedback
means a lot to me and
it can be a valuable
gift to fellow readers
who are considering
this guide. Writing a
review on Amazon is
a simple yet incredibly
helpful way to pay it
forward(Do not worry,
its free!). Scan this QR code to take you straight there!

Your words have the power to inspire confidence in others, just as I've aimed to do with this book. Whether you found the content insightful, the instructions clear, or if you have any suggestions for improvement (I WILL incorporate it into following books), your review will be appreciated.

By sharing your thoughts, you not only assist other seniors in making an informed choice but also support the author (that's me!). Your review provides insights that can guide prospective readers, making their journey with the Apple products more enjoyable and stress-free. If you made it this far, I am offering a digital copy of our next book for all customers that leave a review and email me a picture of their review posted on Amazon! Email me at:
JasonBrownPublishing@gmail.com

Thank you for considering this request. Your words can make a big difference, and together, we can make the Apple world even more accessible and enjoyable for everyone, everywhere!

Thank you,
Jason Brown
400

Made in the USA
Middletown, DE
10 March 2024